The Christ Is Dead,
Long Live the Christ

The Christ Is Dead, Long Live the Christ

A Philotheologic Prayer, a Hermeneutics of Healing

ANDREW OBERG

RESOURCE *Publications* • Eugene, Oregon

THE CHRIST IS DEAD, LONG LIVE THE CHRIST
A Philotheologic Prayer, a Hermeneutics of Healing

Copyright © 2022 Andrew Oberg. All rights reserved. Except for brief quotations in critical publications or reviews, no part of this book may be reproduced in any manner without prior written permission from the publisher. Write: Permissions, Wipf and Stock Publishers, 199 W. 8th Ave., Suite 3, Eugene, OR 97401.

Resource Publications
An Imprint of Wipf and Stock Publishers
199 W. 8th Ave., Suite 3
Eugene, OR 97401

www.wipfandstock.com

PAPERBACK ISBN: 978-1-7252-7784-7
HARDCOVER ISBN: 978-1-7252-7785-4
EBOOK ISBN: 978-1-7252-7786-1

JUNE 22, 2022 10:18 AM

Scripture quotations marked (NRSV) are taken from New Revised Standard Version Bible, copyright © 1989 National Council of the Churches of Christ in the United States of America. Used by permission. All rights reserved worldwide.

Scripture quotations marked (NLT) are taken from the Holy Bible, New Living Translation: Catholic Reader's Edition, copyright © 1996, 2004, 2015 by Tyndale House Foundation. Used by permission of Tyndale House Publishers, Carol Stream, Illinois 60188. All rights reserved.

Scripture quotations marked (NJPS) are taken from Tanakh, The Holy Scriptures by permission of the University of Nebraska Press, copyright © 1985 by The Jewish Publication Society, Philadelphia. Used by permission. All rights reserved.

Sections of this work have appeared in different form as papers or parts of papers in the following academic journals; all copyrights to these versions are held by the author:

"Bloodying God: Crucifixion and the Image." In *Image, Phenomenon, and Imagination in the Phenomenology of Religious Experience*, Libri Nigri series. Edited by Martin Nitsche and Olga Louchakova-Schwartz, series editor-in-chief Hans Rainer Sepp, 209–28. Nordhausen, Germany: Traugott Bautz GmbH, 2022.

"Dry, Weary, Smiling Bones: Finding a 'Yes' through Hebrew Narrative and a Reduced Spirituality," *Religions* 13, no. 1 (2022): 78, https://doi.org/10.3390/rel13010078.

"A Comment on Crucifixion Imagery as Seen from 'the Kingdom,'" *Bulletin of the University of Kochi* 70 (2021): 39–57.

"Facing a Form of/Formed God: Japan's Hidden Christians and Usages of the Image – A Phenomenological Perspective," *Cultural Studies* 8 (2020): 31–72.

"Rereading the 'Vineyard' Parable: Squeezing the Grapes of a Fresh Hermeneutic for a Radical 'Kingdom' and a 'Weak' God," *Bulletin of the University of Kochi* 69 (2020): 17–35.

"Approaches to Finitude: Death, Self, Others," *Journal of Applied Ethics and Philosophy* 10 (2019): 8–17.

For all those who wonder

Contents

List of Illustrations | viii
Acknowledgements | ix

Part 1	**Man, Son (of)**
Chapter 1	There | 3
Chapter 2	A Life: Human | 7
Chapter 3	A Life: Beyond | 11
Chapter 4	A Life: Considered | 36
Part 2	**The Real in Ideas and Images**
Chapter 5	A Theory of *Notion/Event* | 47
Chapter 6	The Image and the Idea | 58
Chapter 7	A (Special) Case Study: Japan's Hidden Christians and the Image/Icon | 67
Chapter 8	Viewing the Cross from "the Kingdom" | 81
Part 3	**Parables and Pictures**
Chapter 9	Hermeneutics: Storytelling and Re-Telling | 103
Chapter 10	Art and Interaction(s) | 131
Part 4	**Temporality: God/"God" Here, "the Kingdom" Now**
Chapter 11	Afterliving | 173
Chapter 12	(Honestly) Facing Finitude | 191
Chapter 13	Sacrificial Nonsense | 223
Chapter 14	Death Is/Was Birth | 245
Part 5	**A Peace-Making, a Re-Making**
Chapter 15	Endless Construction | 254

Bibliography | 289

List of Illustrations

Figure 1: Peitro Perugino, "Agony in the Garden" (1483–1493)

Figure 2: Albrecht Dürer, "Agony in the Garden" (1515)

Figure 3: Carl Bloch, "An Angel Comforting Jesus before His Arrest in the Garden of Gethsemane" (1873)

Figure 4: Nikolai Ge, "On the Mount of Olives" (1869–1880)

Figure 5: Heinrich Hofmann, "Christ in the Garden of Gethsemane" (1890)

Figure 6: William Blake, "Job Recounting his Experiences to his Daughters" (1825; 20th print)

Figure 7: Pietro Perugino, "Agony in the Garden" (1483–1493); redux

Figure 8: Albrecht Dürer, "Agony in the Garden" (1515); redux

Figure 9: Carl Bloch, "An Angel Comforting Jesus before His Arrest in the Garden of Gethsemane" (1873); redux

Figure 10: Nikolai Ge, "On the Mount of Olives" (1869–1880); redux

Figure 11: Heinrich Hofmann, "Christ in the Garden of Gethsemane" (1890); redux

Figure 12: El Greco, "Christ on the Cross, in a Landscape with Horsemen" (1610–1614)

Acknowledgements

First and foremost I would like to thank my family, and especially my wife and daughters: light and life for each day. Appreciation must be given as well to Eric Uhlich for his help with the images and good advice on all things graphic, and to Matthew Wimer, Jonathan Hill, and George Callihan of Wipf and Stock/Resource for their patience, kindness, skill, and diligence. I also wish to express gratitude to Doctor Vincent Pastro and Doctor Hitoshi Fukue for their kind words of encouragement at the right times; gifts they probably did not even notice. Mention too must be made of Doctor Joël Joos, friend and colleague at the University of Kochi, who has quietly encouraged me to pursue my own path in research and academic life; and further to the university at large for its faculty support. This work has also been supported by a research grant from the Japan Society for the Promotion of Science, reference number 21K12829. I owe a substantial intellectual debt to the founding scholars of the Jesus Seminar at the Westar Institute, and to Doctor John D. Caputo, Doctor Walter Kaufmann (of blessed memory), and Doctor Daniel Boyarin: all of whom I have never had the pleasure to meet but their style and thoughtful, persistent querying have influenced me deeply. Finally to the great Other, the I-know-not-what, the being or force or sense or call beckoning us to become ever better; may it be so.

Part 1

MAN, SON (OF)

Chapter 1

THERE

"Forgive those neighbors who have wronged you, and then your sins will be forgiven when you pray. If people harbor anger against each other, how can they expect healing from the Lord? If they do not show mercy toward people like themselves, how can they seek pardon for their own sins?"

SIRACH 28:2–4

". . . forgive us our sins, as we have forgiven those who sin against us."

MATTHEW 6:12

"If you blow on a spark, it flares up, and if you spit upon it, it will be quenched; yet both come from your mouth."

SIRACH 28:12[1]

WE SEEK A RETURN, we seek a remission, above all we seek a reconsideration of this Jesus: that first century Palestinian Jew (and we shall henceforth call him by his Aramaic/Hebrew name Yeshua[2]), but so too that "Jesus" as the ever-idea this particular proper noun has come to represent. Yeshua's efforts were not a quest to form a new religion, although he did probably seek to form—or to ground—a faith of sorts: in

---

1. All three quotations taken from *Catholic Holy Bible* (NLT).
2. By using the name "Yeshua" and not "Jesus" we already move to re-situate what have become automatic and default mental associations built up over centuries of adding to and foisting upon that certain term, and thus we help thereby to humanize and de-mythologize—to concretize—the real man and his real (reality-building) teachings. This is not to downplay the figure of Christ, nor the potency of that image or the singularity of that legacy (and the image will prove central to our study), but it is to make of him a man, it is to remind ourselves of his manhood and fragilely human personhood. Incarnate—what a word! Yet we may perhaps concede it if we add the following addendum: "incarnate" as we all are, incarnate as "made in the image of" indicates; Yeshua was perhaps wiser, stronger, freer than many of us: guide, teacher, rabbi, sage, son, brother, friend. Resurrected? In thought? In blinding light? In *idea*? . . . We get ahead of ourselves.

himself, perhaps, yet not in the sense of person or object; rather as representative of a way, a symbol or model of another, alternative means by which to be a Jew and to live Jewishly. (One of many alternative Jewish modes of being within the ripe context of first century Roman occupied Palestine in fact; but for us the simple presence of these varied options carries more argumentative weight than whatever definitional details might be offered.) This faith which signifies the Yeshuan version of being-in-the-world is the kind of faith one might have in a signpost: it is a trust, a willingness, a go-and-see; and it is that attitude—that *comportment*—which allows one to follow its directing and thereby potentially be "renewed" by the life-path so trod: a moulding of mind through a re-orientation of certain tendencies within human thought. This is not the only "salvation" available to those who seek such (it is not even *any* "salvation": an abstraction which we will anyway later contend there is no need for), but it is a good "soteriology," and perhaps even a fulfilling one. This "brand" of Judaism (if it may be so labeled) we assert here at the outset as at least beneficial in part, but probably not in whole (naturally arguable: this is our position (and see Chapter 15)), while making no claims for exclusivity or even preferability over others who might wish to promote other partisan positions. We wish to merely offer some perspectives; and while we admit non-expertise in matters Judaic, we think that nevertheless the reasons for the positive appraisals to be made and the placement of the ideational package will become clear enough as we proceed, keeping our Yeshua within the Jewish context wherein he dwelt.[3] Ours is neither to "prove" nor to "establish" (although it may be to clarify), but rather to renew, to redeem, to re-commit; and then to (re)start afresh from the same beginning. For what, we ask, could be more thoroughly Jewish than a return?

    What we know, then, what we sense, is the *feel* of this prodding and the need for this return, this effort to put Yeshua back into the flesh he wore and the words and concepts back into lives gone and here unadulteratedly, without the built-up distractions—the glaring, blinding lights—of substitutionary image-imaginings or posthumously designated gateway assignations, to make a connection between the dirty and dust covered peasant orator with honeycomb turns of phrases that still touch legions of those Yeshuan acknowledgers who find beauty and perhaps even truth in the way he signaled—regardless of divinity claims—those who are yet convinced the old message has something to offer our mad, maddening world. We therefore wish to draw a bolder restitutionary line that sends the crucifix back into the Star of David, to (re)place both of these weighted markers within a single loop, a single spinning circle, a merciful cycle of grace lent and taken. If, as has been suggested, the modern Occident really is a product of self-hatred, of the Christian at war with the Jewish self who gave her birth,[4] then we strive for nothing less audacious than forgiveness; should we

---

3. However, these same points on Jewish paths and what Yeshua offered his contemporaries have been made by those with vast expertise in matters Judaic; see for instance Boyarin, *The Jewish Gospels*.

4. On this see the recent, and most interesting, Nancy, *The Banality of Heidegger*.

dare cry for regeneration we must show it. The prefatory prayer reads: ". . . as we have forgiven those who sin against us": that "as" ought not to be read like "since" but rather "to the extent that," "to the level that"; or, in other words: Forgive us God/"God", only insofar as we have braved to, toiled to, broken ourselves to—*freed* ourselves to—forgive others.

Yet let us not be misunderstood: The coin is two-sided but weighted on one, and for those who find what is honorable in Yeshua's message it is likely not so much a matter of forgiving fellows as it is a matter of pleading to have forgiveness extended (historically), and maybe too of forgiving siblings (of whatever shape or form) remembering that on this usage the identifier "Christian" means no more—but no less—than another moniker for what we wish to subvert into a notional grounding of Yeshuan-following-(respecting/appreciating)-Judaism, and thus as well forgiving whatever self-hatred and/or self-denial may or may not be found. Our received lineage marks errors without and within: this is to be expected. On the present neither Christian-nor-Jewish viewing (but of course both "Christian" and "Jewish") fault is not found so much as explorations are sought. The "you" here is blameless, the "we" have wronged and continue to wrong; this is regrettable, and a request for a way back (a renewal, a return) is made. Although our proposal, as shall be detailed, will not comprise any orthodoxy but rather a nebulous "positioning," the effort too will not be for a fully inked document; instead something more akin to the physicality of Jacobean striving. We love and pore over the letters—let us admit as much—but in midrashic fashion we hope to sparkle them with a life of otherly, more open interpretations, with a presentation of unbounded and unapproved exegeses. What we really wish is to offer a daily call of instructive ever-mystery, perhaps in the spirit of: "Hear, O Israel! The Lord our God, the Lord is one//Blessed is God's glorious majesty forever and ever";[5] and thus however the locator "God" might be understood; whatever might be found implied in a title such as "Lord." There are parts of Yeshua—parts of the received Yeshuan residue—which, we think, might help gesture us there. We shall try.

We are in a tradition, a series, a chain, a link, and we realize that. We search for *re*-newal, *re*-birth: not a new, not a birth; those doors have probably closed. We have come a long way, and perhaps not how such was intended; at any rate it is time, I think, to look over our shoulders. Emmanuel Falque reminds us that "the necessity for a renewal of theology, whether Jewish or Christian, should not occlude the riches of its

---

5. The *Shema Yisrael* of Deuteronomy 6:4 and its response (the verse can also be seen translated as "The Lord is our God, the Lord alone"; the daily prayer often uses "Adonai" (God's/"God's" pronounceable name, as opposed to the Tetragrammaton) instead of "the Lord"); on the meaning and centrality of this prayer (with a link to the words themselves), see Marx, "Hear, O Israel (Sh'ma Yisrael)," *ReformJudaism.org*. Accessed September 21, 2021. On this topic too—and how wonderfully appropriate for our venture—see Mark 12:29: "Jesus answered, 'The first is, "Hear, O Israel: the Lord our God, the Lord is one; [the following verse continues Yeshua's statement; he has been asked which commandment is "first"]." *Thinline Bible with the Apocrypha* (NRSV).

past" (and these words we will revisit),[6] and Graham Harman too that "an absolutism of reality may be coupled with a relativism of truth."[7] We are not here arguing for "hard truths"—not in a strict sense at any rate, not in an empirical-universal TRUTH sense—but we will make claims for a "truth" that is nearer the heart than any set of data may achieve, and far more observable. We will first spread a topsoil of history, a contextualizing and situating, and then stepping thereon begin an engagement with an extended proposition, embarking on a discussion of broader comprehensions than contemporary prejudices tend to favor in order to cast a gaze at another (fully deflated) Christology, at the image and the icon the figure-person has become, and at an alternative numinousness or numinosity (numen-ology?): at a "kingdom"-ology that tries to make (another) sense of what that "kingdom" is/was in proclamation and practice. In coming down from those heady ontology-flaked clouds we will find mostly a phenomenology, a life lived in a slow dance (maybe a stroll) with the transcendent, a life alongside an/"the" other/"Other." Ours is not a theological undertaking definitionally speaking, rather a philosophical one: a philotheology that roots itself in experiences past and present, revealed and hidden, Western and Eastern, real ("real") and imagined: ideational, conceptual, notional, symbolic; *hermeneutic*. We set out to explore, not to offer conclusions. We know simply that we know not; but we shall see what we find.

---

6. Falque, *The Guide to Gethsemane*, 52.
7. Harman, *Weird Realism*, 14.

Chapter 2

A Life: Human

THE SIMPLE EFFORT TO arrive at an historically accurate—or at least one that might be reasonably so—biographical picture of Yeshua is a challenge that has never been far from controversy, and little wonder given how very dear to the hearts of well over a billion this man, the image(s) of this man, the idea(s) of this man, have been and still are. Moreover, in the absence of much which we would like to have by way of record keeping, such are primarily what we are left with: images, ideas, concepts, assumptions: sometimes merely guesswork. John Dominic Crossan puts our mnemonic position succinctly when he writes that, "When today we read his [i.e. Yeshua's] words in fixed and frozen texts we must recognize that the oral memory of his first audiences could have retained, at best, only the striking image, the startling analogy, the forceful conjunction, and, for example, the plot summary of a parable that might have taken an hour or more to tell and perform."[1] We are left with pieces of pieces, the ossified topsoil of a pedagogical program fed by subterranean mulch unique enough to sustain the broad socio-religious movement it did over the decades it took before anything started to be affixed to paper.

Even such shaken and stirred accounts as this carry originary ingredients however, and they can indeed contain real substantive weight, as the great strides made in recent decades towards the recovery of a "historical Christ" indicate; we wonder: how much are the researchers engaged in this area now able to relate to us? Additionally, having taken on what we determine to be applicable or beneficial, how may these details assist in the ongoing personal experiences many of us have (think we have, feel we have) in relation to a "living Yeshua" (living idea, living image) and/or the teachings we have received? What might we learn of the flesh and blood Yeshua, he who actually walked the roadways of first century Palestine? These are delicate but crucial questions, yet I fear that a(nother) caveat must be inserted here before we delve in any further: I am neither a New Testament nor even a Near Eastern historian, and lest this study be misjudged, let me state outright that I do not pretend to be; as

---

1. Crossan, *Jesus*, 65.

Part 1 | Man, Son (of)

indicated, ours is a philosophical effort, the field of scholarship in which I do claim (or anyway comfort myself with) some measure of professional, academic, and experiential qualification, and thus we shall only glance at what those in the associated areas have written, and that for the sole purpose of grounding what will become a primarily phenomenological and metaphysical (yet one ontically so) trek through the thickets, as it were; and on the way we shall try not to mistake the forest for the trees.

To begin then. A number of scholars and groups have attempted over the years, and increasingly so from the twentieth century onwards, a reconstruction—a profiling—of Yeshua the man, and the general agreement (where such there is; perhaps putting it as a quote-unquote "agreement" would be more fitting) is that he was a Jewish itinerant teacher of humble background who gained a widespread following in the particularly apocalyptically leaning climate of Roman occupied Israel at the time, during which a strain of Jewish sages akin to John the Baptizer (perhaps a more proper rendering of the "John the Baptist" nomenclature) are thought to have anticipated an imminent "end of the world."[2] For a long while it was thought that Yeshua too was probably an "end is nigh" type of prophet—and he may have personally accepted such prior to his own teaching period—but that interpretation has been challenged and appears (at least as far as I can tell) to be on the decline.[3] Yeshua was deeply concerned with "the kingdom of God," but with *bringing* it, not waiting for/expecting God/"God"[4] to push into history and make it happen.

This man Yeshua was evidently a peasant, a member of the teeming and socially immobile underclasses; nowhere near being a properly accredited and trained religious leader, figure, or authority. He was not of the priestly caste (the Jewish Temple still stood during his lifetime and national religious life remained centered around it and its cycle of events, although there was some tension between an "establishment" Temple-centered mode and a looser "every person" mode such as that championed by sects like the Pharisees), he was neither scholar nor "credentialed" exegete, was almost certainly illiterate, and may not even have set out to instruct on his own authority until after the death of John the Baptizer (Baptist), of whom he had probably been a follower. He was thoroughly a Jew—born and raised, "dyed in the wool"—and his

---

2. For some very accessible starters into the study of the historical Jesus I recommend the following (in order of publication): Crossan, *Jesus*; Funk, *Honest to Jesus*; and Ehrman, *How Jesus Became God*.

3. On this point of Jesus not being an evangelist of apocalypse see also Funk (ed.), and the Jesus Seminar (group), *The Gospel of Jesus*, particularly the notes to Chapters 1 and 2 found on pages 91–92. A very interesting take on the figure of Jesus can also be found in Harold Bloom's interpretative essay attached to Marvin Meyer's revised translation of the Nag Hammadi text *The Gospel of Thomas*. Bloom indicates other intriguing scholarly sources and ideas about Jesus in his essay as well; see Meyer, trans. and intro., *The Gospel of Thomas*.

4. We shall use this linguistic device of scare quotes (God/"God") in reference to the divine throughout, but not because we think Yeshua thought thusly. Rather, ours is an attempt to dissociate from the reader's mind whatever extant presumptions might exist regarding what divinity "is," to highlight these assumptions which are so often deeply buried, and thusly jarred (we hope) to be more open to the philotheological explorations we wish to make in our study.

efforts appear primarily aimed at reforming the version of Judaism (one of many at the time, and—we shall argue—yet (in some ways, at least)) as lived by those who were his sociopolitical peers (i.e. the downtrodden), and within that the theological framing of a person's relationship with God/"God" that it taught: that is, the manner and means of such relating, the *how* of one's being with God/"God". His was an anti-authoritarian, anti-(or anyway disregarding of)priesthood, anti-brokered, a countryside versus city, a farmer versus scribe, an "expendable" versus "elite" fashion of Jewish spirituality.[5] As John D. Caputo reminds us, Yeshua himself had never heard of this thing called "Christianity,"[6] and nor indeed would anyone for some decades to come following his (self-giving?) execution. (In our study's final portions—to give it all away and ruin things right from the start—we shall attempt a similar, but far more inadequate (incomparable, really) gesturing for a re-consideration of what a "Yeshuan-ism" and God/"God" within and without such might entail.)

That thing, that "Christianity thing," was to appear in the world much later, either by way of the invention of the church's early missionary Paul (and via his disagreements with the movements' other initial leaders) or, if one is interpretively differently inclined, through the transformation brought about under Constantine the Great, the fourth century Emperor who instituted the faith as the new state religion, and thereby—bit by bit—unifying a landscape of beliefs and rituals as diverse as the far-flung Roman Empire itself.[7] Yet whenever the "official start" is taken to be, it was clear enough by the second century that the burgeoning group of Jewish Christians who had embraced the changes to practice and understanding of Jewish Law and being that Yeshua advocated had come into sufficient conflict with/distance from the re-ordering of Judaism(s) that was then coalescing around the rabbinic (synagogue and yeshiva oriented) model following the destruction of the Temple complex in Jerusalem[8] that a split was bound to happen sooner or later. When it did finally take place the process of Yeshua's exaltation probably sped up—perhaps remarkably so—and the man who had been an orator of reformation, a healer, a teacher, a sharer of bread, became not only a "son of God" (a common enough term in the classical world for someone praiseworthy or remarkable in some way, and—incidentally—a label only then quite recently officially bequeathed by the Roman Senate on Yeshua's close historical predecessor and founding emperor Octavius Augustus[9]), but actually and literally raised from the

---

5. Crossan, *Jesus*, especially emphasizes the social reformer aspect of the historical picture scholars have been able to put together of Yeshua's ministerial life.

6. See the wonderful Caputo, *The Weakness of God*.

7. Biographies on the famous emperor are not hard to come by; I enjoyed Grant's well-known title *Constantine the Great*. Much of this initial unification, as regards dogma but also some structural and role implications, resulted from the First Council of Nicaea convened at the behest of Constantine in 325 CE; for a very, very brief overview see Editors of Encyclopædia Britannica, "First Council of Nicaea," *Encyclopædia Britannica*. Accessed January 20, 2020.

8. Funk discusses this briefly in Funk and the Jesus Seminar, *The Gospel of Jesus*.

9. Crossan, *Jesus*, discusses this in his book's opening.

dead, thereafter to be transported directly to Heaven before his gathered witnessing disciples like the prophet Elijah is said to have been, only without the intermediary chariot being required.[10] This narrative has gained such commonplace that it is largely taken for granted, either accepted at face (faith) value or rejected out of hand as so much "superstitious poppycock"; yet our inherited thought-worlds did not have to be this way, and understanding the trajectories at play in the manner we do by this simple sketching covers over a great deal of important nuance. Crossan, again putting the details into a more proper perspective, informs that:

> By the end of the second century of the common era, two hundred years after Jesus, *rabbinic* Judaism, like *catholic* [that is, "universal"; not what we today call the Catholic Church] Christianity, was deeply involved in retrojecting its ascendancy onto earlier history; it would later be as difficult to discern any earlier plurality in one as in the other. . . . It would, in truth, be difficult to say, had Moses woken from slumber around 200 C.E., which of the two would have surprised him the most.[11]

There were Judaisms and Christianities. Christianity *was* a Judaism. Christianity yet *is* a Judaism if we can unfasten the rabbinic model from that position of definitive article (the "the") it has achieved, while also re-Christologizing (in many ways de-politicizing) the church model from the position it has achieved; and hence we endeavor some steps towards each in the below. I think, therefore, that both of the reduced reactions to this "Christianity thing" (yes/no or faith/dismissal) miss some truly fascinating notional elements hidden beneath and within the storytelling of Judaism(s) writ large, of God/"God" as comprehended by our Hebrew "forebears" (ancestors in all sorts of ways, reckoning by lineage in blood and/or (taking liberties here, and asking the forgiveness of genetically-genuine Jewish readers) by spirituality), and thus let us dwell a short while on this "risen" in "risen Lord" as that is most obviously what appears to set Christianity apart from other Judaisms. Or does it?

---

10. The story of Elijah's ascension can be found in 2 Kings 2:3–9. A cup for him (for his return) is left out at Seder (Passover) celebrations, a tradition I confess to find quite moving.

11. Crossan, *Jesus,* 223; emphases in the original

Chapter 3

A Life: Beyond

THIS ASPECT OF RESURRECTION is central to virtually everything connected with Christianity as it is commonly understood in its present form, and so it naturally benefits our project to focus on it at slightly more length than the shakiness of the historically claimed witness accounts might warrant; I believe it is possible to both disconnect the person Yeshua from the abstracted position he has come to have (i.e. "Yeshua" the idea), yet to still consider the historical dead man as a "resurrected" wayfinder in a manner which not only fails to conflict with contemporary rational sensibilities (and does not call to mind any unsettling zombie-esque tales) but that is also in fact much closer to the original comprehension of Yeshua as "risen Lord" when seen ("seen!": comprehended) in the setting from whence such came.[1] For this journey we progress by going backwards, returning to the New Testament for our query/quarry, attempting to read it as it is and without the later addition of taught or enforced exegeses (while nevertheless recognizing that the New Testament itself is an exegesis: a collection and commentary purposely chosen for a particular portrayal). In other words, we make efforts for "other" words: for the same words but transformed in association, efforts to remove whatever filters may have been given us, efforts to approach the text (admittedly in translation) with a clearer pair of eyes. If we do—if we can—what is there to be found?

The epistles of Paul are the oldest documents in the canonical New Testament, easily predating even the earliest (officially approved) Gospel: that of Mark (more on that book and its possible, but non-surviving (at least in an extant format), predecessor in the below). In the first letter Paul wrote to the church at Corinth, he outlines that Christ is resurrected—risen again after having been assuredly dead—and that

---

1. We will later argue (in Chapter 11) for a position which takes Yeshua as presuming his own physical (fully corporeal) resurrection as divine reward following death (which we will also argue he did not/could not foresee with absolute prescience, albeit he certainly would have been aware of the risks he was under). This, we will propose, is similar to the view presented in Second Maccabees. Note that this is at odds with Paul's view as presented in this chapter, which appears to have more Platonic elements; Yeshua's could perhaps be characterized as less "Hellenized" than Paul's and more in line with typical Jewish understandings of the biological body and its ontological place.

if such is not the case then the whole edifice of Christianity (framed as their belief; "Christianity" as such naturally did not yet exist) is for nothing, essentially meaningless.[2] Of course Paul does not think that to be so; therefore the resurrection is real and must be real; but how? "Risen" in what form? He goes on:

> [42]So it is with the resurrection of the dead. What is sown [the physical body] is perishable, what is raised is imperishable. [43]It is sown in dishonor, it is raised in glory. It is sown in weakness, it is raised in power. [44]It is sown a physical body, it is raised a spiritual body. If there is a physical body, there is also a spiritual body.[3]

We might wish to take issue with a point of Paul's logic here since the fact of a physical body is not a necessary cause for (does not necessitate) a "spiritual body"—whatever such may be—even if (a giant "if") it is a *sufficient* cause for one (and no argument is provided for that as well), but such is beside the point at present, and indeed in many ways separate (or separable) entirely. Rather, what is important here for our concerns is not whether there absolutely "is" a spiritual body (in any sense), but instead the fact that Paul evidently understands Yeshua's body to have been raised *not in a physical way* but in a *spiritual one*, and the vision he claims to have had of the postmortem Yeshua is not of a man walking around as the Gospel tales have it, but of a bright light, the identity of which Paul does not even recognize until a voice from out of that luminescence informs him.[4]

The nuances here call for a pause, and for caution. For those of us who read the New Testament, and maybe especially for those who tend towards reading it in the sequencing of its constitutive books, there is a constant risk of falling prey to the natural tendency to provide coordination and alignment amongst the texts where there is none—at least not originally—and to see the cobbled together collection as a seamless singularity rather than what it really is: a hodgepodge produced by bickering bishops ensconced in politics and group dynamics, chosen over a series of years and using as possible inclusions only the volumes that were then to hand[5] (documents which were, additionally, authored over a number of decades for a number of reasons under a number of circumstances, with many not even entirely penned by a single individual nor free of unauthorized appendices). As Hans-Georg Gadamer would remind us, any book stands in a history—even the great ones that manage to stand outside

---

2. See 1 Corinthians 15:13–14: "[13]If there is no resurrection of the dead, then Christ has not been raised; [14]and if Christ has not been raised, then our proclamation has been in vain and your faith has been in vain." *Thinline Bible with the Apocrypha* (NRSV).

3. 1 Corinthians 15:42–44; *Thinline Bible with the Apocrypha* (NRSV).

4. The story of Paul's conversion is related in Acts 9:1–19 (technically I suppose ending with verse eighteen; verse nineteen is essentially a coda), and his name change from Saul to Paul is recorded later in 13:9 (interestingly given as an aside: "But Saul, also known as Paul . . . ") *Thinline Bible with the Apocrypha* (NRSV); see also Funk, *Honest to Jesus*, 259.

5. Thus excluding from the very start, and that by default, books such as those which were much later to be discovered at Nag Hammadi, Egypt.

history[6]—and with the Bible as we have it (in the Christian usage of that title: the Hebrew Bible (Tanakh), possibly the deuterocanonical books, and the New Testament texts[7]) we have not merely the stacked lineages of each work on its own, but as well the interactions and placements within the ordered official collection(s) determined at much later dates.

We tend to forget these details though, and when we open the cover to read we may see an order where there is at heart a chaos, or anyway a series of literary blocks that were not necessarily meant to be adhered together. Thus we again might see but not "see," we might look backwards and think it forwards, we might focus in on a piece and proclaim it a whole. Are our intentions in this format of approach merely indicative of a comforting fiction? Is the reading of these ancient books with modernly-blinded eyes (and with an eye to the modern) no more than a reassuring delusion, calibrated to make life's vicissitudes more tolerable? There must be more at stake in taking up these matters of faith, in grasping these matters of faith *in faith;* and indeed I think there is, I am very happy to concur with that: there is a world more at stake, a living "world" of a life unfolding through its foundational (its accepted, its applied) ideascapes, the essence of which reach into the core of one's being. Yet at times these ideas do need re-examining, and I believe that we in this particular Western and Semitic tradition find ourselves in that situation at present. (Incidentally, I would also argue these same points not only for a Yeshuan-styled or a Yeshuan-inflected Judaism but for every faith—including the faith of no-faith—and although we will explore this specific unraveling in more depth in the next chapter, for now we may simply state that within the specificities under consideration what is pertinent is not so much Yeshua the man as "Yeshua" the idea, the figure(ized) "Yeshua"; and such is not even really about Yeshua/"Yeshua" at all, rather the taken conceptual and therefrom the built perceptual.)

The elusiveness regarding his vision which Paul reports—the non-recognition of Yeshua as Yeshua in post-resurrection form—was not unique to his writings, and this same acknowledged (or alleged) lack of surety extended even into the narratives of encounters had with Yeshua when portrayed as being present humanly (in the image of a human or "as" a human) by those who supposedly (in the received traditions) knew him personally in life and then claimed to have seen him that way after death.[8]

---

6. Gadamer, *Truth and Method*.

7. Some might here wish to claim that either or both of those last two in our list are "unauthorized appendices." Let us be lighthearted about all this!

8. I stress here the physicalist aspect rather than something vague like Paul's "bright light," and please recall that these other narratives were written some decades after Paul's; the evolution at play is something we will need to dwell on. Notice too, however, that these could well have been entirely conjured fictions by the authors of the books, for not all resurrection stories in the New Testament allege a first person witness by the teller of the tale ("real" or otherwise), and in fact most of them do not: e.g. the canonical Gospels give us Cleopas and a companion on the road to Emmaus, Mary Magdalene and the other Mary at the tomb, Peter running to the tomb, "all the disciples" (at a home gathering first, then at the Ascension scene; and we might wish to check ourselves if we assume that "disciples" necessarily

For instance, in the recounting of the risen Yeshua's appearance to Mary Magdalene in John 20, or the story of the followers who saw him on the road in Luke 24, or again the disciples who related witnessing him by the sea in John 21; in each of these anecdotes none of the subjects knew who he was although Yeshua is not described in any instance as a "light" or other non-humanoid shape but instead as a person, a fully biological entity, or anyway an apparition in such a fully corporeal form. While I do not think we can read any of these incidents as undiluted history, there is something very interesting going on in the narrative arc wound through the New Testament anthology.

Developmentally the so-called "resurrection faith" that took root and grew amongst those who had adopted Yeshua's teachings during his period of ministry, as well as with the further second-order (so to speak) believers who heard the message indirectly via others as it spread throughout Palestinian social circles in the first century CE, is thought to have begun with the Mary Magdalene retelling (however much or little historicity is a part of that retelling), and since her tale as it is expressed in John 20 matches almost perfectly with the salient features of the oldest divine-human interactive narratives recorded in the Tanakh (that is, the Hebrew Bible; we will consider those accounts shortly below), I think it is worth quoting in the complete here despite the presence of many fictional elements and the further complication of John's penmanship being situated as the last of the four canonical Gospels, and therefore the most chronologically distant from the purported events themselves (again, however much reliability there may or may not be within the received text; the Gospel of John is believed to have been written around the end of the first century).[9] The relevant verses are:

> John 20:1–2, 11–17: [1]Early on Sunday morning [or, as in the Greek, "on the first day of the week"], while it was still dark, Mary Magdalene came to the tomb and found that the stone had been rolled away from the entrance. [2]She ran and found Simon Peter and the other disciple, the one whom Jesus loved. She said, "They have taken the Lord's body out of the tomb, and we don't know where they have put him! . . . [11]Mary was standing outside the tomb crying, and as she wept, she stooped and looked in. [12]She saw two white-robed angels, one sitting at the head and the other at the foot of the place where the body of Jesus had been lying. [13]"Dear woman, why are you crying?" the angels asked her. "Because they have taken away my Lord," she replied, "and I don't know

---

means eleven males (excepting Judas Iscariot) à la the church taught "twelve disciples")). The book of Acts—likely authored anonymously (production is disputed) but credited to "Luke" since it is a two-part work with that text (with "Luke" in quotation marks/inverted double commas because again the actual author is definitively unverifiable)—gives us Paul again, a vision to Stephen at his martyrdom, and a voice heard by Peter; but then conversely we have John, in what is ostensibly his own accounting, and thus not all the stories are of the "this happened to so-and-so" variety.

9. Funk and the Jesus Seminar, *The Gospel of Jesus*; see especially the Notes to the "Pillars and Pioneers" epilogue on pages 105–6 and those for the Gospel of John on page 112.

where they have put him." ¹⁴She turned to leave and saw someone standing there. It was Jesus, but she didn't recognize him. ¹⁵"Dear woman, why are you crying?" Jesus asked her. "Who are you looking for?" She thought he was the gardener. "Sir," she said, "if you have taken him away, tell me where you have put him, and I will go and get him." ¹⁶"Mary!" Jesus said. She turned to him and cried out, "Rabboni!" (which is Hebrew for "Teacher"). ¹⁷"Don't cling to me," Jesus said, "for I haven't yet ascended to the Father. But go find my brothers and tell them, 'I am ascending to my Father and your Father, to my God and your God.'"[10]

Situated within these sample resurrection accounts of the New Testament we can trace a clear move between Paul (written earlier) and the Gospels (written later) towards an ever more robust assertion of physicalism, and this raises some intriguing lines of inquiry. Before we examine those aspects though we must engage in a reinforcing of the realignment of probable presuppositions heretofore sought and doubly called for now. Even having noted the pairing of "Paul (written earlier)" with "the Gospels (written later)" I find that I need a moment for the nuances to really sink in since long years of habit and—likely in the case of those raised in Christian homes and/or cultures—instruction too have established the automatic ideational reaction (the default setting) of taking the four Gospel accounts to be foundational to Paul's works, and not the other way around, due to the episodes their authors' treat as being situated further back in the overall narrative framework of the self-expression of the religion's claimed genesis. By this I do not simply mean that the books can be found at the beginning of the New Testament as it is now bound by book manufacturers (although of course they can), but rather that the stories given in the Gospels are positioned in chronological years prior to the ministry of Paul as taken by a linear perspective: Matthew, Mark, Luke, and John present themselves as telling the reader about Yeshua's life as if they were written by a journalist at the scene; and then we have Paul penning his epistles quite openly as one "born late,"[11] while addressing his audience in the contemporaneous fashion that letters naturally employ (a voice from the middle of the first century); if we therefore read the Gospels on their own assertions instead of as being at the earliest many decades "after" those "events," we are mistaken. It is only too easy to mentally mesh what are actually the separate aspects of Paul as later convert to (one of) the alternative version(s) of Judaism(s) (i.e. the emerging Yeshuan faith) and his subsequent self-establishment as missionary to Gentile groups—a vocation that included the drafting, forming, and sending of all those instructional missives to the varying and scattered Christian communities across the extant Mediterranean

---

10. "Woman" as a form of address is most unfortunate (even with the "dear" added); but the text was written in a very different time and place, and I suppose the modern English translators wished to stay close to the language of the original; this quotation is from *Catholic Holy Bible* (NLT).

11. See 1 Corinthians 15:8, where Paul writes of Yeshua's self-revelation to him: "Last of all, as to one untimely born, he appeared also to me." *Thinline Bible with the Apocrypha* (NRSV).

world—with the timeline the Gospels base their narrations around. In fact the opposite is the case, and thus bears remembering: however much nonfiction is mixed up in the fiction of the Gospels (or vice versa if one prefers: "however much fiction is mixed up in the nonfiction"), Paul actually wrote the documents that became the bulk of our New Testament years and years before those Gospel accounts and their timelines were created, copied, and distributed in written and thereby determined forms,[12] and it was from Paul's conceptual masonry that the later constructs of fortified thought would primarily be built and, perhaps regrettably, thereafter ossify: he was the primary literary midwife during the Yeshuan movement's birth pangs, even if his was only one of many oral voices providing its evangelization.

In summary of these tokens we have only really glanced at, Paul's "bright light" changed into, over the course of many years, a human man: first (evidently) in a form somewhat akin to a specter ("Don't cling to me" as above, raising the natural question of *could not* cling?), and then into a personhood as seemingly bodily substantive as you or I (e.g. Yeshua tells the doubtful Thomas to go ahead, reach out and touch him in John 20:27, or eats a piece of cooked fish in the presence of his disciples in Luke 24:42–43). The repositioning required of oneself to observe with a more acute awareness than is usual these all too often glided-over textual details (overfamiliarity a primary culprit) is a striking intellectual exercise—it is an effortful unwinding of received wisdom and patterns of thought; a potentially painful procedure—but it will prove worthwhile and may be more enlightening yet as we take this path deeper down.

Crossan thinks that Paul's vision was a trance experience, and as such that which is, by definition, not revelatory of new information but a fusing of previously held information (although we may add that logically this fresh junction could itself be quite expressively novel). He then adds that the theological results Paul reached about his vision (or trance, or revelation—let us leave our judgment open) were only one possibility amongst many: "Maybe we should keep *trance* [Paul and his conclusions], *lifestyle* [the conclusions about Yeshua's message deemed most important to his fellow peasant followers in maintaining "the kingdom"], and *exegesis* [the conclusions of scholarly followers who went back into the existing Hebrew scriptures to search for

---

12. There were naturally many oral accounts in circulation, but I think it wise to exercise caution regarding such and to remind ourselves that these competed for listeners' attention and acceptance in both overall scheme and in detail; Crossan's remark quoted a few pages earlier concerning the teachings of Yeshua probably goes double for the biographical stories that were being passed on about him; for the reader's ease here again is what Crossan wrote: "When today we read his [i.e. Yeshua's] words in fixed and frozen texts we must recognize that the oral memory of his first audiences could have retained, at best, only the striking image, the startling analogy, the forceful conjunction, and, for example, the plot summary of a parable that might have taken an hour or more to tell and perform." Crossan, *Jesus,* 65. Even for those who knew him personally and engaged directly with him, how many life events—tens of years after their occurrence—would have been perfectly or near perfectly retained? Further, how many would have remained untainted by other (promotional) considerations, especially in the absence of anything like our "just the facts" modern value towards the presentation of a significant personage? (An attitude which is replete with self-deception and not infrequently hypocrisy, as we will study below regarding unavoidable biases and layers of interpretation.)

what could be applied to Yeshua—a reading *back into*] a little separate from one another—as different options and combinations for different followers and different groups within earliest Christianity."[13] This is a significant offering: it is a potential meme of an idea (in the term's older, non-internet sense), and if pulled out is quite remarkable. If Paul's vision of a bright light and voice that proclaimed itself to be Yeshua's was effected by Paul's own internal psychology—as a trance event would be (externally triggered or not)—and yielded up not a pristine *quantity* of data but a pristine *quality* (i.e. a new comprehension of elements already epistemologically held), then the basis of Paul's entire doctrinal hermeneutics becomes something entirely other than what it has traditionally been taken to be. How much weight are we comfortable giving to Paul's experiential claims about his vision? How do we wish to deliberate his perhaps more Hellenized Judaism (and thus demoting of the physical/literal and promoting of the spiritual/allegorical[14] (hence possibly at odds with the writers of the Gospels, who may have had more Palestinian aligned body-centric views))? By Paul's own admission this "light/voice" is foundational to his entire message, and then that of course to the full development of the Christian religion as we have it today, conceptually shorn (or anyway constantly striving to be, one way or another) of its point of fact Judaism.

Thus I must repeat the question: How much can we lay (or build) on this avouchment of a direct divine interaction? Again, this seems to me to be a matter of faith, and therefore only answerable individually (how near or far one is willing to go, or one feels oneself able to or compelled to go; by whatever source or means), but merely allowing ourselves to really think it through is instructive, particularly when held against how we might otherwise take and apply Yeshua's message as far as we are able to reconstruct and contextualize it. Moreover, the meaning of Yeshua's personhood and being becomes more clearly alternatively analyzable; e.g. either as the above mentioned fellow peasants adjudicated, or perhaps as how the contemporary scholars did: for the former the practical aspects involved with this life now were especially highlighted (living better in "the kingdom"), while for the latter the advent of the historical appearing of the man over against other facets was focused on, including— importantly—resurrection issues ("he came then" with "he will come once more"; manifestation into eschaton, skipping over Yeshua's death and its conjoined topics).[15] There is additionally quite some variance in the descriptions we have of Paul's vision between what he himself summarizes and what is conveyed about him by other/ another writer(s). For comparison, we have the abovementioned fifteenth chapter of

---

13. Crossan, *Jesus*, 190; emphases in the original (aside from the bracketed emphasis, which is mine).

14. This is a point repeatedly stressed by Boyarin in his *A Radical Jew*.

15. Boyarin, *A Radical Jew*. Crossan's account has the literate and elite priestly Yeshuan followers concerned mostly with his role as an occasion already predicted/prophesized, and then as a yet-to-be-realized *parousia* (a return, a second coming). There is of course room in this for the atonement aspect which was to become so emphasized as Yeshuan-Judaism coalesced around a core, but I would like to point out that there is also room for this notion of a required and (quite literal) substitutional sacrifice *not* to be involved.

Part 1 | Man, Son (of)

First Corinthians, where in verses three through eight Paul merely claims that "I also saw him," or "he appeared also to me." Here is the relevant passage in both the New Living Translation and the New Revised Standard Version (respectively):

> 1 Corinthians 15:3–8: ³I passed on to you what was most important and what had also been passed on to me. Christ died for our sins, just as the Scriptures said. ⁴He was buried, and he was raised from the dead on the third day, just as the Scriptures said. ⁵He was seen by Peter and then by the Twelve. ⁶After that, he was seen by more than 500 of his followers at one time, most of whom are still alive, though some have died. ⁷Then he was seen by James and later by all the apostles. ⁸Last of all, as though I had been born at the wrong time, I also saw him.

> 1 Corinthians 15:3–8: ³For I handed on to you as of first importance what I in turn had received: that Christ died for our sins in accordance with the scriptures, ⁴and that he was buried, and that he was raised on the third day in accordance with the scriptures, ⁵and that he appeared to Cephas ["Peter" in Greek], then to the twelve. ⁶Then he appeared to more than five hundred brothers and sisters at one time, most of whom are still alive, though some have died. ⁷Then he appeared to James, then to all the apostles. ⁸Last of all, as to one untimely born, he appeared also to me.[16]

There are a number of interesting things going on in this passage, and we point firstly to the reference to Paul's having *received* the teaching that he thereafter imparted; it seems based only on this reading (ignoring for the moment the rest of the Pauline corpus) that he was apparently told by someone(s) of the burgeoning church's message and not that it had been revealed to him: notice that the visionary part succeeds the "passed on to" or "received" part, and that the closing merely mentions the event almost in passing—"I also saw him," or "he appeared also to me"—such that nothing of a divine communiqué is emphasized or even expressed. (While I admit that the "received" could conceivably be taken in a revelatory sense, the "passed on to me" phrasing is far more indicative of an earthiness (so to speak); the Greek Paul uses in the epistle is *parelabon* from *paralambano*: "to take into close association," "to gain control of or receive jurisdiction over."[17]) Moreover, he was evidently told about it in some detail given the components enunciated, and then there is as well the repeated insistence on the pedagogical package's alignment with what were then accepted scriptures; but now we pause to ask: Accepted by whom? Whose sacrality? Such texts as those being cited would have been Hebrew given both Paul's own ethnicity and cultural background and the fact that the exegetes we have been discussing

---

16. *Catholic Holy Bible* (NLT); *Thinline Bible with the Apocrypha* (NRSV).

17. *The New Greek/English Interlinear New Testament*, trans. by Brown and Comfort, ed. by Douglas and Bryant, 606–7; Danker, rev. and ed., *A Greek-English Lexicon of the New Testament and Other Early Christian Literature*, 767–8.

were Jewish academics who became Yeshuan followers or associates of the Yeshuan groupings and then searched through the holy documents they already had to find hints of him therein; how appreciative of all this, therefore, would Paul's mainly Greek Corinthian audience have been?[18]

Note also the differentiations between Cephas/Peter as first and foremost, followed by "the twelve" (or "Twelve"; Cephas/Peter by implication being outside (above?) this grouping), and then the apostles; with James—by (some) tradition(s) Yeshua's own brother—lumped in as a kind of first amongst those apostles (and not "the twelve"), or possibly as occupying a middle position between "the twelve" and the apostles (depending on how inclusively we take that "all" in "all the apostles" to be), hinting already at an hierarchy within the Yeshuan ministerial ranks and probably a patriarchical assertion too since neither of the Marys would have been likely to make the cut of this undefined "twelve." (More on that in a moment; but consider also the fact that the Greek for what is "followers" in the New Living Translation and "brothers and sisters" in the New Revised Standard Version (verse six) reads simply as "brothers" in the original; yet this, on the other hand, is not necessarily limited to men as the term is broader in Greek than in its English equivalent.) Caution is additionally called for by this very aspect of "the twelve" as being non-delineated: it is possible that this phrase from Paul could have included women; and I mention this because the Gospel narratives from which we take our own authoritative listing of who is whom in "the twelve" were again written well *after* Paul wrote his letter. (In unwrapping our minds how liberating we find it to think on these altered timelines! Although Paul's record on women is indeed sketchy, I believe it well worth pondering that he might have had many women leaders in mind here; and then to think further on what such indicates for those who take Paul seriously today.) Then, lastly, we have Paul's almost whispered "I also saw him" or "he appeared also to me": why no details about the bright light? Why be so vague? *How* was Yeshua seen by or appeared to Paul (in what manner)? The same way that he is claimed to have been (or done) for Peter, "the twelve," the five hundred, James and the apostles, or in a different way? Very different? Slightly different? Nothing is clear.

Our questions then deepen by Paul's other own accounting given of his vision and change of ritual orientation (or allegiance, or affiliation: from Pharisaic Jewish[19]

---

18. The letter is addressed to "the church of God" at Corinth, to "those who are sanctified in Christ Jesus" (1:2), and although this (almost certainly) would have included some ethnic Jews it would have been a primarily Gentile grouping (see 12:2 with its "you know that when you were pagans," something a born Jew would not and could not ever have been), and the book is centered around Gentile concerns regarding the new faith; see Lander's introduction in Levine and Brettler, eds., *The Jewish Annotated New Testament*, 321-2.

19. The Pharisees were a very interesting intertestamental group (we should try to forget the image much of the Gospels give us of them): composed of laypeople and scribes rather than of hereditary priests, the Pharisees—as opposed to the Sadducees, who were the traditional religious authorities and were a priest based grouping—accepted the Oral Law as valid, sought to apply reason and personal conscience, and held beliefs very much in affinity with what came to be widespread in Yeshuan circles:

Part 1 | Man, Son (of)

(affirming both Written and Oral Torah) to Yeshuan-Jewish (with arguments being made over what to do with/about the Law)): namely, the one found in Galatians, a letter to another predominantly non-Jewish audience and a book that scholars (generally) agree was written before First Corinthians.[20] In it we find the following description, once more citing the New Living Translation's version and that of the New Revised Standard Version, in that order:

> Galatians 1:11–17: [11]Dear brothers and sisters, I want you to understand that the gospel message I preach is not based on mere human reasoning. [12]I received my message from no human source, and no one taught me. Instead, I received it by direct revelation from Jesus Christ. [13]You know what I was like when I followed the Jewish religion—how I violently persecuted God's church. I did my best to destroy it. [14]I was far ahead of my fellow Jews in my zeal for the traditions of my ancestors. [15]But even before I was born, God chose me and called me by his marvelous grace. Then it pleased him [16]to reveal his son to me so that I would proclaim the Good News about Jesus to the Gentiles. When this happened, I did not rush out to consult with any human being. [17]Nor did I go up to Jerusalem to consult with those who were apostles before I was. Instead, I went away into Arabia, and later I returned to the city of Damascus.

---

viz., worship was not Temple dependent nor composed of animal sacrifices (rather prayer and study), the acceptance of a Messianic hope, bodily resurrection, and angels and demons (a thousand bells ring for us!); see "Pharisee," *Encyclopædia Britannica*; and Kohler, "Pharisees," *Jewish Encyclopedia*. Both sites accessed March 18, 2020. In thinking on all this we might wish to consider Paul a Yeshuan even before he was a Yeshuan (the Pharisee-and-Yeshuan-Judaic affinities abound), but of course what is really going on is the reinforcing of multiple first century Judaisms and the (re)alignment of what has been labeled "Christianity" within the more apposite categorization of "Jewish," at least in a faith-oriented sense if not a strictly ethnic one. (I might comment here that I for one, and for what such is worth, consider it unfortunate that "Jew" is so often used with exclusively ethnic connotations (while I nevertheless respect and understand the crucially identitarian and particularist elements involved), and that it can hardly be valuable or appropriate to ever write or speak of "the Jew" as if such could exist in the uniform way implied, in the first century or any century (most appositely and especially our own). What is certain, though, is that however "Jewish" a non-ethnic Jew may be, the crushing weight of facing relentless prejudice and living within an astounding history (both positively but of course negatively too) will remain firmly outside the comprehension of those born into other lineages: An impossibility. Raphael writes eloquently on this general topic in a short pieced titled "Reflections on anti-Semitism," *The New Criterion*, 20–4.)

20. Perhaps the timeline is put best by the non-specific wording of Cohen's introduction to The Letter of Paul to the Galatians in *The Jewish Annotated New Testament*, where he writes that: "This letter shares language and themes with Romans and Corinthians, but the relative sequence of these letters is uncertain." Levine and Brettler, eds., *The Jewish Annotated New Testament*, 373. In the introductions to Galatians and First Corinthians in the *Catholic Holy Bible*, however, Galatians is cited with a date of "Around AD 49" and First Corinthians with "Around AD 56"; *Catholic Holy Bible* (NLT), pages 1239 and 1215, respectively. An internet search mostly confirms the later dating of First Corinthians as well, although all aspects considered I must admit I am happiest to agree with Cohen and remain on "uncertain." Boyarin, for his part, takes First Corinthians as something of a situational "corrective" to the Galatians message regarding the gender issues discussed therein (Paul thinks the Corinthians have taken things too far), but also suggests there might be some merit to the idea that Galatians was written while Paul was staying in Corinth; see Boyarin, *A Radical Jew*, especially Chapter 8.

> Galatians 1:11–17: ¹¹For I want you to know, brothers and sisters, that the gospel that was proclaimed by me is not of human origin; ¹²for I did not receive it from a human source, nor was I taught it, but I received it through a revelation of Jesus Christ. ¹³You have heard, no doubt, of my earlier life in Judaism. I was violently persecuting the church of God and was trying to destroy it. ¹⁴I advanced in Judaism beyond many among my people of the same age, for I was far more zealous for the traditions of my ancestors. ¹⁵But when God, who had set me apart before I was born and called me through his grace, was pleased ¹⁶to reveal his Son to me, so that I might proclaim him among the Gentiles, I did not confer with any human being, ¹⁷nor did I go up to Jerusalem to those who were already apostles before me, but I went away at once into Arabia, and afterwards I returned to Damascus.[21]

In this passage Paul very explicitly writes that everything he learned was by direct revelation, not a whit from a human source, and although this seems to contradict the First Corinthians account we might be generous and find a way for it not to: for instance, we could think that the Corinthians had already heard of his revelatory experience from the Galatians (the Graeco-Roman world being as connected as it was, and if we grant too that Paul indeed sent his letter to the churches found in the region of Galatia (now Turkey) prior to the one he sent to the city of Corinth, we may find this plausible) and hence Paul felt no need to repeat that claim. (Although we now wonder, why not repeat it, really, given the authority such would register?) Yet even so, willingly extending that much, it is still hard to grant fully considering that what Paul remarks was "passed on to" or "received" by him in his epistle to the Corinthians is of a far greater scope than what the voice attributed to the bright light narrative states, and furthermore in that bright light recounting Paul is thereafter (post-vision) almost immediately met by (and presumably not only "met" but was instructed by/spoke with) one Ananias, a follower of Yeshua in Damascus, the city where the text explains Paul had been bound when he was struck by his vision, and where he then maintains a fast in a temporarily blinded state for three days, waiting. ("He remained there blind for three days and did not eat or drink"; Acts 9:9 in the New Living Translation, see also below—and notice once more a failure to "see," a motif repeated again and again in these stories.) While there is the above "returned to" caveat regarding Damascus (Galatians 1:17; but what is all this about Arabia, kilometers and kilometers away?), indicating having been there before—and perhaps truly enough such was forthwith following the vision—we remain in the dark about what to make of Ananias, the man who was purportedly sent by God/"God" to get Paul started on his new life. Paul certainly tells us nothing, but one would think—all things considered—that he would, or ought to.

These details of encountered personages, location, downtime, visitation, et cetera, however come not from the epistles but from the conversion story as it is relayed

---

21. *Catholic Holy Bible* (NLT); *Thinline Bible with the Apocrypha* (NRSV).

Part 1 | Man, Son (of)

in The Acts of the Apostles, and we must therefore now turn to it, acknowledging that the source for this crucial and foundational relation of Paul's shifting from (one of) the more standardized Judaism(s) of his day to the Yeshuan-Judaism movement initiated by his claimed/felt/experienced vision of a resurrected Yeshua is nothing penned by Paul himself (despite his obvious productivity), but is rather to be found in this other book best known simply as Acts (full title: "The Acts of the Apostles"), a text traditionally attributed to either Luke or to whomever the anonymous author was of both Luke and Acts since those books are clearly linked even if their authorship is sometimes called into question by one New Testament scholar or another.[22] The vignette is from chapter nine, quoted from the same two versions and in the same ordering:

> Acts 9:3–6, 10–12: ³As he [Paul; at this point still before his name change and therefore referred to as Saul] was approaching Damascus on this mission [of persecution, see the Galatians verses above], a light from heaven suddenly shone down around him. ⁴He fell to the ground and heard a voice saying to him, "Saul! Saul! Why are you persecuting me?" ⁵"Who are you, lord?" Saul asked. And the voice replied, "I am Jesus, the one you are persecuting! ⁶Now get up and go into the city, and you will be told what you must do." . . . ¹⁰Now there was a believer in Damascus named Ananias. The Lord spoke to him in a vision, calling, "Ananias!" "Yes, Lord!" he replied. ¹¹The Lord said, "Go over to Straight Street, to the house of Judas. When you get there, ask for a man from Tarsus named Saul. He is praying to me right now. ¹²I have shown him a vision of a man named Ananias coming in and laying hands on him so he can see again."

> Acts 9:3–6, 10–12: ³Now as he was going along and approaching Damascus, suddenly a light from heaven flashed around him. ⁴He fell to the ground and heard a voice saying to him, "Saul, Saul, why do you persecute me?" ⁵He asked, "Who are you, Lord?" The reply came, "I am Jesus, whom you are persecuting. ⁶But get up and enter the city, and you will be told what you are to do." . . . ¹⁰Now there was a disciple in Damascus named Ananias. The Lord said to him in a vision, "Ananias." He answered, "Here I am, Lord." ¹¹The Lord said to him, "Get up and go to the street called Straight, and at the house of Judas look for a man of Tarsus named Saul. At this moment he is praying, ¹²and he has seen in a vision a man named Ananias come in and lay his hands on him so that he might regain his sight."[23]

---

22. The introductory entry for The Acts of the Apostles by Gilbert in the previously mentioned *Jewish Annotated New Testament* lists authorship as "written by the author of the Third Gospel, traditionally identified as Luke. The two works (Luke-Acts) have a common literary style, narrative parallels, and thematic similarities . . . The attribution of Acts to Luke . . . first appears in the second century." Levine and Brettler, eds., *The Jewish Annotated New Testament*, 219.

23. *Catholic Holy Bible* (NLT); *Thinline Bible with the Apocrypha* (NRSV).

Prior to pondering (wandering? meandering?) the specificities of this account—which are quite remarkable in the broader context we have been examining—allow me to add as an aside that this story is later retold twice in Acts, once in chapter twenty-two (verses six through sixteen) after Paul has been saved by a Roman tribune and group of soldiers from a crowd he had angered with his preaching (the crowd is portrayed as Jewish, one of Acts' unfortunately frequent polemical instances of Yeshuan-Judaism apologetics sought via a denigrating of "the Jews from Asia" (as here, see 21:27) or "the Jews" from elsewhere, or just "the Jews"), and the other time in chapter twenty-six (verses twelve through eighteen) when Paul is brought before King Agrippa (ruler of Judea; at this point in the book Paul has made his way to Jerusalem) after again being involved in/causing a public disturbance. That these other accounts agree on their main points while differing in some minor details from that found in chapter nine and quoted above is interesting of itself, particularly given that these three versions fall within the same book which is thought to have a single authorship—and therefore could have been given stronger parallels if so sought—but such do not directly concern our study.

Now for this snippet from chapter nine, in which we actually find not one distinct vision/numinous injunction being referenced, but three: firstly the light and voice, then Ananias' divine instructions delivered in his own vision, and then the mention of a second vision by Paul folded into Ananias' vision wherein he is told that Paul has been informed about/prepared for him. Note again that Paul does not write about any of this himself, and in Galatians even asserts in the strongest terms that no human taught him the message he delivered; the lack of alignment between these tales purportedly about the same event (Paul's conversion) cannot help but raise doubts. While it is the case that Acts does not overtly state that Ananias *taught* Paul anything, surely a visit by a Yeshuan believer who is credited with providing the healing prayer that restores Paul's eyesight would have resulted in at least a few subsequent words about how Paul might change his thinking, and in the chapter twenty-two version of the story Ananias is actually quoted—by Paul—as having told him to "be baptized," have his "sins washed away," and "call on" Yeshua's name. Arguably any one of those points would fall under the rubric of instruction, and taken together almost present a miniature early church catechism.

To me though the real question that lingers most is why Paul himself only uses terms such as "appeared/saw" and "revelation," stripped of any drama and almost proud in the implied claims of self-sufficiency (only Paul and God/"God", no mere mortal pedagogy at play). On the one hand, Paul writing for himself in the way he does appears designed to establish his authority, and perhaps given his background of previous persecution and very public disbelief he felt the need to do so. On the other hand, the writer of Acts putting it the way he does places Paul within the context of a larger and pre-existing (already cohesive) single group (which the earliest Yeshuan followers, spread throughout the wider Roman world and using different texts, performing different services, and almost certainly emphasizing different aspects of what was anyway hardly a uniform doctrinal code could scarcely pretend to); although in its development Acts too does elevate Paul to a lofty position. It might be that in this the Acts author was more concerned to promote the whole, whereas Paul was oriented to promote himself. The additions of a bright light, blindness and healing, extended fast, et cetera, could also be mere fictions appended on for effect; certainly the storytelling in Acts is more enjoyable to read than Paul's braggadocio. Finally, it is possible that Paul either did have a "bright light" vision or believed himself to have had one (and we will later argue that this distinction between "had" and "believed oneself to have had/have" makes no pertinent phenomenological difference) and told such to whomever later penned the book of Acts: Paul is thought to have died between 62-64 CE and Acts to have been composed at least after 70 CE but probably in the early second century;[24] overlap was possible. The issue of how well remembered such a relating would have been by the time it was recorded is of course applicable here as well—as in many other instances within scripture—but again I would like to stress the absence of any remote necessity for us to read any part of these texts as historical, in either a "hard" or a "soft" version. Much can be taken from them even if they are entirely fictive; although one would think that at least kernels of historicity exist here and there to varying degrees. Whatever the case may or may not be, it is this "bright light" that has remained in our imaginations, and it is from this jumping off that the later(ly written, narratively earlier) spectral and/or bodily resurrection accounts of the Gospels developed.

The story that seems to have begun this luminescence to ligament trend—if I may be forgiven the rhetorical flourish—is that of the empty tomb found in the final chapter of Mark (sixteen), which again is the oldest of the narrative Gospels but still was not written until around or slightly after the year 70 CE, making it roughly forty years separated from the death of its main character and purpose: the man Yeshua. (An incidental point on dating: Yeshua's birth is recorded for us as being in the time of Herod the Great, who died in 4 BCE,[25] and thus if the New Testament accounting of Yeshua's ministry beginning when he was thirty years old[26] is accurate (or close to accurate) then we have a date of somewhere approaching 30 CE for his crucifixion, regardless of the length of the ministry itself.[27]) This Markan tale of the abandoned

---

24. On Paul see Sanders, "St. Paul the Apostle," *Encyclopædia Britannica*. Accessed March 17, 2020. The dating for Acts is from the same introduction by Gilbert in Levine and Brettler, eds., *The Jewish Annotated New Testament,* 219. The introduction in the *Catholic Holy Bible,* however, puts the date earlier at "Probably between AD 63 and 70"; *Catholic Holy Bible* (NLT), 1167.

25. Some useful contextual information can be found in this brief biography: Perowne, "Herod: King of Judea", *Encyclopædia Britannica*. Accessed November 11, 2019.

26. This from Luke 3:23, which reads flatly, "Jesus was about thirty years old when he began his public ministry" in *Catholic Holy Bible* (NLT); and, "Jesus was about thirty years old when he began his work" in *Thinline Bible with the Apocrypha* (NRSV).

27. There is some controversy over this detail; the Gospels of Matthew, Mark, and Luke refer to one Passover (an annual event) during Yeshua's public time of teaching, while John refers to three (or

burial cave, however, is thought to have been the author's innovation as it seems unbeknownst to Paul—raising yet more questions about Paul's interpretation of the resurrection and perhaps too of his asserted revelation—and even in its Gospel telling the story ends properly with Mary Magdalene and Mary the mother of James seeing an angel—not Yeshua—at the tomb and fleeing in terror (up to verse eight); the rest of the chapter (verses nine through twenty) has been attributed to "Pseudo-Mark," i.e. another author entirely, someone who went back at a point afterwards and affixed a second conclusion.[28] However many writers were involved, the trajectory itself is certain: Paul's very vague "appeared also to me/I also saw him," to Acts' "bright light" ex post facto attribution to Paul's resurrection experience, to Mark's "empty tomb/proclaiming angel" (written possibly contemporaneously with Acts but probably before Acts, yet not about Paul), to Pseudo-Mark's "he [Yeshua, and recognizably so as the context makes clear] appeared first to Mary Magdalene[29] . . . after this in another form [another form?] to two of them . . . later he appeared to the eleven themselves [the remaining disciples, minus Judas Iscariot; here again clearly as Yeshua]" (Mark 16:9, 12, 14). Robert Funk summarizes the direction that the relaying and comprehension of the resurrection narratives took in the first to second centuries this way: "as time passed and the tradition grew, the reported appearances become more palpable, more corporeal. They gradually lose their luminous quality and take on aspects of a resuscitated corpse."[30]

Given the time span involved (with even the oldest of the New Testament biographies composed decades after the events described), the desire, and certainly too a felt need, to present Yeshua in a miraculous light by a burgeoning community (both in

---

possibly two, some have suggested one reference is actually to another festival). What is pertinent for our discussion is the linear development of the ideas involved in resurrection rather than the period of ministerial length per se, but interested readers who desire to forego scholarly minutiae may see the following websites for a general picture: Pelikan and Sanders, "Jesus," *Encyclopædia Britannica*; and "Ministry of Jesus," *Wikipedia: The Free Encyclopedia*. For two decidedly biased accounts, see also Hunter, "Why do we think Jesus' ministry lasted 3 years?" *Daily Bible Study Tips*; and Staples, "The Length of Jesus' Ministry and Daniel 9," *Jason Staples*. All sources accessed January 21, 2020. On the whole, considering John's more effluent interpretative push as compared to the other Gospels, and too Mark's closer alignment with the purer "Sayings Gospels" such as Q and the *Gospel of Thomas* (both of which will be referred to much more in our following text), I think it more likely that the authors of the *Britannica* entry are possibly correct in emphasizing that Yeshua's public career was short, maybe less than a full calendar year, although maybe slightly more. Yet what an impact it had! Crossan, *Jesus*, 25, also indicates that we do have solid dates for Pontius Pilate's service as prefect of Judea (from 26 to 36 CE)—this is the man whom the canonical Gospels have acting as judge at Yeshua's trial—and hence Yeshua must have died somewhere within that timeframe; moreover, given the average lifespan for men in the region at the time (twenty-nine years, again according to Crossan, *Jesus*), a birth late in Herod's reign and execution in the early to middle portion of Pilate's rule would fit the pieces together quite neatly, with Yeshua being killed at full adulthood and probably beyond his years of intensive physical labor.

28. Funk, *Honest to Jesus*, 259–60; Funk and the Jesus Seminar, *The Gospel of Jesus*, 111; footnotes to Mark 16 in *Thinline Bible with the Apocrypha* (NRSV).

29. What prominence for her! As many have lamented, what a shame the church did not manage to keep its somewhat proto-feminist early leanings (or anyway the sparks thereof).

30. Funk, *Honest to Jesus*, 260.

terms of numbers and in ethno-cultural makeup) that found itself wishing to put distance between their own group and the other Judaisms, which by then had also begun coalescing around the new post-Temple rabbinic and more fully synagogue-centered framework, gathering atop groundwork helpfully laid by the same Pharisees whom the New Testament assails. Moreover this latter orthodoxy/emerging orthodoxy of a "mainline" Judaism was itself motivated to eject the Yeshuan-Jews with their alternative interpretations of the Law in order to assist in fostering the uniformity sought; this situation of "goodbye/good riddance" was thus very much a two-way street.

There was a further consideration involved as well: the inevitable increasing Hellenization of the Yeshuan community as it ceased being a purely (originary) Judean and ethnic Palestinian Jewish faith which resulted from the influx of Gentile converts (hat tip to Paul)—people who brought with them their own pre-existing ideas about the divine and divine/mortal intermingling—meant that with each of these various elements in deeper play as the years passed from the first century to the second, we can (and should) consider from our vantage the prior Pauline understanding of resurrection as likely the theologically "purer" one, at least as far as those first believers are concerned, compared with the later Gospel tales ("purer," that is, in the sense of it being less politically motivated and influenced). This despite, or possibly because of, the opacity and overt mysticism that is part and parcel of Paul's personal comprehension as expressed in 1 Corinthians 15:42-44 (what, after all, *is* a "spiritual body"?). For the sake of refreshing our memories, and since too in the light of the foregoing examination of Paul's ever-unclear explanations of his resurrection vision/revelation we are now better equipped to handle it, I think it worth repeating the argument Paul presents in that section, however logically garbled it might appear from our own (modernly biased) perspective. Here then is the passage once more, this time citing both the New Living Translation and the New Revised Standard Version (respectively), as we have for our other Pauline and Paul-related portions:

> 1 Corinthians 15:42-44: [42]It is the same way with the resurrection of the dead. Our earthly bodies are planted in the ground when we die, but they will be raised to live forever. [43]Our bodies are buried in brokenness, but they will be raised in glory. They are buried in weakness, but they will be raised in strength. [44]They are buried as natural human bodies, but they will be raised as spiritual bodies. For just as there are natural bodies, there are also spiritual bodies.

> 1 Corinthians 15:42-44: [42]So it is with the resurrection of the dead. What is sown [the physical body] is perishable, what is raised is imperishable. [43]It is sown in dishonor, it is raised in glory. It is sown in weakness, it is raised in power. [44]It is sown a physical body, it is raised a spiritual body. If there is a physical body, there is also a spiritual body.[31]

---

31. *Catholic Holy Bible* (NLT); *Thinline Bible with the Apocrypha* (NRSV).

A LIFE: BEYOND

If we take this passage as a type of keystone for that on which Paul's own understanding of "bodily resurrection" rested, we can apply the sort of incorporeal and aethereal (and therefore non-bodily in every physical sense) conception outlined here towards his recounting of the vision upon which he based his "conversion" referenced above. This abstraction, incidentally, would not be out of line with strands of contemporary Jewish religious thought, particularly amongst the subset of scholars to which Paul belonged: the Pharisees (see, e.g. the self-proclamation he makes in his letter to the Philippians (3:5): ". . . a Hebrew born of Hebrews; as to the law, a Pharisee"; or in words assigned to him in Acts 23:6 by that book's writer: ". . . 'Brothers, I am a Pharisee, a son of Pharisees.'"; both verses from the New Revised Standard Version).[32] We can now, resting on the preceding, think our placement of the word *conversion* in the quotation marks/inverted double commas as we have done in this paragraph apposite because seen in this light Paul did not so much change faiths as he moved from one Judaism into another. This is naturally a very controversial point, and it will have to be argued and re-argued throughout our study, but my contention is that given the nature of the world in which Paul was embedded it was his acceptance of Yeshua as ultimate atoning salvific sacrifice (and "atonement" is another point we shall have to argue, and in that strenuously against a simple and literal version; see Part 4 below, especially Chapter 13) that was the real difference with other Judaisms at the time; certainly not the aspect of resurrection we have been exploring, and not even resurrection as comprehended in the "spiritual body" ambiguity which he asserts for each of us at death and, apparently, in which he took his revelatory vision of Yeshua to be composed. He thinks something happened to him that convinced him the Yeshuan-Jews were correct in their claims; probably he did not think it a "bright light" himself (else he most likely would have described such in his accounting(s)), but he assigned that experiential "something" to be an intervention by a risen Yeshua who was no longer of perishable, dishonorable, weak flesh, but had ascended to the opposite qualities in his postmortem state of (re)new(ed) life. The soteriological implications Paul took will, as remarked, need to be returned to, and such are most obviously an issue of deep variance with Judaism(s) as we know it (/them) today and therefore comprise the largest obstacle to our project of re-enfolding Christianity into Judaism; but at this moment we will table those matters and maintain a focus on resurrection(-al) options.

There is another advantage too to this Pauline "appeared/saw" (and leaving it at that) indefiniteness: such does not require the incredulousness on our part that a forthrightly physical resuscitation viewpoint demands, like that made by the

---

32. The notes given to this section of First Corinthians in *The Jewish Annotated New Testament* state further that: "Rabbinic literature speculates about the form of the resurrected body (whether naked or clothed, reconstituted from dust or repaired, like or unlike a mortal body, et cetera); Roman-period Jewish epitaphs suggest that some understood resurrection as purely spiritual and incorporeal." Levine and Brettler, eds., *The Jewish Annotated New Testament*, 349. It should be pointed out here too that the other major group of legal scholars at Paul's time, the Sadducees, did not accept bodily resurrection or even an immortal soul; see "Sadducee," *Encyclopædia Britannica*. Accessed March 19, 2020.

Part 1 | Man, Son (of)

narratives given in the Gospels. Admittedly this is not really an argument in favor of it so much as it is a relief not to have the more extreme cognitive load made (especially to those of us who perhaps exercise our reasoning a bit overmuch and cannot simply suspend thought to "just believe"; I realize this failure of "pure faith" will appear pathetic to some and valiant to others, but there it is), to be able to accept Yeshua as a spiritual guide, as someone with a real experience of the divine who had meaningful and applicable teachings to share—valid even across these millennia—without also having to take the leap into what is often euphemistically labeled a mindset which is "childlike" in its acceptance. Perhaps this unburdening will not affect many who consider Yeshua's ministry valuable, and perhaps it is simply wrong and there really *was* a straightforwardly physical resurrection of the man, but in the absence of evidence one way or the other—indeed, in the impossibility of evidence—the case that we have tried to put forward strikes me as being a compelling one. (I should add that I think a stance along these lines is one that Funk and other New Testament scholars who have taken this journey with far greater expertise than I have (again, ours is a philosophical undertaking) might also accede to, or at least acknowledge as sober and sound.) Experts and arguments aside though, a re-examining and re-working of the many ways a term like "resurrection" might be understood is a task we may find worthwhile if we are thoughtful, with or without existing belief, and indeed an operation such as this is even welcoming in one degree or another. The entire "risen L(l)ord" edifice could well be a fiction, an imagining that got stretched and stretched, yet it could also be taken in a less literal but nevertheless experientially potent manner: Yeshua "reborn" conceptually and thereby phenomenologically—and what that consequently does/might do for one in the lived moments of a life passed.

The notional picture is however more nuanced than Paul's vague gesturing, by no means clear even in his (Acts appended) "bright light," as an additional return to the wider historical background and conceptual climate of first century Palestine indicates in the way that it renders the proffered "solution" darker (or murkier) yet. The problem we now encounter in this regard, as I see it, is one to be found within the texts of (rabbinic) Judaism itself; that is, the then slowly coalescing version of a mainstream Judaism which was composed of the other Judaisms that were (mostly) not of the Yeshuan disciples' variety(-ies). (I wish to stress here (again and again) how extremely blurred the lines between these sections of Jewish religious society were at this juncture—in Palestine and the Diaspora—, a point made forcefully by Daniel Boyarin,[33] and one we will have cause to return to further in the below.)

The *earliest* of the shared Hebrew scriptures for this group/these groups describe God/"God" as indeed being seen in very physical and "real" ways by a number of prophets (and even by regular people) throughout Israel's past, clearly much along the same lines as to how the risen Yeshua was reported to be perceived in the canonical Gospel tellings, which—not incidentally—were the *latest* of those within the New

---

33. See Boyarin, *Border Lines*.

Testament narrative-documentary tradition (and a long ways from Paul's rather tame (by comparison) reported vision). James Kugel outlines the many instances in the oldest parts of the Tanakh where a theophanic event—God/"God" appearing before a person—is related quite matter-of-factly; and I do not mean in the "burning bush" sense (although in that sense too), but very much as a fellow *homo sapiens sapiens* standing there with two dusty feet on the ground. Moreover, and extremely intriguingly, in most of these cases the subject/viewer involved did not at first realize the other before them was in fact God/"God" until the climactic story moment comes and her or his eyes are dramatically "opened" such that she/he is suddenly able to "see" (in both of the same meanings that English grants to this verb: as visual perception *and* as mental comprehension).[34]

Paul's Acts' assigned "bright light" vision of Yeshua involved as well the later dropping of "scales from his eyes" whereupon "his sight was restored" and he was baptized into the Yeshuan-Jewish faith (once more, narratively this happened after his spending three days in a total fast while blinded; by textual implication the condition was a result of the radiance of the light that felled him en route to Damascus; for further contextual placement of this story within the gathering of other resurrection relatings, The Acts of the Apostles has been dated to around 70–90 CE and is therefore approximately contemporary with the composition of the Gospel of Mark).[35] Paul's inability to see is given as quite literal in this account, but must have been allegorically purposive too since one cannot miss the overt symbolism, particularly within the setting of it as a "conversion" tale. The reader will notice further yet how these exact elements are precisely those involved in the Mary Magdalene vignette that was quoted above, emphasized especially in its verse sixteen where Mary "turns" (realizes, has her eyes "opened"), and also—as mentioned too—in Yeshua's strikingly odd remark (odd when we take care to pause and make note of it) not to cling to him in its verse seventeen. Was that last line perhaps a literary hint by the author, an indication to understand the expressed resurrection in terms that yield only an illusion of (solid) corporeality? Such would be more akin to how Paul appears to have understood his

---

34. Kugel, *The God of Old*.

35. The "happy ending" of restoration to our Pauline Damascene tale quoted in part earlier might be the verses Acts 9:17–18, in *Catholic Holy Bible* (NLT): "17So Ananias went and found Saul. He laid his hands on him and said, 'Brother Saul, the Lord Jesus, who appeared to you on the road, has sent me so that you might regain your sight and be filled with the Holy Spirit.' 18Instantly something like scales fell from Saul's eyes, and he regained his sight." *Thinline Bible with the Apocrypha* (NRSV) expresses the same as: "17So Ananias went and entered the house. He laid his hands on Saul and said, 'Brother Saul, the Lord Jesus, who appeared to you on your way here [i.e. to Damascus], has sent me so that you may regain your sight and be filled with the Holy Spirit.' 18And immediately something like scales fell from his eyes, and his sight was restored." On the dating of Acts see: The Editors of Encyclopædia Britannica, "The Acts of the Apostles," *Encyclopædia Britannica*. Accessed January 23, 2020. Incidentally, and as noted above in Chapter 3, the first mention of Saul as "Paul" (that is, his name change) occurs in Acts 13:9 with the simple locution "Saul, also known as Paul." (This phrasing can be found in both the New Living Translation and New Revised Standard Version, and, I would guess, in many other versions as well.)

vision if our analysis has been sound. As for the concurrent Markan version of the Marian tale, short of the existence of a miraculous auditory recording bequeathed to the writer of Mark (or a whispering in the ear or the like) the dialogue as we have it is obviously not a verbatim one, and thus we are left to wonder why (we are prompted to contemplate why) this precise wording—of all the possibilities—may have been willfully included. Here and throughout scripture (Hebrew, Greek, Aramaic, Latin, Yeshuan . . .) there are depths to be explored that are inextricably tied to the personal experiences of the authors as they interacted with their faith(s), their Jacob-esque "wrestling with God."[36]

Yet between the oldest Hebrew narratives and the retelling of visions of Yeshua as a (re)interpreted physically resurrected and divine Jewish messiah[37] there is a wide gap

---

36. Genesis 32:22–30. What is of remarkable note in this section, and precisely in line with our present argumentative movement, is not only Jacob's struggles with the divine but the relating of such as being first described as Jacob wrestling with "a man" whom—astonishingly—is unable to break free from Jacob's grip even after putting his hip joint out of socket. Jacob demands a blessing and to know the man's name before he will release him; he then receives the former and has his own name changed from Jacob to Israel, but his partner pointedly refuses to reveal his personal identity, saying only (mysteriously) "you have striven with God and with humans, and have prevailed" (verse twenty-eight). Jacob thereafter calls the place where this confrontation occurred "Peniel" (meaning "the face of God"), since, he says, "I have seen God face to face and yet my life is preserved" (verse thirty). Jacob's eyes were thus similarly "opened" post-exertion—or was this a mistaken appropriation of divinity to the other? Absolutely the reader is made to conclude the prior choice in favor of a true revelation. Quotations are from *Thinline Bible with the Apocrypha* (NRSV). Kugel, *The God of Old,* comments on this passage as well. It is worth comparing this account from the Tanakh, where it forms 32:25–31, and where the "striven" verse (here twenty-nine) reads: ". . . you have striven with beings divine and human" and contains this footnote around the "beings divine and human" phrasing: "*Or* 'God (Elohim, *connected with second part of* 'Israel") *and men.*" Thereafter the "Peniel" verse (here thirty-one) has this wording: "So Jacob named the place Peniel [another footnote: "*Understood as 'face of God.'*"], meaning, 'I have seen a divine being face to face, yet my life has been preserved.'" *Tanakh* (NJPS). The labeling of "Peniel" yields the same, yet note the ambiguous "beings divine and human," which indeed could intend the plural reference only for the latter "human" but is not as explicit as the New Revised Standard Version's straightforward "God and with humans" thus leaving room for multiple "divines"; and moreover this possibility seems strengthened by the translation's use of the indefinite article in "a divine being face to face" rather than "God face to face." (Note that Hebrew only has a definite article, and so the *lack* of an article in the text may be rendered with an indefinite article in English.) Have we been given a theological (interpretive) insert by one version or the other? It does appear so; nevertheless, the overall point we wish to make in this section within our own study remains (i.e. a theophany and a revelatory "seen!").

37. Again, the Gospel accounts of these tales were written forty-some years after the events purportedly described, and although that is not a great deal of time scientifically speaking (despite the fact that for human lives (and memories!) the amount certainly weighs heavier), they were nevertheless penned under starkly different socio-historical circumstances. The claim that Yeshua "fit the bill"—so to speak—of what the messiah should be is also a very contentious one, and the New Testament as we have it is therefore filled with arguments to this effect—whatever our own eyes may "see" in it, a fair reading of the New Testament does not find it *proclaiming* (i.e. as in announcing the known) Yeshua as messiah so much as it *contends* that he is such—while many other texts of the time that are not to be found in Yeshuan-Jewish literature give arguments against. The scholarly field is vast, but the traditionally dominant view on the messiah within what became rabbinic Judaism is of a potent descendent of David who would bring triumph and unity to the Jewish people (politically or otherwise); however this too has proven not to be nearly as unitary as once thought: a stone discovered in Israel to have first century BCE Hebrew writing on it was recently analyzed and the conclusion was reached that it describes a

in which centuries passed that witnessed more and more books being composed by Hebrew writers expressing the Hebrew numinous comprehension, out of the bounty from which thenceforth a collection of some would be compiled into a (more or less) single set of holy writ, and along this literary-conceptual journey any previous notions of a human or human-like apparition of the divine gave way to God/"God" appearing in a storm, or a fire, or a calamity, or latterly not at all in a visible manner, and then finally of course the conclusion that God/"God" is not only *never* seen but is not even *see-able* became the default norm. Anyone would tell you in that era (as perhaps now too) that God/"God" is "felt" in the mind—or the heart or the stomach, depending on culturally based descriptive inclinations—, and not perceived by the eyes, that God/"God" is interacted with in an inner fashion, and not an outer one.

This idea of a more removed, perhaps "higher," God/"God" took root—gained intellectual traction, was ontologically and culturally embedded—and in that it became taken for granted, an assumption from which one started rather than worked one's way towards. Yet what presents itself to me as an absolutely fascinating possibility in this ideational progression is that the very movement amongst the early Yeshuan-followers (and even, it seems, amongst at least some of their preceding Judaic messianic communities) to claiming visions of Yeshua as physically—as literally *bodily*—resurrected might have in practice been a return (and most probably an unintentional one) to these same ancient understandings and reports: throwbacks, if you will, by certain

---

messiah who would *physically suffer and then rise from the dead after three days(!)*: given that the artifact predates the historical Yeshua, what this indicates is that such ideas regarding the messiah were *already* part of the cultural zeitgeist when Yeshua lived and taught—they were there and ready to be affixed to him or to anyone else—and were indeed antecedently applied to independence leaders against the Romans at the (linearly precedent) time of the stone's inscription, just as they would later be to Yeshua. We are so accustomed to the concept of Yeshua as a radically re-understood suffering and resurrected messiah—something new, a historical break, perhaps foretold but never realized—that we might fail to appreciate how startling this earlier dating really is. The label "messiah" moreover kept getting applied in the centuries that followed, e.g. Simon bar Kokhba, founder of a successful—yet short-lived—Jewish state in the second century CE (in this case not, however, of the "suffering" type); also too, and on the other hand from bar Kokhba but along the same "atonement" lines in which Paul took Yeshua, there is the Maccabean rendering of the defiant priest Eleazar who is held up as a paragon to emulate in his martyrdom and of whom the first century CE text Fourth Maccabees states (quite astonishingly in its substitutional forthrightness) in 6:26–30a: "26When he [Eleazar] was now burned to his very bones and about to expire, he lifted his eyes to God and said, 27'You know, O God, that though I might have saved myself, I am dying in burning torments for the sake of the law. [cf. Yeshua's plea as in Mark 14:36, Luke 22:42, and Matthew 26:42, where he asks for his coming Passion suffering to be removed, yet resigns himself to God's will.] 28Be merciful to your people, and let our [i.e. "my" at this point in the story: Eleazar was the first of a group arrested and tortured to death by Greek soldiers of the Seleucid Empire acting under order of Antiochus IV] punishment suffice for them. 29Make my blood their purification [!], and take my life in exchange for theirs [!!].' 30After he said this, the holy man died nobly in his tortures"; *Thinline Bible with the Apocrypha* (NRSV). I emphasize all this neither to reduce Yeshua's uniqueness nor his peculiar message, but rather to try and place him in a much needed wider context. On the archeological/historical portions (and some hermeneutical comments) of the foregoing, see: Ethan Bronner, "Ancient Tablet Ignites Debate on Messiah and Resurrection", *The New York Times*; "Simon bar Kokhba", *Wikipedia: The Free Encyclopedia*; both accessed January 29, 2020; Boyarin, *The Jewish Gospels*; and Kirby, "4 Maccabees", *Early Jewish Writings*. Accessed March 23, 2020.

groups of Jews to the manner in which their ancestral other groups of Jews wrote and talked about meeting with God/"God". Everything was right there to be read inside the received texts already familiar, and if (they might have thought) the transcendent had not manifested on these mortal shores for some while, then really what was that? Time is nothing to a timeless God/"God".

If these new-old interpretations were indeed a comprehensive return, we may be led to wonder further if that could also speak to a deeper veracity for a physical (even if only in appearance, i.e. a non-substantive but a visual) resurrection. Would that also fit with Paul's "appeared"? More provocatively, are we able to take these fervent beliefs at their word(s)? We need not accept them ourselves (or we might), but the groundwork laid for these understandings does appear to indicate that we may wish to concede the reports were at least taken as genuine by their sources, their writers, "factually" (empirically) relating the experiences of their delineators; whether expressed in the third person or the first, such were seen/"seen". This indulgence (tolerance?) on our part would moreover not negate Paul's more nebulous take on a "spiritual body" since again the post-Pauline "body" in question may only have looked (or been understood as, et cetera) physical in form while actually being (compositionally, metaphysically, ontologically) "spiritual." Possibly not a walking reanimated corpse or otherwise an object remade in fleshiness, but an image that presented itself to the viewer (by whatever means psychological and/or inspirational) as being absolutely human rather than as something fuzzily alluded to ("I saw"; Paul), luminous ("bright light"; Acts), or otherwise aethereal. The question here, that upon which everything hinges, is how we are to (how we *decide to*) take the phenomenology as it has been outlined.

Remembering—imagining—once more the particular historical climate in which these recordings took place deepens the likelihood of such an abstraction forming and rapidly spreading within the budding community still further. It is worth recalling—it is even crucial to recall—that this entire scene of Yeshuan church building and the excommunicating of Yeshuan-Jews from what were also becoming "mainstream" Jewish communities was occurring around and within the timeframe of what would prove to be the initial stage in a series of major Jewish national military struggles for independence from Rome (the First Jewish-Roman War of 66–70 CE), the period that the classical historian Flavius Josephus records in his *The Jewish War*.[38] These times called for a messiah—desperately so—and the label was bestowed frequently and competitively. Only a few decades earlier when Paul was writing his letters to the burgeoning group of Yeshuan believers scattered throughout the Mediterranean basin that war had yet to begin, Jerusalem had yet to be besieged, and the Temple complex had yet to be destroyed. Deliverance was still somewhere off on the horizon, not even imaginatively in sight. Hoped for, not looked for; yearned for, not fought for.

Although there were movements in other directions, such as the reforms the Pharisees sought which emphasized prayer and study over sacrificial rites, the primary

---

38. Available in a revised and paperback edition as Josephus, *The Jewish War*.

weight of Pauline-era Jewish life remained centered around the singular Temple locale and its practices—and that particular place was in fact overwhelmingly essential to the dominant urban and elite form of the Judaisms that existed then. (Which form, not incidentally, was a primary target of Yeshua's peasant-centered ministry;[39] if Paul was a Yeshuan before he was a Yeshuan (as we have suggested), was Yeshua a Pharisee without ever realizing it? Delicious thought!) As an example of this centrality, consider that every single Jewish male was required to visit the Temple three times a year: at the festivals of Pesach (Passover), Shavuot (Weeks, or Pentecost), and Sukkot (Tabernacles, or Tents, or Booths).[40] Every man, at the same time, every year and three times a year. Whether or not one actually did so (and from a practical point of view it seems highly improbable that such ever happened to the universal extent commanded), and even whether one was a male who had to pack up and leave or a female who farewelled a family member(s), the impositions thus engendered would mean that the Temple and its importance would never be far from any individual's mind. One would need to plan the whole year—and that of one's family—around such, from large details to small, and the more so if one happened to live some distance from Jerusalem.

We must never forget, and can probably never overestimate, how unconditionally indispensable that collection of buildings and rituals were to the people—symbolically at the very least—and then suddenly the entirety was reduced to nothing, destroyed, the very heart and soul of the nation ripped out and shredded, the identity-granting and meaning-making core of traditional priestly Judaism fully eradicated, erased, vanished like smoke. A given Israelite may herself have disdained the religious caste and cared not one whit for the Temple and its activities, but she still would have *known* it and felt it ideationally in her selfhood. If the messiah were not already "on the battlefield" when that happened then absolutely one would need to be conjured. It is at precisely this earth shatteringly historic crux that the Gospel accounts and their completely physical flesh-and-blood risen Yeshua stories start to be written; however it might have been that previous years of Yeshuan-Jewish believers took (or did not take) the idea of a resurrection (something we might never be able to know in any granular detail), suddenly these specifically bodily narratives appear, and not only in the New Testament Gospels that later had the stamp of canonical approval placed on them, but in other Gospels and similar concurrent texts as well.[41] Yet these burgeoning/emerging Christian works are not the sole contemporary documents that begin

---

39. This is most evident in Yeshua's "kingdom" teachings, which we will explore in Chapter 9.

40. A simple explanation of these can be found here: Kohn, "What Are Pilgrimage Festivals? Three major holidays mentioned in the Torah: Passover, Shavuot and Sukkot", *My Jewish Learning*. Accessed November 11, 2019. Most versions of the Torah (the five books traditionally accredited to Moses (Genesis, Exodus, Leviticus, Numbers, and Deuteronomy), split into weekly readings with supplementary passages from the prophets and/or narratives) will also contain commentaries explaining such events; my copies are Plaut, gen. ed., *The Torah*; and Lieber, sr. ed., *Etz Hayim*.

41. A recent and fairly extensive collection of these books can be found in Ehrman and Plese, eds. and trans., *The Other Gospels*.

to (re)make claims for people once again "seeing" God/"God" in a physical form:[42] rather, it was a much more extensive Jewish trend, a multiple Judaisms trend.

Kugel informs us that, "In rabbinic writings from the second to the sixth centuries CE, God is frequently represented as having appeared to human beings, sometimes in altogether human dimensions . . . Time and again, God is presented in rabbinic texts as appearing in human form—indeed, this is one of that literature's most striking traits."[43] The Temple was gone, many of the Judaisms had little idea what to do with themselves—most prominently the collapsing (or already collapsed) ex-priestly version—and were still only making headways towards reorganizing around a central rabbinical format and formulae for worship; every Judaism needed God/"God" to be at hand. Moreover, exactly at this very delicate moment, this turning point, Yeshuan-Judaism asserts itself as the brand new and newly branded "Christianity," a Judaism replete with an increasingly divergent set of practices and comprehensions; but then not only as one more variant version of Judaism, and not even only as an alternative understanding of what it meant to be a Jew and to serve God/"God" as a Jew, but indeed as an entirely new way of life centered around a whole new identitarian conceptuality (Gentiles welcome!). No more synagogues; rather now churches. The Temple had been destroyed, and the argument thence went: Did such not speak to the necessity of a new worldview, and did not this was-Jewish-but-has-become-other-thing called "Christianity" offer a path out of the conundrum faced, providing fresh answers to the very troubling questions pressing in from all corners?

Admittedly the most we can offer from our twenty-first century vantage point on what it may have felt like to live under such conditions is speculation, but it seems quite probable that in regard to this specific change—from Paul's resurrected "saw," to the "blinding light" of the author of Acts (which, while remotely possible, I think it highly unlikely this description was something the author heard from Paul), to the Gospel narratives' walking and talking and eating and drinking (and touchable) in every way physical "man as we knew him"—the impetus (overtly or not) could have been as a means of emphasizing within the wider socio-historic context both Yeshua's nearness to God/"God" and/or his "factual" divinity. This is, not coincidentally, also exactly the sort of notion that would have been highly desirous for a group seeking to radically shift the existing Jewish ritualism and theological comprehension amongst which it dwelt and from which it had begun to consider itself separate. That such should happen within the psychological framework of the Temple's destruction at the hands of the Romans makes perfect sense once we pause to reflect on how world-movingly (new "world"—in the complete Heideggerean sense—creatively) shocking that act would have been for first century Jews of every conceivable stripe, regardless of social standing, adherence to the Law, or depth of individual belief. It was a

---

42. Or more technically in a modern Yeshuan-Jewish sense: seeing the resurrected Yeshua as God, or as a form of, or sign of/from God.

43. Kugel, *The God of Old*, 101–2.

A Life: Beyond

culture-wide total tragedy akin to little else in history (though sadly not the only one the Jewish nation was to undergo).

Returning our discussion to the present, what we perhaps have today are options for how we might approach the concept of Yeshua's resurrection (note: not options for types or forms of resurrection *tout court,* rather options for types or forms of *how we might think of the claims made as to this resurrection*—how we might think of the thoughts, our ideas on the ideas): 1) Paul gives us one abstraction that could be applied to any "seeing" (i.e. as a "spiritual body," whatever that might mean and possibly even meaning different things at different times and circumstances); 2) Acts another that points in the general direction of a physicality but in that is still more of an emptied gesturing; and finally, 3) the Gospels give us a third which—in line (in conjunction?) with the rabbis—is both a return to a more ancient understanding of theophany and is also evidently one based on human psychological and emotional need. These triune traditions, during and after their mutual entwining, appear to be telling us that when the bottom falls out God/"God" shows up—conceptually and experientially—in a way that is as "real" as necessary for those crying out to/for the divine.

Of course none of this is verifiable as far as the authentic figure of Yeshua goes; we will never have a foolproof proof of anything that might definitively segregate documentary myth from documentary fact (that is what faith is for; and not for), but ours is a philosophical study and thus whatever the historicity was or is or could be or might have been—et cetera—our primary concern is with the interactions people had (and still have) with these notions, the interplay of accepted/adopted concept and experienced/expressed lifeworlds. It is *being* that is our playground—human being—existence in these bodily forms which we know "from the inside out"; while almost continuously failing to really know: the mystery, the beauty, the maddening fog of our mortality and limitations. Meditating on the cogitations and implications induced by these thoughts is useful, helpful, for our very human vulnerabilities I think, and these are topics we will return to in Parts 3 and 4 when applying the (to be) proffered hermeneutical principles to Yeshua's "kingdom" teachings and to a positioning within finitude and final finish. Prior to any interpretative suggestions though, a methodology must be properly laid out; for that we will need a denser theoretical foundation on which the nexus of ideas, images, and what may form (a) "reality" for an individual/group can be based. That will form our efforts in Part 2. Firstly, however, to close out this Part 1 we will try to make some summative remarks on the person Yeshua, the self-qualified rabbi and self-appointed pointer of a way ("the Way" as it became) that shook and built a world/"world" in a manner no Roman army could ever dare dream.

Chapter 4

A LIFE: CONSIDERED

AN APPEARANCE, A BRIGHT light, an impression, a vision, an apparition, graspable physical flesh; in the end all these assertions are distractions really, arguments likely designed to found and fortify claims of messiahship amidst circumstances of high demand and multiple options for supply; originating claims that were not, as it turns out, even that original.[1] The purveyors of these arguments may well have believed them, or anyway believed them at least to a certain extent, and then perhaps (but perhaps not) exaggerated or expanded or extrapolated freely on what they felt or heard in order to establish stories that were deemed convincingly "true" even if not (acknowledged with a wink and a nudge?) empirically true. It is only really we, on the other side of both the Enlightenment and the Scientific Revolution, who think that "good news" (i.e. "the Gospel", from the Old English "god spel") need be "factual"; and furthermore, we might ask (with Pontius Pilate?[2]): What is the true anyway? True to whom? What counts as empirical, as factual; what as real? On what grounding, by whose data, interpreted how and when, where and why? What is the definitively and the absolutely real, the real-y real? Are there absolutes, universals? These are questions of theory, of ontology, of the ontic versus ontology, and we will need to return to them in our study's next major Part; for now, as remarked, and given that our concerns have heretofore been historical, let us attempt an historical placement: and that—the history woven into this idea—is tragic. No loss has been suffered for the ink spent (no meaningful loss I would argue, from a "big picture" perspective), but the blood and lives taken on

---

1. The reader is once more referred back to the note in Chapter 3 on that first century BCE stone stele with its haunting, nagging, and increasingly potent the more one dwells upon it, details of a messiah who physically suffers, dies, and returns to life three days later.

2. This was put to Yeshua by Pilate in the trial scene narrated in John 18:28–38. The figure of Pilate has been historically verified as the Roman prefect of Judea from 26–36 CE (during Emperor Tiberius' reign; see the note above), and so we can at least conclude that much of the tale as factually established. Yet did Pilate really say this? Did he utter the very words? Judgments on the "empirical truth" of that are not likely to satisfy literalists—but therein we have it, for the story is a good and compelling one regardless; is that not enough? Must we have a voice recording of Pilate's every syllable to move our hearts, or cannot rather the imagined moment of it accomplish the same?

the basis of this and related notions are horrifying, and have compounded exponentially that first bodily giving on the cross: crushingly, needlessly, far, far too frequently. How many? To what end? Why has there not been an *end*?

We find ourselves like Walter Benjamin's angel, capable merely of looking back with weeping from the present, powerless towards the past even as we recognize its terror,[3] sensing that today instead of reflecting in reverse we must rather steady ourselves for the great effort to turn, to extend our gaze and our stride forward. The resurrection faith is (and can "only" be; but this "only" is by no means a belittlement) at core a *faith*—without qualification—and thus accepted or rejected as such and in whatever manner understood (i.e. resurrected *how?* physical is not the only option); and while beliefs are undoubtedly experientially self justifying, in this particular case we find an unintended loss is incurred if taken literally, a spiritual and ethical subterranean (sub-aware, unnoticed, perforce contained while concealed) relinquishing of one's responsibility which accompanies a considering of Yeshua to *be* God/"God" in the dogmatic manner taught by officialdom. This dereliction of one's duty, I wish to suggest, is part and parcel with a "full faith" as such becomes a distancing necessarily effected between the Yeshuan "kingdom" message as taught and the corollary realm of a personal, effortful adoption of it: the taking up of, the taking upon oneself of this "kingdom" creation disappears into an obfuscating soteriology. Yeshua in his ministry pointed always to the "Father"—to God/"God", ungendered; I employ the masculine here merely to cite the tradition—but if he (Yeshua) himself is an avatar/version/form of the same and singular God/"God", then it appears impossible for his message not to be consumed beneath the resultant image of the man (God/"God"-man), and then additionally for the fleshy and sweaty and stinky (as we each are) human personage that was the man not to recede in turn into a remoteness so sequestered that we feel it unthinkable to emulate. If he was/is God/"God", how can we be like him? Why even try? Well, we can *try*, but . . . The exemplar shifts into an extraterrestrial, he who (merely) thought differently and tried to teach us how to think differently too transforms into he who was so substantively other as to transcend substance itself, the Word become flesh (John 1:14), but never really—and yet always—both Word and flesh. Is it *homoousios* (same in essence) or *homoiousios* (similar in essence)?[4] Again,

---

3. I refer to the somber imagery (based, it seems, on Paul Klee's painting "Angelus Novus" (1920)) of his famous essay "On the Concept of History," recently re-printed in a new edition of *Illuminations*, ed. and intro. by Hannah Arendt, see pages 196–208. On the connection with Klee's work interested readers may also wish to see Jeffries, "The Storm Blowing from Paradise," *Verso: Blog*. Accessed February 07, 2020.

4. The metaphysical usage of the Greek term *ousia* ("substance," "essence," "matter," "gist," "nature," "being," "entity," "quintessence," et cetera) goes all the way back to the Golden Age of philosophy, and was later picked up by none other than Martin Heidegger (not surprisingly, given Heidegger's insistence on a Graeco-German connection). In relation to Yeshua it became a central aspect of the First Council of Nicaea and its weighty Nicene Creed of 325 CE; the brief "Christian Theology" section of the "Ousia" *Wikipedia* entry gives a nice overview: "Ousia," *Wikipedia*. Accessed March 26, 2020.

Part 1 | Man, Son (of)

lives have been taken over this—murder, destruction—and we, with Benjamin's angel, stand aghast.

More than that, what is the "essence"? What is the how and the where of it; and what in all these Greek iotas (the "*i*'s" have it . . .) has happened to our Yeshua? When we encounter Krishna in *The Bhagavad Gita* we do not, after all, try to be him; we purely worship him (and eagerly take his instruction).[5] If Yeshua is Krishna—the divine absolutely present, yet apparently "just" that Pandavan chariot driver[6]—then there is no question of living as he did: we cannot, we are too flawed and we know it. Hence we resignedly judge that we cannot even make an attempt, for who could come close to matching him? Thereby Yeshua's repeated message of realizing/building God's/"God's" world now in and as this world now is drowned beneath the waves of the "end times" and the "second coming" when "all shall be made new" (again, far more on this in Parts 3 and 4). As with much else in phenomenological and notional interaction, of which we shall have a great deal to consider in the following, the concept or image imagined or perceived (or both) becomes a directory symbol for generating and sustaining a sense of awe—yet this is a distancing awe—and thus so in particular when it comes to matters sacred. Yeshua the revisionary visionary becomes Christ the spirit-figure and God/"God"-figuration, abstracted away to the highest heaven, from which vantage the words he spoke—Yeshua's earth-bound and earth-centered message—simply cannot take the rarefied air, tumbling back down in silence instead, only to then vanish amidst the feet of we mortals who stand and stare with our ears blocked and our faces upturned, un-"see!"-ing.

This attitude, the over-reverence, the blinding, burying, tragic projection of it, is thereby nothing short of a betrayal of the very Yeshua who as teacher and guide, as first century rabbi and in every century since, spent and ultimately gave his whole being in the effort to convince others to do towards God/"God" as he did, to approach

---

5. Two editions that I can recommend to varying degrees and for varying reasons are: Mascaró, trans. and intro., Brodbeck, new intro., *The Bhagavad Gita*; and Lakshmanjoo, comm., Hughes, ed., *Bhagavad Gita: In the Light of Kashmir Shaivism*.

6. The parallels of world faiths surely reflect the contours of human nature: one is reminded of Matthew 13:54–57a, "54He [Yeshua] came to his hometown and began to teach the people in their synagogue, so that they were astounded and said, 'Where did this man get this wisdom and these deeds of power? 55Is not this the carpenter's son? Is not his mother called Mary? And are not his brothers James and Joseph and Simon and Judas? 56And are not all his sisters with us? Where then did this man get all this?' 57And they took offense at him." *Thinline Bible with the Apocrypha* (NRSV). We can easily imagine those around Arjuna muttering similar things about his supposed servant while they waited for the battle to begin in the narrative scene as it is set. With regards to the other similarity found, the claim of the divine as absolutely present, such would seem to apply whether the divinity were "activated" or not: it has been explained to me by a professional clergy member that prior to beginning his ministry Yeshua was still God/"God" but was not "turned on" (if you will), and that was because God/"God"(in/as Yeshua) needed to completely experience being human in the Trinitarian aspect of Son while simultaneously being divine in the Trinitarian whole (please notice the nuance in that explanation: God/"God" *needed?* Maybe *wanted,* but . . .). These types of discussions are as old as the Yeshuan faith, although they are markedly *not* the faith, I think, of Yeshua himself; and that is what we will seek to get back to in our study in order to make the argument for a Yeshuan return to Judaism.

the divine with nothing in between, no mediation requisite nor—indeed—called for.[7] We can, Yeshua told us, and we should.[8] This is one of the pillars, I think, of the called for and yearned for "kingdom of God," a form of permanent Shabbat (Sabbath), or the time/place/way-of-being in which all is made into the sanctified and sanctifying holy day of rest.

In good faith then, and in the goodness of faith, I would like to request the reader's indulgence to dispense a little happily spilled ink on this before we progress further, to grant me the liberty of extending out a few words. I feel the need to ask for forbearance, for tolerance, for patience because I well realize how delicate these matters are; yet as with everything of the heart we must be open and honest, first and foremost willing to listen, to consider, and then to decide (or not) one way or another. I make no call to change minds (nor see any need to; God's/"God's" grace abounds), simply to share my own.

Let us therefore spiral back to the historical wells we have plumbed: those of the man Yeshua (sketchy and necessarily brief) and of the ideas/faiths concerning his resurrection (speculative but more analytically workable). It is perhaps easy for us, particularly from our digitized and self-congratulatory "modern" viewpoint, to straightforwardly dismiss the type of "savior" and "Son of God" assertions that have been made about Yeshua in the course of the birth and growth of Christianity as a phenomenon distinct from both Yeshuan-Judaism as it was and from what has become our Judaism(s) of today (the dominant rabbinical version of familiarity).[9] We could of course merely label the Gospel narratives as fictions and drop them into the trash bin as we might a disappointing paperback bought while jetlagged and groggy waiting for a connecting flight, but I think we might be missing something if we do; and that on at least three fronts.

For one there is the potential in these stories—however "unreal" they are (those quotation marks/double inverted commas are to be returned to)—to trigger something in us; and that the more so if we do not take them in the shallow yes-it-happened literal sense that many apologists would have us do. Anyone who has read a good novel can attest to this. Secondly, there is the actual history of the centrality these tales

---

7. Funk, *Honest to Jesus,* emphasizes this point.

8. In this personalization of practice and directness of approach Yeshua does ring once more—in my estimation—with the sounds of a Pharisee, although naturally there were many differences too, as a further study of his lifestyle exhortations will reveal. Still, Saul/Paul the Pharisee as an unwitting Yeshuan and Yeshua the sage as an unwitting Pharisee has a wonderful symmetry that I cannot help appreciating.

9. I think it appropriate to continue to use the parenthetical plural, although now mainly for emphasis and nuance; while splits within Judaism do naturally remain (both between and within Orthodox and non-Orthodox forms), the differences between the wider socio-historical situations of now and then could maybe best be described as along lines of substance and approach between adherents and their practices; but then also a difference of degree could perhaps be indicated too. Unfortunately a more detailed study of Judaism's development since the first century is beyond our scope at present, but a few of the works cited so far could provide inroads, especially the books by the historian of religion Daniel Boyarin.

have had in our shared cultural heritage and the important roles they have played in the general trajectory of Western civilization. We noted earlier how the West may be characterized as self-hating (or this has anyway been asserted),[10] how we in the so-called "Christian world" are obsessed with "overcoming" the very selfhood which we cannot overcome precisely because it is our selfhood: we are "Jews" in many aspects of mental framework and approach if not strictly in ethnicity, and we had better learn to admit it (and would probably benefit greatly from *feeling it,* I might add). If we have been trying to "erase our faces" in the Foucaultean sense[11] then we have failed miserably and thank goodness for that. One learns nothing from running from oneself but very much from honesty towards oneself, an adage most of us tend to appreciate upon reaching adulthood (which, it seems, Michel Foucault might never have . . .). Finally, whatever we may think about what the authors of the New Testament books and the non-canonical but still Yeshuan-centered alternative works thought themselves (regarding the canonical: specifically here Paul and the Gospel writers, but also including Acts; regarding the non-canonical: those many other Gospels and varied documents outside of the New Testament proper, such as *The Gospel of Thomas* (to be studied here), *The Acts of Paul and Thecla, The Gospel of Truth,* et cetera), the experiences they reported and interpreted were clearly of enormous significance to them and thus bear pondering if for no other reason than the microscopic view thereby lent on the human condition; which is naturally reason enough. Ours is—let us recall—a phenomenological study; or at least it is aiming for such (whatever my own failures heretofore and henceforward might be).

We will therefore try not to miss, and indeed to take seriously, the grandiose avowals made by these apostles and evangelists concerning their teacher who was arrested, crucified, and thereafter—postmortem, if one can believe(!) it—was said to have commingled, communed, and communicated with these same "witnesses" in the treble role form of man-God/"God"-savior. This we will do by initially setting aside the God/"God"-savior portions of that label in order to better examine the "man"—the *human*—part because what that aspect, that person, had to say and do prior to his execution was evidently of such tremendous import that it left a mark on the lives surrounding his own deep enough for those others, those first and second-order followers (and third and fourth and fifth, and on down the line) to accept and admit and proclaim a literal bodily resurrection; and then even beyond that ideational nod to further carry out a reshaping of the entirety of their existences and identities centered around that core premise. They really believed; and in believing they reformed not

---

10. See Chapter 1 above; also Nancy, *The Banality of Heidegger.*

11. Miller includes this quote in his biography of Michel Foucault: "'More than one person, like me no doubt [for clarity, these are Foucault's direct words], writes in order to have no face'"; *The Passion of Michel Foucault,* 123. See also the refreshingly critical (but for that the more balanced?) review of Miller's book by Kimball, "The perversions of M. Foucault", *The New Criterion,* 10–18; available archived online and accessed March 26, 2020.

only their individual lifeworlds but that of a significant portion of their birth societies. This is obviously quite remarkable.

We might however think they overdid it, that they went a bit too far especially concerning those identitarian lines; and we might think too that just as at present we risk much by a forthright dismissal of their legacy, they too risked—and lost—much by the dismissal of their own, the denigration of the legacy into which those who worked to establish Yeshuan-Judaism had been born, i.e. that of the multiple Judaisms of their inhertied contexts. Although the mid-first century (and thereafter) Yeshuans could well have started the inter-Judaic fight that resulted in the eventual term "Christianity" in order to differentiate themselves from culturally superior "rivals,"[12] let us now—so painfully belatedly—put an end to it, ask for forgiveness, pray that it is received, and set about to (re)build this "kingdom" idea(l)/lifeworld in good common practice and good common condition: forming it, finding it, realizing it is/as already here.

Yet how so? Many steps are required, and the current undertaking is simply one tiny wobble in an effort to begin. In the chapters that follow we will seek to craft ontological and hermeneutical tools that could well suit this project, but the doing of it will—and must, really—remain up to each of us in the daily passing of our beings and selves as we forge such, as we (re)mould and (re)make these "me's" and "I's," out of the ingredients we have received.[13] A first attempt, perhaps, involves the re-figuring of the figure: We have already witnessed how many ways the claims to resurrection were actually made, that the adoption of Yeshua as "risen" in an agreed upon and church-wide doctrine was anything but uniform, and indeed that it evolved greatly over a span of decades (centuries if one counts the "essence" or "substance" arguments within this category). Whatever the reasons for the idea advancing as it did (and we must remember that such reasons were deeply embedded within the specific and unique socio-historical and political circumstances of the time and place(s) where they occurred), it was and is an abstract: traceable, translatable into more than one reading, interpretable into far more still. This is not a "take it or leave it"; Yeshua could be "alive" to us while absolutely and irrevocably dead; we could stand before the exhumed remains of a two thousand or so year-old corpse (whatever might be left) with a DNA report proving beyond doubt that this inert matter used to be called Yeshua and walked around Roman Palestine remarking about this and that while he touched her and him, and still find the room in our hearts for his "spirit," and that without there even being a *spirit* in the kind of quasi-ontological manner the term is often

---

12. Boyarin, *A Radical Jew*, explains how the earliest Yeshuans/Christians were entirely in the position of the disadvantaged underdogs vis-à-vis the Jewish community(ies) within the wider Roman world.

13. On the self as made and re-made readers who take no offense at my own "self"-citation may wish to see Oberg, *Blurred*.

taken. (In Part 4 we will consider death as total annihilation, and finitude—possibly surprisingly—as welcome balm.)

"Living" in this sense—in the way in which words, inspiration, beauty perhaps, live—may not be enough to motivate us to pray *to* Yeshua's spirit, but it could surely be sufficient to cause us to pray *for* a Yeshuan spirit—and that, I think, is something much more in line with Yeshua's ministry than what we have currently (this to be argued in Part 3 below). The point here is that we can appropriate without "accepting," and even in our present quest to be the "Jews" we are (a quest which the reader may after all reject; our study is merely an argument for the (positional) return of Christianity to a more accurately aligned and defined Yeshuan-Judaism (in mentality and in praxis), and thence to the Judaism within which it (we argue) definitionally belongs); we can admit that Yeshua had—and has—very much of value to impart about living in touch and in tune with the numinous, whether we take that as indicative of an Otherly present/existential divine or not. This relates to the question—that ultimate question—of being, of the manner and placement of our being-in-the-world, of what we open and what we close, what we allow to be disclosed or what we (mostly inadvertently) keep enclosed.

It may, however, be feared that if we take Yeshua into our hearts and minds as a purely human sage who died a very long time ago and now lives only in the appreciative sense indicated above, then the temptation to dismiss him altogether would be impossible to resist. Is this "taking" not really too reductive? We like our favorite poet, but would not think twice about carrying her "spirit" around with us (although we probably nevertheless do if we read her often enough). Additionally there is the element of baggage: we have been raised to accept, or have grown up in the cultural thickness of, a Christology so exalted that it seems to demand a firm yes or no, it seems to brook no in-betweens and does not play nicely with ditherers. One is either with us or against us, the powerful majority seems to stress; the dominance of the official church in our shared Western (and in many ways global) societies and histories is simply too overbearing and has crushed too much under its weight for far too long. While in the New Testament we find Yeshua remarking that "my yoke is easy, and my burden is light,"[1] the sheer cultural, social, and economic juggernaut (and all that has gone with it) of the church has been anything but, for good and for ill. We might therefore wish to push the pendulum the other way, to just drop Yeshua full stop and be done with it, be done with him: if he is not God he deserves no more notice than any other historical figure who might or might not have been as (or more) interesting. Yet such would be a shame—ethically, experientially—because Yeshua was not only a Socrates, he was not only a Jewish Cynic,[2] he was not only a (or even The) Bud-

---

1. Matthew 11:30; *Thinline Bible with the Apocrypha* (NRSV).

2. Crossan, *Jesus,* presents a very compelling case for understanding Yeshua this way, and seems to (at least on my reading) emphasize his ministry as more about social reformation/revolution than anything else. I think though that the "lifestyle of the heart" (or of the "mind" or "spirit") dimension is

dha, he was an icon of such towering that each of these stands in a relation to him that the modern individual must gauge for themselves, regardless of what could be the questionable justification for this extraordinarily widespread judgment of import. Moses and Muhammad were ethicists par excellence, and the systems they built are composed of more detail and nuance—truly societal in their breadth—than anything done by Yeshua; and yet it is the adages of the wandering Palestinian peasant that can be taken up and taken to heart with a subtlety of choice that otherwise might be hard to discover, as we will try to highlight in Part 3 when we offer some variant readings on "the kingdom" parables, art and imagery, and how such may be interacted with.

Still, all of this about words and lives is not a competition, and I certainly do not wish to raise one teacher over another nor make anything near an assertion of exclusivity. What I do wish to stake a claim to, and perhaps the reader will come to agree, is that there is hidden value to be discovered in the work of this man Yeshua, and if we can unearth it (*resurrect it!*) then we may also find the effort both worthwhile and twenty-first century applicable. From there, and this is almost undoubtedly more controversial, I would have us who value Yeshua's legacy then leap back into an embrace of Judaism/"Judaism" (although perhaps the embrace will not be returned . . .), as Yeshuan-Jews/"Jews" of the heart, as it were, as being aligned with one (surely non-Orthodox) version of the Jewish way-of-being/way-of-relating.

Finally too, on this note of existing, if I may also be so bold as to simply make an assertion at this yet early juncture, I would like to go so far as to suggest that the nurturing and blossoming involved in the creation of a sage like Yeshua really ought to be a point of pride for the undeniable spiritual genius of Hebrew culture, of its brilliant and untiring quest to ever-discover (to *wrestle with:* that famous imagery of Genesis 32:22–30;[3] as above, and to be examined again in our study's closing Part 5) the absolute divine. Where and amongst who else on this good Earth could compare with it, save possibly for the Subcontinent with its thinkers, teachers, texts, and tics of being?

To conclude: at this nexus within our human story, since there is almost nothing we can really know that approaches a solid reliability, a steely confidence, about the person Yeshua who lived and breathed and sweated and stank and laughed and loved and drank and ate (beyond, that is, the vagaries and "knowings" we have outlined), what we interact with today if we are inclined towards Yeshuan-Judaism in the (hoping to) return/reversionary sense I have been highlighting—or again if we are in/of Christianity in a more traditional parlance (which terms I would have us change), or even if we are simply situated within Yeshuan-Jewish outlooks and ways—is not a partner that may be labeled Yeshua "properly speaking," but rather is the *idea* of Yeshua ("Yeshua"), the spirit of it/him, and it is the ontic influence that this notion holds that produces in us and in our lives one event after another. Paul demonstrated

---

just as—or possibly even more—compelling than the external behavioral and structural aspects.

3. The patriarch Jacob and his wrestling with a partner whom might be God/"God", might be an angel, might be a . . . See again the note in the previous chapter.

this by his own mannerisms, the author of Acts by others, and the Gospel writers by yet more (et cetera, et cetera); and as for them, so for us: this influence of the idea is what transforms into its/"his"—Yeshua's "himself"—reality. This is a point that needs argumentation, and it will be provided at some length in the next chapter. As a foreshadowing, then: In the most crucial sense, I find the analyses of these points leading to the conclusion that the ontology makes no difference whatsoever in any lived awareness (religious or not). No justification for believing is necessary, merely one's experience and the unfolding thereof, including in both the personal and the communal aspects.

We will therefore attempt a "belief": an adoption of this spirit—this "spirit"—in a large or small way, to one degree or another; and from it we shall see what we find. Hence, as any believer of whatever stripe or faith might also be challenged by another to give account for one's held beliefs, we will accept that too; we realize far more philosophical work is needed for the preceding, far more *philotheologic* work. Yet as we likely know too, objections demanding proof of the numinous tend to boil down to little more than exercises of the "she said/he said" variety, and they leave both parties either agreeing to disagree or somewhat off-put. There is not much point in engaging in such, and the labors we have before us (and behind us) are not meant to provide anything more than thoughtful possibilities. I do think though that such are more than enough, and that they provide the impetus needed to go on.

There are abundant other reasons the reader may decipher to engage with one's (religious or irreligious) experiences within one's life/lifeworld (here including the faith of no-faith within the panoply); and the more so if we are brave enough to truly appreciate finitude and the utter cessation of the self at death, as we have gestured towards in the above. No afterlife, no consciousness, no lingering identity, none whatsoever. Thus, accordingly, we shall need to add this consideration of confronting the end and the erasure of "me" with the necessary juxtaposition of a rejection of the atonement model of Yeshua's execution that such calls for to the areas to be explored in our following Yeshuan return to ("our") "Jewish" self(ves). These latter analyses, however, will need to wait until Part 4; for now, having worn the reader's patience entirely thin, let us move instead to Part 2 and a study of the notion/event, the image-idea, and the (or rather, and *some*) metaphysics of the "real."

Part 2

THE REAL IN IDEAS AND IMAGES

Chapter 5

A THEORY OF *NOTION/EVENT*

WE HAVE THUS FAR introduced the idea of the idea, which—tautology though it may seem—is of an order deeper than its expression belies, and that due entirely to the formative influential aspects thereby rendered on a human mind. Douglas Hofstadter describes how physio-biologically the brain operates automatically, silently, on one level, and with the functioning of awareness (e.g. in reflection, in thinking) found separately on another. Compositionally the first level is that of the neuronal and associated interactive networks which form the physical dimension whose data processing and cross-communications are interpreted by other areas within the physical organ, that from which raw results are thereafter fed into and yielded up to the "higher" level so experientially familiar as one's inner flow, the noisy jack-in-the-box "voice" which does not—seemingly—even leave us alone during sleep.[1] It on this latter and largely abstractional-oriented dimension of awareness and probative thought, the layer of the notional, in which "we live and move and have our being" (as Paul says with regards to Yeshua when addressing his Athenian audience in Acts 17:28);[2] it is from here that we, as the type of animal we are and using the equipment bequeathed to us, engage with the world that surrounds; and thus, it might be extrapolated, our environments too are bifocal: the natural one into which we are bodily placed with its more primal imperatives of survival, reproduction, pain avoidance, and pleasure pursuance; and then the creational one into which we are mentally placed, with its perhaps similar imperatives but conducted on a scale of far different scope. Both surroundings, it will be understood, are ever re-generating and re-generated. We live in the world and we live in our ideas; but more than either of these (more than both) we live in the world

---

1. Hofstadter, *I Am a Strange Loop*; Damásio also explains the physical dimension of consciousness well, using the device of "neuronal maps"; see especially his *Self Comes to Mind*. For an argument along these lines that finds consciousness to always be a part of the human condition, even when an individual has passed out or is in deep sleep or otherwise "unconscious" by common usage of the term, see my *Blurred*.

2. *Thinline Bible with the Apocrypha* (NRSV). Paul actually states (or rather, is made to state by the author of Acts) that this is a quote from "some of your own [the Athenians'] poets."

as shifted as comprehended, the world as "seen" through the lenses of our ideas, and thus *the* world becomes *a* world—this is a point we will revisit.

Consider Yeshua; consider the idea of Yeshua; consider Yeshua *as* an idea. We have (loosely, broadly) examined the epistemological side to the life of Yeshua from an empirical standpoint and found it wholly holey (and not even really that holy), which led us to a (tighter, narrower) examination of the same Yeshua from an *experiential* standpoint and there—here—we found it amazingly detailed, rich, and varied, as the alternative views on resurrection in and after the first century of our Common Era indicated, and as our (still many) conceptual options point towards today. The ways to understand are as wide as the potential for belief itself (or as restricted: *we* unfold or do not, and we must never forget that), and those ways are the midwives for our numinous phenomenological lifeworlds. Thus it is into the idea and what it does to us—or can, could, might (should?) do—that we now must dive, for only once re-surfaced from this "deep end of the pool" will we be in a position to (re)think the words of Yeshua (or those accredited to him; as we shall see it does not really matter whether they were literally spoken by him, by another, or by no one at all) and therefrom purposefully (re)apply them. We rise and mount the springboard.

In beginning our discussion on the conceptualizations we hold and which (en)hold us, we must note forthwith—straight out of the gate, as it were—the cruciality of the twinning factors of embeddedness and reception, the traditions and heritages in which we stand. Any present reaction is an historically based and situated one, composed of linkages that mentally bind, and perchance blind, fetters on perceived possibilities, on what is and/or might be; and we, of course, are not Harry Houdini able to miraculously wriggle free. To think anew one must first understand anew, have one's "eyes opened," "turn," and "see" as our characters in the theophany tales of Chapter 1 did. This naturally is not only a matter of effort but also of exposure, and if one's situational circumstances do not offer (or perhaps even actively block) such, then however much effort is expended it frankly might not be enough. There is, I think, an element of luck in the opening of one's mind—in untethering one's old ideas and in meeting new ones—although too the more one strives for such the more likely one is to happen upon that certain key which grants passage through the door; for the good or the ill, we might add. Thinking, feeling, living: all these make an approach, the external the internal, the internal the external. Whether we appreciate it or not, the world is the one we see ("conceptualized" is conceptual-*eye*-zed), and therefore we must renewedly seek to "see" if we would move beyond the default of was-born-into and had-handed-over. One other impediment is also worth mentioning here at the outset, and that is the inevitability of some enclosure, some impossibility to break out; or, to put it in words of which Martin Heidegger would likely approve, the (limited) possibility of the possible. In respect to another—but very much aligned—context, Heinrich Wölfflin has written that, "Not everything is possible at all times, and certain thoughts can only be thought at certain stages of the development."[3] While Wölfflin's "the development" in this quote was framed in the topic of art history, it could just as well be about humanity writ large: we are definitively stuck in the conceptual frameworks out of which we comprehend the world around us (again this is a pivotal point, and one we shall need to return to).[4]

Thinking on this interplay between thought and experience, between the *how* of the internal and the *why* of the external, and prior to proceeding to an explanation of the psychological and cognitive bases upon which these comments are grounded, I would like to request a consideration of what I will call the notion/event—simply for the reader to mull it over, to grant it a bit of time on its own in the cerebral sun, unaided and absent the multidisciplinary accoutrements which will follow and which will (I assure) provide sustaining evidence. I label this offering as "notion/event" instead of what might seem the more natural "notion-event" because I hope to capture by that slash the interchangeability of the elements involved, rather than a buried nuance of dependency such as a dash would imply. A notion, I am arguing, is an event[5] is a notion, an ideascape is a world composed of a hemmed in horizon; this, it will be understood, is to remark that such is "a" (and not "the") "world" (and not world/planet) with boundaries. To expound and expand on this, let us explore what I find to be an enlightening passage from a book by William Lycan.

In *Consciousness and Experience* (1996), Lycan comments on the manner in which quale[6] function as forms of personal (or perhaps personalized) "facts," arguing that a person's introspection works on second-order representations of first-order psychological states, yielding tokens that have both referents and modes of internal presentation and thus give to the subject phenomenal information that is unavailable to an outside observer or researcher.[7] These "facts" should of course not be understood as *facts* in the strict evidentiary sense: they are instead internal informants

---

3. Wölfflin, *Principles of Art History*, ix.

4. On these ideas of frameworks and reductions, see Feyerabend, *Against Method*; and, far less wonderfully, Oberg, "Thinking Unempirically," *Philosopher*. Archive accessed October 10, 2019.

5. A philosophical capital "E" would not be inappropriate, is in fact apropos, but I have read too many philosophers who do not capitalize the term no matter what they mean (I offer no excuses: we are a disagreeable lot), and anyway "event" both reads better and is likely more widely familiar than "Event."

6. A perceived and/or experienced quality and/or property—the famous "what it is like." My *Blurred* contains a detailed consideration of qualia re: consciousness issues and an argument against the (in)famous "gap" contention between neuronal function and emotional experience (that old—goodness how old!—brain/body "hard problem," as it's been more recently labeled); see Chapter 5: Consciousness, Qualia, and the Self. Nagel's earlier work is fundamental to these discussions, and I offer an alternative reading of his "what it is like" that is grounded on an understanding of *type* as opposed to the more minutiae based accounts such as Chalmers'. Some crucial background reading may be found in (limiting myself here): Nagel, "What is it like to be a bat?" in *Mortal Questions*, 165–180; Nagel, "Panpsychism," in *Mortal Questions*, 181–95; Jackson, "Epiphenomenal Qualia," *The Philosophical Quarterly*, 127–36; Chalmers, *The Conscious Mind*; Damásio, *The Feeling of What Happens*; Damásio, *Self Comes to Mind*; and Dennett, *Consciousness Explained*.

7. Lycan, *Consciousness and Experience*, see pages 100–1.

and are neither dependent upon nor even really accessible from the (shall we say) "hard" world of the physical sciences, of the non-minded dimension(s) to the cosmos in which we minded animals spend our little emotional and cognitive lives. Herein is a hint already of a "real" that is not *real*, because as reflection on it indicates this "felt-by-me" is through the process of interior data building "*real-enough*-for-me," foundational enough, sufficient and in most cases quite probably also satisfying to the individual in question. Lycan then extends this line of query through the term "intentional inexistents": items that are representatum given within a mind as a "physical" object but are actually more in line with concepts; the important difference—if I read him correctly—being in how one perceptually understands and thinks about versus any recordable empirical state.

To illustrate this Lycan cites the example of the sky as a "blue thing," although, as he writes, "no one thinks that there is any nonexistent *physical thing* up there. But I contend that there is a nonexistent physical thing up there: It is an illusion. Vision represents 'the sky' as an object. Poets write about it. Visually, the sky is *a canopy*, or the *vault* of heaven."[8] We of course know what he means: we have spoken and felt similarly, we may even be doing so now merely in the reading of such. It is this holding of certain phenomenal information about "the sky," then, that causes us to perceive it and thus also to feel it (and this feeling, allow me to add, is a facet of our study to be remembered since it will prove singular a little later on) as a particular object, as a celestial ceiling, despite knowing only too well that scientifically speaking the atmosphere above our heads consists of a number of gaseous layers, and that the blue color the sky imparts to one's eyes is a function of how the sun's light passes through those layers along lines more refracted to blue wavelengths than to red. Experientially, liv*ed-ly,* this knowledge is "tabled" in the everyday: as the saying goes, "out of sight [sight to "sight": our "seen" yet again!], out of mind"; yet there is still arguably a particular form of "realism" in operation here, only it is a subjective and phenomenological rather than an observable realism;[9] and furthermore, despite the subtle phenomenal, internal, and immeasurable details related to my experience of this "sky thing" as compared with yours, the impact it and much like it plays on each of our daily lives is clearly of existential value. These thoughts alone are perhaps enough to justifiably anchor the manner in which the conceptual attains a degree of reality, but let us nevertheless press on for there is far deeper to go.

There is no such "blue sky thing" hanging solidly and uniformly above, there is no such object nor invariability; we realize this, and yet experientially that seems

---

8. Lycan, *Consciousness and Experience*; see the discussion on pages 152–3. The quoted section is taken from note 9 on page 189 to the aforementioned text; emphases in the original.

9. At least, it is not observable from a "neutral" or "third person" stance; although very interestingly we may note that such are so commonly human animal type experiences that they are therefore nevertheless quite easily describable, and out of a description alone a reader or listener may even generate their own, sight unseen as it were; but not, of course, un-"seen," to return to our biblical refrain of "see"-ing as comprehending as *awakening*.

to matter very little, almost not at all, as our lives beneath "it" roll out quite well and the days tick away without ever having to take stock of the gaseous layers piled up to the exosphere. Those days—what of them? Our sun goes up and comes down, and we mark it a "day"; only naturally the sun neither goes up nor comes down as we are now well aware (and this awareness has become "natural" to us in a way it never could have only a few short centuries ago); the sun does not move at all while the Earth we stand on does: physically, rotationally—but not phenomenally. We *feel* one but not the other, we *know* one and we know the other, only one *knowing* is not the other *knowing*. There is knowledge and then there is knowledge; knowledge and "knowledge." These ideas, our little sketches, of the sky and the sun shape how we dwell here in simple but yet profound ways, and the consequences of our shared folk thought are easy to grasp and apply, perhaps even appearing too obvious for comment. Yet I wish to take this further because I find that the abstract hidden in play, in plain "sight" (to "see!") is quite profound. Towards this end I hope to build a case that what matters in a human life is not perforce (or even frequently) dependent on what might be assigned to the so-called "objective facts," to the empirical and demonstrable of the sky's varying levels or to solar stasis, to press instead that indeed such data are for us largely irrelevant since we assign truths based on phenomenological experiences, and moreover within the confines of a single sensorially driven life that truth (or "truth") is entirely sufficient for its holder, however many accusations of material mismatch, subjectivism, or relativism may be thrown against it. For me in this world which is only "mine" the emotional carries far more weight than the empirical, and each having been or done in my personal past casts its long shadow.

Let us attempt to draw this out. An idea is never simply that, never merely an ephemeral floating, a cloud carried on the mind's breeze. A human being feels, and not only does that deepen the experiential elements involved in external factors such as what happens to one or how one behaves, but extends as well to the thoughts one maintains and the valuations upon which such rest, being formed and then in turn forming and re-forming as assertions and determinations give rise to further cognitions: breeding, shaping, twisting, transforming one's mental backdrop in an endless cycle. These feelings are furthermore interactive along both axes that Hofstadter mentioned: the neuronal (we might label this the "silent" or "spontaneous" position and, as will be detailed shortly, consists of one's intuitive judgments along with other factors), and the cognized (the "noisy" and "purposive" position, analysis done with active engagement, one's reasoning and one's critical—or even one's banal—thinking).

Moreover, due to the automaticity of the brain's built-in systems it is impossible to disentangle the intuitive judgments and emotive reactions of the former axis (or plane or layer) from the latter, there is simply no chance for a "pure" reason or an "objective" logic because the analyses carried out will inevitably be performed using data provided within the same brain using the same parts that have already conducted the body's sensorial and primary processing (i.e. the primal: those survival promotion, organism thriving based procedures). However dry a fact or datum one may wish to present or encounter, it will be sifted via an organic network that has cast its verdict and expressed its appraisal through intuitive and emotive means that do not even need to *bypass* one's awareness for the simple reason that they *preclude* awareness: the intuitive reactions and judgments (from a simple flight/fight to a more complex disgust-avoid or appeal-approach, and on and on) come first, often with accompanying emotions, and thereafter the slower and more laborious frontal lobe critical faculties may (or may not) be brought to bear. In relaying his research results in this area, Jonathan Haidt highlights the common experience of finding oneself having done something, reacted somehow, and then only after the fact of its completion retroactively assigning what appears to be a logical reason for it.[10] In sum, we are biased, from top to bottom, from head (brain!) to toe.[11] The "notion" of notion/event is therefore not merely an intellectualization, it is a composite of the felt and the apprehended, experiential in the broadest possible meaning of whole person: every sense attuned, the so-called mental and the so-called physical; and this necessarily because the mental is simply one other form of the physical. Any rationality or logical operation will ever carry its intuitive and emotive luggage: an idea is never merely thought without also being concurrently felt, reacted to, interacted with. In turn this calls forth the event.

What Christianity has therefore done (and I do not think willingly, but gradually, quite naturally: an accretion) is taken the man Yeshua and turned him into the *idea* "Jesus," the "Son of God" as a/the/our "atoning sacrifice" and thus "savior of humanity." This undertaking, decades—centuries—in the making (we might mark the First Council of Nicaea as its initial endpoint;[12] there was—and ever is—more controversy to follow), effectively and astoundingly took a real walking, eating, drinking, laughing, stinking, meat-and-bones meandering mendicant and preacher of ethics, expounder of a way-of-being, and tore any postmortem historicity loose, replacing it with what is in effect an *idol* (I do realize how provocative this language is, but I find the push a needed one), an *image;* and it is *this image* that is engaged with today, not the man and—sadly—not (much of) his teaching.

In the reversal we are attempting here we therefore seek a transport of Christianity back into a Yeshuan-Judaism, and then (will try to) argue that although we maintain the "Yeshuan" adjective—that is, a nuance of outlook, a difference of practice gratefully received from Yeshua (what I take to be so important, a wellspring of wisdom)—we nevertheless yet have, yet *are,* within Judaism. Towards this end we have already examined the first of the barriers to this would-be movement—resurrection

---

10. Haidt, *The Righteous Mind*; see also Haidt, "The Emotional Dog and Its Rational Tail," *Psychological Review*, 814–34.

11. It is interesting to note here how long a history this "perspectivism" has in philosophy (especially in the Eastern traditions), although not of course the related neuroscientific and psychological research that have since reinforced it. In the modern Western tradition its strength probably stems from the groundbreaking (and scholarly discomfiting) work of Friedrich Nietzsche; see his *Beyond Good and Evil*.

12. "First Council of Nicaea," *Encyclopædia Britannica*. Accessed January 20, 2020.

A Theory of Notion/Event

narratives—and henceforward will also contend with what has just been raised: the image's central position. From thence a re-examination and an otherwise-oriented hermeneutics of "the kingdom" shall be offered before facing the second of the primary barriers: namely that of the so-called atonement. For all this we now have—I hope—what will prove a helpful tool in our theory of the notion/event.

This positing, if it is worth using, can highlight how the conceptually accepted generates the dimensions of reality that are experienced by creatures capable of abstract thought through the interplay involved in the brain's networks. Perhaps for animals operating only on an amygdala and the limbic system, sensorial input yields nothing more than the materially given—the here and now, as it were—but that is not the world a human being encounters. We think, constantly, and what we have come to assume (quite probably without even realizing it) about Yeshua, or about the Buddha, or about Lao Tzu or Socrates or Muhammad, or anyone or anything else along metaphysical planes on whom (on which) a mental background might be formed, such thereby births the physicality of our encounters—the assumptions (backgrounds) making themselves "felt" behaviorally and perspectivally—and in involving ourselves with these forthcomings we deepen the inhabited ideascape of personal (personal-*ized*) enclosures even as their contours are stretched and their boundaries are warped through additional experiences and exposures. Change is the rule for this process (and indeed for everything); but it is a change that arises from a foundation.

Yet what lies beneath this grounding, behind these interactions, reactions, ideas, and the crossroads between? What kind of "reality" is under discussion? What does it mean for a concept to be en-structuring for a life? At this point the reader will likely already be recalling Edmund Husserl's framework of "horizon," and his student Martin Heidegger's expansion and reworking of that into "world," the essential encircling of cognitive perception that is involved in these very famous notions with their indications that one can really only think so far (up to the point of "horizon"), cannot practically see all the angles at once (Husserl's well-known example of the impossibility of studying every facet of an object simultaneously), and that this is due to the qualities (again, inescapable) of situational embeddedness and conditional contexts within which we spend our days ("world"). Together these elements create and continually shape the outlooks from which we comprehend the environments and movements of our day-to-day lives, establishing all that we are even *capable* of comprehending.[13] The ideas we cling to influence the viewpoints we have; and this whether we "cling" to them or merely have them running on default, as it were, the barnacled detritus of childhood acculturation. These taken-for-granteds generate intuitive judgments and prejudices which thereby color and warp and morph one's interpretations of one's

---

13. Some starting points for interested readers could be: Husserl, *The Essential Husserl*; Smith, *Husserl*; Heidegger, *Being and Time*; Heidegger, *Basic Writings*; and Sembera, *Rephrasing Heidegger*. The primary and secondary literature for each is vast, but one can grasp their core concepts of concern fairly readily.

surroundings, both physical and notional. An inhabited ideascape is not a separate condition from the natural environment: it is a de facto part of the very same, and is bound by equal socio-historical, geographical, epochal, economical, et cetera, et cetera, contributing factors as is the individual herself.

A great deal of contemporary psychological research has borne these conclusions out, with Haidt's "Social Intuitionist" model (gestured at above) being particularly explanatorily effective, along with Daniel Kahneman's more recent work.[14] The core conception in this is again precisely that: the concept, the belief, the idea, the abstraction; however one wishes to splice that which is then reified into the concrete *thus-es* encountered moment by waking moment; such are the very cornerstones of the phenomenology of a life as lived out. What we think filters and blocks what we see—what we are able to see (to "see!")—and therefrom what we decide and choose, how we exist and behave: lenses on the world as experienced, guides and directors.

Even so, while the above might be accepted as operationally apposite from a neural point of view, it may be doubted how we could therefore assign a "reality" to functions such as these in the same or similar vein that we do for physical objects which are grasped in the hand. How real is "real"? How real does "real" need to be? That word "hand" naturally brings Heidegger back to mind (his to-hand and at-hand), and so let us think a bit more about the philosopher's work. In an extremely interesting study of his oeuvre that situates its core in neither of the cornerstones of Being nor Dasein,[15] but rather in the tool, Graham Harman examines the metaphysical implications of the as-structure[16] and declares it to be "derivative of the tool," that: "The objects of Dasein's understanding cannot be regarded as mere extant appearances; the 'as' necessarily arises from some prethematic reference, from the sphere of *world*, the occluded underground zone of execution or tool-being."[17] Harman's broader purpose in this examination is to demonstrate that the human form of existence is hardly the only aspect to Being in the universe, that Being is wide and is additionally not even limited to animate creatures, but instead that what we take to be the rickrack of

---

14. Haidt, *The Righteous Mind* and "The Emotional Dog and Its Rational Tail," *Psychological Review*, 814–34; Kahneman, *Thinking, Fast and Slow*; Kahneman, "A Perspective on Judgment and Choice," *American Psychologist*, 697–720; see also Dijksterhuis, "Think Different," *Journal of Personality and Social Psychology*, 586–98; and Osman and Stavy, "Development of Intuitive Rules," *Psychonomic Bulletin & Review*, 935–53; and too the classic study by Tversky and Kahneman, "Judgment under Uncertainty," *Science*, 1124–31. From a (more or less) purely philosophical perspective there is additionally the pleasingly straightforward Ryle, *The Concept of Mind*; and in a different academic tenor but still an echoing: Polanyi, *The Tacit Dimension*.

15. This is a highly technical and detailed term of Heidegger's which is usually no longer translated from its original German; for our purposes here we can simply elide it as "the self".

16. A key point for Heideggerean analyses regarding interpretation: the designation of X as something for something. (It is actually a deeper concept than this briefing belies, and Harman's move here is to situate it in usage (i.e. ontics) rather than in existence (i.e. ontology).)

17. Harman, *Tool-Being*, 42; emphasis in the original.

A Theory of Notion/Event

our environs, the "junk" or "stuff" or "pure objects," are themselves creatures—in a sense—of multiple ontological layers.

This is a rather stunning overturning of typically pinned down terms, and whether Harman is successful or not in this endeavor is probably open to question, but the application of these notional prods to a phenomenological analysis such as ours can provide an avenue towards the idea and the image, significantly the idea-as-image, that is worth exploring. In the approach we hereafter take to items or "tools" (using the Heideggerean vernacular we are in), let us therefore also bear in mind the following from Harman: "The tool isn't 'understood'; it *is*. It can be understood only *because* it is, and such understanding can never adequately mirror its being."[18] There is a hint here of a "real" beyond or beside the (standardly) real, and I think such will prove revelatory for how the resurrection of Yeshua was and has been comprehended, and with that the taking of the man as being himself divine/Other rather than as a guide to, or a pointer of, the divine/Other. I fear, then, that we must struggle on with this a bit more.

To continue: It is apparent enough how a hammer is real, and given a certain frame of mind we may even be willing to grant further delineations to the same hammer's (form of) reality, but a hammer is of course a *physical* object, while with the idea (the idea-image) what we are seeking is how something as immanently nonphysical as it could have a realism beyond what is demonstrated in the world via the expressive behavior of the holder of said idea. In other words: Does the idea *itself* have a (form of) reality, or only the empirical effects wrought through the medium of a "real" creature's movements stemming from the idea within whom it is contained (i.e. as a result of; to one degree or another)? Is the idea *real*, or only the measurable aftermath of what I do because I happen to think that way? One more quote from Harman should suffice to put us onto our next step: "Anything, prior to erupting in its explicit form, is real simply by exerting its efforts in the cosmos, by breathing its life into a world that would not have been the same without it."[19] The reader will no doubt see ("see!") where this is heading. An idea, pushed on and out, can fit this category, and because it can the world turns on ideas; which, we remember, can be/are idea-images, pure images, *breathing idols*.

Consider a situation in which a group of soldiers constructs a defensive fort in the desert by using nothing but bulldozers to move the sand around (and minus any extras such as timbers for support beams or the like). Have they created something new? We are likely tempted to reply that they have, for naturally they have erected a fort where there was none before and therefore it, at least, is a new object. Yet is it? The thought experiment is Peter van Inwagen's, and he actually answers in the negative, arguing that all that has occurred is a rearranging of the "furniture of the earth without adding to it," and that to assert otherwise would be to place two distinct

---

18. Harman, *Tool-Being*, 182; emphases in the original.
19. Harman, *Tool-Being*, 219.

objects spatially coincident, something he terms "incredible."[20] The sand and the fort are the exact same object(s), differing only in modal and historical properties, in what has been done to the non-minded by the minded; van Inwagen summarizes that, "we speak of the persistence of artifacts the way we do because of covert reference to intelligent beings' activities, to histories of maintenance."[21]

The illustration might appear to be a step back from the reality of an idea—as an image or otherwise—but the pertinent factor to be taken here, I deem, is the subtle interplay of how we speak of these events and the accompanying physicality, and therefore how we think of such, and therefore speak again. To van Inwagen the fort described above is a "virtual object," yet it is still an *object* and, to repeat Harman, one that certainly does exert itself in the universe we jointly inhabit. Virtual or not, real—in any sense—or not, the fort is felt and makes itself felt, it is expressed and expressive. It is that exertion and its influence, its generated interactions with those (with us) intelligent beings that can arguably provide the ontological substance we have been querying. The effects are real enough—or "real" enough, or real "enough"—in whatever form they happen to come, and for the phenomenology of a Christian believer this does count double: Yeshua, for example, if taken as a/the "risen Lord" thereby morphs from man into idea-image (*ideal* idea-image), and hence almost without noticing becomes for the adherent not an assisting focus for one's prayer and love and devotion directed to the Father (again, using the traditional language for God/"God" ungendered), but instead a focus for *himself*: he now as "He," resurrected and co-equal with the "Father" as standardized Christianity post Nicene has had it; and that in a way Yeshuan-Judaism did not set out, and Yeshua the sage-cum-rabbi certainly never put forth. Even in such lofty assertions as those assigned to Yeshua by statements like the Gospel of John's famous "I am the way" (John 14:6, "Jesus said to him, 'I am the way, and the truth, and the life. No one comes to the Father except through me.'"[22]), we have Yeshua motioning his listeners to God/"God" and not to himself as God/"God". Yet that is nevertheless precisely what was made: Yeshua *as* God/"God", the as-structure, and if we follow Harman this is a usage claim just as much as it is an identity claim, and therefore—therefrom—Yeshua is "used" in the idea-image (the Christian definitionally idolatrous) manner of that of worship or supplication-recipient object/entity. This is obviously an astounding transformation, and it is little wonder that it took centuries of church intra-communal discussion and argumentation to bring about. We are here in our study trying to (move towards) an undoing of this—or at least a loosening—and that for the sake of Yeshua's message and its continuing relevance (so I judge) to the ethical and social dimensions of human existence.

20. van Inwagen, *Material Beings*, 124–5.

21. van Inwagen, *Material Beings*, 134–5.

22. *Thinline Bible with the Apocrypha* (NRSV). This is in response to Thomas' question about how they (the disciples) might know the way to where Yeshua is going to "prepare a place" for them (from verse three).

A Theory of Notion/Event

To close out this section on theoretical keystones, we return to that other most famous phenomenological philosopher (and, appropriately enough, Heidegger's own teacher) Husserl, to very briefly glance at his thoughts on the "physical thing" and "conscious of" as taken from his *Ideas I*: "Thus the physical thing is said to be, in itself, unqualifiedly transcendent. Precisely in that the essentially necessary diversity amongst modes of being, the most cardinal of them all, becomes manifest: the diversity between *consciousness and reality*."[23] Surely there is a direct link here to the idea as image and as idea-image, as object and the connected concept(s), albeit—again following Husserl—any given encounter will provide only a one-sided facet of that perceived. The physical thing not only contains its transcendence (beyond its corporeality), but is existentially that very transcendence, and because so the distinction with consciousness (i.e. the felt-by-me) is possible. Continuing on, Husserl states, "Necessarily there always remains a horizon of determinate indeterminateness, no matter how far we go in our experience, no matter how extensive the continua of actual perceptions of the same thing may be through which we have passed."[24] We find once more (only of course with Husserl as predictive, written far earlier) Harman's "occluded underground zone," via Heidegger's tool-being, via Husserl: these are the depths of unqualifiedly everything to which we lack access. We are bound in by our (Husserlean) horizons, encloistered by the (Heideggerean) worlds of our embedding, forever trapped by the happenstances of our conditions; but let us not mistake such for absences. This after all is simply how we human animals are, and nothing can be done about it.

The idea adopted, the image incorporated, touches us, imparting a reaction, a phenomenological moment, a movement that spins itself out in myriad ways with that selfsame embeddedness throughout the course of the life in question. There is an unpinpointable reality here: an imprecise existence within an existence which nevertheless casts its net over the definable and measurable of the being, over the carnal and the perceivable. This is the living idea, the expression of the idea-image, the notion/event unfurled, unleashed. This is the hidden power of the phrase "risen Lord," and it unmade everything that was Yeshuan in its re-birthing of man to idol.

---

23. Husserl, *The Essential Husserl*, 73; emphases in the original. This is taken from *Ideas: General Introduction to Pure Phenomenology*, Volume I (*Ideas I*, 1913), Section 42.

24. Husserl, *The Essential Husserl*, 75. Taken from *Ideas I*, Section 44.

Chapter 6

THE IMAGE AND THE IDEA

THUS, WE CHARGE, WHAT was done to the memory of Yeshua following his execution by the Roman authorities turned the man and his message into a new Golden Calf,[1] it took what he offered as revelation—like Moses before him—and set that to one side, preferring the concreteness of an image that could be worshiped outright to the more onerous demands of a differential way-of-being; as Exodus starts the tale (here firstly from the Tanakh, with our earlier used biblical sources to follow):

> Exodus 32:1–2: ¹When the people saw that Moses was so long in coming down from the mountain, the people gathered against Aaron and said to him, "Come, make us a god who shall go before us, for that man Moses, who brought us from the land of Egypt—we do not know what has happened to him." ²Aaron said to them, "Take off the gold rings that are on the ears of your wives, your sons, and your daughters, and bring them to me."[2]

There are some intriguing points to be realized from this passage, and parallels to be discovered. To begin, I would like to draw the reader's attention to a very slight, but for that profoundly significant, nuanced variance to the translations between our two considered religious traditions. In this modern and "purely Jewish" (that is, as understood by contemporary conventions) rendering we have "against Aaron" in verse one, whereas in the Christian versions (again, as taken under contemporary conventions) the same phrasing is put as "around Aaron." The Hebrew could apparently go both ways (I am more than willing to trust the experts), but how altered the provided meaning becomes thereby! Here is the same section as presented in the New Living Translation and the New Revised Standard Version, respectively, with some comments added to the second—largely repetitive in its wording—in order to strengthen the cut and reach of what I hope to explore in the below:

---

1. The story of the Israelites' (in)famous construction of this idol essentially right after the astounding mass theophany at Mount Sinai (God's/"God's" reported self-revelation to the gathered *entire nation*) is told in Exodus 32; we quote the first two verses below.
2. Exodus 32:1–2, taken from *Tanakh* (NJPS).

Exodus 32:1–2: ¹When the people saw how long it was taking Moses to come back down the mountain, they gathered around Aaron. "Come on," they said, "make us some gods who can lead us. We don't know what happened to this fellow Moses, who brought us here from the land of Egypt." ²So Aaron said, "Take the gold rings from the ears of your wives and sons and daughters, and bring them to me."

Exodus 32:1–2: ¹When the people saw that Moses delayed to come down from the mountain [or—transplanting—when the Yeshuans saw (but for that perhaps did not "see"?) that the anticipated second coming of their "risen Lord" was delayed], the people gathered around Aaron [the recognized and extant local authority figure(s)—let us put in here the late first and early second century CE church leaders], and said to him, "Come, make gods for us, who shall go before us [the believers needed a justification—why had Yeshua not returned in triumph? what reason to linger?—but too they needed a structuring of church, a hierarchy, rites and rituals, a defined set of dogma to provide some grounding if they were to carry on for the long term]; as for this Moses, the man who brought us up out of the land of Egypt [as for Yeshua's "kingdom" message and his peculiar way of life, the new being-in-the-world that he taught], we do not know what has become of him ["We cannot keep at it! Give us some simple and clear routines to follow."]." ²Aaron said to them, "Take off the gold rings that are on the ears of your wives, your sons, and your daughters [the leadership remarks: "Give us our worldly necessities, fund and support us so we can focus on these issues."], and bring them to me ["We will make what you want, something of solidity and an easily perceivable substance."]."³

Bring me/us your gold, the hierarchy instructs, and I/we will take away your burden of thinking and living for yourselves on the detailed but open model of Moses, or the delicate and imprecise model of Yeshua, bequeathing you something much easier in lieu. It is hard, they admit, this orienting around a non-imaged basis; I/we (they) know that, I/we know too how difficult it is to make sense of that man whom we call prophet or brother, and/but singular leader, and/but master or lord. I/we will therefore make you an image, an idol in all but name, an idol of a calf, an idol of Yeshua, an idea-image that will be placeable there before, that will be directory and directing of each spiritual impulse, emotion, intuition. It will be a/the conceptual concretized: this molten gold you offer will be cast and cooled, formed, dried, and displayed.

Each lineage gives us a Golden Calf; yet note again how subtly crucial is the line betwixt the Tanakh with its "gathered *against* Aaron" while the other two have "gathered *around* Aaron." As a non-Hebrew scholar I can only repeat my assumption that the "against/around" wording could travel in either direction when translated (as, indeed, the implications of the term might do exclusively within English), yet the

---

3. *Catholic Holy Bible* (NLT); *Thinline Bible with the Apocrypha* (NRSV).

alternatives achieved resonate with remarkable depth. It is a picture of a leadership compromising ("against") versus one complicit ("around"), a reluctant and a perhaps feeling forced—an afraid—authoritative echelon ("against") as opposed to a willingly participant and actively engaged—a guiding—top rank ("around"). There could even be a more sinister motive at work (and if so one would think—one would hope—an unaware and unrecognized motive): an anti-Hebraic-religio sentiment[4] on the part of the Christian translators rendering the Hebrew scripture into English. If so, would such not also be a part of the general "was Yeshuan-Jewish but has become Christian" self-hatred that was alluded to in the above?[5] Another query that presents itself: Did the burgeoning church require a more tactile divine in order to meet the needs of its increasingly Gentile congregations with their backgrounds most probably rooted in Greek forms of adoration? Or rather was it due to the potency with which an image can touch any human being, Gentile or otherwise? Or both, or other, or all and none? What really is the power of the image? What is the breaking forth of the life transforming abstraction embodied within and constitutive of the idea-image? What might be and has been done? We will need to explore how very flexible the idea of Yeshua became as it spread, as its seeds that were sown in multiple imageries disparately but commonly grew, and for that we will take the extreme example of Japan's Hidden Christian communities of the seventeenth to nineteenth centuries with their unique and highly object-oriented version of the faith; transitionally, though, first a few general reflections on the image and the idea, its place and its experiential punctuating.

An image can reinforce the mental configuration—the "world"—one exists within, or it can unsettle, turn, and dislodge. It speaks through the ideas and associations that it elicits, as we have seen/"seen" in the preceding, and it does thusly (necessarily) due to the multiplicity and interconnectedness of the conceptual-perceptual networked cosmoses held within any one human mind. We are creatures of the abstract—again, as above—and this is simply how we work: an unavoidable, *inescapable*, facet of human being. This is a point aptly made by Jean-Luc Nancy regarding the image in art, as considered generally and in its place for us, when he writes that the mixture of "life and activity" we know is "less a sensuous world than an intelligible world of markers, functions or uses, and transitivities—in the final analysis less a world, perhaps, than a milieu, an *Umwelt*."[6] (That final "less a world," by the way, should be taken in the standard Earth-world sense, rather than in the Heideggerean

---

4. I do not wish to use "anti-Semitic" here, although such may certainly be involved, because a part of this study's overall goal is to allow the Jewish religious sense to speak for itself away from the cultural and ethnic boundaries that are indeed nevertheless also a definitional part of it (as difficult as such an "away from" might be for us to imagine from our current historical setting). This is in some regards a Pauline/Hellenistic motivation to be sure, but would not God's/"God's" "dwelling place" "be" encompassing enough for "Jewish" non-Jews? I would anyway like to think so.

5. Nancy, *The Banality of Heidegger*.

6. That is, "life-world", the "world as experienced": the term is a Husserlean one and is very connected to (originary of, in the phenomenological lineage) Heidegger's "world"; Nancy, *The Muses,* 18; on *Umwelt* see Husserl, *The Essential Husserl,* and Smith, *Husserl*.

"world" sense extrapolated from *Umwelt*.) Here again we find the borders around an existence, its parameters or "horizons," to use what is probably the most famous of Husserl's specialized labels, and it cannot be stressed enough that what we are therefore capable of comprehending arises not (fundamentally) out of the perceptually accessible, but rather from the contextual foundations that ground the mental approach, the notional landscapes which are at present inhabited. If we do not think it then we are unlikely to be able to see it—"see" it!—and how disturbing it can be to see/"see" that which was hitherto unthinkable. (Purely now on the work of art: this is an aspect at which provocative images may best excel, if such are indeed enabled (through whatever means) to bring forth further or revelatory fresh ideas/idea-images.) Even so "ocularly" blessed, even so shaken, however, any ontological transition within a mind (hence within a life) will necessarily be gradual, due to the cocoons of established thought patterns which become encrusted with age and customization—and too the naturally large role played by one's acculturation—and thereby difficult to break through; although not impossible. The image and the idea thus dance together in the inspiration imparted and in that taken: the idea becomes an image, and an image cannot but evoke an idea.

In a later work Nancy notes that the image "is an imprint of the intimacy of its passion (of its motion, its agitation, its tension, its passivity) . . . The image touches me, and, thus touched and drawn by it and into it, I get involved, not to say mixed up in it."[7] An image, we might tentatively conclude, appears then to work—to do its work—firstly in the way that it is already comprehended (perhaps better: *pre-*comprehended), but then secondly it does so in the way that it beckons one to re-understand, in its producing forth of the summoned and the presently felt (whether conceptually or emotionally (or both)), to stimulate a growth and to nudge towards a further becoming. One reacts to and interacts with the image before one only via the means one now has access to—that much is clear enough, we cannot after all begin from nowhere, not even in those cases where we are shocked into the unforeseen (e.g. by provocative art)—but what is thereby birthed and/or conjured is another (notional) creature, a beast with a lifespan of indeterminate longevity: it is a living new start with an unknown end, and it may provide previously unimagined methods of interacting. The voiced call of interplay between self and image-idea/idea-image thence uttered may or may not echo—it rings, it fades—depending on how the individuated existence thereafter unfolds. An encounter with an image always becomes a "me-plus-this," but for . . . ? A yawning opening, yet a "maybe"/"may be" that has its possibilities ever restrained by the details of extant embeddedness (and therefore not a "wide open" opening—we each have our "horizons," each our confines of "world"). A potential of, from, with history; a "what" held by the "somewhere" from which one is currently positioned: we can only shrug and carry on.

---

7. Nancy, *The Ground of the Image*, 7.

Part 2 | The Real in Ideas and Images

On this aspect of historical rootedness, Arthur Danto—in a thoughtful consideration of art's broad sweep—has remarked, "One can without question imitate the work and the style of the work of an earlier period [mechanically, reproductively]. What one cannot do is live the system of meanings upon which the work drew in its original form of life [conceptually]."[8] That which has been done can always be re-done by hands sufficiently skillful; that which has been thought can always be re-thought by minds sufficiently nimble (imaginative); but the indwelling of a fully embedded "world" can never be achieved: there are simply too many factors related, too many details underscoring and establishing, too many ifs, ands, buts, ors. Perhaps this complexity is a gift for us, a grace; it is at any rate something of a miracle. In reflecting on this at our still early stage in the present dwelling upon the image (image-idea) and idea-image, we might for the moment summarize by calling these proposed image reactions a type of a (poetically) perspective "couplet"; the interactions at play and their emergent result(s) are "works" or "products" buried in the primal and existential system of meanings that is a functioning human brain: a form irreplaceable and irreproducible, a completing and a complementing; one could not be had without the other, one would not be whole without the other.

Towards this, and moving us slightly back in the direction of our Yeshuan-Jewish focus, Abraham Joshua Heschel—writing about prophecy rather than imagery, though still making a point which I think is very apposite to our concerns—proposes that a difference lies between "descriptive" and "indicative" words, the prior having specific referents while the latter category "merely intimate something which we intuit but cannot fully comprehend."[9] In this, he explains, indicative terms bring out "not so much a memory [i.e. of the referent, as a descriptive term would] but a *response*, ideas unheard of, meanings not fully realized before."[10] Auditory evocation, if you will: new ideas, new images, new image-ideas/idea-images, the importation of the notional through a medium freshly deployed, the immanence of the other(-than) carrying the manifestation of the never-thought; even, as here—religiously, in or with (by?) the sacral—of the ineffable. One hears/reads/stands before the idea-image and it . . . Sometimes nothing, at other times a universe explodes—*one's* universe explodes. The abstracts we live in seem limitless, but our study sadly must narrow itself off (whatever my verbosity), and thus we nod a thanks but farewell to Heschel, keeping to mind (but not to ears) the image as more strictly visually formed.

Perhaps, if we wish to stay thematically adhered to the Christian, we next picture the empty cross of the Protestant, or the embodied crucifix of the Catholic: How might previous alignments and allegiances affect the conceptuality and emotionality triggered by such, particularly for their partisans? What does a seeing ("seeing"?) entail; what is that like for the believer versus the non-believer? What *is* the "what it

---

8. Danto, *After the End of Art*, 203.
9. Heschel, *God in Search of Man*, 181.
10. Heschel, *God in Search of Man*, 182; emphasis in the original.

is like"?[11] These too are bound by and formative of "horizons," "worlds," and we may venture that perhaps (and as otherwise from the various Christian groupings) Judaism—throughout its rich history and its multiple Judaisms—with its strong ethos of anti-imagery is meant precisely to allow, maybe foster, an ever-evolving conceptual "wrestling with" relationship of humanity towards the divine;[12] an openness that runs counter to the tendency—the (per)forced reaction—of association and meaning assignation onto the image that defines and thereby limits both it and what it does to the interacting subject. Such a purposely non-limiting approach may indeed be a much better fit with the historical Yeshua's "kingdom" message than the currently common Christian style of strict enforcement of dogma as interpreted hierarchically (however many layers the hierarchy may have, and even if only two or three);[13] this is an area to be explored at some length in the chapters which follow. (I should add that I think Judaism—ours today and theirs then—naturally has its hierarchies too; my point here being only the potential appositeness of an anti-imagery sentiment as applied to human-divine relating.)

We *homo sapiens* are, however, intensely visual and sensory creatures, and it is no wonder that very many of us have chosen to situate ritual practices and numinous experiences along these lines of "sight." Consider, for example, the employment of iconography in the Orthodox Christian tradition. In a work specifically on the phenomenology involved in Eastern Orthodox liturgical rites, wherein the surrounding church walls and iconostasis are heavily decorated (we might call this *populated*) by imagery, Christina Gschwandtner refers us to an argument of Jean-Luc Marion's on the feel one has of being "viewed" by an icon when before it, writing:

> Marion argues that in gazing at an icon I experience another gaze weighing upon mine; I experience myself as being seen . . . This is visually manifested by the inverse perspective employed by icons, which create the experience of our being envisioned by them instead of the Western perspective of objective contemplation by the viewer.[14]

Contemplating this, imagining the feel of it, raises some interesting possibilities regarding the me-plus-this(image). For one, being "viewed" in this way might have any number of elicited emotional responses: judgment, shame, unworthiness or embarrassment amongst the more negative; love, support, sympathy with or generous pity amongst the more positive; and these would seem to concur strongly with the

---

11. That is, the qualia; see the explanatory note to the discussion of Lycan in the previous chapter.

12. À la Jacob in Genesis 32:22–30; see again the preceding note on this section and some approaches to translating it (and thereby interpreting it!) in Chapter 3.

13. I am thinking here of certain Protestant denominations that claim egalitarianism, yet there is always a "knowledgeable" teacher of some sort—how could there not be in human sociality?—and thus a form of default ranking. Perhaps (unprogrammed) Quakers come closest to equality here.

14. Gschwandtner, *Welcoming Finitude*, 114; the Marion passage under consideration can be found in Marion, *God Without Being*, 17–18.

associative juxtapositions raised by the depicted saint or avatar or sacred aspect et cetera, in question. The idea one holds reaches out through the image-idea/idea-image so powerfully as a result of this added layer gained from a sense of being actively "viewed" by the (an)other that the experiential ceases being a purely internal affair and becomes a fully other-engagement, a proper *interaction* in a way that an empty cross would (almost certainly) not be able to induce. Psychologically one might be prodded in a nearly limitless manner by such an arrangement and confluence of affective forces, particularly in the charged atmosphere of a communal religious setting. Yet these comments are not meant to assert that a spurring of this sort is not real; they are clearly "real" as an instance of the notion/event, which as we have tried to argue are very much real/"real" enough: a life, a life-world, and possibly a radically life-altering one at that.

The potency here waxes or withers with the fervency of the ideational adherent, "my god" becomes "my God" becomes "God immanent": a marker, a reminder, a moving tribute, a manifestation, a theophanic event. Again, Judaism's genius (if it so be) may lie precisely in the prohibition of this ever potentially misleading-ness, this misdirection tied up with and within instances of imagery. Amy Whitehead has explored the distinction between a fetishistic understanding of religious statuary and an animistic one (and we can broaden the labels used to apply to iconography more generally, I think): for the former a *non-representation* qualifies the image, and hence for the believer (the holder of the idea) worship with or toward or through the image is an issue of "the spirit of the matter"; whereas for the latter *inhabitation* qualifies the image (it is achieved in/by the image) and so worship is rather one of "the spirit in the matter."[15] On this further, Kugel relates how widespread the animistic sense alluded to here was in the ancient world of the Near East (and surely elsewhere), "the gods . . . *were* the images. That is, the gods lived inside their own statues."[16] Expounding on how this notional "lived inside" was apprehended he explains that:

> There is a group of ancient Mesopotamian texts that describe the production of divine statues. The image was indeed fashioned by human artisans, but then it was said to be "born", brought to life . . . While it was being shaped, it was indeed a statue, the image of Marduk, and it was so called. But once finished, it was not called an image; now it was Marduk himself.[17]

Judaism has since its beginning worked endlessly against such mental attitudes taking root within its members, and although this anti-imagery was for long ages of human social history a primarily or nearly universally unique feature of its communal ritual life, before we get ahead of ourselves by claiming some kind of singular spiritual

---

15. Whitehead, *Religious Statues and Personhood*, 120; she is referring to a work by Peter Pels that argues for distinguishing in this way: "The Spirit of Matter," in *Border Fetishisms*, 91–121.

16. Kugel, *The God of Old*, 73; emphasis in the original.

17. Kugel, *The God of Old*, 84.

dispensation for the Jewish comprehending (while neither disclaiming it)—that is, for the Judaically framed "horizon," "world," *Umwelt*—let us recall, let us "see" again, how very many of our Hebrew narratives were tales of an actual physical manifestation of the divine; only such were appearances that were not static, not statuary nor iconography, yet perhaps arguably nevertheless "habitations" in some instances (e.g. one could make this case for "burning bush" type manifestations[18]). Notwithstanding, these stories called for and called upon a mental "turn" of realization/recognition from their participants (the characters involved), and then of course we readers witness the archetypal reaction of prostration before the wholly/*holy* other who is suddenly known to be present. For the ancient Israelites, Kugel muses, God/"God":

> was not to be represented in an image, *not* because He did not have a body, however, and not because He could not be seen by people. On the contrary: perhaps making an image of Him was forbidden precisely because the fact of His *appearing* among human beings, His being revealed, was . . . such a crucial item.[19]

In this ideascape (for these people at this time) God/"God" would come and commune—right there, as real as real can be (none of our messy "real"-ness afoot)—the material and spiritual worlds were not so thickly separated, and thus perceptional space had to be left for the unknown, the as-yet undisclosed, the (in Heideggerean terms) still covered-over. It would be no blasphemy (it is absolutely not intended as such) to label this an area left to and for the imagination: conceptually unbound and therefore non-confining in its non-defining: the divine could *be* as we exist moment by moment, as we stretch out our hours and days in the interplay of seeking the transcendent while we do; for those of us who choose to do. Any determined representation would and must fail beneath such an understanding; an image of the living can at best capture a moment of that life, a moment which is now already gone.

An image wants,[20] and to produce an image is to affix an abstraction onto it by the sheer fact of creation. Its descent into the world (so to speak—but maybe *ascent* if we take Harman's "erupting" to heart[21]) will, after all, be done *for* something by *someone*, and therefore intention is not a question of "if" but of "how much," of "how well related" and how "successfully" communicated (this, by the way, is an interesting and controversial question within art criticism, closely connected to interpretation

---

18. See Exodus 3; of special interest here—conceptually, theologically, slippery slope-ally—is the wording shift in subject from verse two's "*An angel of the LORD* appeared to him in a blazing fire out of a bush" to verse four's "*When the LORD saw* that he had turned aside to look, *God* called to him out of the bush"; *Tanakh* (NJPS); my emphases.

19. Kugel, *The God of Old*, 106; emphases in the original.

20. A full treatment of this may be found in Mitchell, *What Do Pictures Want?*

21. As in the quoted text which was given above: "Anything, prior to erupting in its explicit form, is real simply by exerting its efforts in the cosmos, by breathing its life into a world that would not have been the same without it"; Harman, *Tool-Being*, 219.

and the subject-object dialogue). Inevitably the maker's mark will be on the made, the conceptual associations and juxtapositions of the mind behind the hands that have moulded hanging there heavily, indelibly, about the item's contours (its "shoulders," whatever shape such might have or take). A viewer or experiencer may well mistake the idea of—the idea underlying—any given image, and in that the image-idea/idea-image compound might "fail" in the (desired or sought) expressive sense, but it will be there, tethered to its manufacturer's "horizon" of comprehension just as it is to its viewer's "horizon" of elucidation. That which is "seen" is not only what can be seen visually but what can be understood given the networked embeddedness of the interacting creature, an area we have stressed repeatedly in the above. The same indeed goes for "images" which are purely auditory, or even only mental; but now we pause, because the mental—the *idea*—is of course really the boiled core of it, the uncrossable threshold for a human being: here, and no further. The image speaks worlds through its idea(s): it speaks life and death, instantiation and dissolution, an endeavored immanence of the transcendent. Is it any wonder it so beguiles? Judaism very wisely gave it a flat no—and Yeshua was without doubt a fellow denier—but then his followers, wise in a different way, said yes, and history was re-born. Let us explore a special case of this.

Chapter 7

A (Special) Case Study
Japan's Hidden Christians and the Image/Icon

As we have sought to argue—or at least to hint at or gesture towards—there is a certain tremulousness in Christianity (in what that construct became as against the Yeshuan faith, that is: we mean here an instability within the faith *in* (the figure) Yeshua that developed as we know it today instead of the faith *of* (the person) Yeshua, which was (is) really a Judaism later usurped), and perhaps this shakiness extends most from the inarticulate nature—the *inarticulability*—of the Christ emblem at its notional heart; that marking which seems to lend itself fairly easily to syncretism. If such is indeed a definitive quality of the broad system called "Christianity," then it would help account for the comparative ease with which the religion has so frequently crossed borders and cross-planted itself ("Cross"-planted, to employ a central image and to jumpstart us on the below) across peoples and through centuries. Our project of an enfolding, of an attempt at (re)unification, is really therefore a reduction: we seek a far lower or lesser Christology that is grounded more firmly in the individual-assage (the historical), along with a "weaker" theology (to be discussed), and a humble request for forgiveness and acceptance in return from the heart of contemporary Judaism. Thence we hope (we pray) to a togetherness.

One marginal and marginalized group that provides an excellent example of both these trends of flexibility and inexactitude which we have claimed mark the development of Christianity is the Hidden Christians of Japan's well-known (and well romanticized) feudal period; and hence, despite the conceptual brutishness that the movement displays when viewed from a modern perspective, they can assist our efforts in signaling a way into a settled unsettledness, a comfortable vagueness; although we will take and arrive at far different conclusions (and much less emphasis on ritual) than they did. For this we will begin with a brief biographical sketch for the purposes of framing, move to an examination of the Hidden Christian's usage of disguised Marian and other Christian iconography, and then wrap back into further ruminations on the place and potential of the (en)pictured phenomenologically and numinously, furnishing the stage already constructed with the intertwining of image and idea: that pairing which will not leave our sight ("see!") for the remainder.

Francis Xavier, one of the co-founders of The Society of Jesus (better known by the membership title of "Jesuit"), first brought Christianity to Japan in 1549 CE, landing in Kagoshima, a city on the southernmost point of the southernmost of the four main islands (Kyushu) on August 15th; appropriately enough the Feast Day of the Assumption.[1] The new belief system was welcomed by many Japanese—mostly but not entirely of the lower classes—and it enjoyed a rapid expansion over the following few decades, particularly in the various regions of the island of Kyushu and in and around Kyoto, eventually attaining a number of converts large enough to cause the government concern about spreading foreign influences from the influx of Western ideas and values which inevitably accompanied the priests and their teachings, unapproved—and therefore threatening—notions that were thought to be entering the minds of the populace.

Counteracting political decisions were therefore made, steps taken that favored increasing social control, and thus beginning in 1587 with the unifying *daimyo* lord (a powerful samurai leader, much like a baron) Toyotomi Hideyoshi's edict banning Christianity, the long and uneven persecution of those who adopted the religion started upon its winding historical path. The European missionaries were soon pushed aside and ever further from the nation's urban centers, resulting in the Jesuits relocating their seminary for the training of indigenous Japanese priests from Kyoto to the remote island of Ikitsuki in Nagasaki Prefecture (essentially the middle of nowhere, and painfully inaccessible). Even that drastic step was not to last, however; the first shogun of a fully united and centralized Japan—namely, Tokugawa Ieyasu, effectively ruling behind the scenes by this point—signed an edict in 1614 that expelled every foreign priest and shuttered each church: effective immediately, everywhere, and this was reinforced shortly thereafter by the then-established second shogun in the Tokugawa line—Hidetada—in 1616.[2] The stage was thereby set for an extended trauma for Japan's Christian believers, one that surfaced and sank throughout the remainder of the Edo Period (1603–1868) and until the early years of the Meiji Era (1868–1912).

This 1614 edict proved to be a turning point for the seriousness with which the authorities addressed the "Christian problem." Thereafter every family unit across Japan was required to register at its local officially designated Buddhist temple in a manner very similar to how each resident is required to register at one's relevant city hall today. This system was expanded further in 1638 following the Shimabara

---

1. Turnbull, *The Kakure Kirishitan of Japan*, 28. The Feast Day of the Assumption refers to Mary's ascension, the day she is believed to have been bodily taken to heaven at the end of her life and thus avoided physical death.

2. Turnbull, *The Kakure Kirishitan of Japan*, 31, 34. Hidetada's rule from 1605–1623 overlapped with his father's (Ieyasu) in practical terms despite the latter's technical abdication of office in 1605. Formally, Hidetada was head of the bureaucracy from 1605 onwards, although his father retained much influence and power until his death in 1616.

Rebellion,[3] an event that appears to have greatly disturbed the national government. In that ill-fated, would-be revolution spanning the mid-winter months of 1637–1638, some forty thousand peasants revolted against their local *daimyo* ruler's policy of arresting the wife and daughter(s) of any man who could not pay his taxes, which were exorbitant (and one can imagine the dreadful treatment that befell those wives and daughters following their seizure by local soldiers). This underclass protest took the form of farmers arming themselves with what they could and occupying Hara Castle en masse with their family members. Eventually every single one of them, including the children, were massacred by the *daimyo's* troops; but more than the act of armed defiance itself—there were many disturbances related to overly high taxation in feudal Japan at the time—what set this particular instance apart was that the peasant "army" carried a battle flag with the Portuguese for "Praised be the Blessed Sacrament" written on it,[4] identifying themselves not only as subversives, but as Christian subversives. This had the additional effect of influencing the shogunate to decide on a cessation of trade in goods—fearing further derivative foreign influences stemming from such activities—with all nations and outside enterprises save the Dutch East Indies Company,[5] for whom the famous artificial island of Dejima was constructed as a sort of holding pen for the grouping's staff to live and labor exclusively within, located in what was then Nagasaki Harbor but has since become landlocked amidst greater reclamation work.

The registration system was then expanded once more in 1671 to include births, deaths, marriages, adoptions, change of residence and/or occupation. This procedure came to also feature an annual review conducted by the temple designed to ensure a family's non-Christian status (and interestingly the legal framework of Japan at the time treated a whole co-dwelling familial unit in the same way that modern codes consider a single individual). The process itself involved each household member ritually stepping on a so-called *fumie* artwork of Christ or the Virgin Mary[6] as a means of demonstrating non-belief in the faith,[7] following the logic that if one were willing to literally step on Christ's or Mary's visage then one could not possibly consider either to be sacred. Initially, confiscated Christian objects and images were used for this purpose, but in later years craftsmen were drafted to produce the items outright, and in at least one instance the manufactured piece was judged to be so beautiful that the official functionaries convinced themselves the artist had to be a fellow believer;

---

3. Turnbull, *The Kakure Kirishitan of Japan*, 40–1. The city of Shimabara is located in the peninsular southeastern part of modern day Nagasaki Prefecture.

4. Whelan, trans., intro., and ann., *The Beginning of Heaven and Earth*, 8–9.

5. Whelan, trans., intro., and ann., *The Beginning of Heaven and Earth*, 8–9.

6. This label was sometimes reversed in the Japanese syllabary to read *ebumi*: meaning either "stepping picture" or "picture [for] stepping," respectively (written, again respectively, thusly: 踏み絵 or 絵踏み).

7. Turnbull, *The Kakure Kirishitan of Japan*, 41; see also note 32 on page 241; Whelan, trans., intro., and ann., *The Beginning of Heaven and Earth*, note 2 on pages 69–70 to text on page 9.

otherwise how could he have made such a moving work? The man, in fact a Buddhist, was arrested and then executed.[8]

This raises the pertinent issue of icon possession and usage amongst the community of Christian believers who persisted in their practices following the prohibition of the "foreign" faith. If one is an underground worshipper, why run the risk of having incriminating evidence lying about? One simple answer might be that they were taught thusly: the Jesuits' catechism for Japanese converts[9]—called the *Doctrina Christian*—encouraged numerous sacred images to be placed on family altars,[10] and in another guidance text issued to adherents regarding the persecution of Christians (titled *Readiness for Martyrdom*) the missionary authors stressed that neither acts purporting to be non-Christian but actually Christian (e.g. carrying and using a Buddhist rosary instead of a Christian one for the associated Christian prayers) nor false apostasies (e.g. verbally declaring oneself non-Christian while mentally maintaining one's belief) were ever permitted, although it was considered acceptable to not confess if not asked, and to hide whatever Christian items one possessed.[11] Hence the combination of being encouraged to make use of physical objects in one's religious life and practice, together with the discouragement (indeed the active instruction against) applying non-Christian items for Christian rituals may help to account for the enthusiasm for iconography that we find in Edo Period Christianity, although our thoughts on the image-idea/idea-image likely will make us deem there is more to it than merely that; and indeed, as already indicated, Japan's Hidden Christians did in the end do just what they ought not to have done: use non-Christian statues and other icons as foci for Christian worship. Moreover, they not only "used" but enthusiastically embraced these items.

---

8. This incident is related in Fujimura, *Silence and Beauty*, 115–16; the full details of this story (not given here) likely contain at least some elements of fiction as it appears to come via a historical novel by Yoshiro Nagayo called *The Bronze Christ* (1927). The protagonist in the book, Yusa Hagiwara, was a metalsmith who made fumie during this period, and twenty of his original pieces are known to remain today.

9. I admit to once needing to look this term up, and so for the sake of similarly unfamiliar readers: A "catechism" is a book or other document that contains a summary of the church's teachings and rites (traditionally in a question-and-answer format), those beliefs and rituals perhaps popularly known as the "sacraments" but technically including more than the core seven sacraments of the church; see Walsh, *Roman Catholicism*, 3; and cf. the motto on the Shimabara Rebellion's battle flag referred to above.

10. Whelan, trans., intro., and ann., *The Beginning of Heaven and Earth*, note 2 on page 69.

11. Certain readers might remember the U.S. President Bill Clinton's "Don't ask, don't tell" directive of 1993, which served an analogous avoidance of the real issue at heart; for the above, see Turnbull, *The Kakure Kirishitan of Japan*, 34–5. Interestingly, this *Readiness* text (most probably) arrived early on in Japanese Christianity in 1557—a mere eight years after Francis Xavier's first arrival—and it thus predated the official ban on Christianity. Although later Christians who lived under that ban were likely not familiar with the document itself, its tenets had clearly been taught to them and were apparently both accepted and applied.

A (Special) Case Study

Bodhisattva statuary (roughly: enlightened beings who forestall nirvana to help guide other sentient beings to enlightenment[12]) in particular quickly became popularized as Christian reverential aids (although with a certain additional style and flair taken from Japan's indigenous Shinto religion), and it is easy to imagine how the practicalities involved could have led practitioners to the conclusions they did. If one has been instructed to employ objects ritually by one group of authorities (church), but has also been prohibited from having certain objects while still allowed to have others by another group of authorities (State), then it is a fairly short step to using the accepted items to secretly practice the forbidden acts which have become a significant part of one's life. Yet the query remains: Why make use of an icon at all? Does not the First Commandment and its inclusive condemnation of making a likeness of God apply? Furthermore, if one were to nevertheless employ an image of some kind, even what appears to be a safe legal option (e.g. a statue of the Bodhisattva Goddess of Mercy Kannon mentally disguised for use as a substitute for the Blessed Virgin Mary) would still run the risk of having its true purpose discovered by someone at some point—be it an inquisitive neighbor or an unannounced visit from a samurai guard (both not uncommon occurrences under the Edo Period's surveillance policies)—and that was not the only item that the Hidden Christians employed: painted scrolls of the saints, paper crosses, string rosaries; these and others were central and more transparently Christian parts of the ritual lives of the hidden faithful. Within this symbolic and camouflaged milieu it was the figure of Mary, whether in a Kannon version or outright, that became fundamental to Japan's believers, a point from which I think we can discover an instruction on the arc of Christianity towards potential syncretisms and, yet again, on the overwhelming flood that is the image-idea/idea-image.

When Xavier and the other Jesuit missionaries first brought Christianity to Japan in the sixteenth century the theological concepts of Mary as both Virgin Mother and Immaculate Mother were already fairly well established although not yet dogma,[13] and certainly would have been taught to the new believers. In Japanese hands this shortly gave way to a deeper exaltation of a feminized divine that merged the new with pre-existing notions of deity/nature as spiritual mother (taken from Shinto), likely as a result of the position of Japan's long-standing mythological character *Amaterasu omikami,* the nation's imperial lineage founding Goddess of the Sun, and/or residing

---

12. However, this is not the only definition of a Bodhisattva; some strands take these entities as people on their way to Buddhahood, or as those who have become enlightened or taken vows towards such and seek to assist others (views and interpretations vary). See Silk, "Bodhisattva: Buddhist Ideal," *Encyclopædia Britannica.* Accessed July 01, 2021. Silk's overview referenced here emphasizes the aspect of "one on the way" as a Bodhisattva, but it also mentions the "savior deity" role some play in local cultures due to a mixing of extant mythologies with Buddhist teachings.

13. The notion of Mary's immaculateness (as bearer of the immaculate Christ) was a controversial idea within the church until around the mid-fifteenth century, whereafter it gained ground doctrinally and became official dogma in 1854; see Walsh, *Roman Catholicism,* 148. The Assumption of Mary, incidentally (as referred to above), also became official dogma in a similar way in 1950 (Walsh discusses this on the same page).

emanation of the "great spirit of the universe of the great circle."¹⁴ If indeed the first (and perhaps current) Christian converts in Japan were inclined to already consider the numinous in a maternal rather than paternal dimension due to this background, then the figure of Mary would quite seamlessly be both accepted and probably even promoted, and thereby too would it be further freely associated with another previously transplanted recipient of folk (if not technical) apotheosis: Mahayana Buddhism's Bodhisattva Kannon (*Kuan Yin* or *Guanyin* in Chinese), an enlightened being definitionally connected with mercy.¹⁵

Shusaku Endo—famous author of the novel *Silence* and native son of Nagasaki Prefecture, Japan's Christian heartland—argues in one of his nonfiction works that the Jesuits' own adherence to Mary, conjoined with their missionary directive of "substitute not destroy" when endeavoring to spread the Christian message to other cultures, helped prompt them to emphasize Mary from early on in their proselytizing actions in Japan, doubtlessly encouraged the more by the convenient and attractive fit of the divine mother concept within the special circumstances granted by the presence of a Supreme Goddess (i.e. *Amaterasu omikami*) already "at the heart of Japanese religion." Moreover, as Turnbull points out, "The association of Mary with pre-Christian ideas, and the easy identification of her with Kannon, a devotional tradition so similar that camouflage was hardly necessary, facilitated still further a process of transformation [Turnbull's discursive context is on the transition of the Hidden Christians' ritualisms from a sacrament based form (following church rites and directives) to a personally/popularly based form (following the religion's outlawing)]."¹⁶ This conceptual slide was enhanced by the ban itself, which compelled believers to disguise their prayers to Mary by making them through alternative means, and the ready usage of Kannon statues and images as substitutes evidently had great appeal for reasons of symbolic proximity and the practical advantage that should a neighbor or other resident be curious about one's potential Christianity, appearances would point merely to Buddhism and the worship of Kannon; after all, the statues genuinely were Kannon statues, and they had additionally been manufactured for the sole purpose of being such; whatever intentions may have been put onto the pieces by Japanese Christians would

---

14. On *Amaterasu omikami* and other Shinto notions of divinity see Yamakage, *The Essence of Shinto*; the "great spirit of the universe of the great circle" discussion can be found on page 131 in Yamakage's book. Further, Fujimura, *Silence and Beauty*, 75–6, emphasizes how for the well-known novelist and thinker Shusaku Endo this was a crucial factor in the Japanese context as it pertained to Christianity.

15. While Kannon is most often called the "Goddess of Mercy," ontologically she is not a Goddess per se as Buddhism does not consider Bodhisattvas to be divine; see the note above. On this point, strictly Buddhism neither denies nor acknowledges God(s)/"God(s)"/Goddesses/"Goddesses," et cetera, but instead focuses on individual efforts to achieving enlightenment on one's own power and thus freeing oneself from the cycle of birth, death, and rebirth. See again Silk, "Bodhisattva: Buddhist Ideal," *Encyclopædia Britannica*. Accessed July 01, 2021. On core Buddhist teachings generally, and written for a popular audience, there is Hagen, *Buddhism*.

16. Turnbull, *The Kakure Kirishitan of Japan,* 106; Turnbull references Endo, キリシタン時代：殉教と棄教の歴史 [*Kirishitan Jidai: Junkyo to Kikyo no Rekishi*; The Christian Era: A History of Martyrdom and Apostasy (title trans. provided by Turnbull)].

not be those of their maker(s). A practicing Hidden Christian could hope that by this manner direct questions might thereby be avoided. Thus we have Exhibit A of the abstractional blending and associated image travelling which we have alleged in this case study; more awaits.

While for another culture that might have been the end of it, here the situation becomes murkier still due to the additionally extant (and so ancient as to be completely culturally ingrained) Shinto systems and thoughts related to *goshintai* or *gozensama*, those which involve an object that is literally (in the full sense: what the terms definitionally mean when translated) "the body of *Kami* [we note: *Kami* indicates "God" or "sacred" or "divine" or "ineffable" or "numinous" or "mystery" or even "Other"; there is no direct English for this extremely vague but pervasive Japanese word]"; and furthermore "Like a body it [that is, the *goshintai*] contains the spirit of *Kami* when it [the spirit] comes down to manifest its presence in this world."[17] Hence these are visible divine "homes" that can contain—but importantly do not always contain—the *Kami*'s spirit (and such dwelling could too be something like a sacred space, not necessarily a physical object). The preceding are background and presumed pieces of knowledge, non-examined data for anyone raised within a Japanese cultural context, and hence however much it might have been (or is) taught to either Shinto or Christian believers that the ritually employed religious materials were (are) purely symbols or temporary vessels of a transcendence, in practice it proved (and proves still) simple enough for the blocks of "mere matter" to be thought to have acquired religious power in and of themselves, resulting in an approach to the statue or icon that blurs the boundary between praying *to God* via an assisting item, and praying *to the item* itself.[18]

What then did these Kannon/Mary statues and icons (known as "Maria Kannon" in Japanese) look like? A number of examples of the Kannon statues are on display in Nagasaki City's "Twenty-Six Martyrs Museum,"[19] most of which were manufactured in China and are of ceramic make, but a few of which were produced in Hirado City, Nagasaki Prefecture, having been ordered at the time by locals. The general imagery is of a serene and very peaceful feminine figure, seated or standing with eyes closed, a crown and/or shawl covering her head. She appears to be deep in meditation, with

17. Yamakage, *The Essence of Shinto*, 66.

18. Turnbull, *The Kakure Kirishitan of Japan*, highlights how this is the case amongst the surviving Hidden Christian communities who endeavor to keep the traditions of their ancestors in the religious objects they employ, actually praying *to* the *gozensama* objects and considering *those objects* to answer their prayers, rather than making an appeal "to God as symbolized by the *gozensama*"; see page 106.

19. The museum is located on a hill across from the modern Japan Railways Nagasaki City central train station, a mount which served as the site of the crucifixion of twenty-six Christian believers—including two young children—who were forcibly marched there from Kyoto after having had their ears and/or noses cut off. The group was a mix of foreign missionaries and Japanese believers, and their public execution was intended as a warning and an encouragement not to accept the alien faith; and that if one had already accepted it then to quickly renounce it. The crucifixions took place on February 5th, 1597—relatively early in the period of persecution—and at the time the location provided an unobstructed view clearly visible from Nagasaki harbor: both domestic and foreign arriving ships would not have missed the scene. I visited the museum and memorial situated out front on August 27th, 2019.

hands folded or with her right palm extended openly towards the viewer in a gesture of greeting and benevolence.[20] Some of the statues—we can imagine this type were likely favored—depict a child held in the Goddess'/woman's arms, and one done by a Japanese artisan rather than a Chinese sculptor (and furthermore made of clay instead of ceramic) takes the form of a very human-looking woman with her kimono opened at the chest and an infant child suckling at her exposed breast. If this object were considered as an icon of Mary and not Kannon such a representation would certainly have shocked, and possibly appalled, any contemporary Europeans who came across it.[21]

Statues were not the only icons used by the Hidden Christians however; hanging scrolls decorated with paintings of Mary and other stalwarts of the faith—particularly the Apostle Paul or indigenous martyrs and/or heroes of steadfastness in the face of the Tokugawa repression—were also used, placed on the rear wall behind an enclosable and therefore disguisable home altar (e.g. within a hollow in an external wall or perhaps in an internal load-bearing beam) very much akin in form and size to a Shinto *kamidana* ("God shelf": these are essentially model sized household shrines typically placed on their own shelf in an auspicious part of the home, complete with various votive objects[22]). A somewhat famous Marian painting that has survived the centuries is titled "Our Lady of the Snow" (*"Yuki no Santa Maria"* in Japanese) and is noteworthy for its mingling of a Western artistic style with Japanese colors and techniques, overlaid on traditional Japanese *washi* paper. Crosses placed on or near the altar were too made of paper, folded in a manner not unlike other *origami* items, and even rosaries were formed from similarly disposable material such as string or wound paper, knotted to create shapes like the beads used to count repetitions in the cycle of Hail Mary prayers.[23] The act of displaying a scroll or multiple scrolls on a wall behind a constructed centerpiece is not where the similarities with a Shinto home altar end

---

20. Unfortunately the museum does not allow photographs to be taken, but many samples may be found online at: "マリア観音 [Maria Kannon]", *Google Images: Search*. Accessed November 12, 2019.

21. Thus providing a telling example of how different Japanese sensibilities were (and remain) even amongst the subset of cross-cultural co-religionists we are considering. To a Japanese Christian the baby Yeshua nursing from Mary's breast was completely fitting in its earthiness, with no hint of sacrilege surrounding; to a devout European believer the nudity of the holy mother and the excessively human aspect of the savior were areas to be shunned.

22. Yamakage lists three considerations for setting up a Shinto household shrine: "1) It can be set up at a high position. 2) It can be at a floor level that has three or four steps. This is called 'the Floor for Kami' (*kamidoko*). 3) It can be kept in a special niche (*tokonoma*) with a hanging scroll and the name of Kami written on it." Yamakage, *The Essence of Shinto,* 84. The votive objects might include miniature decorative mirrors, offering trays and artificial food/drink offerings, incense holders, et cetera.

23. These items can be viewed at the aforementioned "Twenty-Six Martyrs Museum" and also at the "Christian Museum" connected to the Oura Cathedral in Nagasaki City—the first church to be rebuilt following the relaxation and then lifting of the ban on Christianity as the shogunate fell and was replaced by the Meiji Era (1868–1912) with its restoration of direct imperial rule to Japan (supplemented by councilors and other trappings of nineteenth century royal governing practices such as were common in Europe). I visited this museum on August 27th, 2019, as well.

though, for the overall appearance, judging by the replica at the "Twenty-Six Martyrs Museum," is quite alike with its raised dais (three steps and a platform) that supports a statue—as a Shinto *kamidana* would support its shrine—and that has offering bowls carefully arranged in front of it. In the case of the Hidden Christians these would have contained saké, sashimi (raw cut fish), broiled fish, and steamed rice. That food and drink oblations were placed before a statue in an act of supposed Christian worship is surprising enough, but what is more striking are the lengths these believers evidently went to in keeping—even celebrating—physical objects in the practice of their faith despite the prolific risks owning such posed to their persons,[24] and even despite the aforementioned First Commandment's prohibition on making images of God/"God". Granted, the images placed and sacrificed to by the Hidden Christians were not *of* God/"God" per se, but as has been remarked, these images were nevertheless *prayed to* (and not only prayed *towards*) and were clearly the recipients of much care and attention. Our Exhibit A is now—before our very eyes ("seeing"!)—transforming into Exhibit B, and so let us dwell a moment longer on our case study to explore some of the image-idea/idea-image ramifications fermenting within these syncretic trajectories.

We have already demonstrated the practice of Hidden Christians in praying to their statues, pictures, and other representata as non-Christian Japanese might do with a more typical *goshintai* or *gozensama* (and here again please allow me to me stress the difference between praying "to" and praying "towards": *to* is directed at the object itself, *towards* at the idea or concept or signifier as represented or symbolized by/through the object), but is the habitation of an "other"/Other as thus implied by the act of prayer conducted this way thereby an aspect of Shinto beliefs influencing—perhaps in an unrecognized manner—the practices engaged in? It does appear (at least on my own analysis) that such is what is occurring here, although I doubt the ritual process itself was ever overtly taught to the Christian converts by a local Shinto priest in the ordinary course of their lives prior to the time of converting to the church; or even, really, taught to those who either never altered their religious affiliation and simply practiced Shinto in the way of their forebears; or, moreover, even to those who were raised in Hidden Christian homes following an earlier generation's change of allegiance but still grew up in the religio-cultural environment of Shinto quite by the accident of being Japanese: Shinto simply does not typically *teach* unless one seeks it out informally or joins a specific training program of some sort.[25] Yet this facet (or feature) of habitation as considered by Shinto is there to be discovered, for as Yamakage

---

24. Turnbull, who visited the "Twenty-Six Martyrs Museum" in the course of his own research, comments on this aspect too; see his *The Kakure Kirishitan of Japan*, 104, 107–8.

25. In my experience of living in Japan for two decades now, and in speaking with Japanese people, Shinto priests perform very little instruction in their duties related to the public. This is presumably both a result of the non- (in some ways anti-) orthodox approach of the religion and its absolute social pervasiveness. It *is* Japanese culture, and therefore (in many or most Japanese eyes) needs no annotation. Many Western commentators would label Shinto shamanistic, although I think it has a more deeply theorized set of theological principles than that term usually implies.

explains, the mirrors often placed within shrines and in front of home *kamidana* altars become receptive to the descending spirit of *Kami,* and therefore its/Its (i.e. the *Kami's*) "spiritual vibration permeates the surrounding area,"[26] and furthermore the mirror or other *yorishiro* (a "divine home" or "divine summoner" such as a sacred tree) can act as "antennae" for the spirit of *Kami* to come into. Moreover, once so possessed the mirror (tree, et cetera) acts as a pathway for prayers to be heard.[27] The *Kami* is in the object and the object directs one to the *Kami.* Having been born into the cultural milieu of Shinto as presented by Japanese society, the Hidden Christians would not have had to work out any of the aforementioned explicitly, such would have simply been second nature—the presumptive thoughtworld, an unvoiced voice prompting and shaping comprehensive terms—and whether the figure involved were Mary, Kannon, or a decorative mirror, we can regard the approach taken as singular and uniform; and that by default (assumed).

There is, however, a certain degree to which the figure of Mary appears to have had a particular and enormous appeal for the Japanese Christians of this period. In the near total absence of copies of the prohibited Holy Bible, the Hidden Christians did eventually produce a sacred text of their own, titling it *Tenchi Hajimari no Koto* (roughly, "things related to the beginning of heaven and earth"), a book that reads very much like a mixture of Japanese folklore and (somewhat distorted) narratives taken from multiple sections throughout the Bible; the original believers, we must remember, were almost exclusively taught in an oral manner by the European missionaries who had visited them, and even at the best of times (that is, from the believers' perspective) there were few printed Bibles available for study by those converts who actually could read, with precious fewer still following the advent of official government persecution. In this treasured homespun work of the *Tenchi*—a single community copy of which was probably read out loud only at group settings on special occasions, if it was read at all and not kept permanently concealed—Christal Whelan relates that the Virgin Mary "becomes one of the persons of the Trinity. The entire paternal Judeo-Christian tradition is turned gracefully on its head and feminized . . . The character of Mary is that of Great Mother and shaman."[28] From a standard Christian perspective this is a disturbing exaltation of Yeshua's earthly mother, even given her (Roman Catholic) church sanctioned status as "Queen of Heaven," an exemplar and model for we mortals, yesterday, today, and tomorrow.[29] To a non-Hidden Christian mind—but still a Christian one—putting Mary as co-equal with the God(/"God")head would be little short of heresy; indeed, it would *be* heresy. Yet there it was, growing out of

---

26. Yamakage, *The Essence of Shinto,* 78.

27. Yamakage, *The Essence of Shinto,* 80.

28. Whelan, trans., intro., and ann., *The Beginning of Heaven and Earth,* 31–2.

29. On Mary's official position in the Catholic Church see DeTurris Poust, *The Essential Guide to Catholic Prayer and the Mass,* 9, and Part 3, especially Chapters 9–11; and Walsh, *Roman Catholicism,* 147–8.

conceptual grounds that had been watered but not, through the twists of historical fate, well tended.

Similar thinking can also be found in regards to Mary's place within this group and periodic situation depicted in the famous novel *Silence*, in which the plotline follows a Portuguese missionary's travails within the same broad contextual setting. Endo notes in that work how—in the words of the priestly main character—"these poor peasants [i.e. the Japanese converts] honoured the Virgin above all. Indeed, I myself since coming to Tomogi [a tiny village in Nagasaki Prefecture where he is washed ashore after being secreted into Japan via ship from Macau and is then fortunately sheltered by a group of Hidden Christians] have been a little worried seeing that the peasants sometimes seem to honour Mary rather than Christ."[30] Once more, Mary is understood not so much as the way to the Son (as church dogma has it), but as an end in herself. A divine or, at a minimum, semi-divine entity—how could such be fostered within Christianity? By token it naturally could not, but by the selfsame "natural" development into (a form of) Christianity out of local roots it is an indication (and perhaps more than that) of the effortless slide into syncretism that was proposed above. Whether this trait is a result of the complex (and often confusing) aspects of Trinitarian doctrine or of something(s) else is beyond the scope of the present chapter to answer, but we may speculate, and those thoughts may help us understand the situation more clearly. Strictly with the Hidden Christians of the Edo Period, the likely reasons for Mary's appeal have been gestured at in the pre-figuration and assumptions of Goddess within Shinto (and therefore Japanese culture), but there remains for us one other factor which runs the line between the object itself and the thinking about the object itself that will need to be addressed before we make some final remarks regarding the philosophical abstractions involved in this (and other) iconography: that of the split between the eras of "pre-art" and "art" in cultural trajectories.

Arthur Danto distinguishes a historical time marked by "pre-art" considerations (as pertaining to the abstractional approaches people took to images and other manufactured items), and an "art" time (and further too a "post-art" time, starting from the late twentieth century onwards), whereby the first designation comes to apply—in the case of religious objects—to those produced before around 1400 CE (in the Western world), and this because the purposes held by the makers of the works were not aesthetic but purely spiritual in intent—only later did the paintings, sculptures, et cetera, come to be viewed with eyes willed towards an appreciation of outward beauty per se rather than towards numinous assertions and/or implications.[31] Prior to that shift people simply thought differently: a religiously themed painting was not "art," it was a helper in one's faith. Although it is obvious that Japan's Edo Period (1603–1868) in

---

30. Endo, *Silence*, 72.

31. Danto, *After the End of Art*. Antecedents to this idea however go back at least to G.W.F. Hegel and his *Lectures on Aesthetics* (the first from an 1818 course, the last from 1828/29), although the notion is quite likely older still.

its entirety exceeds Danto's benchmark in terms of calendar count, when questioning whether it would be better placed in the "pre-art" or the "art" category in terms of the thinking processes people likely applied in regard to objects perceived, we must remember that Danto's was a comment made about European conceptualizations, and that for Japan—given its unique (purposeful) stoppage of any societal development during its "closed country" era—the year of 1400 itself is of far less importance than the considerations it signifies. While modern Japan has an ancient culture of beauty and the study thereof, and indeed already had one during the Edo Period as well (a detail that remained important throughout the Tokugawa years and was often celebrated by the Tokugawa rulers and elite classes), at exactly what point within the Japanese framework a willfully religiously oriented item might have been approached as an artwork instead of as a spiritual tool I must admit that I am not sure; still, given the Tokugawa government's general stress on Buddhism as the official faith, and the nationwide employment of temples and priests for purposes of social control, it is presumably safe to mark this "pre-art" to "art" notional transition (i.e. the "thinking behind the gaze," as it were, at least as directed to Buddhist statuary and other iconography) as probably not occurring in Japan until after the end of the shogunate, and thus certainly after the benchmark of 1400.

Kannon statues were therefore probably taken throughout the long Edo years only in their maker-intended meanings as spiritual aids instead of as pieces of art, except of course by the Hidden Christians, who still used them religiously but did so in the unintended (that is, unintended by the likely creators) meaning of becoming stand-ins for the Virgin Mary. From a conceptually applied point of view however, there is really very little difference here as the processes involved were mere shifts from one Goddess of Mercy (Kannon) to another (Mary, in her further exalted form of "Goddess Mother"). The mental emphasis for both groups (that is, the "Kannon as Kannon" group and the "Kannon as Mary" group) were additionally centered on a personally held faith assisted by the usage and/or the presence of the item, and not on the craftsmanship and beauty-oriented appeal of the item as perceptually regarded or intellectually considered. On this note of thinking/thinking-about, we may appreciate as well Hans Belting's relation of how (in a discussion specifically focused on the Virgin Mary) for a believer the representational accuracy of an icon has little to do with the inherent power of the iconography.[32] As long as it is a symbol-for, or (more potently?) dwelling of, a transcendence in authority or entity, then one might imagine almost any sufficiently communicative physical form as befitting: if it called to mind the "right" idea then whatsoever image-idea would be enough to "get the job done." A Kannon statue would therefore have been a justificatory match for the Hidden Christians wishing to maintain a devotion to Mary in a visual and tactile way, and this made the stronger by the statue's established association with mercy (Kannon as

---

32. Danto, *After the End of Art*, 52; Belting, *The End of the History of Art*; see also Belting's more recent *Likeness and Presence*, where Chapter 3 especially deals with Marian images.

the Bodhisattva of Mercy) along with the "feminized" divine features described in the foregoing (serene womanly visage, the wearing of a crown and/or shawl, often holding a baby or young child).

In regards to what would be most apposite if the conceptual direction taken by Hidden Christians were truly better in line with animist (i.e. habitation: the "spirit in the matter") rather than with fetishist (i.e. non-representation: the "spirit of the matter") conceptualizations[33]—and whether acknowledged or recognizably taken (or not taken) by the believer her/himself would make no difference to this point, the background mental influence is what is paramount—the "spirit in the matter" aspect that appertains during those moments the statue were in use would be that of "Mother Mary's," and none other: animist. It would, moreover, associate in precisely this way since the object was prayed *to*, actually beseeched *itself* attitudinally by the worshipper and not, as would be the case by a contemporary Christian approaching a statue or icon (that is, if church teachings on this matter were properly understood by the modern-day participant), prayed towards or through. Whatever the piece may have looked like on the outside, to the believer it/It (or rather "she/She") would be Mary on the "inside," inhabited, and with everything infused that such entailed. These statues were for the Hidden Christians not only numinous tools, but *numinous themselves*, spiritual beings themselves, and the psychological projections juxtaposed by the acceptance of this conceptualization would bequeath multitudes of gradations on the object, meanings overlaid not only *onto* but *into* the icons and related images. There can be few clearer examples of the image-idea/idea-image (and indeed the notion/event) than that rendered in the above by this particular group from within the confines of their peculiar cultural-historical setting.

We have proposed that Christianity taken separately from the Judaisms out of which it arose, and too as its own system and image-idea/idea-image (which is of course what every "system" essentially is; whether religious, political, et cetera) has an inbuilt abstruseness to it, an abstracted wobble that one might charitably label recondite or, less generously, imprecise; and that this is (at least partially) a result of the shoehorning of divinity onto the rabbi/sage Yeshua: this was a thing done, and it can be undone (for the betterment of the Yeshuan message, as we shall contend); as it stands it is a making-into which requires vast loads of other notional freight to first be unpacked. For those without the antecedent preparation (by upbringing and/or culture), that task could be an overwhelming one. It is perhaps little wonder then that the Hidden Christians, with wholly different presumptions about the transcendent, proceeded as they did: syncretistically, creatively, making it up as they went along (and—to gingerly step on a few toes—in that surely following in the footsteps of the early church as they forged a new path from both Judaic and Grecian modes and thoughts). The image here is so heavy with idea that it cannot but give birth to an

---

33. Whitehead, *Religious Statues and Personhood*; Pels, "The Spirit of the Matter," in *Border Fetishisms*, 91–121.

otherness: it must create. Might an image be found without an idea? Not in these quarters, and not only via Hidden Christians. We again must admit the greatness of the "No" that Judaism has leveled against the pictured; but simultaneously we must also acknowledge the potential cogency of any image-idea/idea-image, and particularly those for such charged subject matter as spirituality provides. Might we therefore sculpt our own "Maria Kannon," taking one established mark or figure and via an adjusted approach having it/causing it to prompt differing intuitions and "readings" from out of and within us? In the next chapter we shall attempt just that: the adherence of an alternative notional core to an icon that is similarly nearly buried beneath itself.

Chapter 8

Viewing the Cross from "the Kingdom"

"The creation of an image can be just as much an abomination as its destruction . . . In other words, iconoclasm is more than just the destruction of images; it is a 'creative destruction,' in which a secondary image of defacement or annihilation is created at the same moment that the 'target' image is attacked."

W.J.T. Mitchell[1]

WE MAY WISH FOR a pure image, idea-free, a non-representative figure, nothing but a form, a shape, a percept of valueless and empty content, an ideationally unbounded *thus,* something (some-"thing") that would be oblivion: Kazimir Malevich's "Black Square" (1915).[2] Yet as that famous painting itself shows, oblivion itself is a concept, laden with presuppositions, assumptions, and interpretations; it is anything but a blank. Under this condition of the ungraspable, impossibly out of reach true void or null, what may be done? Shall we give up, stop trying, tuck ourselves away in our (comforting) assumptions? It appears there is simply no way out from/of our minds. Unfortunately—or perhaps fortunately, depending (and everything depends . . .)— this may well be an inescapable fact of human biological hardwiring. As Douglas Hofstadter has outlined with regards to contemporary advances in the cognitive sciences and understandings of brain functioning, we are creatures of the abstract,[3] born to operate on that level, stuffed so full of notions that even our best attempts to evade them only result in more. (Think, for instance, of language and its buried associative networks, each connected to an ever deeper milieu, each attempt to explain becoming only further enmeshed in the preconceived; then imagine the effort that would be required to communicate without language, beyond language, and how even exclusively

---

1. Mitchell, *What Do Pictures Want?*, 16 and 18, respectively.

2. For a good introduction to the artist and some of his more important works, see Néret, *Kazimir Malevich (1878-1935): and Suprematism*. Groys, the somewhat "trendy" philosopher of art and media, also discusses Malevich in his *In the Flow*; there, see Chapter 4: "Becoming Revolutionary: On Kazimir Malevich," pages 61-74.

3. Hofstadter, *I Am a Strange Loop*.

physical gestures would still become ensconced in hermeneutic complexes). Each promising escape from ourselves reveals yet another dead end. Abstractionist artwork (e.g. such as Malevich's "Black Square"), for instance—and especially those done for expressiveness over explicitness—inevitably elicits the question: "What does it mean?" Or, for viewers sophisticated enough to ask instead "How does it make you feel?" the response remains replete with encumbered phrases: "surprised" (and then the associated ideas and signifiers); "perplexed" (again the associated ideas and signifiers); "joyful" (once more the associated ideas and signifiers); "lustful" (here too the associated ideas and signifiers . . .); one cannot simply *feel*, it leads unceasingly to pronouncements, and thereon to this cognitive "bridge too far." We cannot help ourselves, and this incapability to purely turn off can be stifling. Hence, however much we may wish to laud a prohibition of the anyway un-imageable (God/"God"), ideas are tied to images and images to ideas—we *will* somehow think the divine—thus one might indeed be determined the wiser to throw in the towel as it were, to go ahead and make use of these markers and graphs that litter our lives. Such, precisely, is what Christianity has done (has chosen to do); and in that remarkably so.

Our task now is an attempt to re-work and re-fashion the faith's (the system's) most central image-idea/idea-image into a glyph that is arguably more compatible with Yeshua as we have come to know him in the above, and will come to know him better yet in Parts 3 and 4 below; we seek to forge a Yeshuan-Jewish icon that has been de-idolized: which is to offer it as de-*idealized*. For this we of course take the cross, nothing less would do, and in that specifically focusing on its embodied form, before we thereafter attempt to secure a "kosher-ized crucifix." (A pause here to reassure the reader—whose patience is gratefully acknowledged—that no offense is meant by this phrasing, although its possibility is certainly recognized.) What we will strive for in this undertaking is a re-tuning of the idea as matched with the image; a taking of the image with another idea, and hence making it (we hope) a generator of yet different ideas for us which, I think, would prove not only more apposite but more beneficial to the time, place, and modes of modern life than that which we have inherited. We want to see ("see!") the crucifix differently. If we can, such would be—not without some irony—another small step forwards in our effort to re-envelope Christianity within her mother Jewish fold.

The cross/crucifix itself is naturally a shorthand, a signpost to an entire cosmos of meanings and, if adopted—if taken "to heart" (another figuration)—it is an instantaneous transport to an affective and conceptually drenched mode of existence. In this the cross is not unlike a great many other avatars (the Star of David, the Om, the star and crescent, an open palm with the dharmachakra wheel, the Buddhist sauwastika), and such have long fascinated social scientists from a number of fields. In addition to the more commonly considered theoretical constructs that have arisen along these lines (namely, those of the idol and the fetish, as explored above), W.J.T. Mitchell has argued for the adoption of a third—the "totem"—yielding a triune model that (re) admits this particular conceptualization as a symbolic analytical device. In effect, a move like this would establish a further layering onto the image-idea/idea-image matters with which we have been concerned, and it is thus well worth considering. We have, after all, asserted that Yeshua himself has been made into an idol, and further that the icons of Christianity would (quickly) come into fetishistic understandings as regards their use and approach (i.e., the "spirit of the matter"; with the exception of Japan's Hidden Christians, whose worship probably better fits into an animistic mould: the "spirit in the matter"[4]); how, then, might this "totem" apply here?

Mitchell writes that "It [the totem] also names a revaluation of the fetish and idol. If the idol is or represents a god, and the fetish is a 'made thing' with a spirit or demon in it, the totem is 'a relative of mine,' its literal meaning in the Ojibway language."[5] (Notice that for Whitehead the placement of Mitchell's reading of fetish would more properly fit into animism—"a spirit or demon in it"—for our wider point at present, however, this is mostly irrelevant since we are now examining the totem as an identifier.) This is a remarkable linguistic quirk: "a relative of mine," linking the totem with a member/individual well beyond the merely associational and into the familial. It is a kin bond, a genetic bond, a heritage and historical lineage bond, and on our topic it would imply the taking of the blood of the crucifix "within one's own veins": the Eucharist as imbibed mentally. The emotive and self-forming facets of such should be clear. Moreover, totems, Mitchell writes, although made yet take on an independent life and thereby "seem to create themselves, and to create the social formations they signify."[6] The embrace of the (embodied) cross I think, and even further of the whole atonement scheme (to which we will return later in our study), therefore has its deepest ramifications along these identificatory lines; and in that the below will contend accordingly that what this whole process of the idolization of Yeshua, with its exalted symbolism of what was at the time merely an everyday and entirely unnoteworthy tool for execution, achieved most prominently was a demarcation of difference: a raising up—literally, as a crucified prisoner would be—of a bastardized version of Yeshua's message onto its mutated Golgotha, which thence became (incredibly) a "city built on a hill," a "light set forth on a lampstand," and one never to be "hidden under a bushel."[7]

It is important, and quite applicable particularly in the case of Christianity (although again we must except the unique category of Japan's Hidden Christians, as the previous chapter explored), to note as well how the totem is approached by its holder ("bearer"?) otherwise than is an idol or a fetish. Émile Durkheim's foundational work

---

4. Whitehead, *Religious Statues and Personhood*, 120; Pels, "The Spirit of Matter," in *Border Fetishisms*, 91–121.

5. Mitchell, *What Do Pictures Want?*, 98; the final reference to the linguistic origins comes via Lévi-Strauss' work *Totemism*, 18.

6. Mitchell, *What Do Pictures Want?*, 105.

7. See the parable portions in the synoptic Gospels where these analogies are made: Mark 4:21, Matthew 5:14–15, and Luke 8:16.

in this area outlines that the "attitude toward the animals or plants whose name he bears [i.e. the totem, narrowly understood here as a clan referent; we shall attempt to take the concept more broadly] is by no means the attitude a believer has toward his god."[8] Rather, the totem is a representatum for a grouping or a people, a pointer whose concept is far more potent than it itself could be (the being-ness of the clan Crow outweighing the image of a crow used emblematically or decoratively, or for that matter of any living crow found in nature). For the Christians this totem mark of the crucifix would go on to even become a portent, delineating a future of otherness (first as forced, then as enforced), which became a self-fulfilling prophecy of dominance, and therefrom—presumptively, interpretively—of Christianity's "rightness," "righteousness," "providence," "blessing," "victory"; all the while, we find, hiding its true character as a "secondary image of defacement," as our chapter opening quotation put it.[9] What I mean by this is that the cross de-"faces" (metaphorically and—stretching it a bit—literally) Yeshua because it betrays both the man's actual teachings and the depth of his Judaism (as one style amongst multiple first century contemporary Judaisms). It defaces (using the term more standardly) by swapping out Yeshua for Christ ("Christ"—figure, image, image-idea/idea-image: idol). We will try, therefore, to put the Jewish "face" of Yeshua back into perspective, and place it once more onto/into Christianity—as a Judaism—via a journey through this very totem, this sign of a man hung on a cross, in light of what he (probably or perhaps) said prior to his meeting with that cross. In this task we may make some progress too towards an un-idolizing (a de-idolization) of "the Christ." For clarification: in the present chapter we will not try to dissect Yeshua's teachings so much as we will merely glance at them, gazing only enough to adjust the lenses with which we see the image (image-idea/idea-image) of the crucifix; in our study's next two chapters we will move more fully into an exploration of Yeshua's "kingdom" preaching and the Christology that was foisted upon him—through but more so against his message—from a conceptual standpoint.

It was argued earlier (in Chapters 5 and 6), and this will provide the starting point for our work to follow, that due to the psychological penetration and subsequent effects thereof that a concept can elicit on and from its bearer, such may be determined to have a degree of realism that might at first blush seem impossible from the aethereal elements involved.[10] As discussed, ideas are commonly thought of as mere mental phenomena, passings not existing anywhere in the world, and certainly not nearly as concrete as the images which express or indicate them; but this, it was found, belies the condition. An idea—particularly in the case of the notion/event—can and often does become the foundation for innumerable actions, for entire lives, livelihoods,

---

8. Durkheim, *The Elementary Forms of Religious Life*, 139.

9. Mitchell, *What Do Pictures Want?*, 18.

10. In addition to the ground covered here, see relatedly (although in the context of a study on the self, coincidentally also a sixth chapter (six, incidentally, being traditionally associated with the material)) Chapter 6: "Metaphysics and Time: The Reality of a Realist Self and Its (Re-)Making" in Oberg, *Blurred*.

and ways of being, through which the root abstraction(s) continually manifests; but these are not the whole of the relationship either: for not only the praxis of "done in the name of" but also the doxastic of simply "name of" is determinatively ontic in its own right, and such flows out into individually embedded situations via myriad ways and means. The lived image-idea/idea-image; the notion/event expressive and expressed; the building and the inhabiting of a "world"; an empiricism of the unseen and immeasurable; which of course bursts the very boundaries of the "empirical," yet the phenomenology nevertheless points us squarely there. Taking this further still, we might then venture that an idol/fetish/totem could be just as internal as external, *object*-ivity be what it might; but then perhaps that is pushing things a bit too far even for us. At any rate, these theoretical bases of the notion/event with the corollary image-idea/idea-image provide the stepping stones for our picture-esque "kingdom" journey, and so let us return to it.

Yeshua the sage was nothing if not an idea-dealer and remarkable notion narcotic, but the crucified portraiture of him that has been laden with intellections piled and piled over the centuries is something I think he himself (from what we can tell) would have shivered at. What has been constructed out of the dead flesh of the living man perhaps does more to lead *away* from the teachings, really, than towards; and the "atonement" reading of the cross—the "for the sins of all" diktat nailed to the cross—(to which we shall return) has so badly blinded us to what are the core, and truly revolutionary, ethical aspects of the rabbi's discourse that we can now see/"see," I am afraid, little else. Yeshua's "kingdom" guide for I-you and we-God/"God" has been swallowed up by the Golden Calf he was later made into.[11] Such a result is tragic. The present chapter will therefore seek to provide new intuitions for those moments we happen to encounter the crucifix or cross, to help in taking it neither as totem nor idol, but instead to understand it as a fetish that—as a "made thing"—can be un-made, re-placed (or ignored); and thus liberated we may then be able to put our flesh and blood teacher back amongst his fellows. With him also, perhaps, we might place those of us who would try to build "the kingdom" of which Yeshua spoke with our likeminded compatriots, completely without regard to whether we "are" Yeshuans or not; indeed, without regard to whatever identificatory name tag we might choose to affix (be it Yeshuan-Jewish, Orthodox Jewish, non-Orthodox Jewish, Muslim, Jain, Hindu, Buddhist, humanist, deist, motivated atheist, concerned citizen, et cetera, et cetera . . .). With these reformed reactions, these altered automatic intuitive judgments, we will try to find instead a fresh hermeneutic for the far too familiar iconography that the embodied cross has become (that stale, well past its due-date picturing). In short, an

11. We can imagine the early church constructors of this doctrine saying something along the lines of Aaron in Exodus 32:24 when he tries to defend himself to Moses: "It's not our fault! We only called Yeshua savior, and then all these other things just came out that way!" (For those interested, the actual verse reads: "So I [Aaron] said to them [the Israelites], 'Whoever has gold, take it off!' They gave it to me and I hurled it into the fire and out came this calf!"; *Tanakh* (NJPS). Readers will recall the fuller context and discussion of this scene at the opening of our Chapter 6 above.

effecting of a "creative destruction" of the image (image-idea) that may take us—we hope—into "the kingdom"; or at least into a better understanding of it. If we can learn to perceive Yeshua hung through another set of eyes, what might result?

Robert Funk (whose work we met earlier in Chapters 2, 3, and 4) was the founder of a group of biblical scholars that included both professional clergy and lay academics, calling itself the Jesus Seminar.[12] Their self appointed mission was to study the teachings and deeds of Yeshua in order to ascertain with as much confidence as possible what were and were not likely to be historically accurate. Of all that has been attributed to the person who lived in first century Palestine and wrote nothing down himself,[13] what did he really say and do? As sketched above, that appears the best we can manage—a *sketching*, and one with many empty spaces at that—but in a listing of their results of probable authenticity, one can nevertheless find many parables and aphorisms which provide a set of teachings (including proverbs, caricatures, et cetera, amongst other proclamations), totaling ninety-six in number.[14] Based on these, Funk makes a series of suggestions on how Christian theology and church structure (bearing our contemporary situation in mind) might be brought more into line with the actual (or anyway more credibly actual) views expressed by Yeshua whom—we should remember—never set out to found a new religion himself.[15] These include:

1. Understanding Yeshua as a secular sage[16]

2. Adopting an unmediated relationship with God and thereby taking the priesthood and clergy as against Yeshua's teachings; moreover, as mentioned, accepting that Yeshua himself did not seek to establish either a church or a mission, and that the later institutions of power and hierarchy that developed were imposed upon his teachings for justificatory purposes[17]

---

12. Information on this group, now defunct, may be found here: "Jesus Seminar," *Wikipedia*. Accessed July 02, 2019. Together the Seminar produced three main works, while many of its members have also published research independently. The primary reports are: *The Five Gospels* (1993; the four canonical Gospels plus the *Gospel of Thomas*), *The Acts of Jesus* (1998), and *The Gospel of Jesus* (1999). These efforts and much else related to them continue in The Westar Institute; see their home page at: *Westar Institute*. Accessed July 06, 2021. I should disclose that I am a Scholar member of the group (there are also Praxis (clergy related) and Associate (general) memberships).

13. There is a line of argument that no man called Yeshua ever existed at all, that the entirety is pure legend, a phantom summoned by the person who became Saint Paul in order to root his own teachings more authoritatively. However, the consensus among New Testament scholars appears to be towards an actual historicity of the figure, albeit this to various degrees and manners depending on the views of the academic in question.

14. See page 326ff in Funk, *Honest to Jesus;* and also Funk and the Jesus Seminar, *The Gospel of Jesus*.

15. In this he very much parallels his earlier forebear reformer Siddhartha Gautama, the Buddha.

16. Funk, *Honest to Jesus,* 302.

17. Funk, *Honest to Jesus,* 311; the "no mission" part is especially apposite in light of our broader purposes. If Yeshua did not want Christianity he must have been after an otherwise-Judaism; let us honor his wishes and think about what might (and what might not) be done. How to shape today's church?

3. Asserting that no one anywhere can have any claims to special privilege[18]

4. Eliminating external rewards and punishments; there are only intrinsic ones[19]

5. Completely abandoning the notion of a blood atonement, of Yeshua as the "sacrificial lamb" required to appease a grudge-bearing God[20]

A particularly interesting result of meditating on just these five points of Funk's full twenty-one (he calls them his "theses") is that it becomes clear how an adoption of them (the idea) would completely shift the experiential effects (the idea-image) that crucifixion symbolism or representata (the image) may have; or, at least, the power to do so is therein contained. On this too consider what such a notional re-attunement would mean along totemistic lines: Here Yeshua was foremostly a person like you or me (far more remarkable of course, but completely and only human), concerned with relating better to the divine from within the circumstances of his surrounding culture. He was wiser perhaps, freer certainly, but his death becomes the result of political and social forces, sought by neither his adherents nor himself, and above all not demanded by God/"God" as part of (or the entirety of) some necessary and otherwise unavoidable (even the preferred(!) version as some have it) salvific plan.[21] If this is so, then the picture of his execution accordingly transforms into what it probably was witnessed as at the time: a gory tragedy. Furthermore, if the many agonies and pains were not to (transactionally) win Heaven for a fallen humanity, then the awe I take in perceiving his broken body risks degenerating into a kind of—if not an outright and not merely "kind of"—grotesquely masochistic schadenfreude. On the other hand, if the crucifixion presents the execution of a reformer rabbi/sage (following Funk, and many others too), then how much "savior" might remain in this image/image-idea as totem? Again, there could still be reverence ("awe," as just noted), yet probably not worship, except in the stretched or reduced sense of how one might "worship" at a great teacher's feet.

---

18. Inclusive of both entitlement type claims (e.g. elitism, titular) and ethnicity/group type (e.g. "sole holders of the ultimate truth," "saved versus unsaved"); Funk, *Honest to Jesus*, 311–12.

19. E.g. getting rid of afterlife concerns, desires for worldly gains, et cetera. Funk, *Honest to Jesus*, 312.

20. Funk, *Honest to Jesus*, 312. On this point see as well Caputo, *The Weakness of God*; and our Chapter 13 below.

21. This is not to discredit the position of Yeshua's death as ultimately being a noble self sacrifice (if it was), but instead it is to move the perspectival focus—when considered from the historical man's own point of view, that is—to an *accepted* (as in: agreed to) end rather than a *desired* end; and, moreover, as a dying suffered through without the (pre- or presciently held) hindsight yielded by the resurrection addendums of the Gospel narratives. Even if we were to maintain a high(er) form of Christology in which Yeshua (somehow) completely foreknew the resurrection (Funk would no doubt dispute this), phenomenologically—on this higher view—as "fully man" (which too is a part of the high Christology of God/"God"-man) his anguish would still not thereby have been lessened; on these and related queries (written indeed from a rather high Christology, at least on my reading of him) see Falque, *The Guide to Gethsemane*.

Nevertheless, there is clearly an identitarian distinction that could still be found here, one that draws apart from other Judaisms while resting within Judaism broadly speaking. Pausing for a moment on this aspect of breadth, let us also be frank in admitting that even today there is hardly a single "Judaism" to be found, and naturally the same could be asserted for every major religious movement encompassing a variety of peoples, places, patterns, and practices. There already are, and always have been, Juda*isms,* and a Yeshuan-Judaism could (our argument is *should*) be counted as simply one of them. This would not remove the totemism of the embodied cross so much as it would (possibly) push for a replacement. The idol and fetish aspects would likely melt out of the image, but if a Yeshuan-Jew yet wished to keep this as a glyph (rather than, say, an image of the Sermon on the Mount, or preaching by the lakeshore, or something), it could be accommodated. Perhaps in that it might be felt in a "fight the powers that be" manner, as Crossan emphasizes is a hallmark of Yeshua's ministry;[22] but we get ahead of ourselves, and it is to that ministry to which we must return.

The reader might be finding these thoughts heretofore rather incredible; or offensive. What believer, of whatever type or to whatever degree, could accept the historically based reductions (the shrinking) that Funk and his colleagues have arrived at? Furthermore, where is the beauty of faith? Must we limit ourselves to taking the cross as an at best tragically heroic act (a happenstance: faced with its possibility a grim acceptance was the response), or an at worst terrible mistake (a miscalculation: pushing the authorities finally too far brought an unwanted and unexpectedly swift judgment)? Does looking on the crucifix displayed call for an attitude of indifference in order to avoid misinterpretation, or at least to put some distance between the ingrained traditions we have had handed down to us versus a more research grounded vision of Yeshua?[23] To perceive the occupied cross must do more than leave us neutral; emotionally, even only empathetically, its appearance is far too prodding, regardless of any connected—or none whatsoever—devotional commitments. Or so it seems. In a brief, but I hope sufficient, examination of some of the less commonly quoted "kingdom" teachings that set Yeshua apart from his contemporaries, let us attempt to perceive too a few of the associated mindsets of the milieu he moved within, reaching back from our embeddedness now to that of then, to the women and men who surrounded, with the ideas they carried as real and meaningful (their own notion/events). Again, it is perhaps through such efforts that we might best approach a view of the crucifixion that could—maybe—approximate theirs (in interpretation, certainly not in experiential impact), and from thence an otherwise which we may take for ourselves. For this, I should add, we need not strictly endorse Funk's suggestions, not

---

22. Crossan, *Jesus*.

23. Or indeed with Yeshua as a maybe-Christ, one in competition with others before, during, and after his own time, as we saw ("saw!") in Chapter 3; this was highlighted especially in that chapter's note on the lateness of production of the canonical accounts, the astonishing first century BCE stone tablet, and the continued affixation of messiahships for many years to come.

even in the minimized listing that was cited, but maintain them as possibilities which may prove helpful.

In Chapter 2 when we considered the historical picture of Yeshua the man (and only as a man), we emphasized that although the popular imagination of his ministry was for long centered on an "end of the world" message, it is—as a result of much further research—thought now that he is more properly described as having been really more of a religio-ethicist than anything else. His concern was most probably *bringing* "the kingdom of God" via reformed social frameworks and actions, not awaiting its dramatic appearance in flashes of lightning and peals of thunder (a picturing, not without coincidence, that brings to mind the revelation at Mount Sinai;[24] and most definitely such would have for Yeshua's listeners and those who also/or followed other teachers too, such as John the Baptizer (Baptist), who—we noted—*was* an apocalyptic sage.) Yet whether or not Yeshua himself was an apocryphal preacher (and although the general direction has moved away from this understanding there does remain contention on the point), and too whether or not his listeners yearned for an evacuation of Roman imperial forces from their lands or merely shrugged their shoulders at the political realities of the day, what seems a sure truism then, now, and five hundred millennia from now (if we are still around) is that human animals project their hopes into the future, optimistic to a fault, and ever craving for a "better than." We might call this coming glory "utopia," we might call it "social justice," we might call it "commune," or we might call it "the kingdom of God."

In Yeshua's day, by his proclamations, it was that last—"the kingdom"—but today, under different terms, we might label it "the event," and in that turning not be far off Yeshua's mark. Caputo, in his analysis of Yeshua's teachings as a "to-come," finds in them an accounting of a lived situation that does not perhaps "exist" but "calls," they form a set of prescriptions that "express the multiple hopes and desires that we want to keep as open-ended as possible so as not to block their future, lest we prevent the event and close off the incoming of what is coming."[25] "The kingdom," as Yeshua unveiled it (on this comprehension of his work), always beckons us to do/be better, to

---

24. Exodus 19:16–19, "16On the third day, as morning dawned, there was thunder, and lightning, and a dense cloud upon the mountain, and a very loud blast of the horn; and all the people who were in the camp trembled. 17Moses led the people out of the camp toward God, and they took their places at the foot of the mountain. 18Now Mount Sinai was all in smoke, for the LORD had come down upon it in fire; the smoke rose like the smoke of a kiln, and the whole mountain trembled violently. 19The blare of the horn grew louder and louder. As Moses spoke, God answered him in thunder." *Tanakh* (NJPS). What an image-idea! Were it not for the prohibition on imagery, surely a blazing mountain replete with thunder and lightning would make for a robust iconography expressive of an omnipotent and strength-displaying view of the divine—if such were desired; but then, in the face of Roman oppression, would that not be exactly what was wanted in first century Israel? Particularly by the lower classes who provided the mainstay of the adherents of folk lecturers like Yeshua and John the Baptizer (Baptist). The following chapter of Exodus 20, by the way, gives us the Ten Commandments. (The first instance of such, that is: Deuteronomy 5 has another listing.)

25. Caputo, *The Folly of God*, 85.

get closer to it—to its building—and to the perceived accompanying satisfaction and fulfillment that would follow if we could.

Simultaneously with this gesturing hand and its onward urging, however, is Yeshua's (surprising) pronouncement that "the kingdom" is already present, that it actually does "exist," and it does so right in this instant, all around, we simply have to open our eyes to see it. (In Heideggerean terms we might say it is to-hand, yet still awaiting at-handedness.) A logion from the non-canonical Nag Hammadi text *The Gospel of Thomas*—which has been dated to the middle of the first century or somewhat later,[26] making it possibly the oldest of the Gospels—contains this teaching:

> *Thomas,* Saying 113: His followers said to him, "When will the kingdom come?"
>
> [Yeshua replied] "It will not come by watching for it. It will not be said, 'Look, here it is,' or 'Look, there it is.'
>
> Rather, the father's kingdom is spread out upon the earth, and people do not see it."[27]

Here it is, now, "spread out upon the earth," surrounding, supporting, composing our ordinariness; what is required is only to live it, to *be* it. This implies both a perspectival shift and a behavioral adjustment; nothing that seemingly lies beyond our power though, nothing that requires a great blow of the horn and a descending of heavenly thunder, lightning, fire, or chariots.

At the same time—and here again there is a simultaneity of nuance, another fold within the "royal" ("kingdom") conceptual origami—"the kingdom of God" is a full negation of the everyday, of business as usual. Caputo calls it "the contradiction of the 'world' (*cosmos*) [i.e., in the ordinary and non-Heideggerean sense of the word "world," as it is used metaphorically for hierarchical structures and relations], which is the order of power and privilege and self-interest";[28] a sentiment summarized nicely, of course, in Yeshua's statements asserting that the "first will be last, and the last will be first."[29] "The kingdom" will not only *not* come in an act of power (it is "already here"), it will not even be based on power, and the powerful will not be amongst its significant figures: they will, rather, be "last."

It is perhaps in dwelling on this point of privilege and relation where the effrontery of the crucifixion taken as a symbolic image of both sacrificial love and total

---

26. See the chapter introduction to the same in Barnstone and Meyer, eds., *The Gnostic Bible*, 43–4.
27. Meyer, trans. and intro., *The Gospel of Thomas*, 63.
28. Caputo, *The Weakness of God*, 48; emphasis in the original.
29. See Matthew 19:30, "But many who are first will be last, and the last will be first"; also Matthew 20:16, "So the last will be first, and the first will be last"; Mark 10:31, "But many who are first will be last, and the last will be first" (the perfect parallel here of Mark 10:31 with Matthew 19:30 gives this phrasing of the statement much more authoritative historicity); and finally Luke 13:30, "Indeed, some are last who will be first, and some are first who will be last." All quotations taken from *Thinline Bible with the Apocrypha* (NRSV).

transcendent triumph (required and accepted blood offering = redemption = salvation = Heaven) most forces its way to the fore. The preacher of "the kingdom" as a "to-come" better way of existing on this good Earth, as already present reality (is possible now), and as social complex not grounded in authority and command, has had his many lived and uttered complexities compressed into a marker of the method by which he happened to be killed. The process is offensive; or at least would be were it not so historically inscribed. It is this pictured hanged man with an accompanying "atonement" reading—a comprehension which essentially ignores the social message of "the kingdom"—that is today met most often with a mixture of reverence and guilt by Christians ("my God, who gave his life for unworthy me"), and (at least a little) resentment by everyone else, due to the many global tragedies that have been historically committed in the name of Christianity and/or Christian political entities. Quite simply, the crucifix as image and its associated contemporary interpretive idea is nothing other than a disservice—a disrespect, a disgrace—to "the kingdom" vision and the man who stood for and offered that vision. If we would only stop long enough to take note of it, we might recognize how much a juxtaposition done in this vein requires from us a re-reading of that same cross, both for the sake of "the kingdom" and for the legacy of him who bequeathed it. If we can do that, if we can attempt such a revivification, what form might the image-idea/idea-image of the stretched and shattered man take?

Unfortunately, aside from tradition, there is another obstacle blocking our path to renewal. We have grown so accustomed to the kneejerk hermeneutic of the icon of Yeshua executed as being the summit of his pedagogy—to viewing his murder as the foreknown and inevitable endpoint, of which he himself was aware, and to which he purposefully trod[30]—that we are prohibited right from the outset of even being capable of more fittingly "seeing" it. We think we know, and thus we do not remotely know. Our presumption in the taking of the cross as *the* indicatory sign (identifying totem) of a transactional "sacrifice" to which he purportedly (necessarily) pre-assented,[31] has blinded us to the breathtaking revolution that was being urged on his audiences in the many "kingdom" proclamations Yeshua made, in the annihilatory not/no/non/never towards the entirety of standard human history, of our species' full mode of sociality and structure, that was couched therein. Yeshua wanted to tear it all down, every bit of *this*, and in return for that teaching what we have done to the man is to present him time and again as flesh torn up. The crucifixion we encounter is now,

---

30. In the below (Chapter 11) we will suggest that Yeshua might well have had a belief in corporeal resurrection as divine reward for martyrdom (or beyond only being reward for martyrdom and covering reward for fidelity too?) and hence "courted" it in some sense (a belief along these lines is exemplified by select sections of the deuterocanonical text Second Maccabees); but even if he did, such would have been at best an expectation—and at least a hope—and thus would not qualify for the kind of strong epistemic position we are considering here.

31. To this we may further append how the taking of the Passion narratives through the additionally distorting lenses of the Resurrection narratives have done nothing to help divest the conceptual air.

in our collective error, a disruption and a barricading, an overlay of an entirely other image-idea/idea-image onto the associated man's (the crucified man's) self-birthed "kingdom." We have buried the man while announcing him resurrected; the irony of this folly should not be overlooked (let us "see" it!). This person named Yeshua burst onto the complex of his time and place and declared to anyone who would listen that things were just fine, do not worry, love each other and trust the divine, break down or disregard the formations of hierarchy and the walls that such have erected between you and God/"God", between you and you—and it ended in a bloody shambles. (The Gospel refrain "Anyone with ears to hear should listen and understand!"[32] rings now for us.) What does that shambles really depict? The church, and Western heritage generally, have taught us to take it for everything; could this be right, or even one of a few possible "rights"?

Let us try to clear our minds (our *eyes*) and think some more on this. Caputo's deconstruction of the call (the event) in/of "the kingdom" contains the very practical consideration that we ought to, in his words, "Make no mistake, there is only one world, in the sense of what Heidegger calls 'being-in-the-world,' [again, this is as per the standard usage of the term "world," lest the Heidegger reference add confusion (yet more) to our muddied waters] but within it the kingdom and the 'world' are its tensions [i.e. "the kingdom" as how things could be, and "the world" as how they are]"; and Caputo states further that, "the issue is not so much with what name we are to call God, but what the name of God calls for, what it calls upon us to do."[33] This is a shift away from a concern with "God as being" to one of "God-as-indicator (as shorthand) for how to be"; and then the additional query: How might we become that? This is the call of "the kingdom," the call of "the name (of) 'God'", as Caputo would later put it.[34] In other words, this is the shaping of a new perception won through a fresh conceptuality, as we have been arguing; it is an erecting-of made possible by the ocular surgery of the mind. We have asserted that an idea can carry enough substance such that it attains to the creational, to a world-building (and now we *are* using "world" in its Heideggerean sense, as the full expansion of Husserl's "horizon") for its bearer within the world (the vulgar "world" again) outside one's window. This response to the call, this openness to the event and "the kingdom," is a particular form of what may conceivably be labeled a "faith community" (and at that non-denominational: of whatever faith, or even the faith of no faith), yet one that is not so much marked by a withdrawal from this everyday world of being-in-the-world as it is by the establishment of a "world," a biosphere that takes the form of an alternative psychological being-thus, even while it lies within—as it must for we human animals—the broader confines of a physical being-as.

---

32. As the *Catholic Holy Bible* (NLT) puts it; see, e.g. Matthew 11:15, 13:9; Mark 4:9, 4:23.

33. Caputo, *The Weakness of God*, 37 and 39, respectively.

34. The phrasing and punctuation for "name of God" goes through a few permutations in Caputo's work: this particular abstracting of "God"-as-call-as-concept can be found in Caputo, *Hermeneutics*.

Viewing the Cross from "the Kingdom"

In the light of this "kingdom" preaching that the New Testament (and contemporary non-New Testament (non-canonical) Gospels) has assigned to Yeshua, its applicability, and especially its only too admittedly unverifiable nature (Again, as we stressed in our encapsulated look at the historical Yeshua, we can ascertain merely to degrees of likelihood what he may have actually spoken, and this especially since he wrote nothing down himself, and what was written about him was only done so many years later.), let us consider a further Caputo-ean provocation: "The narratives of the New Testament are more true, not less true, because their truth is beyond the truth of correspondence. Truth is not a correspondence with being but its parabolic intensification beyond being's achievements."[35] What kind of a "truth" might be in play here? Does it matter whether or not there is any alignment between the empirically verifiable and the claimed experiential? We have considered similar questions already in our study in Chapter 5 above on the notion/event, and based on our conclusions there, we can notice here how the question whether anything recorded in the narratives have actual historicity to them or not is a rather unimportant one—at least as far as phenomenological concerns go. What does matter (and matters greatly) is what we might choose to build upon such revelations (again, the phenomenology becomes central), and those structures are notional, they are ours to take and "see/see!" via whatever means may stimulate us, be they crucifixion imagery or otherwise. The real heart of the issue, of course, is the nature of that stimulation. The cross when perceived could mean something else entirely from how we have so far comprehended (been moved by) it: if the idea behind an image is transformed, then the felt reality generated by that image alters as well—and with that change, quite possibly, a(n other) life.

Here we may be reminded of another picture and another personage, often depicted at the foot of the executed Yeshua, or weeping over his dead body taken down from the cross, or—and certainly these must be the greatest in number amongst the many artworks that have survived in our collective heritage—as a young mother holding her child in arms: naturally this is Mary, herself (narratively at least) a paradox, the "container of the uncontainable" as she is described in the Eastern Orthodox tradition.[36] In the truths (or, if one prefers, "truths") of the empirically untrue, in the truths revealed through the non-referential tales of the Annunciation, Nativity, et cetera,[37] we find in Mary—in the words of Mary DeTurris Poust—a "scared girl, knowing what awaits her if she ends up pregnant and unmarried, freely choos[ing] to say 'yes' to God."[38] The Mary figure in our pages demonstrates for we readers (and probably

---

35. Caputo, *The Weakness of God*, 16.

36. Caputo, *The Folly of God*, 21.

37. Not a few dare to puncture even deeper and label these "wholly fictitious," or somewhat derogatorily "fairytales"; yet in no way do descriptions like these remove or reduce the potency of the stories when/if a person takes them (experientially) to heart, nor indeed with regard to their meaning-making qualities for an individual's life as lived.

38. DeTurris Poust, *The Essential Guide to Catholic Prayer and the Mass*, 99.

initially in the early church for audiences whom only listened) a submission, a surrender; and this act too is demonstrative of "the kingdom," it is exactly what Yeshua calls for from each of us: personal abandonment to the divine, releasing one's individual desires and concerns into trust, patience, faith.[39] Mary's acceding to this bit of inserted Graeco-Roman mythology (the god(dess)-human impregnation trope) within a Hebrew context quite probably illustrates this facet of "the call" better than any other type of character could. Again, DeTurris Poust: "Without knowing all the reasons or what the eventual outcome will be, she agrees."[40] She does not know, cannot know, but purely says to God/"God", "You have me, I will do it." It is only a story of course, but that *only* when remarked about any fiction conceals the affective impact a chronicling can produce in the reader/listener. Who amongst us has not taken a leap like Mary's at some point in our lives (that is, a "yes" to an unknown, not to a bodily fertilization!), be it for whatever reason—secular, religious, otherwise—aimed at whatever objective? In its theological/ethical sense this is "the kingdom," and in its philosophical/metaphysical sense it is "the call," the openness to the event. We understand how Mary feels and how she responds. It is surely this aspect of her general approachability that so endears and attracts—beholds, clenches—believers and non-believers alike.

The image of Yeshua crucified might have more uplifting associative effects along lines such as these too, if we are able to shift the idea of him into a reduced (or eliminated) exaltation and take the man simply as a man, as a person who also said "yes" during his struggles with God/"God" (and moreover as someone who did indeed so struggle), throughout his carrying the heavy load of bespeaking "the kingdom," and of trying to have that message truly be *heard*: that is, taken to heart and not merely to ear. Towards this it might even assist our notional realignment to think of the Yeshuan accounts in a robustly non-corresponding way, as entirely invented or very nearly there, as tall tales that yield (tall) truths/"truths" precisely because they are not true in the way that "water = H_2O" is true. Although, as outlined above, there is certainly good archeological and anthropological grounding for the personhood of Yeshua, issues of historicity may be tabled or set aside ("bracketed" in the Husserlean sense), at least temporarily, in a purposive mental move aimed at promoting alternative praxes stemming from other intuitive reactions (percept input and the resultant image-idea/idea-image): in other words, ignore the "facts" of Yeshua until one is able to react differently to the image(-idea) of Yeshua (some readers will already be there), and then perhaps

---

39. Yeshua's words (likely actually said by him, or anyway something to their effect, rather than being latterly "put into his mouth") on the "birds of the air" and "lilies of the field" come to mind here: Matthew 6:26–30, "26Look at the birds of the air; they neither sow nor reap nor gather into barns, and yet your heavenly Father feeds them. Are you not of more value than they? 27And can any of you by worrying add a single hour to your span of life? 28And why do you worry about clothing? Consider the lilies of the field, how they grow; they neither toil nor spin, 29yet I tell you, even Solomon in all his glory was not clothed like one of these. 30But if God so clothes the grass of the field, which is alive today and tomorrow is thrown into the oven, will he not much more clothe you—you of little faith?" *Thinline Bible with the Apocrypha* (NRSV).

40. DeTurris Poust, *The Essential Guide to Catholic Prayer and the Mass*, 99.

go back and re-assess the whole from the newly won vantage point. An overly strong act such as this might be necessary to shock us out of our old habits and the details we have always told ourselves. For if, as Kyle Takaki has written (echoing issues in self and embeddedness studies[41]), our "perceived reality consists of a narrative cloud of possibilities anchored by what actions we-did-and-could-have-taken,"[42] then it might be that we need to work most on a re-seeing/"seeing!" of the cross through a focus on that "could-have-taken," attempting decisions and behaviors which would manifest as acts of "the kingdom" rather than the status quo. The rebel rabbi/sage we know from the embodied cross may have been killed and in that way silenced, but in a viewing of it, or upon a viewing of it (e.g. as a happening upon, an accidental or unintended sight of it), we might train ourselves to recognize only a *seeming* victory for the powers that be (the world, the top-down, the authoritative and hierarchical complexes) since the message itself remained, and thus hope. The crucifix—that scene of bloody and brutal execution—then becomes triumph in this life and not in the next:[43] ironically, beautifully, encouragingly. Again, the empirical question fades far into the background of the phenomenological one, if the epistemology is there.

This, though, requires a deeper movement into "the kingdom" as a way of life, as a being-in-the-world (our regular "world" here once more; that is, the vulgar usage) wherein the "unruly rule" of "the kingdom"—its flipping of existing human hierarchies and social superstructures—allows for a setting in which, as Caputo puts it, "the wondrous works of the kingdom are worked. By the impossible everything happens."[44] Let us not, therefore, after all wholly jettison the narrative content the church has for so long promoted amongst us; for what could be more impossible than divinity incarnated and subsequently slaughtered at the hands of we dirty mortals? By each notion of God/"God" transcendent nothing whatsoever; and yet, to be sure, "the kingdom" is not about transcendence, rather immanence: this moment, today. It is, as we have remarked, about simply being, "be"-ing. Still, in that being, in that—in this—very now, we can and should make room for the impossible in our facing of/up to the world we are in, and the old "atonement" story may help remind us of that by looking to the hanged Yeshua (either as created character or actual past personage; on this aspect the antecedent "Yeshua was" makes no difference) with an acknowledgment of the audacity of passing such off as "God/'God' dead" (an interpretation that has served its purpose), and then recalling the further temerity of "the kingdom"

---

41. On the mutual interweavings and cross-fertilizations in this area, see Oberg, *Blurred*, especially Chapter 2.

42. Takaki, "Bullshit, Living, and the Future," *Journal of Philosophy of Life*, 32–51 (41).

43. We shall, in fact, argue in the following (Chapter 12) for approaching death as the complete annihilation of the self, and hence there is no "next" of concern—not now, not then. We "know" this, of course, but it is another rock stuck in the sole ("soul") of our shoes, a legacy of both previous religio-cultural traits and Descartes' very long reach; on this see Oberg, "Approaches to Finitude," *Journal of Applied Ethics and Philosophy*, 8–17.

44. Caputo, *The Folly of God*, 63.

Part 2 | The Real in Ideas and Images

preaching that brought the series of events about (an interpretation whose service will probably always remain "till kingdom come"). The line, we may note, from Yeshua's public ministry to his public annihilation is a remarkably straight one; and that no matter whether one believes it as foreordained and fulfilling of some external sacral demand, or as the natural outcome for leaders of real or potential lower class revolts in Roman occupied Palestine. It is the modern tragedy of the crucifixion pictured that none (or anyway few) of these living "kingdom" ideascapes are prodded in contemporary minds by it, and that what are instead relayed through the tellings and retellings are taken to be physically/literally ontic rather than phenomenologically ontic. Thus it is that many who cannot stomach the purportedly unquestionable aspects (what the believers insist upon) shrug their shoulders and reject what might otherwise be valuably offered from these stories as only so many worthless magical imaginings. A veracity, however, need not correspond to anything measurable to bequeath value, and the lived benefits of an imagination (yours, mine, his, hers; let us not concern ourselves with sources) require no miracle above a single (mental) step beyond, a turning of idea, a refining of vision.

Another logion from *The Gospel of Thomas* has this teaching:[45]

> *Thomas* (Leloup), Saying 83: Yeshua said:
> "When images become visible to people,
> the light that is in them is hidden.
> In the icon of the light of the Father
> it will be manifest
> and the icon veiled by the light."[46]

We might take this to indicate the distracting qualities that an image can have, the veiling results it can bring to buried inner verities ("light"), truths—as we have been considering—that are better described as "felt" than as "known," truths that are perhaps only "truths." Concepts and associations become laden and burdened (indeed *burdensome, burdening*), and whatever was meant is lost in the mists of history; not only intentions but intuitions too are covered over. Yet in a re-turning back, if the necessary shift can be made to that inner, to bringing out that inner pointed at here,[47] then the internal light itself dims—or overwhelms—the obscuring effects that the image had theretofore induced, and the abstract lying within is made as concrete as the image fixed without. The idea-image takes, and gives, its reality. What is the "inner" of the crucifixion? Of how we have reacted to it?

---

45. Using now a different translator; I prefer to quote from these sayings rather than from other early Gospels because *Thomas'* non-canonical status might grant it a deeper power to surprise than what is found in the New Testament, despite the text's having become quite well-known in its own right.

46. Leloup, trans., intro, and comm., *The Gospel of Thomas*, 45.

47. Another "kingdom" teaching: the need to make the inner and the outer as one (Logion 22); see Leloup, trans., intro, and comm., *The Gospel of Thomas*; and Meyer, trans. and intro., *The Gospel of Thomas*.

Viewing the Cross from "the Kingdom"

It may be partly our familiarity with human suffering—our own, but also that of others—which very naturally causes us to cast so much into and onto the crucifixion when we are confronted by it, to take the image in the way that we tend to do. There can be no doubt, after all, that when gazing upon a painting such as El Greco's "Christ on the Cross"[48] one's heart is filled with an awe and a dread, an empathy that might have nothing to do with the "atonement" based thought of "This was done for me." The pain expressed on the figure's face beneath the crown of thorns crammed tightly round the head, the agonizing look of the eyes cast towards the sky, the needle thin arms and emaciated body with its ribs, hips, knees so prominent in its wasted state, loincloth barely covering the waist with too little flesh to support it, blood trickling from the nail prominently pounded into the crossed feet. Who could fail to be moved by such a sight? To then affix additional associative labels such as "sacrifice," "injustice," "innocent," "substitute" to this image only intensifies the excoriating mental discomfiture of the viewing. It is small wonder that many are brought to tears, particularly those faithful who ascribe to a full Christian orthodoxy, and hence for whom the icon carries its complete traditional interpretative weight, that tonnage of "this for me personally, in my stead, the punishment I deserve but can now avoid."

To otherwise believers and to non-believers too though, that thought and those labels will at some point probably surface when face-to-face with an image of the crucifixion, particularly if raised in a context that either supports that inherited understanding or that acknowledges it as a part of the surrounding dominant culture. For example, if we have been raised in a Christian home but would not claim the religion for ourselves, then of course such would be at the forefront of our minds, and the connected conceptuality would color and influence (some might claim "taint") each reaction and affective flow. Yet even if we have been raised in a Muslim or Jewish or Hindu or Buddhist (or atheist, agnostic humanist, et cetera, et cetera) home in a Western country, then although we may not be (as) likely to make the mental "for me" leap, we would nevertheless be aware of it, and that mere knowledge would thereby lend its emotively causational arc to the experience (a notion/event). Extending further, if we have been raised in an other than Christian home in a non-Western country where Christianity is perchance a minority religion, a repressed religion, or a non-existent (as practiced) religion, still in this globalized twenty-first century we would almost certainly be aware of the story behind Yeshua on the cross since it has been so repeatedly and so widely presented throughout the history of our Common Era. The idea has created its reality and now feels inescapable, forcing the query: Could all of this really be a "natural" response, a default and necessary reading of an event, one which grew out of the universally human condition of how we experience pain?

---

48. An example of the work can be found online here: "File: El Greco—Christ on the Cross, in a Landscape with Horsemen—1610–14.jpg." *Wikimedia Commons*. Accessed April 21, 2022. We will have occasion to view this painting ourselves in the course of our own study; see Chapter 13 below.

Such does seem doubtful. Countless thousands were crucified by Roman soldiers and we feel nothing for their anonymous faces and nameless deaths. Similar imagery of later Christian martyrs might stir in us something akin to that felt when considering Yeshua's broken body but not to the same degree, since with them the thought (if we have it) is not a "for me," but rather a "for him": they died for Yeshua, for Yeshua's memory, in his honor (it is supposed), or as a witness to him (by which the more accurate rendering would be "as a witness to his message," and/or "as a witness to his (avouched) being-hood of divinity"). In considering that, we might have to recognize—or at the very least entertain—the uncomfortable analytic step that this entire "atonement" hermeneutic was possibly only a tactic, a game of the church fathers to distinguish themselves and what they sought to build out of, and away from, the synagogues and Judaic culture and customs whence nearly the whole of Christianity was established.[49] The "Passover sacrifice" motif as applied afresh to the figure of Yeshua granted its designers a new establishing moment in the same way that the original narrative of the Passover rite of Exodus did (both grounding notion/events): in the latter it played the role of the Israelites' foundational ceremony as a people freed from Egyptian slavery and released/sent forth by God to construct a nation and land that would be a signal of ethno-communal priesthood purposed to demonstrate divine will and law for every other grouping on the planet; in the former it asserted the annulment of the Exodus model, and its simultaneous replacement by the (universalist) theme of a once-and-for-all human oblation to appease divine anger/judgment/displeasure and thus (re)establish the proper mortal-immortal relationship,[50] only this time without the exclusionary insistence on a particular "holy tribe." There is no more need for the Temple, the Law, the many detailed practices of the Torah, or indeed even for Israel (and, by extension, the Jewish people and Judaism), because one single sacrifice has consumed the lot of the endless ritual gifts; henceforth a new covenant and a novel (simplified) set of rites.[51] That line drawn—and crossed—by Christianized Jews, by Yeshuan-Jews who would rather not (we might conjecture) be "Jews" in an individually identifying way, provided the schism required for the different frameworks and alternate authorities thereafter founded.

Yet whatever the politics involved may have been (or be), I think there is a call—a further notion/event—within crucifixion imagery that strikes deeper than the "atonement" (conceptual, interpretative) produced feelings of gratitude and guilt, and the

---

49. This, and related thoughts, will be explored further in Part 4: Chapter 13, below.

50. Think, for instance, of the parallels that might be found in the story of Andromeda's being offered to the sea monster to stay Poseidon's wrath in the Greek myth, references to which have been found on pottery dating back at least to the sixth century BCE; see Editors of Encyclopædia Britannica, "Andromeda," *Encyclopædia Britannica*; and "Andromeda (mythology)," *Wikipedia*. Both sites accessed June 15, 2020.

51. Regarding the Temple with its rituals and what some psychological/spiritual repercussions of its destruction in 70 CE might have contributed to the resurrection accounts (and in that traumatically so), see Section 2 in Oberg, "Rereading the 'Vineyard' Parable," *Bulletin of the University of Kochi*, 17–35 (19–25).

aligned fraternal sense of belonging for fellow idea-image adherents, tend to expose: that beneath the body which has been broken and displayed the cry of Yeshua's "kingdom" dream can, and does, still ring—on some level and in some way—urging us to take up the responsibility that is ours, to take down the flesh fastened, and to forge "the kingdom" that is already here, "spread out upon the earth."[52] The image-idea/idea-image is not a frozen one, and although we have the onerous weight of centuries bearing down upon us in the traditional stance, the automatic associations and readings we currently perceive from the cross need not be thusly. We have taken on the icon of Yeshua hung with a particular comprehensive stance—whether by default or by an acknowledged acceptance—and have thereby established the reality that it itself has generated (the ossified notion/event, idea-image). We took the picture presented in the way we were told to take it, and then made it central to our collective (cultural) lives[53] with such vigor that virtually every alternative has disappeared from thought, and therefore lived existence; whether we believe (i.e. agree to) the "atonement" line or not, it is there and everyone knows it (and, really, *only* it: there are no/few variant readings, as just remarked[54]). We walled ourselves in, turned out the lights, and forgot where the exit lies. One cannot help feeling that Yeshua, he whose "kingdom" was envisioned on a freedom from the musts and the have-tos (and too each connected worrying concern), would be heartbroken by this uncanny ability to miss the point, to fail to notice the emphasis he placed on divine love and care right now in the rush to push a divisive viewpoint that sundered its own past and dangled the reward of a salvific portal to an afterlife of bliss as enticement to come onboard. The church pronounced that Judaism's ship had sunk with this finalizing holy self-offering; the rescue craft of Christianity, they claimed, had arrived just in time.

Pearly gates, streets of gold, and mansions in the sky: goodness gracious; who today can still stomach such cockamamie? Who can be swayed by a simplistic tit-for-tat such as this, wherein nothing more than a mere mental nod yields a near apotheosis for some and a horrifying, ceaseless torture for everyone else? With all of the terrors of the twentieth century (and those already of the twenty-first) boiling in our historical memories, and with them the brazen ugliness with which the question of theodicy assaults us, have we not come to a more sophisticated approach? Furthermore, in the light of extensive studies on the self, notions of soul, consciousness/mind investigations, and even the interpolation of what were once purely metaphysical queries into

---

52. Meyer, trans. and intro., *The Gospel of Thomas,* Logion (Saying) 113, 63.

53. Once more, this whether one confesses to be a Christian or not: culturally and historically speaking, in this modern digital age the symbology has spread to all corners.

54. If we disbelieve or disagree we might say "The Christians think . . . " but typically it either simply ends there without another image-idea/idea-image being offered, or it is merely shrugged off as a political execution without ramification outside of Christian understandings. While the latter might be a very weak form of an idea-image (or anyway could be argued thusly), in its disassociation—its dismissal—the concluding result is essentially an ignoring rather than an alternative as such. Compare that with the "kingdom" interpretation we have been offering as a purposively, newly affixed image-idea/idea-image.

biological/psychological ones, are we not ready to at least entertain an ending, a cessation? Would personal finitude, an absolute annihilatory closing, really be so bad?[55] Might we not take a hint from Yeshua himself and ask if God's/"God's" abundance as proclaimed by the pre-crucified rabbinic wayfarer, and as felt and known (ideationally of course, but phenomenologically as well) in this life not be enough?

The hermeneutics remain ours. We have made the image-idea/idea-image by which we currently respond to this emphatically enduring symbol, but we can unmake it, we can call for a notion/event over which we place an ownership rather than remaining tied to (encumbered by) the extant one. Indeed, I believe that we, striving to mark this new millennium, are "called" to do just that; and it is "the call" of "the kingdom" beckoning us on. By this I do not mean a telos, a directing *Geist* or "world historical spirit"; but it might be our particular Zeitgeist, if that term is taken in a reduced sense. This is the moment we have arrived at. We first took hold of, and thus can naturally let go of, the crucifixion mourned as a "kingdom" cut short; it was not and it is not. Yeshua's elucidation of it was, certainly, but there can yet be a resurrection of his legacy in a more substantial way than the legends of corporeal resuscitation have achieved. The cross itself can elicit "the kingdom"; we only need to "see!" it that way. We can, moreover, experience an understanding of the divine broadly via this—or any other—pictorial marker to a degree that is far closer to that which Yeshua sought to usher in than what we have heretofore achieved, and the image-idea/idea-image melding into the notion/event directs us to the methodology involved. In the above approach to the crucifix we have perhaps arrived at some of the "why" as to what the image has meant, to what it has triggered in or from us, but as Caputo teaches, "the kingdom" is really more about the "how."[56] We may therefore henceforward wish to turn once more and ask anew: As seen from this fresh "here," what *might* it mean? That is the setting for the next division of our study, wherein Yeshua's parables and sayings, with their buried—but at times erupting—"kingdom" can be found.

---

55. I must apologize for these additional self references, but see again Oberg, *Blurred*; and Oberg, "Approaches to Finitude," *Journal of Applied Ethics and Philosophy*, 8–17.

56. Caputo, *The Weakness of God*; and Caputo, *The Folly of God*.

Part 3

Parables and Pictures

Chapter 9

Hermeneutics:
Storytelling and Re-Telling

IN THIS CHAPTER WE will seek a deeper clarification of what might be happening in "the kingdom" that Yeshua foresaw in his mind's eye, on the actuality/possibility of it, and what that vision (and its challenge) implied more broadly for the message that he sought to install within the Judaism(s) of his time. From this, it is hoped, our overall argument for a re-installment of Christianity into Judaism—as a version of Judaism, as one of today's yet-existing multiple Judaisms—will be strengthened; although the path before us remains long. We will attempt this by considering three well-known parables, quoting at times from canonical texts but too (perhaps more so) from lesser repeated versions of their tellings, the latter in an effort to try and dislodge whatever familiarity we may have with such, and hence too the subsequent automatic and default thinking about these stories that tends to be generated. Firstly we will examine the "Parable of the Workers in the Vineyard," doing so at some length in order to establish the general hermeneutic approach we will employ, and thereafter turn to the "Parable of the Mustard Seed" before finally analyzing the "Parable of the Great Banquet" (but not the sometimes associated "Parable of the Wedding Banquet" (also called "Wedding Feast"/"Marriage of the King's Son"). For these other relatings we will primarily be working from the texts as found in the Scholars Version produced by the Jesus Seminar, the wording of the *Gospel of Thomas,* and the listings of the so-called "Lost Gospel" Q; for the sake of comparison, we will also provide additional examples from the canon, continuing to take the New Revised Standard Version as our representative of such. Prior to entering the "Vineyard," however, a few short words on Q may be appropriate for readers without background knowledge of the nature of this "work."

Perhaps the most noteworthy aspect to Q is that it does not exist, it is a work labeled as "work" indeed, fully deserving of those double quotation marks/inverted commas, by which we indicate—and this follows along splendidly with what we have already discussed in the above sections on the quasi-real yet somehow still "real"

Part 3 | Parables and Pictures

(substantively so) aspects of images and ideas—that it does not *exist* so much as it "exists": it can be found in the world, but not in a direct manner; it is there but not there, buried but uncovered, readable but not touchable. This naturally requires explanation. The name Q is from the German term *quelle,* which means "source" in English, and is denotative of the hypothetical standing of the still (always?) undiscovered common reference material from which the more than two hundred verses shared by the Gospels of Matthew and Luke (but not Mark) are thought to have been drawn. This "third," or "triangulation" (if the reader will), is considered necessary since scholars have concluded that the authors of Matthew and Luke did not know of, nor have access to, the other's book when each produced her/his own book contemporaneously in the last decade or so of the first century CE (and, as an aside, how delightful it would be to find that one or the other or both had been penned by a woman!), about twenty years after the completion of Mark.[1]

Like *Thomas,* Q is a Sayings Gospel with little narrative structuring (but not absent altogether as it is in *Thomas;* Q does contain some stories and action sequences). In taking the overlapping areas from Matthew and Luke, the reconstruction of a previously (probably) extant document was painstakingly put together by various academics over decades of research; and if such did indeed exist, and was representative of what the faith grouping that produced and/or used it took to be central to their beliefs, then what is perhaps particularly striking (at least for us from our present historical perspective) is its neglect of the passion, death, and resurrection tales that are so crucial to the canonical Gospels.[2] Rather, Q focuses on issues of the social and the relational, on the manner of living that Yeshua taught, and, as the translators and editors Mark Powelson and Ray Riegert write, in Q we are presented with a very human sage: "Jesus [Yeshua; let us keep to that more proper moniker] is neither Christ nor the Messiah but rather the last [that is, "last" for the Q community, as in "most recent"] in a long line of Jewish prophets. He is a charismatic teacher, a healer, a simple man filled with the spirit of God."[3] However, as with the other Gospels, "the kingdom" message is central to the objective of Yeshua's ministry in Q too, as is the responsibility that each of us has to bring it to fruition, the vital part that we play in its building (its budding), regardless of individual position or standing: no authoritative hierarchy is laid out, and the disciples themselves scarcely make an appearance. A single example of the sometimes barbed form this pedagogy can take may suffice as illustration; and while the contents quoted below are of course already with us (being common to Matthew and Luke), taking Q's words here within the altered notional approach that our historical contextualizing has yielded might provide a pleasantly jarring effect:

1. Powelson and Riegert, trans., footnotes, and eds., *The Lost Gospel Q*; this is taken from the preface by Borg, 13–14.

2. Powelson and Riegert, trans., footnotes, and eds., *The Lost Gospel Q* (see again Borg's preface); Yeshua's claimed miraculous birth is also nowhere to be found in Q.

3. Powelson and Riegert, trans., footnotes, and eds., *The Lost Gospel Q,* 28; taken this time from the editors' introduction, titled "The Story of the Lost Gospel Q".

Q18 [Yeshua is speaking]: "Give, and there will be gifts for you. A full measure of grain, pressed down, shaken together and running over, will be poured into your lap; *because the amount you measure out is the amount you will be given back.* [emphasis mine]"[4]

Give and it will be given—but be careful, because only in proportion to one's own efforts. This appears to stand in contrast to the general proclamations Yeshua made of a complete trust in divine abundance (of the "birds of the air neither sow nor reap" and "lilies of the field neither toil nor spin" sort[5]); yet note that this is instead about human—and not God's/"God's"—effort: "measure of grain," "pressed down," "shaken together": all these involve purposive and planned behaviors and results. I believe that this teaching can therefore be read primarily along the social dimension, with the "gifts for you" coming from others, from personal and regular earthly sources: not, then, "blessings from Heaven" so much as "blessings from neighbors"; although, hard as it might be at times, we ought probably to remember too that our neighbors are (or could be!) blessings themselves. This small sample indicates a helpful conceptual pairing, and it is in fact on these dual axes of the social and the divine, the intersecting relational spectrums of human-human and human-God/"God", where I think the parables shift in emphasis and focus, as we will set out to explore in the following. With that in mind, let us therefore take leave of our prefatory comments on Q and delve more deeply into the selected tales below.

---

4. Powelson and Riegert, trans., footnotes, and eds., *The Lost Gospel Q*, 51; from a section of the Sermon on the Mount, emphasis added.

5. See Matthew 6:26–33 (Yeshua is speaking in this passage); a truncated version of the passage was quoted in our prior chapter, but we list it again here for the reader's convenience: "26Look at the birds of the air; they neither sow nor reap nor gather into barns, and yet your heavenly Father feeds them. Are you not of more value than they? 27And can any of you by worrying add a single hour to your span of life? 28And why do you worry about clothing? Consider the lilies of the field, how they grow; they neither toil nor spin, 29yet I tell you, even Solomon in all his glory was not clothed like one of these. 30But if God so clothes the grass of the field, which is alive today and tomorrow is thrown into the oven, will he not much more clothe you—you of little faith? 31Therefore do not worry, saying, 'What will we eat?' or 'What will we drink?' or 'What will we wear?' 32For it is the Gentiles who strive for all these things; and indeed your heavenly Father knows that you need all these things. 33But strive first for the kingdom of God and his righteousness, and all these things will be given to you as well.' *Thinline Bible with the Apocrypha* (NRSV). In Q (51–53), by the way, this reads as: "[51] Jesus spoke to his disciples: 'Don't be anxious about your life. Don't worry about getting enough food or having clothes to wear. Life means more than food and the body is more than clothing. Look at the ravens. They don't plant seeds or gather a harvest. They have neither storehouses nor barns. Yet God feeds them. Aren't you more important than birds? Can any of you, for all your worrying, add a single moment to your life? If worry can't change the smallest thing, then why be anxious about the rest? [52] Look at the lilies that grow wild in the fields. They don't weave clothes for themselves. But I tell you, even King Solomon in all his splendor was not dressed as beautifully as these flowers. If that is how God clothes the grasses, which are green today and burned in the sun tomorrow, how much more will God provide for you. How little faith you have! [53] Don't be blinded by the pursuit of food, clothing and possessions. Stop worrying about these things. Only those who lack spirit and soul pursue them. You have a Father who knows what you need. Set your heart on God and these other things will be given to you." Powelson and Riegert, trans., footnotes, and eds., *The Lost Gospel Q*, 85–87.

Part 3 | Parables and Pictures

The presentation of our first text to consider, the "Parable of the Workers in the Vineyard," will be given here in a translation that may be unfamiliar to some but which is probably closer in sense and nuance to the original language, and has moreover received a far more thorough historical vetting than other versions of the same story. This relaying was produced by the Jesus Seminar, and thus a few additional short introductory remarks (apologies to the reader on all these backgrounds being given . . .) on the group and its processes of working and literature manufacture that relate directly to the subsequently quoted work, and in what the body as a whole set out to achieve when active (and, in other ways by some same and some different members, continues to attempt) will also be briefly mentioned vis-à-vis the above situating of the similarly studiously re-built book of Q.

It is important to acknowledge that the Seminar was neither sponsored nor funded by any institution, be it religious, academic, or otherwise. Its membership was open to anyone with the fitting credentials, and was not only composed of professional biblical scholars. These details ensured that the cohort contained a wide spectrum of views within it (although its intellectualism has been subject to criticism from some professors and clergy), and at its peak it enjoyed roughly two hundred different participants in the biannual debates it held, with around one hundred and fifty full members. The ultimate goal of the group was to inventory and verify the entire catalogue of surviving Christian (and/or what have generally been termed "Gnostic" or "Gnostic Christian") documents prior to 325 CE (the year when the Roman emperor Constantine the Great convened the First Council of Nicaea in an effort to unify church doctrine and scripture), and then to classify each for historical likelihood. This procedure entailed a multi-tiered voting system and resulted in a set of sayings and actions related to Jesus that were (in descending order): 1) undoubtedly said or done, 2) probably said or done, 3) not said but the contents are similar to what was actually said; or not supportably done but still possibly done, and finally 4) not said; or improbably done and most likely fictional. The Seminar then compiled what they concluded to be the most reliable words and deeds of Jesus and published three reports on their results (mentioned in the preceding chapter), in addition to holding a number of public lectures and workshops. These activities continued from its founding in 1985 until the close of its regular work in 2006.[6] The members created their own English translations of the documents they worked with, dubbed it the Scholars Version, and—as related—such will provide the wording for our own efforts.[7] The parable therein reads as follows:

---

6. Funk and the Jesus Seminar, *The Gospel of Jesus;* general information can also be found here: "The Jesus Seminar," *Westar Institute.* Accessed November 11, 2019.

7. For readers who may wish to make a canonical comparison, here is a more traditional translation (Matthew 20:1–16), taken from *Thinline Bible with the Apocrypha* (NRSV): "1For the kingdom of heaven is like a landowner who went out early in the morning to hire laborers for his vineyard. 2After agreeing with the laborers for the usual daily wage, he sent them into his vineyard. 3When he went out about nine o'clock, he saw others standing idle in the marketplace; 4and he said to them, 'You also go into

Hermeneutics: Storytelling and Re-Telling

The Gospel of Jesus 4:4–21:

Vineyard laborers: ⁴Jesus used to tell this parable:

⁵Heaven's imperial rule is like a proprietor who went out the first thing in the morning to hire workers for his vineyard. ⁶After agreeing with the workers for a silver coin a day, he sent them into his vineyard.

⁷And coming out around nine A.M., he saw others loitering in the marketplace ⁸and he said to them, "You go into the vineyard too, and I'll pay you whatever is fair." ⁹So they went.

¹⁰Around noon he went out again, and at three P.M. he repeated the process. ¹¹About five P.M. he went out and found others loitering about and says to them, "Why did you stand around here idle the whole day?"

¹²They reply, "Because no one hired us."

¹³He tells them, "You go into the vineyard as well."

¹⁴When evening came, the owner of the vineyard tells his foreman: "Call the workers and pay them their wages, starting with those hired last and ending with those hired first."

¹⁵Those hired at five P.M. came up and received a silver coin each. ¹⁶Those hired first approached, thinking they would receive more. But they also got a silver coin apiece. ¹⁷They took it and began to grumble against the proprietor: "These guys hired last worked only an hour but you have made them equal to us who did most of the work during the heat of the day."

¹⁸In response he said to one of them, "Look, pal, did I wrong you? You did agree with me for a silver coin, didn't you? ¹⁹Take your wage and get out! I intend to treat the one hired last the same way I treat you. ²⁰Is there some law forbidding me to do as I please with my money? ²¹Or is your eye filled with envy because I am generous?⁸

Before we examine the content here we can note what is missing: verse sixteen as found in the authorized versions of the Bible (again, this parable is from Matthew 20:1–16), which reads: "So the last will be first, and the first will be last," echoing the final verse of the previous chapter: "But many who are first will be last, and the last

---

the vineyard, and I will pay you whatever is right.' So they went. 5When he went out again about noon and about three o'clock, he did the same. 6And about five o'clock he went out and found others standing around; and he said to them, 'Why are you standing here idle all day?' 7They said to him, 'Because no one has hired us.' He said to them, 'You also go into the vineyard.' 8When evening came, the owner of the vineyard said to his manager, 'Call the laborers and give them their pay, beginning with the last and then going to the first.' 9When those hired about five o'clock came, each of them received the usual daily wage. 10Now when the first came, they thought they would receive more; but each of them also received the usual daily wage. 11And when they received it, they grumbled against the landowner, 12saying, 'These last worked only one hour, and you have made them equal to us who have borne the burden of the day and the scorching heat.' 13But he replied to one of them, 'Friend, I am doing you no wrong; did you not agree with me for the usual daily wage? 14Take what belongs to you and go; I choose to give to this last the same as I give to you. 15Am I not allowed to do what I choose with what belongs to me? Or are you envious because I am generous?' 16So the last will be first, and the first will be last."

8. Funk and the Jesus Seminar, *The Gospel of Jesus*, 27 and 29 (documental source material is listed on page 28). The section, chapter, and verse numbering is unique to their report.

will be first" (Matthew 19:30; the preceding part of chapter nineteen has relayed the incident of "The Rich Young Man," i.e. a would-be follower who could not agree to part with his wealth for the sake of the poor).[9] In the Seminar's book this verse is located immediately before the "Vineyard" tale and is given its own titling, reading:

> *The Gospel of Jesus* 4:3:
> *First and last:* [3]Jesus said, "The last will be first and the first last."[10]

The source documents listed for this "first/last" verse are the Gospel of Mark, *Thomas*, and Q.[11] *Thomas*, in some corners even more so than has been the case with Q, has garnered a great deal of attention as a Sayings Gospel, a purely instructional collection of Yeshua's ministry that is entirely devoid of narrative, lacking even the bare bones of Q (e.g. such brief vignettes in Q as pertain to John the Baptist, Yeshua travelling here or there, certain individuals or groups approaching Yeshua for this or that, et cetera) and without any connected events up to and inclusive of Yeshua's execution, which warrants nary a mention in the book. All of this has, of course, already been discussed in our study; but I believe it nevertheless beneficial to recall these details once more, since although we do not need to belabor the differences amongst these resources, it will still be worth citing some of the other *Gospel of Thomas* translations of this same "first and last" saying to act as further supplementary help in understanding just how subtle much of the work in this area can be.

A first example comes from Marvin Meyer's version of *Thomas*: "For many of the first will be last and will become a single one."[12] Another is from Jean-Yves Leloup's, which reads: "Many of the first will make themselves last, and they will become One."[13]

---

9. Both verses are taken from *Thinline Bible with the Apocrypha* (NRSV). Amy-Jill Levine calls this phrase a "floating" line, and notes that it is found in other settings such as Mark 10:31 ("But many who are first will be last, and the last will be first."), Luke 13:30 ("Indeed, some are last who will be first, and some are first who will be last."), and Matthew 19:30, as here; Levine, *Short Stories by Jesus*, 233. We too noted these similarities in the above, and the just quoted references are also from *Thinline Bible with the Apocrypha* (NRSV). Readers will no doubt notice the interesting weakening that Luke lends to this thought with the addition of the two "somes."

10. Funk and the Jesus Seminar, *The Gospel of Jesus*, 27. The title they give their Chapter 4, by the way, is: "Teaching with Authority". Q lists this line separately as well, see Q65: "The last will be first and the first will be last."; in Powelson and Riegert, trans., footnotes, and eds., *The Lost Gospel Q*, 99.

11. Funk and the Jesus Seminar, *The Gospel of Jesus*, 111–16 gives a useful summary of the canonical New Testament Gospels and related ancient documents. A few reminders: Mark is often dated to around 70 CE, Matthew to 85 CE, and Luke to 90 CE. *The Gospel of Thomas* is one of the Coptic language findings from the famous Nag Hammadi cache unearthed in Egypt in 1945, and may—like Q—also have been a source for Yeshua's teachings in Matthew and Luke, with *Thomas* possibly dating from as early as the middle of the first century, making it the oldest of any Gospel we have. For additional information on *Thomas* see the introductory remarks in Barnstone and Meyer, eds., *The Gnostic Bible*, 43–44.

12. Meyer, trans and intro., *The Gospel of Thomas*, 21 (Logion 4:2–3); cf. Barnstone and Meyer, eds., *The Gnostic Bible*, 45, where the translation of Logion 4 also reads as: "For many of the first will be last/ and become a single one."

13. Leloup, trans., intro. and comm., *The Gospel of Thomas*, 9 (Logion 4 (without subdivisions as Meyer gives)). The reader will recall that this is actually a double translation, with Leloup going from Coptic to French, and then the translator Rowe taking Leloup's French into English.

Hermeneutics: Storytelling and Re-Telling

A final mention is Hal Taussig's rendering: "For many who are first will be last. And they will come to be one alone."[14] What obviously stands out in *Thomas* as against the other accounts is the rather mystical sounding "become one/One (alone)"; on its face a phrasing like this may incline us towards a Gnostic interpretation, wherein the material body falls away and/or melts into the purer spirit, and thereby gains release or enlightenment. *Thomas'* early authorship would seem to counsel against such though; Gnostic ideas—although arguably readable into John's Gospel (probably early second century, but maybe very late first)—did not really gain much traction within early Yeshuan followers until at least a century after *Thomas*, if the dating figures are correct.[15] What might this be then? Leloup's "One" has a very neo-Platonic ring to it, akin with Plotinus' teachings,[16] but again those would postdate the issue at hand (although given *Thomas'* Coptic setting within a broader Egyptian-Alexandrian cultural sphere it appears reasonable to speculate on the common currency of the same or similar ideas, or at least the germs of such being present at the time of composition). A "they" whom are "last" that "become a single one" or "one alone," might alternatively be understood in a straightforwardly communal sense: sisters and brothers doing it together, cohesively and non-competitively. The greater "here and now" of this, perceived along more strictly human(istic) lines, are where I think deeper provocations might be found if we are to look, and not only within this parable but—as we will explore—perhaps especially within this parable.

In these *Thomas* renderings there is a neglect of the full reversal which might be noticed, a citing only of the "first to last" (with Leloup's intriguing "make themselves": a subtextual hinting at a purposive social movement hidden within the nuances of the original linguistic rendering?), and the placing of that phrase (i.e. "first-last") in the opposite ordering with that in both the New Testament sources and in the Seminar's *Gospel of Jesus* collection, where it reads "last to first" and then thereafter "first to last." It is, however, precisely this reversing as relayed in the latter, and too the phrase's placement of the last *going to* the first and then the first *going to* the last (voluntarily so?; yet Leloup does have the "make themselves" . . .), that I think is so demonstrative of Yeshua's "kingdom" teachings: the flipping of the accepted default/standardized is what is paramount. If *Thomas* does indeed (and let us admit that our exegesis is quite possibly an over-reading of the text—the initial author(s) may have been simpler in intent) point towards a kind of bottom-up allegiance, that by itself is not nearly as potent as the same *in addition to*: a coetaneous top-down reduction. In the first case we would have the base of the societal pyramid strengthening itself, whereas in the second we would have the same pyramid flattening itself into a rectangle (or even a line!). Which vision is the more compelling? Which potentially closer to Yeshuan

---

14. Hal Taussig, ed. and comm., *A New New Testament*, 15 (Logion 4:2–3).

15. Barnstone and Meyer, eds., *The Gnostic Bible*, contains many excellent overview essays on historical Gnosticism.

16. For an introduction, see Hadot, *Plotinus, or The Simplicity of Vision*; and O'Meara, *Plotinus*.

PART 3 | PARABLES AND PICTURES

thought, as near as we can comprehend it? To seek an answer we must enter the fabled world of the landowner and the workers he hires, and so let us now set foot into the "Vineyard" and search out our own rendering of it.

To start our fresh hermeneutic,[17] our first dig of the shovel in the "Vineyard," we must once more examine this "kingdom" phrasing itself, for the term can be—and often has been—quite misleading, both in a temporal and in a locative sense. While we may "know" that Yeshua taught the advent of "the kingdom of God/'God'" (whether we take that as apocalyptic in nature or not), the terminology itself tends to muddle in modern ears what was almost certainly meant by it when actually uttered by Yeshua. Even his initial Jewish/to-later-become-Yeshuan-Jewish followers seem to have had trouble understanding its conceptual usage (at least, judging by the accounts we have received, which may or may not be of much authentic value), and they of course had none (or fewer) of the intervening years and historical Zeitgeists between them and their teacher that we do. It is interesting to note that in the Scholars Version cited above "Heaven's imperial rule" is used instead of "kingdom of God." Funk, as founder of the Jesus Seminar, explains that the group differed sharply on how to express what Yeshua was getting at when he spoke of God's domain, and that the issue is further complicated by the fact that Yeshua (that is, the historical Yeshua whom they studied) would sometimes employ it to refer to a location and sometimes to an action or a relating of God/"God" with (a) people or land. For their work the group therefore adopted "God's domain" and "God's estate" for a place, and "God's imperial rule" for aspects of relationship. Even this is dissatisfactory to Funk though, as he notes that "It has been extremely difficult to find terms that accommodate both the absolute character of the divine reign and the pacific disposition of Jesus. This problem still awaits solution."[18]

By this "domain" (or "kingdom" or "relating") Yeshua appears to have wished to impart that it was something already present in the world, and meant for everyone; as the early convert, missionary, and voluminous letter writer Paul—perhaps our first and best source for Yeshuan-Judaism as its doctrines coalesced (and, indeed, were shaped by the man himself)—explained the sentiment: "no longer Jew or Greek, no longer slave or free, no longer male and female" (Galatians 3:28),[19] but without Yeshua

---

17. Or anyway somewhat fresh, for indeed "There is nothing new /Beneath the sun!" (Ecclesiastes 1:9) and I would be the first to admit how indebted I am to the many scholars whose works I have read and greatly benefitted from; *Tanakh* (NJPS). This book of Ecclesiastes, incidentally, is sometimes also known by the Hebrew title Koheleth (or Qoheleth), the name of the claimed writer in the opening verses (1:1-2): "1The words of Koheleth [a footnote here reads: "Probably 'the Assembler,' i.e., of hearings or sayings; cf. 12:9-11."] son of David, king in Jerusalem. 2Utter futility!—said Koheleth— /Utter futility! All is futile!" *Tanakh* (NJPS). Robert Alter, in his magisterial re-translation and erudite commentary, prefers the labeling of "Qohelet (Ecclesiastes)"; see his *The Wisdom Books*, 335–391.

18. Funk, *Honest to Jesus*, 88.

19. The full verse in *Thinline Bible with the Apocrypha* (NRSV) we have been using is: "There is no longer Jew or Greek, there is no longer slave or free, there is no longer male and female; for all of you are one in Christ Jesus."

concluding, as Paul's New Testament epistle does, that "for all of you are one in Christ Jesus." To Yeshua at the time of his teaching it was never about himself; instead it was about God/"God" and every human being. Funk summarizes: "In God's domain, circumcision, keeping kosher, and sabbath [sic.] observance [i.e. the pillars of Jewish Law] are extraneous. The kingdom represents an unbrokered relationship to God: temple and priests are obsolete."[20] This aspect of presence and universality, the *nowness* of "the kingdom," we have already remarked on, but I think it cannot be stressed enough. In *Thomas* this is put rather beautifully in the penultimate logion, number one hundred thirteen (quoted in our previous chapter and repeated here in light of current—and naturally still connected—considerations):

> *Thomas*, Saying 113: His followers said to him, "When will the kingdom come?"
> [Yeshua replied] "It will not come by watching for it. It will not be said, 'Look, here it is,' or 'Look, there it is.'
> Rather, the father's kingdom is spread out upon the earth, and people do not see it."[21]

This notion is also found in Q, although worded slightly differently:

> Q79: Jesus was asked, "When will the kingdom of God arrive?"
> He replied, "You won't be able to see the kingdom of God when it comes. People won't be able to say 'it's here' or 'it's over there'.
> "The kingdom of God is among you."[22]

"The kingdom" is already "spread out," it is "among you"—it *is* here—yet at the same time "it will not come by watching for it" (future tense), implying both that "the kingdom" is invisibly present and merely waiting to be realized, but also that we actually have to do some work to realize it: hence both now and to-come, present and future. This dual existence of "the kingdom" is a crucial aspect of the interpretative principle that I wish to expound, and it will be returned to; in the meantime, by way of an example of this manifestation/absence—and as an illuminating illustration of the confusion that can be wrought when we think of this notion in terms of an afterlife or a post-apocalyptic situation—let us visit another aphorism: the "Eye of the Needle." Here it is in the Scholars Version:

> *The Gospel of Jesus* 17:6–7:
> *Eye of the needle:* [6]Jesus said to his disciples, "I swear to you, it is very difficult for the rich to enter Heaven's domain. [7]And again I tell you, it's easier

---

20. Funk, *Honest to Jesus*, 41; on the aspect of its immediacy see also Caputo, *The Weakness of God*, and Caputo, *The Folly of God*.
21. Meyer, trans. and intro., *The Gospel of Thomas*, 63.
22. Powelson and Riegert, trans., footnotes, and eds., *The Lost Gospel Q*, 114.

for a camel to squeeze through a needle's eye than for a wealthy person to get into God's domain."[23]

This rendering is very helpful in the way it demonstrates how "Heaven's domain" and "God's domain"—or even simply "Heaven" and "God"—could be (and frequently were, and really still are) used interchangeably, and not only by ancient authors. Referencing a particular geographical region in a way synonymous with an associated person or group is of course not limited to scripture; journalists employ the identical when they write of "Washington" or "Tokyo" as shorthand for the governments of the United States or Japan. The specific problem encountered by the same trend (and this certainly appears to be a very default manner of indicating, whatever the historical epoch) when it comes to spiritual matters vis-à-vis political or socioeconomic issues, is that even if we intellectually take "Heaven" to be God's/"God's" "headquarters" like Washington, D.C. or Tokyo are for their respective seats of governance, the associative conjunction of a postmortem destination that the word "Heaven" elicits is too firmly engraved in modern minds—we cannot help but to think of it, and whether we do so only at a level below cognitive awareness or not is beside the point. (Indeed, if only at that deep psychological layer then the effects are in fact more pronounced since they go unacknowledged.)

"Heaven's domain," "Heaven's imperial rule," "God's/'God's' domain," "the kingdom"; in the teachings of Yeshua these are each about bringing what is here in this contemporaneous life out into the open: realizing the existent "kingdom" in the everyday, making it happen, making it so real that it is no longer a question of "when" but is rather a nod to this beautiful moment: making a *what could be* into an *is*. It is simply that for some people such is a strenuous undertaking (the rich apparently foremost amongst them; and as will be understood, "the rich" terminology itself is quite probably an abbreviated way to point to those invested in the status quo). The seemingly counterintuitive nature of this teaching is perhaps witnessed by the existence from

---

23. Funk and the Jesus Seminar, *The Gospel of Jesus*, 73. The source is listed as the Gospel of Mark, and there (10:23–25) it reads as: "23Then Jesus looked around and said to his disciples, 'How hard it will be for those who have wealth to enter the kingdom of God!' 24And the disciples were perplexed at these words. But Jesus said to them again, 'Children, how hard it is to enter the kingdom of God! 25It is easier for a camel to go through the eye of a needle than for someone who is rich to enter the kingdom of God.'" Noteworthy here too is the initial future oriented "will be" versus the latter present tense "it is" found within these verses, and the double use of the present "it is" in the Seminar's version. The Gospel of Matthew (19:23–24) has: "23Then Jesus said to his disciples, 'Truly I tell you, it will be hard for a rich person to enter the kingdom of heaven. 24Again I tell you, it is easier for a camel to go through the eye of a needle than for someone who is rich to enter the kingdom of God.'" Once more the emphasis in this translation regarding "entering the kingdom" seems to be on the future tense, and this, I believe, adds to our tendency to misread such texts. Finally, let us look to the same from the Gospel of Luke (18:24–25): "24Jesus looked at him [the rich ruler of the narrative (who is, by the way, the same figure as the "rich young man" in Matthew 19 referred to above)] and said, 'How hard it is for those who have wealth to enter the kingdom of God! 25Indeed, it is easier for a camel to go through the eye of a needle than for someone who is rich to enter the kingdom of God.'" It will be noticed how Luke brings our attention back to the current in this rather straightforward account; all quotations from *Thinline Bible with the Apocrypha* (NRSV).

the fifteenth century (or possibly even earlier in the ninth century) of an argument that the "needle's eye" reference is to a certain gate in the walls of Jerusalem which could only be traversed by a camel if first whatever baggage the animal happened to be carrying were removed and she were then made to kneel down and crawl through the space; but no supporting evidence for such a structure has ever been discovered,[24] and we are left with the feeling that such rhetoric is more of an "explaining away" of the Yeshuan sentiment than it is an explaining of it. Thus we are better served by wrestling with the words as we have them; and as difficult as those words might be to grasp, we may wish to consider that Yeshua's "kingdom" teachings—and really the whole core of his public ministry—could well be an extended attempt to seize the listener (by now become the reader) by the shoulders and shake them/us into agreeing that, "yes! 'the kingdom' can come/is come," and we need not wait for death or a heralding miracle to usher it in. This, precisely, is what I take the "Vineyard" narrative to be getting at. Let us continue our labor in the orchard.

The primary figure in the parable of the "Vineyard laborers" is of course the proprietor, the landowner, he with whom the story begins and ends, and just as it is with taking "the kingdom of Heaven" or "the kingdom of God/'God'" to be related to an afterlife or otherworldly location, it is only too easy to understand the main character here as an allusion to God/"God"; but that, on my reading at least, would be to very much miss the point. Rather, I think that in light of the emphasis we have found on "the kingdom" as (potentially) here, as (potentially) now, this main character is an exemplar of someone who has embraced what Caputo has called the "topsy-turvy" ethics of "the kingdom."[25] He is a person for whom indeed the last has become first and the first last, he is clearly no longer bound by conventional views on what is and is not fair, nor is he restricted by what we might consider to be a "fitting" or "appropriate" attitude towards generosity. He is, in fact, ridiculously generous; though not to a fault, since—as he himself points out to the earliest hired hands who have started complaining—"you did agree with me for a silver coin, didn't you?" (verse eighteen), and "Is there some law forbidding me to do as I please with my money?" (verse twenty). This man, our landowner, he is bringing/has brought "the kingdom" right there into his vineyard through the treatment he renders to those around him. He offers a traditional daily wage to every one of the workers, regardless of the amount of time they put in, and this does seem rather in line with a God/"God" who would offer love, mercy, and grace equally to all: the view of God/"God" that Yeshua espoused, as we have "seen!"[26]

---

24. See Ford, "Bible verses about Eye of a Needle," *Bible Tools.* Accessed November 11, 2019.

25. Caputo, *The Folly of God,* stresses this point especially.

26. A reminder: the quotation marks/double inverted commas are to highlight the double sense of "see" (our "see!") for what I hope has been not only an intellectualization but also a realization. The works of Caputo, Funk, Keller (cited below), and Kugel in particular have helped me to "see!" here, for what such may be worth.

Part 3 | Parables and Pictures

For us, whether we comprehend this divine as God (being) or "God" (ideal), the owner is not a figure or symbol for either: he is a normally human person acting in a manner which God/"God" (as taught by Yeshua) would approve of, he is taking "the kingdom" on board and making an effort to erect it within the confines of his situation and circumstances. This, I take it, is a critical function. "The kingdom" may already be here "spread out upon the earth," but as long as "people do not see it" (Thomas 113)[27] it really does remain as an "if," a "could be," a buried seed or potentiality. It is therefore our duty and our task to make it happen, to notice that "the kingdom" exists in the duality we have alluded to, and hence to exert the necessary efforts to transform that duality into a singularity: into an only "is" and no longer an "if/is." This is an ethical and behavioral challenge that Yeshua is issuing: to overturn the extant social order, to re-work our priorities, to give, give, give, and to treat everyone equally regardless of extenuating details or the ascertainments of whatever status quo we happen to be living under. This is a radical message, and it is one aimed solely at the moment every moment, deciding for the day about the day, and certainly not with a mind for tomorrow—we can imagine that some of the first workers probably would not have signed up with our proprietor again the next day if they took the grousing they gave him seriously—and absolutely not with a mind to any presumed afterlife. Make God's/"God's" "domain" happen, Yeshua seems to be saying, and here is how. That we can *make* "the kingdom," however, indicates that we can also *fail to* make it. If "the kingdom" does not come is that God's/"God's" fault or ours?

Amy-Jill Levine, alone amongst the commentators I have read (and I remind the reader that I am a philosopher and not a biblical scholar, so kindly take that "I have read" with its requisite large grain of salt!) makes a somewhat similar point to the above, but she does so in an overly weak (in my estimation) manner. To her, the landowner is analogous to both God/"God" and a role model for Yeshuan-Jews, a person of means who offers equal pay for unequal work, and thereby the treatment meted out to the laborers is based on a perception of equality that "derives from a sense of justice keyed into what people need to live," so that therefore the "point is not that those who have 'get more,' but that those who have not 'get enough.'"[28] This comprehension of the tale does take the social dimension as being central, but its justice is not "topsy-turvy," or at least not enough; it is instead an operating by the employer that leaves space open for personal benefit, and thus, I think, reduces the aspect of generosity involved. Levine cites later rabbinic sources (e.g. stories from *Semachot de Rabbi Chiyah, Midrash Psalms*)[29] that also promote equal pay for unequal work in support of her stance (in this, by the way, nicely reaffirming for us Yeshua's clean fit within even the Judaisms of the times that followed his own (and hence, we assert, by implication Yeshuanism's fit within Judaism still)), and such are indeed deserving of

---

27. Meyer, trans. and intro., *The Gospel of Thomas*, 63.
28. Levine, *Short Stories by Jesus*, 235.
29. Levine, *Short Stories by Jesus*, 234–35.

thought and analysis, as is the general Jewish ethic of care for the poor (e.g. the Torah's many teachings on concern for the widow, orphan, stranger, leaving the corners of one's field unharvested so as to be gathered by those in need, cyclical debt forgiveness, et cetera, collectively known as *tzedakah*[30]). Yet the anecdotes from these texts are about purely human figures (and hence no doubling of God/"God" with role model as Levine insists upon for the parable), and her cited sources' exemplars act not for the sake of a sociological construction but because behaving thusly is "the right thing to do." Yeshua's "kingdom" prodding is, on our reading, deeper in that its desideratum is not a purely individualized "righteous" praxis but a contribution towards an already/to-be new world of human interrelation. The distinction might appear minute, but it is critical: our fully human landowner is laboring towards establishing "the kingdom"; Levine's is trying to be a "better person" even while representing both an earthly ideal and a divinity. It might be argued that the one leads to the other (a member of society's improvement of self into a broader societal improvement), and we can grant that it may well do so, but what is the intent? What objective is held in the mind of one landowner versus the other? Therein lies our disagreement with Levine, and although it is a small and nuanced one such is, after all, the work of academia and the special niche of philosophical undertakings. This is the *how* of thought and conceptual approach, and as we have sought to emphasize in much of the above, it is on such grounds where "worlds" come to be, and hence (from thence) where this world—our empirical earth—takes shape for we who dwell thereupon. Yeshua, I take it, is here (at least) making a more far-reaching point than Levine outlines for him.

A final detail I would like to add in support is that in Yeshuan-Judaism, at least on the evidence we have for it (however reliable such may or may not be as indicative of the actual words of Yeshua himself), and contra to Levine, those who have really *do* get more, and those who have not really *do* end up with less. Consider, for example, Matthew 13:10–12 and 25:28–29, and the latter's parallels in both Q and the Jesus Seminar's *Gospel of Jesus*, quoted below in that order and with the extra-biblical documents provided for further buttressing of the argument. (On this issue of additional staunchness, by the way, I would also like to comment that one fault I find in Levine's general analytical approach is that she appears to write in such a manner as to consistently treat the New Testament words of Yeshua as if they actually were (consistently) *his* words, and not words that were (sometimes, maybe often?) put into his mouth by others; given her excellent scholarship I get the feeling that she does this without noticing it (or that I am simply wrong and am failing to spot a nuance), but if that is what is occurring in her thinking on these texts—again, we are assuming this is happening without an awareness of it—then such amounts to a passing over of the very historical question which we must never lose sight of lest we mistakenly revert to an unreflective

---

30. For an overview, see Spira-Savett, "Tzedakah in the Bible," *My Jewish Learning*. Accessed August 10, 2020.

default and/or received view: this is another good reminder of the exquisite care called for in each documentary encounter, a point Levine herself would surely agree with).

While Matthew's initial citation (13:10–12) may at first blush appear only concerned with knowledge, the second (25:28–29)—giving the very same teaching and in almost exactly a doubling of the words used (and hence maybe placed there from elsewhere, another "floating phrase" à la the "last-first, first-last"?)—comes from the parable about a rich man who went on a trip and entrusted certain amounts of money to his servants to invest as they saw fit, which is also the context of Q's and the *Gospel of Jesus'* listings. A similar, but contextless, saying can also be found in *Thomas* and is repeated in the Seminar's *Gospel*, it will also be appended to the below along with its *Gospel of Jesus* parallel. I leave it to the reader to therefore conclude for herself whether each of these (Matthew's chapter thirteen quotation included) might not actually have material implications, or anyway meanings beyond the disciple's notional holdings; requesting too that we ourselves be open to the unnerving elements at play even only in Matthew's first placement on purely mental matters (if it is "purely" on those). Yet, on the other hand, as we read and think about what we find we might discover ourselves compelled to reverse those considerations and take the entire set to be not about the material but about the abstract; again, I ask the reader to decide for herself. Here, then, are the teachings:

> Matthew 13:10–12: [10]Then the disciples came and asked him, "Why do you speak to them [i.e. Yeshua's general audiences] in parables?" [11]He answered, "To you it has been given to know the secrets of the kingdom of heaven, but to them it has not been given. [12]For to those who have, more will be given, and they will have an abundance; but from those who have nothing, even what they have will be taken away."[31]

> Matthew 25:28–29: [The rich man, having returned from his journey and learned how his last servant buried the money entrusted to him and therefore earned nothing extra by making profitable financial use of it, is speaking here] [28]"So take the talent [i.e. a coin] from him, and give it to the one with ten talents. [29]For to all those who have, more will be given, and they will have an abundance; but from those who have nothing, even what they have will be taken away."[32]

> Q81: [The rich man, here a nobleman who has been made a king in another land and thereafter returned, is again speaking]: Turning to the others, he said, "Take the silver coins from him and give them to the fellow who turned ten coins into one hundred."
>
> "But sir!" they protested. "He already has a hundred coins."

---

31. *Thinline Bible with the Apocrypha* (NRSV).
32. *Thinline Bible with the Apocrypha* (NRSV).

"Yes," the king replied, "and to the person who has something, more will be given and that person will have an abundance. The person who has nothing of real value will lose even what he thinks he has."[33]

The Gospel of Jesus 4:36–38:

Money in trust: [36]But his master replied to him [the final servant, who only buried the money he was given], "You incompetent and timid slave! So you knew that I reap where I didn't sow and gather where I didn't scatter, did you? [37]Then you should have taken my money to the bankers. Then when I returned I would have received my capital with interest. [38]So take the money away from this fellow and give it to the one who has the greatest sum."[34]

Thomas, Saying 41: [1]Jesus said, "Whoever has something in hand will be given more, [2]and whoever has nothing will be deprived of even the little that person has."[35]

The Gospel of Jesus 4:22–23:

Have and have not: [22]Jesus used to say: "Those who have something in hand will be given more, [23]and those who have nothing will be deprived of even the little they have."[36]

If we should think Matthew's thirteenth chapter to start and stop with epistemological concerns (or vice versa with the others regarding the mundane), the nearly identical wording of chapter twenty-five (13:12 merely lacks the "all" of 25:29) will surely cause us discomfort—and perhaps that is the aim. If these were indeed Yeshua's phrasings then we might expect them to stick in the memory, and the author(s) (possibly also redactors, editors, et cetera) of the Gospel of Matthew may have found themselves putting the terms to parchment with some measure of shock. What was the sage/rabbi getting at? These readings, regardless of whomever might have uttered them (although their inclusion in Q and *Thomas* do, as indicated, provide some support for Yeshuan authenticity) have tossed us into the air once more; we are confused and dismayed, such are truly "topsy-turvy," and we find ourselves in yet deeper want of being shaken loose from the established patterns of apprehension to which we have been bound and chained, of a further breaking out from the comfortable platitudes of which we assume we have a comprehensional grasp. What is really most disturbing, though, is the manner in which this "topsy-turvy" appears a lot like the world we know only too well, and not like "the kingdom" we have determined we know—or wish to know—from Yeshua. It is only "topsy-turvy" because/if it comes from Yeshua; from a newspaper it would be far too (dreadfully) normal. The poor around us *do* end

---

33. Powelson and Riegert, trans., footnotes, and eds., *The Lost Gospel Q,* 117.
34. Funk and the Jesus Seminar, *The Gospel of Jesus,* 31; the full telling is numbered 4:24–38.
35. Meyer, trans. and intro., *The Gospel of Thomas,* 37.
36. Funk and the Jesus Seminar, *The Gospel of Jesus,* 29.

up losing out, the rich *do* take from the poor, and we *do* want to protest that. Maybe each of these sections then are not, in the end, pertaining to the material, but—following Matthew's thirteenth chapter—are truly about erudition. That might be more comforting, but barely so. Our minds cry for a free path through this thicket.

Towards such a conceptual liberation I think a return to the perspectives held by those in history who laid the groundwork and composed many of the founding texts which we currently base our perceptions on will again be of great assistance, and so let us really travel back, the full way to "the beginning." In a remarkably mind shattering work Catherine Keller relates how the creation accounts in Genesis actually do not present God/"God" as having fashioned the lands, waters, sun, moon, stars, et cetera, out of nothing (from a vacuum), but rather through the use of *already existing* materials—i.e. extant with God/"God" itself and not succeeding divine self-existence—viz. a yet formless "earth," a "deep," and "waters" that God/"God" discovered lying round about.[37] These are listed in Genesis 1:1–2, waiting to be noticed by an observant reader who is able to pull the cobwebs of taught interpretations from her eyes and *see* ("see!") what is actually being expressed in the text. Here is the Tanakh's translation, followed by the New Revised Standard Version:

> [1]When God began to create the heaven and earth—[2]the earth being unformed and void, with darkness over the surface of the deep and a wind from God sweeping over the water –[38]

> [1]In the beginning when God created the heavens and the earth, [2]the earth was a formless void and darkness covered the face of the deep, while a wind from God swept over the face of the waters.[39]

"In the beginning . . . the earth *was*" we are told, there it sat, "formless" and just asking to have something done to it like an inviting lump of wet clay tempting the potter. "Darkness" was over the "face of the deep," and so whatever the "deep" might indicate there it was as well—already there—as were the "waters," which although disturbed on their surface by God's/"God's" wind were placid and real enough to be so subsequently unsettled (without God/"God" having done anything to produce them). In addition, the ancients appear to have considered that it took God/"God" more than one try to arrive at a creation which it was satisfied with enough to declare "good."[40] (e.g. As stated at the end of the account in the first chapter of Genesis where we find the summative sentence (here quoted again first from the Tanakh and then from the New Revised Standard Version): "And God saw all that He had made, and found it

---

37. Keller, *Face of the Deep*; see especially Chapter 1 and the discussions in Part IV.
38. *Tanakh* (NJPS).
39. *Thinline Bible with the Apocrypha* (NRSV).
40. Keller, *Face of the Deep*; Chapters 1 and 2 contextualize and trace creation, including comparatively and with references to liberation and gender issues.

very good"; "God saw everything that he had made, and indeed, it was very good."[41] It seems to me that the labeling of "good" in this verse could either be God's/"God's" or the narrator's, but the weight of context tilts it towards being God's/"God's"; and as an aside, looking around ourselves, we may wonder why it is not given a caveat along the lines of being "good enough" or the like, instead of being outright "good"; but then who are we to question God/"God"?)

Although it would be foolish to take such an account in any kind of literal sense as a record of factual events, what would be equally foolish would be to miss the implications of the picture of God/"God" that this reveals and that was, moreover, precisely the one held by Yeshua and his followers and contemporaries:[42] this is the image they had in mind when they spoke of God/"God" and struggled to work out how to relate to God/"God" and to one another in the setting of first century Palestine: of Israel under the Law as it was understood then, of Israel under Roman rule as it was experienced then. This particular comprehension of the divine, moreover, of God/"God" as extraordinarily powerful but not technically omnipotent (i.e. God/"God" only used for the creation what was available, and apparently did so in an unfolding (multiple tries, almost a "guess and check") methodology rather than all at once—and note too how this also points to a divine non-omniscience: if the outcome could be foreseen then multiple attempts would not be necessary), would continue throughout the entirety of the church's founding years; Caputo informs us it was not altered into the current viewpoint of God/"God" able to magically conjure the universe out of a vacuum until the latter half of the second century CE, and then the notional change only occurred in response to a theological controversy at the time.[43] The results of adopting this viewpoint from out of the circumstances of our more "inflated" contemporary perspective vis-à-vis divine actions and epistemology are a comparative "weakening" of God/"God" who, since it (though of course in first century Jewish and Yeshuan-Jewish thought "he") can have neither the traits of omnipotence nor omniscience, and might therefore be in need—albeit in a highly reduced sense of "need"—of our help in order that human events turn out the way that God/"God" wishes. If such background abstractions were held by Yeshua and his listeners, what effect could that have on how we today read the parables told by him? Moreover, what could it mean on ethical and behavioral dimensions for our twenty-first century day-to-day living if we take ourselves and our efforts as co-creative with the divine? (Which, incidentally, is also an extraordinarily Jewish way to see ("see!") things.[44])

---

41. Genesis 1:31; *Tanakh* (NJPS); *Thinline Bible with the Apocrypha* (NRSV).

42. Amongst others Caputo, *The Weakness of God*, emphasizes this; Funk, *Honest to Jesus*, also gives an illuminating account of the "outer darkness" as a visualized field that was based on a perspective of the Earth as flat and as surrounded by varying celestial layers ringing outwards; see page 75.

43. Caputo, *The Weakness of God*; see especially the discussion on pages 75–83.

44. The Hebrew phrase *tikkun olam*, including its interesting historical roots and somewhat divergent present currency, is broadly illustrative of this, and continued reflection on some of the implied ramifications of what is happening within this term reinforce, I think, the point I wish to make here; see:

Part 3 | Parables and Pictures

Firstly, and I think most importantly for we who are concerned with finding a better way to be on this planet, are the participatory demands being placed upon us by such a ground-laying notional stance. If God/"God" works with what is there (*can only* work with what is there), with what is "within reach" for it, then depending on the variables involved it is quite possible—perhaps even probable—that God's/"God's" will might *not* be done. God/"God", in this story, took the "earth" and the "deep" and the "waters" and fashioned the universe as we know it (metaphorically, of course); therefore had a different "earth" and "deep" and "waters" been in place this universe would be one that we do not know: its end product, as with its constitutive elements, would differ, and the final outcomes would have been otherwise. This is not merely an issue for the inanimate, either. Kugel quotes Psalm 139 as an example of a theology in transition during the period of its writing, of an attempt to rectify God/"God" perceived as "out there" with God/"God" perceived as also "in here" (i.e. as pertains divine relation to the human soul/"soul"); I think in following through on some of Kugel's thoughts on this psalm we can also find an application pertaining to our own philotheology as put into practice in our attempt to generate a conceptual transition cum transformation. The central section, which is most related to our hermeneutical and praxis apperceptions (verses thirteen to sixteen), reads as follows (once more from the Tanakh, then the New Revised Standard Version):

> Psalm 139:13-16: [13]It was You who created my conscience;
>   You fashioned me in my mother's womb.
> [14]I praise You,
>   for I am awesomely, wondrously made;
>   Your work is wonderful;
>   I know it very well.
> [15]My frame was not concealed from You
>   when I was shaped in a hidden place,
>   knit together in the recesses of the earth.
> [16]Your eyes saw my unformed limbs;
>   they were all recorded in Your book;
>   in due time they were formed,
>   to the very last one of them.[45]
>
> Psalm 139:13-16: [13]For it was you who formed my inward parts;
>   you knit me together in my mother's womb.
> [14]I praise you, for I am fearfully and wonderfully made.
>   Wonderful are your works; that I know very well.

"Tikkun Olam," *My Jewish Learning.* Accessed July 15, 2020.

45. *Tanakh* (NJPS). It is remarked in a footnote that "conscience" in the Hebrew is literally "kidneys"; this reminds me of how in Japanese sometimes "stomach" is used for the emotional and mental associative organ always rendered "heart" in English. The final "to the very last of them" is also noted by the Tanakh's editors and translators to have an uncertain Hebrew meaning.

> ¹⁵My frame was not hidden from you, when I was being made in secret,
>   intricately woven in the depths of the earth.
> ¹⁶Your eyes beheld my unformed substance.
>   In your book were written all the days that were formed for me, when
>   none of them as yet existed.[46]

Kugel remarks how "It is not clear whether 'secret place' and the 'bottom of the earth' [Kugel uses his own personal translation; in the quoted versions above the same highlighted terms are given as "hidden place," "secret," "recesses of the earth," and "depths of the earth," respectively] are metaphorical references to the mother's womb or instead suggest that human beings all start off as some sort of prefab homunculus."[47] If the latter were the idea, we may note, then such a "prefab" would clearly fall into the same notional grouping (the manner of thinking about or the understanding of) as the earlier "earth," "deep," and "waters": materials already there and available to be engaged, the limited options with which the—thereby also itself limited—work might be done. This is very compelling in the manner in which it situates God/"God" as involved *with* natural processes rather than being in a position to control, domineer, or even disregard them. If Yeshua took God/"God" like this, then his exhortations for the role(s) we have would be far more focused on our *doing* rather than our knowing (and the mind goes back to our reflections on Matthew 13, 25, Q81, and "Money in trust" above).

Kugel continues his reflections on this passage with "The point is that the psalmist is able to conceive of himself as he was back then—mere matter, *stuff*, waiting to be turned into a human being."[48] Again, this aligns well with what we have been considering pertaining to creation more generally, and the "Your eyes saw my unformed limbs," or "Your eyes beheld my unformed substance" of verse sixteen seems to strengthen the argument for the suggested "weaker" view of God/"God" as *needing to* work with the at-hand, and moreover as an abstraction concurrent within the conceptual realities of the period (and therefore too as a possibility for our own slice of history's pie). God/"God" uses or can use only what is there for it to use: This is a perception of divinity working with and within the networked and interlaced cause-and-effect unfoldings of the cosmos; and an apprehension of God/"God", and of God's/"God's" efforts at completing a transcendent will in this way, is precisely the mental turn that I think is called for in "kingdom" teachings if we are serious about discovering modern applications for them. Such a turn is, additionally, quite effectively reinforced by the ideational holding of a "weak" God/"God" (again, these thoughts apply not only to divinity in the "believe in" sense, but also as force, "call" or Event, et cetera): if we wish to bring (make) "the kingdom" we shall have to work for it, and

---

46. *Thinline Bible with the Apocrypha* (NRSV); no commentary footnotes are included.
47. Kugel, *The God of Old*, 68.
48. Kugel, *The God of Old*, 68; emphasis in the original.

PART 3 | PARABLES AND PICTURES

if we wish that God's/"God's" will be done in our societies and on our shared planet then we shall have to work for it. Yeshua's parables did, and I think certainly still do, indicate some extraordinary *hows* for this.

Furthermore, lest the labeling appear offensive or off-putting, "weak" in our usage and as related to the philotheological position we are aiming to construct, is not to any degree indicative of powerlessness: quite the contrary. It is rather to take the impalpable/indefinable (the other/Other "beyond") as being by nature non-enforcing and non-insistent. A transcendent will, whatever such might "be" or mean—and whatever we might consider its source or level or characteristic of "divinity"—might not happen; it might not even have a shot at happening (and clearly this would assist us in responding to the burdens of theodicy questions as well).[49] On this view God/"God" may push or prod, especially if we seek to partner with it, but it does not *shove*. Understanding numinous desires or plans in a sense like this very much places the onus of effort upon us, as remarked, and does so in a way not dissimilar to how Yeshua's emphasis on "the kingdom" as already is/could be indicates that any situational improvements are in our hands. The tools are there, and we are being urged to pick them up: Do we? For an additional envisioning (a "see!"-ing) of all this, let us now look to two more (and more jarring) Yeshuan expositions: the "Parable of the Mustard Seed," and the "Parable of the Great Banquet."

In light, then, of the above, we will first explore the twisting of the "Mustard Seed" as it grows; and so we begin by quoting this brief analogy from the Synoptic Gospels followed by its version in the Jesus Seminar's *Gospel of Jesus,* and thereafter to its readings in Q and *Thomas*:

> Matthew 13:31–32: [31]He put before them another parable: "The kingdom of heaven is like a mustard seed that someone took and sowed in his field; [32]it is the smallest of all the seeds, but when it has grown it is the greatest of shrubs and becomes a tree, so that the birds of the air come and make nests in its branches."[50]
>
> Mark 4:30–32: [30]He also said, "With what can we compare the kingdom of God, or what parable will we use for it? [31]It is like a mustard seed, which, when sown upon the ground, is the smallest of all the seeds on earth; [32]yet when it is

---

49. That is, the problem of evil's existence, particularly if viewed from a stance of an omnipotent and purely good deity as existentially present and caring about human affairs. This is perhaps also reflected in the many implicit "mays" of the Lord's Prayer (or the Our Father), where "[May] Thy kingdom come", "[May] Thy will be done", "[May you] Give us this day our daily bread", et cetera, all contain wishes for such to occur and the acknowledgement that such might not. See "The Lord's Prayer" on the website *Lords-prayer-words,* where explanations for the sections of the prayer are listed beneath the recitation. Accessed September 18, 2019.

50. *Thinline Bible with the Apocrypha* (NRSV).

HERMENEUTICS: STORYTELLING AND RE-TELLING

sown it grows up and becomes the greatest of all shrubs, and puts forth large branches, so that the birds of the air can make nests in its shade."[51]

Luke 13:18–19: [18]He said therefore, "What is the kingdom of God like? And to what should I compare it? [19]It is like a mustard seed that someone took and sowed in the garden; it grew and became a tree, and the birds of the air made nests in its branches."[52]

The Gospel of Jesus 2:19–20:
   Mustard seed: [19]The disciples said to Jesus, "Tell us what Heaven's imperial rule is like."
   He said to them, "It's like a mustard seed. [20]It's the smallest of all seeds, but when it falls on prepared soil, it produces a large plant, which becomes a shelter for birds of the sky."[53]

Q61: What is the realm of God like? How can I describe it to you? It is like a tiny mustard seed that someone tosses into a garden. It grows into a tree and birds nest in its branches.[54]

Thomas, Saying 20: [1]The followers said to Jesus, "Tell us what heaven's kingdom is like."
   [2]He said to them, "It is like a mustard seed. [3]<It> is the smallest of all seeds, [4]but when it falls on prepared soil, it produces a large plant and becomes a shelter for birds of heaven."[55]

The clearest commonalities here are the small size of the seed, the growing of it into a large shrub or plant or tree, and a home or shelter for birds. Between the *Gospel* and *Thomas* there is also the further identical phrasing of "prepared soil," recalling the "Parable of the Sower" with its various earthen types as found in the canonical Gospels (see Matthew 13:1–23, Mark 4:1–20, and Luke 8:4–15), and, if *Thomas* is as old as scholars think it is, then this may in fact be the root of that image's extension by the Synoptic writers into the other contexts in which they employ it (or it may not, this is only speculation on my part). Many commentators have found a resonance with the avian guests taken to be representative of Gentiles entering the/a "new covenant," but such is a bland and somewhat triumphal, self-congratulatory remark to make and so we shall simply pass it by with the following wink as we go (as Yeshua

---

51. *Thinline Bible with the Apocrypha* (NRSV).
52. *Thinline Bible with the Apocrypha* (NRSV).
53. Funk and the Jesus Seminar, *The Gospel of Jesus*, 17.
54. Powelson and Riegert, trans., footnotes, and eds., *The Lost Gospel Q*, 95.

55. Meyer, trans. and intro., *The Gospel of Thomas*, 31. Meyer uses the bent brackets < > to show where he has corrected a scribal error (or omission) from the original Coptic; see his Introduction on page fourteen, in *The Gospel of Thomas*.

says in *Thomas* 42: "Be passersby."[56]). What is of far more interest, and surely closer to the mark when we recall the historical lessons we have learned in the above study of Yeshua's life and the evidence for not finding in the man himself a desire to found a new religion per se (rather instead to promulgate an alternate view of God/"God", and human-God/"God" plus human-human interrelating), is the seed, its type, and what it does/becomes of it. The birds, I think, can be left to the birds; and although such do appear quite frequently in the New Testament, they also appear quite frequently in the outdoors, thus without being specified beyond merely as "birds of the air/heaven" (or just "birds") we need not overly excite ourselves that some wondrous comment is being made to cause us non-ethnic "Jews" to feel as if we too are somehow "special" or "chosen." We are not; but then—and I think Yeshua would agree—no one is; while at the same time absolutely everyone is.

What I think is particularly worth noting about the other elements here is that the mustard seed is presented as "the smallest," as "tiny," and yet it enlarges naturally. Apparently quite easily too, requiring little care as every gardener knows; and the yield of mustard has moreover traditionally been considered to have many health benefits, positives which modern science has reaffirmed.[57] Perhaps, then, we should read thusly: Although we are each insignificant ("tiny") in our own eyes, and likely too in the eyes of others (maybe especially our spouses!), what we are and what we do nevertheless have effects well beyond what we may assume from the perspectives we take of ourselves. The world is a thoroughly interlinked place, a web of connections stretching vastly wider and deeper than might be comprehended by a single lifespan and its experiences, and we therefore simply cannot know the vast good (or, sadly, the potentially bad) that results from what we engage in.[58] We grow, and we do the work that comes to us, hopefully as well as we might; may the birds come and take some shelter therein: any aftereffects are "out of our hands."

In the thinking on "the kingdom" that we have engaged in thus far, we have witnessed time and again how its nudgings are far more towards acting than they are towards believing (although both elements are indeed present), and further how its social relating is geared to being non-wealth and non-rank distinguishing: we are simultaneously urged to share the material and not to care (especially not to worry) about it. God/"God" provides; the natural world knows what it must: the seed grows, birds find rest, medicine is produced, everyone benefits. The sowing/falling into the (prepared) soil is what is needed, which is to indicate the initial act. Be "the kingdom," as it were, and see ("see!") what happens. Levine puts this nicely: "don't ask 'when' the kingdom comes or 'where' it is. The when is in its own good time—as long as it takes

---

56. Meyer, trans. and intro., *The Gospel of Thomas*, 39.

57. Pleasant, "The Benefits of Growing Mustard", *GrowVeg*; also "Is Mustard Good for You?" *healthline*. Both websites accessed July 17, 2020.

58. I stress (in a probably tryingly repetitive way) this aspect of the self's extraordinarily contextualized position in Oberg, *Blurred*, but on a more purely mathematical side as pertains to statistical probabilities and outcomes within complex environments, see also Mlodinow, *The Drunkard's Walk*.

for seed to sprout... The where is that it is already present, inchoate, in the world. The kingdom is present when humanity and nature work together."[59] This of course reminds us also of *Thomas* 113: "the father's kingdom is spread out upon the earth, and people do not see it."[60] Yeshua's teaching here works on both sides of the human-human, human-divine axes of relation: we do what is right by others, placing the seed of self into the ground of society, and then trust to the process. Sooner or later good will come, rest will be found, positives will develop (perhaps surprisingly so), and unforeseen many will enjoy the windfall. *Do*, and then *be*; *be*, and then *do*: act because one is, and so are she, you, they, we. "The kingdom" finds its place exactly where we have and have not been looking for it.

Let us take this mustard "condiment" in hand then as we cross the threshold into the "Parable of the Great Banquet," which again will be presented first from its canonical source (Luke in this case; Matthew has the somewhat similar "Parable of the Wedding Banquet"—see the accompanying note below—but as will be evidenced from a reading of it, such is most certainly not our "Banquet" (although for reasons unclear to me it is often grouped with Luke's "Banquet" in commentaries and compilations)), thence from *The Gospel of Jesus*, Q, and finally *The Gospel of Thomas*, respectively:

> Luke 14:15–24: [15]One of the dinner guests [Luke has situated Yeshua narratively as being at the home of a "leader of the Pharisees" (14:1) for a Sabbath meal; Luke (unfortunately, polemically) plays the setting as the Pharisees seeking to entrap Yeshua], on hearing this, said to him, "Blessed is anyone who will eat bread in the kingdom of God!" [16]Then Jesus said to him, "Someone gave a great dinner and invited many. [17]At the time for the dinner he sent his slave to say to those who had been invited, 'Come; for everything is ready now.' [18]But they all alike began to make excuses. The first said to him, 'I have bought a piece of land, and I must go out and see it; please accept my regrets.' [19]Another said, 'I have bought five yoke of oxen, and I am going to try them out; please accept my regrets.' [20]Another said, 'I have just been married, and therefore I cannot come.' [21]So the slave returned and reported this to his master. Then the owner of the house became angry and said to his slave, 'Go out at once into the streets and lanes of the town and bring in the poor, the crippled, the blind, and the lame.' [22]And the slave said, 'Sir, what you have ordered has been done, and there is still room.' [23]Then the master said to the slave, 'Go out into the roads and lanes, and compel people to come in, so that my house may be filled. [24]For I tell you, none of those who were invited will taste my dinner.'"[61]

---

59. Levine, *Short Stories by Jesus*, 182.

60. Meyer, trans. and intro., *The Gospel of Thomas*, 63.

61. *Thinline Bible with the Apocrypha* (NRSV); cf. Matthew's similar, but markedly different (and frankly disturbingly so with its violent overtones), Parable of the Wedding Banquet (22:1–14): "1Once more Jesus spoke to them in parables, saying: 2'The kingdom of heaven may be compared to a king who gave a wedding banquet for his son. 3He sent his slaves to call those who had been invited to the wedding banquet, but they would not come. 4Again he sent other slaves, saying, "Tell those who have been invited: Look, I have prepared my dinner, my oxen and my fat calves have been slaughtered, and

Part 3 | Parables and Pictures

The Gospel of Jesus 2:9–17:

Kingdom banquet: ⁹Jesus used to tell this parable:

Someone was giving a big dinner and invited many guests. ¹⁰At the dinner hour the host sent his slave to tell the guests: "Come, it's ready now." ¹¹But one by one they all began to make excuses. The first said to him, "I just bought a farm, and I have to go and inspect it; please excuse me." ¹²And another said, "I just bought five pairs of oxen, and I'm on my way to check them out; please excuse me." ¹³And another said, "I just got married, and so I cannot attend." ¹⁴So the slave came back and reported these excuses to his master. ¹⁵Then the master of the house got angry and instructed his slave: "Quick! Go out into the streets and alleys of the town, and usher in the poor, the crippled, the blind, and the lame."

¹⁶And the slave said, "Sir, your orders have been carried out, and there's still room."

¹⁷And the master said to the slave, "Then go out into the roads and the country lanes, and force people to come in so my house will be filled."[62]

Q68: A man once gave a great banquet and invited many guests. As the dinner hour approached, he sent a servant to tell them, "Come, everything is ready now." One by one, they started making excuses. The first guest told the servant, "I'm sorry but I just bought a piece of land and have to go see it."

Another guest said, "You'll have to excuse me, I'm on my way to take a look at five pairs of oxen that I've purchased."

A third guest explained, "I just got married and I can't come."

The servant returned to tell the host about all these excuses.

In a fit of anger, the man shouted, "Go out right now into the streets and alleys and invite the poor, the crippled, the blind and the lame."

Soon, the servant reported back, "I've carried out your orders, but there is still room."

---

everything is ready; come to the wedding banquet." 5But they made light of it and went away, one to his farm, another to his business, 6while the rest seized his slaves, mistreated them, and killed them. 7The king was enraged. He sent his troops, destroyed those murderers, and burned their city. 8Then he said to his slaves, "The wedding is ready, but those invited were not worthy. 9Go therefore into the main streets, and invite everyone you find to the wedding banquet." 10Those slaves went out into the streets and gathered all whom they found, both good and bad; so the wedding hall was filled with guests. 11But when the king came in to see the guests, he noticed a man there who was not wearing a wedding robe [I must interject here; how could he have been appropriately dressed when he had just been called in from off the streets? Matthew's account is indeed a puzzling one.], 12and he said to him, "Friend, how did you get in here without a wedding robe?" And he was speechless. 13Then the king said to the attendants, "Bind him hand and foot, and throw him into the outer darkness, where there will be weeping and gnashing of teeth." 14For many are called, but few are chosen." *Thinline Bible with the Apocrypha* (NRSV).

62. Funk and the Jesus Seminar, *The Gospel of Jesus*, 17.

"Then go farther out to the roads and country lanes," the man responded, "and lead people back until my house is filled. But not one of those original guests will share this feast."[63]

Thomas, Saying 64: [1]Jesus said, "A person was receiving guests. When he had prepared the dinner, he sent his servant to invite the guests.

[2]"The servant went to the first and said to that one, 'My master invites you.'

[3]"That person said, 'Some merchants owe me money; they are coming to me tonight. I must go and give them instructions. Please excuse me from dinner.'

[4]"The servant went to another and said to that one, 'My master has invited you.'

[5]"That person said to the servant, 'I have bought a house and I have been called away for a day. I shall have no time.'

[6]"The servant went to another and said to that one, 'My master invites you.'

[7]"That person said to the servant, 'My friend is to be married and I am to arrange the banquet. I shall not be able to come. Please excuse me from dinner.'

[8]"The servant went to another and said to that one, 'My master invites you.'

[9]"That person said to the servant, 'I have bought an estate and I am going to collect the rent. I shall not be able to come. Please excuse me.'

[10]"The servant returned and said to his master, 'The people whom you invited to dinner have asked to be excused.'

[11]"The master said to his servant, 'Go out on the streets and bring back whomever you find to have dinner.'

[12]"Buyers and merchants [will] not enter the places of my father."[64]

There are many points of interest to this longer parable, but possibly none more so than the starkness of *Thomas'* very different take on it. Prior to thinking on that outlier, however, let us examine the remarkable alignment of Luke, the *Gospel,* and Q. To start with, we can leave aside Luke's framing of the story as a sort of rejoinder to the setting's Pharisee householder (ironically—though one doubts purposely so—holding his own banquet; we recall too that we have even suggested Yeshua himself was a type of "unofficial" Pharisee), and focus instead on the contents of the narrative proper. The invited guests' excuses are the same across the board: land purchase, oxen purchase, just married; the would-be host reacts with anger and instructs his slave/servant to recruit other dinner guests from amongst the disenfranchised and disabled that can be found nearby; thereafter, with seats yet to be filled, to go out again—and seemingly anyone will now do, regardless of the earlier apparently charity based concerns for selection—and bring in still more; and, intriguingly on this concluding aspect, Luke and the *Gospel* have this last grouping be "compelled" or "forced" (respectively) to go

---

63. Powelson and Riegert, trans., footnotes, and eds., *The Lost Gospel Q,* 102–3.
64. Meyer, trans. and intro., *The Gospel of Thomas,* 49.

Part 3 | Parables and Pictures

in and eat, whereas Q has them being "led" (far gentler) into the banquet. Luke and Q then end with the comment that no one originally invited will participate, while the *Gospel* simply finishes with the final set of instructions. If the statement on "none of those invited" was intended by the author(s)/redactor(s)/editor(s) to be a kind of moral or summative teaching, then it is tempting to consider it—as not a few have done—to be an anti-Semitic one about the "chosen people" being replaced in their "chosenness" (especially in Luke with his derogatory setup of the poor Pharisee), and indeed many commentators have produced interpretations alleging just this. As with our birds claimed to be Gentiles above though, let us again underscore how mindless and distasteful an understanding like that is and leave it there. Instead we will attempt to go a bit deeper with our intertwining trio, and then thereafter take another look at *Thomas'* altogether alternative treatment.

We note how in none of these tellings, not even in Luke where our forlorn Pharisee raises the "kingdom of God" wording and makes himself a target by doing so, does the parable start with "the kingdom of Heaven is like" (or some such parallel phrasing), and while this should signal an interpretive caution to us there is still something very "kingdom-y" going on here. Nevertheless, the correlation not being directly made, I think it would be unwise to take our homeowner and feast master here as a signifier for God, and possibly we ought to avoid too comprehending him as an exemplar or a role model in the vein we did with the "Vineyard's" central character. The excuses relayed to the slave/servant are after all fair enough; why react with anger? We are given no background and thus cannot surmise that the guests knew when the date of the banquet would be and should have gotten ready. Perhaps they merely went about their various businesses and then—lo and behold—with terrible timing the meal just happened to fall when X had bought some land, Y had acquired some livestock, and Z had stood beneath the chuppah and committed herself to far more trouble than she could have imagined (I jest!). Surely none of that warrants the lividness described, unless possibly the response was directed more at the idea of the preparations going to waste than it was at the invitees; and, if so, that would appear to furthermore nullify the Luke and Q "none of those invited" assertion: from a generous point of view—and "the kingdom" is a place of generosity—this is a positive result.

In pausing to reflect a bit more on the cancelling of that assumed proposition is where we can also see a "kingdom" ethos peeking through the guest hall curtains of this tale. For one reason or another the man's friends cannot share in the blessings he has at hand; but little matter because that certainly does not mean that no one can: there are needy and no doubt grateful persons just outside the door who would be only too happy to enjoy a sumptuous dinner free of charge (and we recognize that they are neither "compelled" nor "forced" but rather are "brought" and "ushered" in). What is had *will be shared*, and to as many recipients as possible, even beyond the number of the truly needy. Once more, everyone benefits, nothing is wasted: not a morsel spoiled. What there is shall be distributed, as we encountered with the daily wages of the "Vineyard" and the shade from the sprouted "Mustard Seed." More curious to me are those pressuring terms ("compel" and "force") used in conjunction with the final seat fillers in the Luke and *Gospel of Jesus* versions.

A number of possibilities may present themselves if we are creative. With our man taken not as a role model, it could be that he is used here instead to indicate someone whose heart is in the right place (wanting to share), but whose methodology is mistaken (enforced generosity). On the other hand he might indeed be a role model, only of the negative sort: wanting to "do the right thing" so badly that he does wrong in disrespecting others' freedom of choice (e.g. the "I know best" type of condescension that rarely results in bringing about original intentions, no matter how noble they might have been). Similarly this could be a teaching against egocentricity: "Praise me, for see what I have done!" and/or "Look at how beloved I am: my house is filled to the brim!" In these musings we should notice that even if our master is not quite a "kingdom" personage, we may wish or expect him to be: the underlying societal/communal lesson wherein anyone is a (potential) guest and friend remains, and in that the human-human axis of our dual Yeshuan relating is emphasized. Maybe, then, the host here is simply a work in progress; as are we all.

Let us close with the *Gospel of Thomas'* banquet and its oddities. The structuring of the story is obviously the same, and because so we can probably more or less safely assume a common source. The *Thomas* producer(s), however, seem to have something of an anti-mercantile bone to pick, and if so such may be more reflective of the peculiar conditions of the Coptic-speaking group that either created and/or circulated the text than with Yeshua and his Hebrew Palestinian/Aramaic setting as reflected in the first three versions. The excuses are mostly unique, but still with shades of the same: "people owe me money and are coming to pay," "I bought a house and have been called away" (to go inspect it? there must be some connection between those clauses . . .), "my friend is getting married and I have to help prepare for the ceremony," "I have renters to attend to." I suppose that in each of the parable's reported speeches above one could arguably make the case that the overarching theme is an anti-economic sentiment (i.e. aside from the "just married"—and therefore presumably home-focused—the excuses outlined in the literature could be understood as financial in nature to varying degrees), but that line appears especially pronounced in *Thomas*, and the point—in case one were dull enough to miss it—is then hammered home in the conclusion.

With that, moreover, the narrative's emphasis on an indiscriminate and socially responsive and responsible generosity goes entirely amiss; more is the pity. This is one of the rare instances, incidentally, where as a reader I find the otherwise almost always heartfelt and subtly moving *Gospel of Thomas* to be disappointing. If the "Parable of the Great Banquet" is a genuine Yeshuan saying, and given its multiple attestations and historical vetting it likely is, then perhaps when the *Thomas* writer(s) was attempting to recall it she had just been cheated out of some money and was nursing a

Part 3 | Parables and Pictures

grudge. This is a sad thought, but I am glad to have had it and to share it, because it reminds us how the parables of Yeshua—and indeed the broader literary picture of these and every other ancient text, no matter how sacred some may or may not take them to be—are human stories of human relation and should therefore always, always be approached critically while yet open-mindedly. God/"God" might say something to us through anything, but as soon as we enclose it inside the strictures of particular words ascribed to it and fastened to specific conceptual associations, we cease to let anything wholly "holy" purely *be*. Existence flows, and the divine/"divine" voice or call or nudge or whisper—or whatever—must be free to do so as well.

At the close of our parables, our parabolic prancing, what might we discover about this "kingdom"? Possibly the primary lesson is that while there is nothing "fair" about it, such is a thing of beauty: people are paid far more than anyone could hope for, the insignificant rises to unpredictable heights, unexpected gifts suddenly land in one's lap (and belly!): the entire oeuvre is counterintuitive to say the least. Yet what appears to hold it together is genuine concern for one's fellow, and an unwavering trust that at the end of the day (however long or short the "day" might be) everything will be fine. This was also the vision of the medieval mystic Julian of Norwich,[65] and so possibly—just maybe—it is a lesson that God/"God" (again, in whatever way we are able to take that heavily loaded term: as Being/a being; as a call, a force; as an underpinning, a movement, et cetera, et cetera) would have us learn. This God/"God", furthermore, we have argued is "weak" enough (or self-lowering enough) to require our help: it can only use what it finds about itself. If "the kingdom" is to be built, we shall have to dirty our hands and not simply keep them folded in prayer.

In another context, but very much along these ideascapes, the immanent avatar of Krishna—acting as chariot driver—advises the warrior Arjuna: "let thy aim be the good of all, and then carry on thy task in life."[66] Do we know our task? How might we learn it? What else might we learn from it? Let us recall our Yeshuan-Jewish focus, our overall thesis of a re-enfolding within the Judaic tent for this now weathered construct we call Christianity, and henceforth cast our view back onto the figure of Yeshua himself, to the stories told not by him but about him, and to the envisaging such have been given in the received artistic heritage. As we look and think and feel, what happens? Do we "see!" thereby, or merely *see*? In the next chapter we will lay aside the verbal and gaze again as a gaze: a visual perception, a return to the image and the phenomenological enlacing thence brought.

---

65. Julian was a cloistered nun (an anchoress) who claimed to have a series of visions while on what was taken to be her deathbed in the year 1373, after which she fully recovered and then later entered church service; the reference here is to the following passage: "But Jesus, who in this vision informed me of everything needful to me, answered with these words and said, 'Sin is befitting, but all shall be well, and all shall be well, and all manner of things shall be well.'" Windeatt, trans., *Julian of Norwich*, 74. This is taken from "The Long Text" section of the book, which forms the reworking and re-wording of her visions many years after first penning them in what thereafter came to be called "The Short Text."

66. Mascaró, trans. and intro., Brodbeck, new intro., *The Bhagavad Gita*, 19 (3:20b).

Chapter 10

ART AND INTERACTION(S)

". . . for, opposite the sensuous world, the intelligible world is not so much a different world as it is outside the world."

GEORGES BATAILLE[1]

IN THIS CHAPTER WE will concern ourselves primarily with the senses and with their interacting; and amongst the five easily familiar from everyday experience we will single out perhaps the most relied upon for the majority of us—vision—and then further the most often overlooked "sense" (the sixth, as it were) as being the full sense it in fact is: *thought;* which after all is like the other five in the data it provides to the brain and in what the brain does with such; we tend to miss that, I think, since this particular data generator is considerably less noticeable than the others, buried too deeply as it is. What we have endeavored thus far in our study is an offering of alternatives, of ideas otherwise and the place and importance of ideas, of how ideas (notion/events) shape and structure our lives, giving form to the worlds we inhabit (lifeworlds), and creating the cosmoses we indwell and from which we peer outwards, blinking heavily in the conceptual glare. We know these abstractions from the inside, as it were, from personal and day-to-day phenomenology; yet there is another side to these ideas, and its contents are (perhaps surprisingly) every bit empirical and physical, approachable to our non-mental senses, and would even be touchable were they not so tiny. This, then, is an issue of the physiological: but in that out of sight—as we know—makes out of mind, and thus in order to do justice to the artworks (the image-ideas/idea-images) which we will look upon in this chapter, we will firstly need to look upon (to "see!") the brain, becoming neuroscientists before we can become neuroartists; for that prefix, indeed, is the key to everything.

A neuron is a unique form of cell; and mammalian (and other similarly advanced) brains have been blessed with a great array of these organizational master tools. Although they are not necessary for the sustenance of life, neurons are extremely

1. Bataille, *Theory of Religion*, 73–74.

beneficial in the increased efficacy they lend to the organisms that are able to employ them for referential and planning activities, providing representational "maps" for the brain's processing networks to engage with.[2] That the term "network" is plural in the previous sentence, incidentally, is highly significant. Although there is not a single, universally accepted picture of how the brain works, at present there is a consensus which indicates that our brains consist of a vast web of interconnected sections, each in constant communication with the others to varying degrees at varying moments, and the whole is interlaced beautifully and efficiently into what Michael S. Gazzaniga has termed a "constellation of consciousness systems" (this view is loosely known as the modular model of the brain, wherein there is no single central processor or headquarters, but rather many local "offices" that each relate to and link with many others).[3]

A processing network is not, however, a consciousness network; yet the two do work hand-in-hand, and thus if the latter's primary label ("consciousness") is brought into a clearer definition the narrow line between the two should become apparent enough. The difficulty in this, I think, lies in the common usage of "consciousness" or "conscious" to equal "awareness" or "aware"; whereas—if we take what cognitive science offers and judiciously apply it to our thinking on the matter—it would be far better to exchange the vulgar sense of "consciousness" purely for the word "awareness," and then to maintain "consciousness" for the specialist notation of the aforementioned underlying connectivity within a creature's grey matter. Thought, analysis, rationality, et cetera, enter into our lives at the level of awareness, but grounding (supporting, enabling) these abilities is consciousness, or more properly the "constellation" of conscious*nesses,* the entire webbed flowing (pulsing?) of the modes. This in turn entails, furthermore, that consciousness as such might reasonably be thought to be ongoing as long as one of the modal units is engaged in processing work, activities which occur in some areas of the brain even while one is passed out, in deep sleep, or otherwise non-regularly functioning: and hence certainly unaware. To repeat: consciousness is not awareness; awareness is possible because of and reliant upon consciousness; that which is done in/with awareness can however affect the results of deeper processing in the manners described earlier (Chapter 5), through the altering of intuitive judgments and emotional affixations to reactions and responses.[4] It is at this point that we swing back to neurons and must continue our discussion of them and their central place.

The neuronal "maps" mentioned above consist of groups of these cells that activate or deactivate in response to environmentally embedded bodily conditions ("turned

---

2. Damásio, *Self Comes to Mind,* gives much detail on neurons and the "maps" discussed in this section; see especially Chapter 3.

3. Gazzaniga, *Who's In Charge?* For another entirely readable summary of what seems to be the general consensus view (but naturally with differences in the details amongst various researchers and their own accounts), see also: Ramachandran, *The Tell-Tale Brain.*

4. For an extensive argument of the very brief (and somewhat truncated) summary given here, see Oberg, *Blurred,* particularly Chapters 2 and 5.

(or "switched") on/off") is a frequent way the phenomenon is referenced), and the triggers for such include both external situational concerns and internal situational concerns. Through this process the representative tokens that have been produced, and/or have been/are being altered (the "maps"), are employed as a primary means by which the brain conducts its analyses, thus enhancing efficiency and effectiveness. If we recall Lycan and his "intentional inexistents," we can see (hopefully "see!") how our second order thoughts arise from these groups of specialized and mentally directed cellular agents: and on this we tread carefully with terminology because it is important to remember that these cells are not "mental" (in an aethereal sense), they are physical, biochemical: objects in the world quite unlike the Lycan-al example of "the sky" (outlined in Chapter 5). The second order, the thinking, is what our brain does with neurons in order to better move and be in the surrounds in which it finds itself (that is, in which one finds oneself: the embodied you or I): the cognitions, the "turning on/off," gives rise to the resulting conceptualities (signposts and markers) through which we then mentally—via the abstract, higher, emergent level of awareness—experience our lives. It will be clear that what we have discovered is the physical basis for thought, the chemical grounding of mind, the biology of consciousness; and moreover done so in such a way that further speculation on the universality of consciousness as itself a force of nature (such as one can find within strands of panpsychist arguments) is not here necessary. In the usage of and interaction with neuron-composed representational "maps," the areas of data processing within the brain yield the percepts ("qualia") of the multitudinous unfoldings that phenomenologically we associate with thinking, and with the "inner voice" which is our truest companion across these finite years we each traverse. It all comes from these particularized cells.

Returning again to Haidt's psychological model outlined above (see again our Chapter 5), we recall too the role of intuitive judgments and emotional associations/tags in decision-making and behavior generation as expedients for moving a creature towards greater efficiency and an increased likelihood of thriving (or at least surviving). Working with the overarching framework that is emerging from this twin exploration of neuronal "maps" and automatic cognitive processing, we note that while there are many organisms on our shared Earth that do, like us, operate through the rapid and effective layer of intuition as data processor, some do not yet have the specialist type of cells (the neurons), and thus lack the concept generating prowess thereby granted with its attendant notionally based experience of being. While such life forms operate successfully from an evolutionary point of view, they do so shallowly, we might say; non-rationally. For us, and perhaps for other animals near enough like us to also have some degree of neuronal "maps," the self-observed situation of existence is enhanced through further sensual linkages: just as our intuitive judgments are typically connected to our emotions through the systems of organic data processing, and therefore carry an experiential "feel" to them, so too our "maps" become affectively charged; which is to indicate that our thoughts do: those neuronal groupings which when "turned on" become "felt" as mental events that seem to supersede the biochemical status of their origin; this aspect is not, in fact, source but full actuality (i.e. the biology is not *at* the core nor even *in* the core; the "core" is the whole, albeit one commonly mistaken for a part). Again, it is all the particularized cells.

What I am attempting to argue here is that there is no "extra" to consciousness or to mind; it only appears that way in our lived realities due to the means by which our brains involve our selves with our externals: the notional level we operate on as the form of particular data processing animals that we are. By purely empirical considerations, the level of the mental is either an illusion or it is something very close to one (the physics grant only the biochemical); however—and this is absolutely crucial—by *phenomenologically empirical* considerations the level of the mental is not only real (or "real"), it is central: it is the fullness of being. Our mistake is to conclude from this day-to-day factor of human suchness (if we do so conclude, and it is common enough to do so) that what we know "from the inside" must also exist on the "outside"; that awareness (active thinking) must have its parallel in the greater cosmos of provables and measureables. Now perhaps it does; but the question, I think, ought to be kept open since all that can definitively be stated is that the concepts, ideas, notion/events, qualia, et cetera, with which we are intimately familiar *are*—biochemically, scientifically speaking—masses of neurons; and that is it. Our grandiose and wonderful worlds, our universes of thought, come down to a particular type of uniquely functioning biological cell. The metaphysics melts into the physics. God/"God" may not be behind the idea, but a neuron certainly is; yet that does not in turn indicate a response which is an abandonment of *the idea of* God/"God": it might be—and it certainly may feel—that God/"God" is behind the neuron. I do not intend to eliminate any mystery from our world (or further, our "worlds" in the Heideggerean sense) through this analysis and appended musings; I only wish to clarify the positioning for the sake of what is to follow. On that, and hopefully with the received cobwebs regarding consciousness and thinking that our tradition has yielded now brushed away, we undertake the "what is to follow."

We are biological machines built for abstractions; we carry these abstractions into each interaction, engagement, perception of every moment of life; we see and we think we see, and thereby do not truly "see!"; such is our conditioning. The challenge, of course, is to remove these blinders to the extent that we can, and thus we will henceforth experimentally attempt just such an enlightening in the remainder of this chapter, taking the image-idea/idea-image through a series of notion/events, hoping to therefrom shatter the enclosed and learn (to equip ourselves with) a methodology which can later be applied elsewhere as need and desire dictate. For this we will turn again to our main character of Yeshua, and to the conceptual-narrative burdens Christianity has placed on this long dead Jew (that final clause will hopefully be jarring enough for readers who need the shock: what comes next requires preparation).

Art and Interaction(s)

Central to the myths surrounding the historical Yeshua as we have studied him in the preceding is the so-called Passion Week, the period between his "triumphal entry" into Jerusalem[5] and his execution, those sections in the Gospels which demonstrate such exquisite plotting and developmental arc that one could almost say they had been made up: which is naturally the point. Conventional wisdom has it that when a story is too good to be true it usually is, and that certainly applies here; in any literal sense, at the very least, while admitting that there might be elements of historicity involved here and there in the tellings (although we will likely never be able to find out how much and where), and further that whatever the empirical case with such elements as the "entry" device may be, Yeshua does seem to have made his way to the capital and was there executed. Our concern is not with the beginning of this period, however, but rather with a part closer to its end: the scene in the Garden of Gethsemane.

I want to focus on this vignette as we have received it for the primary reason of its relationship(-building) to the artwork that has been created in reference to it. In my view the contents of the Gethsemane tale are so idea-heavy, have become so overwrought and affectively laden throughout the years, that without those particulars the image-ideas/idea-images of the pictures become quite banal, even boring. However, as it shall be argued, if the standard image-ideas/idea-images are jettisoned and the same works are nevertheless thereafter approached again alternatively, a remarkable turn may—could—take place. An instructive move, a switch, a flip, a new appreciation of Yeshua and Yeshuanism (as it were), an indicator of the Yeshuan-Judaism we wish to have (re)considered as a part of the world's existing Judaisms. These concepts, after all, are bound by nothing but the extant shapes of our neuronal groupings, reformulations are imminently possible; and from them, who knows but what might be. I have therefore selected a small number of examples of these images to be examined in the coming pages, and through the accompanying interplays and analyses the above mentioned effort at a riddance of notional limitations and suggestions for other understandings will be made. This is of course not intended to replace one orthodoxy with another, but simply to remove and reply. No reader need, nor should, take any of this (indeed, nor of the entire book!) as anything more than a whispered "maybe," a rumination offered in faith, without force.

To start, let us recount the Gethsemane setting as relayed in Mark (the probable source of all the renditions), then to Matthew and finally on to Luke: the three Synoptic Gospels.[6] We will quote here purely from the canonical material since, as

---

5. See Matthew 21:1–11, Mark 11:1–11, Luke 19:28–44, and John 12:12–19; interestingly, and revealingly, Luke adds an insult to the Pharisees in his telling, followed by a chilling prophecy for the city (verses thirty-nine through forty-four), while John omits the descent from the Mount of Olives portion and has only a very slight jab at the Pharisees. The reader will recall that we have suggested Yeshua himself fits into the general Pharisaic mould of a non-elite, reforming subsection of Jewish teachers.

6. There is a somewhat similar anecdote in John, but it does not name the locale as Gethsemane (like Luke too, which lists only the Mount of Olives), instead placing the events in a garden "across the Kidron valley" (which geographically could still refer to the same place), while also omitting any series

noted, this story appears to be entirely fictional and hence other more historically reliable—and therefore stripped-down—ancient documents (or their reconstructions) do not contain it. The scene takes place in Mark 14:32–42, Matthew 26:36–46, and Luke 22:39–46. In that order then, taking each from the New Revised Standard Version we have been using (and without also citing the New Living Translation as our aims here are not for any textual comparison):

> Mark 14:32–42: ³²They [Yeshua and his disciples] went to a place called Gethsemane; and he said to his disciples, "Sit here while I pray." ³³He took with him Peter and James and John, and began to be distressed and agitated. ³⁴And he said to them, "I am deeply grieved, even to death; remain here, and keep awake." ³⁵And going a little farther, he threw himself on the ground and prayed that, if it were possible, the hour might pass from him. ³⁶He said, "Abba, Father, for you all things are possible; remove this cup from me; yet, not what I want, but what you want." ³⁷He came and found them sleeping; and he said to Peter, "Simon, are you asleep? Could you not keep awake one hour? ³⁸Keep awake and pray that you may not come into the time of trial; the spirit indeed is willing, but the flesh is weak." ³⁹And again he went away and prayed, saying the same words. ⁴⁰And once more he came and found them sleeping, for their eyes were very heavy; and they did not know what to say to him. ⁴¹He came a third time and said to them, "Are you still sleeping and taking your rest? Enough! The hour has come; the Son of Man is betrayed into the hands of sinners. ⁴²Get up, let us be going. See, my betrayer is at hand."⁷

> Matthew 26:36–46: ³⁶Then Jesus went with them to a place called Gethsemane; and he said to his disciples, "Sit here while I go over there and pray." ³⁷He took with him Peter and the two sons of Zebedee, and began to be grieved and agitated. ³⁸Then he said to them, "I am deeply grieved, even to death; remain here, and stay awake with me." ³⁹And going a little farther, he threw himself on the ground and prayed, "My Father, if it is possible, let this cup pass from me; yet not what I want, but what you want." ⁴⁰Then he came to the disciples and

---

of prayers prior to the arrest and focusing almost exclusively on the arrest itself. John's account reads as follows (18:1–11): "1After Jesus had spoken these words, he went out with his disciples across the Kidron valley to a place where there was a garden, which he and his disciples entered. 2Now Judas, who betrayed him, also knew the place, because Jesus often met there with his disciples. 3So Judas brought a detachment of soldiers together with police from the chief priests and the Pharisees, and they came there with lanterns and torches and weapons. 4Then Jesus, knowing all that was to happen to him, came forward and asked them, 'Whom are you looking for?' 5They answered, 'Jesus of Nazareth.' Jesus replied, 'I am he.' Judas, who betrayed him, was standing with them. 6When Jesus said to them, 'I am he,' they stepped back and fell to the ground. 7Again he asked them, 'Whom are you looking for?' And they said, 'Jesus of Nazareth.' 8Jesus answered, 'I told you that I am he. So if you are looking for me let these men go.' 9This was to fulfill the word that he had spoken, 'I did not lose a single one of those whom you gave me.' 10Then Simon Peter, who had a sword, drew it, struck the high priest's slave, and cut off his right ear. The slave's name was Malchus. 11Jesus said to Peter, 'Put your sword back into its sheath. Am I not to drink the cup that the Father has given me?'" *Thinline Bible with the Apocrypha* (NRSV).

7. *Thinline Bible with the Apocrypha* (NRSV).

found them sleeping; and he said to Peter, "So, could you not stay awake with me one hour? ⁴¹Stay awake and pray that you may not come into the time of trial; the spirit indeed is willing, but the flesh is weak." ⁴²Again he went away for the second time and prayed, "My Father, if this cannot pass unless I drink it, your will be done." ⁴³Again he came and found them sleeping, for their eyes were heavy. ⁴⁴So leaving them again, he went away and prayed for the third time, saying the same words. ⁴⁵Then he came to the disciples and said to them, "Are you still sleeping and taking your rest? See, the hour is at hand, and the Son of Man is betrayed into the hands of sinners. ⁴⁶Get up, let us be going. See, my betrayer is at hand."⁸

Luke 22:39–46: ³⁹He came out and went, as was his custom, to the Mount of Olives; and the disciples followed him. ⁴⁰When he reached the place, he said to them, "Pray that you may not come into the time of trial." ⁴¹Then he withdrew from them about a stone's throw, knelt down, and prayed, ⁴²"Father, if you are willing, remove this cup from me; yet, not my will but yours be done." ⁴³Then an angel from heaven appeared to him and gave him strength. ⁴⁴In his anguish he prayed more earnestly, and his sweat became like great drops of blood falling down on the ground [a footnote indicates that verses forty-three and forty-four are not found in every manuscript]. ⁴⁵When he got up from prayer, he came to the disciples and found them sleeping because of grief, ⁴⁶and he said to them, "Why are you sleeping? Get up and pray that you may not come into the time of trial."⁹

Aside from the angel and the sweating of blood in Luke's variation (which, as indicated, are not details widely shared by the oldest manuscripts; scholars even hold them to likely be insertions created by a later scribe[10]), as well as his vaguer geographic setting (somewhere on the Mount of Olives rather than the more specific "a place called Gethsemane" (Mark 14:32, Matthew 26:36)), all three narratives are remarkably similar. However this kinship is not, naturally, necessarily indicative of a grounding in provable and remembered events, and—as will be shortly outlined—quite the opposite appears to be the case here. Instead, the parallelism found in the above point to Matthew and Luke having taken their material from Mark. We have mentioned that amongst the Synoptic Gospels, it is Mark which has the earliest composition date, and furthermore the crossovers between these Gospels are considered by New Testament scholars to indicate each author having access to an existing text(s) from which to draw; such may have been the Q document, or may have been a previous form of Mark, or may have been the *Gospel of Thomas,* or even all three, any combination thereof, or something else we know little or nothing about (recall the shockwaves

---

8. *Thinline Bible with the Apocrypha* (NRSV).
9. *Thinline Bible with the Apocrypha* (NRSV).
10. Funk, ed., and the Jesus Seminar, trans. and comm., *The Acts of Jesus,* 351–2.

created by the discovery of the Nag Hammadi library in 1945, or the repeated findings of the various Dead Sea Scrolls between 1946–1956). Whoever wrote and/or compiled Matthew and Luke (and however many authors and/or editors were involved in that), they need not have known of the other contemporary(ies) at work on their own Gospel either: if I have a copy of *Of Mice and Men* and you have a copy of *Of Mice and Men,* we might each pen a tale celebrating George and Lennie[11] that reads an awful lot like one another's without having met in person, and certainly without ever actually collaborating, particularly if we are both part of a relatively recent social movement seeking new adherents and growth within a competitive transnational ideological environment.

The less noticeable differences are also of interest. Matthew, for instance, expands the prayers found in Mark, adding details of the wording and explicitly stating a third round of prayer whereas Mark is somewhat vague (Mark has a worded prayer in verse thirty-six, a prayer described merely as "saying the same words" in verse thirty-nine, and then Yeshua returning to where the disciples are resting "a third time," versus Matthew's worded prayers in verses thirty-nine and forty-two, and then the outright "prayed for the third time" before again having Yeshua rejoin the group in verse forty-four). Funk et al., in referring to an extensive study on the Passion narratives by Raymond E. Brown, note how Brown "doubts that the Christian scribes who passed on this tradition would have 'claimed to retain memories of the wording' Jesus used. They wrote rather 'in light of the psalms and of their own prayers.'"[12] It is instructive to consider that the writers and preservers of these accounts, in putting their own prayers onto Yeshua's lips, may well have thought they were communicating on an emotionally expressive level instead of a literally informative one; such a perspective is the more enlightening as we approach these words and attempt to find a place for them within the broader contexts then and our own today, particularly since as far as literalism goes the entire sequence is almost without question a copy of the Davidic fugitive tale told in 2 Samuel 15–17.[13]

In that ancient and readily accessible account to Jews of all stripes—at least orally—central as it was within the first and second century Judaisms' communal storytelling (crucial too for the place its characters held within the popular imagination; and indeed continue to hold in many areas today), King David's son Absalom revolts against his father's rule and attempts to usurp the throne. David thereafter flees and climbs the Mount of Olives, is sorrowful and repentant, is revealed to have been betrayed by a formerly close associate (cf. Judas Iscariot), has his servant swear

---

11. Steinbeck, *Of Mice and Men.* I list the original publication information in the Bibliography, but this now classic work has of course appeared in many versions and from many publishers since.

12. Funk, ed., and the Jesus Seminar, trans. and comm., *The Acts of Jesus,* 252; Brown, *The Death of the Messiah,* 225 and 234, respectively.

13. For details and an explanation of the analyses and probability ranking done by the Westar Institute's members on this portion, see again Funk, ed., and the Jesus Seminar, trans. and comm., *The Acts of Jesus,* 132–3 and 150–1.

loyalty to him (cf. Peter, though not in the sections we have quoted), and Absalom's senior advisor (also David's betrayer from the above) recommends that one man die for the whole people's peace, but that when his suggestion is rejected thereafter hangs himself (mirroring both the Yeshuan execution atonement hermeneutic and Judas' suicide; again elements within the wider Passion Week storytelling although not part of the Gethsemane verses cited). The connection being made here, and the propagandistic objective thereof, between Yeshua and King David shines like the sun; and if we can understand that even now then its early hearers in the first and second centuries would have grasped the whole all the more: Israel was under Rome, there were frequent political rumblings and rebellions such as the Maccabean experience and others (see the explanatory note in Chapter 3), and, as Funk et al. summarize, "The empire of which Jesus spoke so frequently [i.e. "the kingdom"] was misunderstood in the popular mind as a renewal of the Davidic kingdom."[14] These Garden dramatics therefore form a story with a point, not a history; and that point—we will argue—has become so read into the images of Gethsemane that nearly every other comprehension of them is blocked; thus too are other possible ways of seeing/"seeing!" Yeshua, his teachings, and Christianity's place within Judaism(s).

Having situated ourselves in the words let us turn finally to the pictures. Gethsemane is frequently taken as a place of deep anxiety, a stance which is typified by Emmanuel Falque in his *The Guide to Gethsemane: Anxiety, Suffering, Death*.[15] Falque's is a remarkable and thoughtful book, but our aims are otherwise than its, and hence our interactions with it will be more akin to the role of foil for our alternative propositions in the proceeding (re)visitations of selected artworks when viewed from behind, as it were, from inside out. Falque centers his analyses of the theatrics presented in the Gospels around the topic of pain; more minutely, around the direct experience of pain, the feel of it as it is known personally (as it only can be known, really: as an expressing-out-from instead of as a describing-from-afar). He writes: "Let all discourse cease and let pain speak,"[16] and in an appended chapter note to this statement he further references Maurice Merleau-Ponty's remarks on phenomenology as a "rejection of science" (e.g. objective labeling, the neutral "how"). Lest we take this "rejection" too straightforwardly, however, I think a sidebar may be necessary to elucidate both Merleau-Ponty's comment and its historical positioning vis-à-vis the contemporary scientific situation (it was originally published in 1945). The section Falque alludes to reads as follows:

> Phenomenology involves describing, and not explaining or analyzing. This first rule—to be a "descriptive psychology" or to return "to the things themselves," which Husserl set for an emerging phenomenology—is first and foremost the disavowal of science. I am not the result or the intertwining of

14. Funk, ed., and the Jesus Seminar, trans. and comm., *The Acts of Jesus*, 150.
15. Falque, *The Guide to Gethsemane*.
16. Falque, *The Guide to Gethsemane*, 88.

> multiple causalities that determine my body or my "psyche"; I cannot think of myself as a part of the world, like the simple object of biology, psychology, and sociology; I cannot enclose myself within the universe of science. Everything I know about the world, even through science, I know from a perspective that is my own or from an experience of the world without which scientific symbols would be meaningless. The entire universe of science is constructed upon the lived world, and if we wish to think science rigorously, to appreciate precisely its sense and its scope, we must first awaken that experience of the world of which science is the second-order expression.[17]

My understanding of Merleau-Ponty here has him asserting the primacy of one's internalizations as the grounding upon which attenuated symbolisms and signs are founded, that for human consciousness (that is, in the sense of one being "mentally aware of" as we have described, rather than as the brain's automatic processes to which one does not have recourse in awareness) first and foremost there are those internal *thuses*, the elements which have come to be called "qualia." Essentially, therefore, the quoted section here is addressing the so-called problem of mind, something about which the science of Merleau-Ponty's era had very little to offer, leading to a prejudice against whatever empirical research *might later* have to propose as time and the study involved marched on, a bias which unfortunately has lasted—outlasting its applicability—and is still to be found amongst many philosophers today. In our opening we sought to indicate how the brain's usage of neurons and representational "maps" may account for (is our best bet to comprehend) the workings of those mental operations which, although feeling mysterious and aethereal from the "inside" abstracted conceptual level upon which awareness functions (the *organic* network's accessing of the *organic* groups of "maps"), are indeed cellular (neuronal) and biochemical in form and expression. Instead of "rejecting" or skirting around the science then, I think we ought rather to go back to experience *through (the science of) experience:* let pain speak as Falque proclaims, certainly, but let it speak from its established voice that we may know it the better through all its layers and levels of operation, of communication. There is no reason to shut ourselves off from this.

Suffering, trauma, hurt: these are the analytical angles that Falque employs to consider what Gethsemane has to offer. He writes seemingly more or less from the established orthodox position of taking Yeshua as a personage who is at once fully divine and fully human, as him foreknowing his own crucifixion and as being accepting of his status as atoning savior and establisher of a new covenantal human-God/"God" form of interaction (i.e. a high Christology: the reader is reminded that we will make efforts to argue against the received "atonement" hermeneutic in what follows; and that, moreover, the possibility of Yeshua having had a personal expectation of physical resurrection as reward does not equal the foreknowing of his crucifixion, nor the being

---

17. Merleau-Ponty, *Phenomenology of Perception*, lxxi-lxxii; Falque's notation is on his page 150, note one to Chapter 11: "Suffering Incarnate," in Falque, *The Guide to Gethsemane*.

certain of a resurrection such as that portrayed in the Gospel accounts: see the note on this in Chapter 8 above). Confronting the Garden from this vantage, Falque concludes that "there is nothing artificial or excessive in the attempt that I consider theologically well-founded to describe here a *metaphysical experiment by God* in which he shares the extremes of human anxiety in the face of death."[18] Falque argues that this anxiety, moreover, should be taken immediately as it happened, and not via the position of the later resurrection; the point of view, the divine perspective, is that from within the "experiment," it is one of the present (now-moment) and not of hindsight or projection (now-from-then). The reader will recognize that there are however some problems with this, primarily in relation to claims about divine epistemology.

To start with, there is the basic consideration that nothing short of a lack of omniscience and omnipotence could justify a need to engage in an "experiment" of this sort,[19] particularly if God/"God" were considered to "be" Yeshua at the same time that God/"God" "is" transcendent Other (as mainline Christianity teaches). It may be that Falque wishes to differentiate the "feel" (emoting) of something versus the "knowing" (intellectualizing) of something, following perhaps the line of "descriptive psychology" and "to the things themselves" that Merleau-Ponty (via Husserl) highlighted in his assertion of the need for the aforementioned "rejection." It may also be that Falque is offering something like what Heidegger did in his breakdown of what eschatology (regarding the *parousia* (i.e. Yeshua's "second coming")) meant for Paul in First Thessalonians: that it is a lived notion and therefore, in being lived, cannot be segregated out from its context, its "original complex of enactment":[20] which is to indicate that this type of idea is never only an idea, and therefore cannot be removed from its relational aspects.[21] Paul functioned from behind and within the lens of an end-of-time perspective; maybe Yeshua did similarly for human-pain: the abstracted and juxtaposed *feel* could not be split into what would be a *knowing*, and hence even God/"God" (the incarnated God/"God"-man) had to go through it to truly apprehend it. (Perhaps; but again—and for clarity—this is not our position.)

These traces of others might be in Falque, or in the background to Falque, and the details are indeed provocative, but they hinge on axes that are not as stable as they may appear. If, for example as the neuronal model demonstrates, there is no actual core distinction between the (physiologically grounded) "feel" of something and the (physiologically constructed) "idea" of something (which, after all, is an issue of

---

18. Falque, *The Guide to Gethsemane*, 46; emphasis in the original.

19. We would agree with the absence of these "omni's" of course—as has been discussed and will be returned to—but that is not the stance of the theological and Christological position from which Falque appears to be writing.

20. Heidegger, *The Phenomenology of Religious Life*, 79.

21. Heidegger, *The Phenomenology of Religious Life*; see especially page 78: "In talk without qualification of 'ideas,' one misrecognizes the fact that the eschatological is never primarily idea. The content of the idea may certainly not be eliminated, but it must be had in its own (relational) sense. The enactmental understanding from out of the situation eliminates these difficulties."

knowledge: an idea is a knowing-held) in the human case where the commonly imagined difference stems from the conceptualized mode being taken as it typically is, then therefore—biochemically speaking—said alleged distinction is illusory,[22] it seems more than fair to wonder if the same might not apply for the divine; and that with or without omniscience. If everything "feels" like something simply due to the associated intuitional (data processed) labeling and conjunctive affective mechanisms, what would stop God/"God" comprehended existentially[23] (and especially in the whollyabled way that God/"God" is presented as being in Christianity) from "knowing" X through the proper cognitive restructuring without having to incarnate and thereafter undergo ("feel") X in a surely incomparably reduced human body? (This doubt alone highlights many of the problems with the traditional way God/"God" is cognized; we shall have cause to return to theological metaphysics later, though unfortunately a full study shall have to await a future work.) Moreover, if Yeshua is taken as God/"God", and if God/"God" is both omniscient and exists outside of time (and each must be so considering the dominant Christian interpretations that Falque writes from), then acknowledged in the moment or not, that resurrection on the "other side" of the Garden would be there; even if suppressed in thought it would be there (although we might grant that omnipotence would also permit a willed forgetting; but then we run down paths that become so fanciful as to be terminal-less). Perhaps Yeshua-God/"God" purposefully blocked such from surfacing every time it arose while in Gethsemane in order to more fully experience the felt anxiety as deeply as possible; but this is a mere speculation—and an idle one at that—for the basic historical conundrum remains that none of this ever happened: as mentioned, the entire Gethsemane setting is a replay of the David/Absalom tale. These are stories upon stories, ideas in enactments, public relations and advertising; yet certainly instructive still.

If we therefore take this notion of an "experiment" conducted by God/"God" through the temporal being of Yeshua (for these initial comparative analyses understood not strictly historically but more in line with the Gospels' "Jesus" figure), of a/ the God/"God"-man in (intense) anxiety but with at least some degree of resurrection foresight, then how might we respond to Gethsemane themed artworks? Let us take some examples[24] and conduct a kind of ideological litmus test with running descriptive commentaries on the proffered intellectual perspective in order to determine how well it may withstand an analysis sundered from the weight of "right because received" (tradition); in this we will follow the chronological order of year(s) of production,

---

22. We might also add that it is thence experientially illusory, at least once the more apposite mental stance is taken and the "feel" of it shifts.

23. That is, as a creature rather than as a "call" or event (or Event, depending on how one applies the philosophical jargon).

24. The paintings (and woodcut and engraving) reproduced here are in the public domain and were retrieved via Wikimedia Common searches to ensure open copyright status. Please see the Bibliography section for full image file details. Artist names and production years are noted in the text.

but not to make a developmental argument, rather merely for appeal to our naturally linear inclinations. Here is Peitro Perugino's "Agony in the Garden" (1483–1493):[25]

Figure 1: Peitro Perugino, "Agony in the Garden" (1483–1493)

Around the figure of Yeshua praying (strangely pictured on top of a large rock and not at all "a little farther" (Mark 14:35, Matthew 26:39) or "about a stone's throw" (Luke 22:41) away from the inner circle of disciples he chose to accompany him), we have the solely Lukan comforting angel, the soldiers coming to arrest him, and the city visible far in the background. Foremost are the reclining future apostles and church fathers, who appear quite at peace, and this raises a further important aspect of this work: the face of Yeshua, his expression, his absolute lack of distress as he gazes at the angel, whose errand of solace hardly seems necessary. To find any anxiety here—which is not only a matter of concern for Falque, but again the Synoptics each stress this point (see Mark 14:33–34, Matthew 26:37–38, and Luke 22:44 above[26])—we must conceptually read-in that which is not visually represented, we must project what we

---

25. Image taken from "File: Pietro Perugino cat20.jp." Pietro Perugino, Public Domain, via Wikimedia Commons. Accessed April 21, 2022.

26. Although we note that Luke's verse forty-four (along with verse forty-three) was, as indicated, likely a later addition to the Gospel. Moreover—and interestingly—Luke has the disciples "sleeping because of grief" (verse forty-five); where is such grief here?

think we know, and what Perugino too would surely have known, having heard and/ or read the story himself any number of times (I am not sure of his Latin literacy nor textual access; the latter element seems historically most in doubt). Why then not display the suffering directly supplied to Yeshua by the referential texts used as the basis for the painting? The logic "behind" this painting, whether acknowledged by the artist or not, seems straightforward enough: it is obvious that one cannot have (omniscient) foreknowledge of one's future resurrection and glory—as the church taught and teaches Yeshua embodied—and still have the requisite anxiety that Falque's argument calls for. In the Davidic tale from which the Gethsemane telling appears to be derivative, however, such does make sense: David had no idea how his son's rebellion would play out; but this is not the case for Yeshua, and without it the alleged "experiment" would seem to collapse as well since the sought after experience-feel could not be had in full. The picture appears to be aimed at eliciting worship and reverence; which although theologically important amounts to taking the Garden scene from a stance of hindsight more than anything else.

Another facet which may also be related is the church's mandate, fully developed by the medieval period preceding Perugino's career, that established the use of images and icons under the aegis of likeness between model and representation (think here along the lines of Platonic Forms, the philosophical theorem which essentially provided the metaphysical grounding to overcome the Jewish prohibition on imagery vis-à-vis divinity), such that—as Belting puts it—"God and Christ, the model and living image, are one and the same God" meaning that veneration of an (appropriate) image was not "idol worship" but rather adoration of God.[27] For an image of Yeshua comprehended as God/"God"-man to therefore reflect the "Form/ideal" of God (which it would need to), demonstrations of fragility would appear not only out of place but indeed heretical. Yet those very weaknesses (if human emotion can be labeled as such) are precisely the compelling points about Yeshua as incarnation, as "the Word made flesh" (John 1:14),[28] and this highlights the core difficulty that Christianity has always had—particularly from within the high Christology that the movement developed into—in its assertion of a dual nature to this peripatetic rabbi that was somehow simultaneously and always omni-everything "God Almighty" and "everyday neighbor" down the street. Christian theologians have never ceased to struggle with this, and there is little wonder why; one can hardly blame Perugino for the expansive visage he produced, but it is not "agony." Additional examinations of other artworks may, however, point in other directions, and perhaps we can thereby get closer to Falque's "experiment" while also garnering insight into what the original Gospel tales may

27. Belting, *Likeness and Presence*, 150–54; see especially page 154.

28. The full verse reads: "And the Word [this is Yeshua as the "logos" of God, eternal and co-existent with God; cf. John 1:1, "In the beginning was the Word, and the Word was with God, and the Word was God."] became flesh and lived among us, and we have seen his glory, the glory as of a father's only son, full of grace and truth." (There is also a footnoted alternative reading of "Or *the Father's only Son*".) *Thinline Bible with the Apocrypha* (NRSV).

have been seeking to impart to their hearers and/or readers. Let us not forget our own imparted (or trained) position in this attempt; as Heidegger counsels: "knowledge of one's own having-become is the starting point and the origin of theology."[29] Might we be better served by recognizing and then severing that which lingers of whatever heritage we may hold and instead approach these pictured first century stories in a less "high" manner, or ought we to continue to think in the more reformatory than exclusionary means of writers like Falque? Which is to ask: shall we jettison the nuances, or only differently emphasize them? How might we see/"see!"?

The next production is Albrecht Dürer's remarkable woodcut of 1515 also titled "Agony in the Garden".[30] Here Yeshua is represented in a positioning akin to how the Gospel stories relay the scene, being physically separated from the disciples and visually alone, although again there is the presence of the comforting angel which is purely a token of the Lukan narrative (evidently an attractive one for many artists and/or listeners/readers), and—as mentioned—most probably not even an originally Lukan feature at that, but instead an addition that occurred at some point far later in the document's evolution. If one looks very closely at the image there are what appear to be approaching soldiers in the distance (in the center left and beside (behind) the tree at whose base Yeshua's companions are sleeping: shown walking under a type of awning or gate), but these are difficult to make out, and there are no urban or otherwise settlement-type elements visible further out in the distance. Importantly however—and evocatively—Yeshua's face is far more clearly troubled in this work, taking us closer to the meaning and, perhaps, one of the prime "morals" of the setting. (Note that even the angel here also bears a look of true concern.) In this we may venture that whereas Perugino might have favored the *God* portion in the dyad of God/"God"-man when he painted Yeshua—and whether this alleged "favoring" was done with any purposive awareness or not is a separate issue from the phenomenological one of viewing; although admittedly not wholly unrelated as it motions towards the creator's intent and thence to arguments about interpretation—Dürer may instead be found within the scope of the opposing pole: that of "man" (with the question of purposive awareness here too remaining open; probably we will never be able to know conclusively in either case).

---

29. Heidegger, *The Phenomenology of Religious Life*, 66.

30. Image (below) taken from "File: 64 Agony in the Garden.jpg." Albrecht Dürer, Public Domain, via Wikimedia Commons. Accessed April 21, 2022.

Part 3 | Parables and Pictures

Figure 2: Albrecht Dürer, "Agony in the Garden" (1515)

If we view this work with the high Christology with which we are now historically familiar after centuries of church teaching on the matter, we will likely experientially interact within the hermeneutical boundaries (image-ideas/idea-images, notion/events) that Falque argues for with his "experiment," a concept that he (and indeed Christianity) follows all the way out to being a full conveyance of the human to the divine through the person of Yeshua: an incarnation-dependent transference, as it were, a thoroughfare of human "suchnesses" that would otherwise not be possible, not even—by this line—for God/"God" (Falque uses the French term *passage* for this movement). Here then is Yeshua presented as God/"God"-man but acting with a primacy on the human variable so that the non-immanent divine side can better acquire the "what it is like" (the qualia) of anxiety, suffering, and death (Falque's book's subtitle, after all).

Although outside the scope of our immediate pictorial concerns, from the Garden scene Falque takes us in this particular comprehension to the cross as well, writing: "It is such powerlessness [with respect to Yeshua-God's/"God's" *allowance* regarding crucifixion: that is, letting it happen despite the ability (the power) to prevent it; this too we shall argue against in the below] that remains always woven into human finitude, with its law of corruptibility, to which God himself, right to the end and without ever disposing of it, consents"; and "In suffering this world the Son conveys to the Father (a passage) the weight of finitude experienced in his death."[31] Once more, however, things began to fall apart if we are serious about Yeshua as God/"God"-man, and by this view of him we must be so attuned. For here too the same epistemological problems arise once even a suppressed or, at least, reduced knowledge on the part of Yeshua is acknowledged within the imagined or accepted confines of the general narrative framing (God/"God"-man = God/"God" and man = divine attributes from the God/"God" side = presence (somehow) of omniscience or a degree of foreknowing that is imparted to the currently humanly experiencing man side). In Gethsemane the resurrection always looms on the horizon, no matter how dark the moment may seem, and with that a triumph: certain victory from the death-to-be/death-already-overcome.

For our part, being merely human, we may fervently believe in our own postmortem "new life" or "rising from the dead" or "call forth from the grave" or what have you (i.e. Heaven (of some sort), possibly reincarnation, et cetera), but we cannot "know" it in the sense that God/"God" is claimed to know (perfectly and definitively, unerringly),[32] and hence if Yeshua is the/a God/"God"-man in the fullest manner in which he is purported to be by the viewpoints behind these artworks, seemingly behind Falque, and behind Christian exegesis, then there is never any question in the matter; therefore too the absence of true or honest anxiety, agony, suffering, and the rest. We have been instructed to perceive these images through notional lenses that simply do not fit, and we therefore understand them askew, we fail to "see!" for the forced affixations involved. This sadly reduces the impact that might be, the potency possible where a fully anxious, agonized, battered and broken Yeshua kneels and prays, not beckoning anyone to take himself as lord, not foreknowing anything except the probable outcomes of the Roman judiciary: simply one individual in worried distress, crying to an unseen God/"God" who at the best of times is only ever felt in subtlety. *Would this not be enough?* That question raised (hung on its own displaying cross), let us leap forward to productions from three and a half hundred years later, to paintings from perhaps the last era when the church could still compete for a central position in broader society prior to its fully succumbing to the present niche standing it has, a

---

31. Falque, *The Guide to Gethsemane*, 52 and 77, respectively.

32. The reader is asked to remember and apply these same thoughts when we later speculate on the kind of resurrection expectation/hope Yeshua the man as purely man might have held, and what such may thereby have accomplished or implied phenomenologically for him.

time of massive disbelief on one hand against a clingingly fervent faith on the other: the nineteenth century.

The final three images we will engage are all from this period, and each takes Yeshua central, eschewing other earthly participants, including even the presence of his chosen disciple companions as the Gospel stories narrate. What is somewhat revolutionary in the bearing brought to thought and approach in regard to these works is their station within the wider historical arc—the transitioning—of art in the West as outlined by Belting: the argument that imagery began its long cultural march as productions of religious iconography not merely first and foremost but only and entirely, but that thereafter, under the weight of numerous developmental pressures, eventually shifted into the aesthetical emplacement with which we are familiar today. It is therefore apposite to be arriving at this mental turn in our own (rough) juncture here in the course of the present study as well, between a philosophical foundation and an application. Dürer's years too were something of a bridge in a larger process, with Belting noting that the currently accepted "humanist definition of art" is one that "was just being formed in the age of [Martin] Luther and Dürer,"[33] an epoch in which (culturally, sociologically, politically; at least in Europe) "Except in the Reformed churches, the dividing line was not between the religious and secular image. It separated, rather, an old concept of image from a new one . . . People did not experience two kinds of images [i.e. a religious kind and a secular kind] but images with a double face, depending on whether they were seen as receptacles of the holy or as expressions of art."[34]

At this point we might think back to the medieval church's Plato-inspired rules on model and representation discussed within the confines of Perugino's work above, and also of the church's objective for these pictures to be pedagogical concept-carriers, to be image-ideas/idea-images in the complete sense we have sought to elucidate in exploring the relation between suppositions and sketchpads—as it were—in the preceding. (Which is a sense that on our argumentation stretches beyond the narrowly didactic purposes of the church in its employment of these works, but it is nevertheless theoretically applicable.) Prior to this time, then, a painting of a Gethsemane scene, or a crucifixion, or a Madonna with child, or any other biblical expression, would have been mentally associated by its viewers (image-idea) with the theological purport of its representation, whereas during the transition Belting outlines the very same artwork might either be taken in that spiritualized interpretation or in a more beauty-oriented framework (the "double face"; again the image-idea/idea-image, but now in a branching form). Then, finally, following this thought-historical movement to the contemporary setting from which the primary locus is neatly "art"; admitting that a work may still be taken to have sacrality to (or with, or in) some degree. In every case it is the initiating image-idea/idea-image that informs the notion/event of the interaction and structures the phenomenology, importantly including the cognition involved. On

---

33. Belting, *Likeness and Presence*, 459.
34. Belting, *Likeness and Presence*, 458.

that latter aspect of cognition, it should be clear that—as Belting guides—"The new painting called for a hermeneutics of art of the sort that had been applied previously to literature . . . A picture is no longer to be understood in terms of its theme, but as a contribution to the development of art."[35] This "part of"—the "contribution to"—is earthshaking in our notional undertaking with regard to these images: it splits the experiential perspective we have been pursuing of individual-to-piece, of the "looking across the frame," or the "co-glancing," or the "exchange," between person and form into the much vaster distance of an evolutionary flow. Our eyes become so widened to the light that it becomes blinding; yet we may blink, for our focus need not expand thusly in the moment (although these issues ought yet to be borne in mind), we have the liberty of blocking out (tabling) these side concerns to remain with Yeshua in his hours of travail in the Garden narrative, since it is from that angle which we hope to learn. This reduction is purposive (and moreover Husserlean in methodology[36]), and we realize that anyway the entire Gethsemane tale is a fiction: thus (hopefully) justified, we progress with the goal of seeing how to "see!" differently yet.

Carl Bloch's "An Angel Comforting Jesus before His Arrest in the Garden of Gethsemane" (1873)[37] is a very interesting example of the potential involved in what Belting labeled the "double face" since the painting extends quite easily to secular appreciation; more so, I think, than the two earlier works we examined which were completer expressions of the Gospel stories and hence perforce more explicitly religious in tone and comportment. Bloch does include the angel found only in Luke's version, and as a central element as the title indicates (yet again we have this angel—what attraction these creatures seem to hold for us mortals!), but in a less stylized and more naturally "human" posing and posture. Intriguingly as well Yeshua is portrayed as actually leaning on the angel's knee, being physically supported—held up—by the otherworldly comforter. The implications of this bodily arrangement are nuanced and deep, and there is moreover a pleasing (to me, at any rate) non-genderedness to the angel, a kind of binary-ism that lends itself to female or male assignation (but not in the halved way such as how Lord Shiva and Mother Parvati are pictured in the Ardhanarishvara;[38] here rather as more of a could-be-this/that depiction). A tree rests in the near background, and further beyond a bit more vegetation, but additional "garden" facets are not to be found, and the darkened setting almost places the scene on an astral plane, as if we were viewing lonely figures stranded on an asteroid flinging itself through space with a pair of contemplative guests its only inhabitants.[39] What is potentially most evocative in the setting, however, is the facial expression that Yeshua

---

35. Belting, *Likeness and Presence*, 459.

36. Husserl, *The Essential Husserl*; Smith, *Husserl*; see also Chapter 5 in the preceding.

37. Image (below) taken from "File: Gethsemane Carl Bloch.jpg." Carl Bloch, Public Domain, via Wikimedia Commons. Accessed April 21, 2022.

38. For generalities and an overview, see "Ardhanarishvara", *Wikipedia*. Accessed October 13, 2020.

39. One is reminded of Antoine de Saint-Exupéry's *The Little Prince*.

is given, one of marked anguish and a foreboding of ill to come. In gazing we cannot perhaps imagine "sweat like great drops of blood" being shed any time soon (Luke 22:44; although the reader will recall this verse is almost without question an appended scribal flourish not to be found in the original text), but we can place ourselves within the mentality of someone who knew what the Romans did to troublemakers—particularly of the political sort, and any "kingdom" message could easily have been heard by the authorities that way—and for that omniscience (alleged or assumed) need not be within our agenda.

Figure 3: Carl Bloch, "An Angel Comforting Jesus before His Arrest in the Garden of Gethsemane" (1873)

Indeed, it is precisely because omniscience need play no part in this work (fore*boding* better than fore*knowing*) that our typical antecedent conceptualities prohibit truly meaningful comprehensions of Bloch's painting. If the idea-image we hold prior to an interaction with this wonderful example of artistry follows the traditional reading-in of Yeshua as God/"God"-man and the resulting existential role he held as conveyor of human experience to a (somehow) otherwise incapable of feeling/realizing deity such as the "experiment" comprehension sets forth, we find in Yeshua's delineated repose and setting—probably from the presence of the angel—an uneasiness that is only on this side of a punishment already acknowledged as merely temporary—albeit necessary—and then inevitably followed by unsurpassable glory. This is a mere "no pain, no gain" assessment, as if Yeshua were about to hit the weights for a strenuous workout after which he would feel great; oppose that to an articulation of *dread* in the piece (an imprecise fear: a deep-seated apprehending of "I know not what, but goodness here it comes"), and the punch of a purely Earth-*born* and ever Earth-*bound* Yeshua begins to reveal itself. Yet here we are getting slightly ahead of our plan, for the implications of an ulterior notional framing will be reserved for the later revisiting of these pieces. At the moment let us only conclude that high Christology gives us a low appreciation, and it robs the potential inherent in this rendering of the Gethsemane fable.

Along similarly restive and graspable lines (if we allow ourselves, if we re-program ourselves) is the astounding imagery in Nikolai Ge's "On the Mount of Olives" (1869–1880),[40] a work that bespeaks an almost gulag pathos in a pre-figuring of Aleksandr Solzhenitsyn done in brush rather than pen.[41] Were it not for the title we might have little idea who this portrait is meant to represent, and we certainly would not be thinking of a particular setting and story, of surrounding anterior and contemporary events. Nowhere are the disciples to be found, there is no angel (thank you, Ge!); Judas Iscariot, the soldiers, and Jerusalem in the distance are each likewise absent. Environmentally too we may never think in terms of the Mediterranean basin or wider Middle East as the foliage and geological elements strike one as being more akin to high latitude climes than to those nearer the equator, perhaps reflecting Ge's own personal acquaintance more than his imagined view of the locale he was painting. Yeshua's face is half covered in shadow, but what we can make out of it indicates pensiveness, a mood of reflection or contemplation; we might find anxiety present, particularly in the setting of the brow, but such, I think, is a reading-in of what is visible (taking the work's title and thereby mentally applying what we know of the associated tale) rather than a reading-out or a more proper interpretation of what has actually been produced. Still, it is moving, and that combined with the worn through fabric and almost skeletal hand resting on what may be mid-leg in this apparently kneeling posture (again, the shading is heavy in the relevant part of the picture since the light source is coming from the left side) is evocative of a trouble felt and expressed.

---

40. Image (below) taken from "File: Nikolay Ge 021.jpeg." Nikolai Ge, Public Domain, via Wikimedia Commons. Accessed April 21, 2022.

41. Solzhenitsyn, *The Gulag Archipelago, 1918–1956*; first published in English in 1974.

Part 3 | Parables and Pictures

Figure 4: Nikolai Ge, "On the Mount of Olives" (1869–1880)

Contrasting the viewable in this artwork with the thought, putting our interpretative weight on the conceptual side of the inevitable image-idea/idea-image, does much—in my view—to ruin the affective output of this piece. Instead of a man who is carrying a personal weight and worry alone as he wanders through a lightly wooded wilderness, we are confronted by (we *confront ourselves with*) the savior of humanity God/"God"-man in the midst of his lifelong—that is, while sojourning as (half) mortal: "lifelong" only in the sense of the somewhat prison sentence-esque "time served" spent on our shores and away from his true Heavenly abode—transference of the experiences of creaturehood to the divine force who/that fashioned such (but allegedly cannot, nevertheless, fully comprehend the same absent said transference: the "experiment" model). From that abstracted angle we might conclude that the Yeshua we find here does not even seem to be in the midst of his real travail; that things have not gotten quite so bad for him just yet. We expect to see "deep grief" (Mark 14:34), "grief and agitation" (Matthew 26:37), "sweat like great drops of blood" (Luke 22:44), or a "comforting angel" (Luke 22:43) providing a solace that can only come from a supernatural domain (never mind that the last two verses were insertions into the Lukan tale; for us today, who have now received the book in this form for many centuries, they are part and parcel of the ingrained (hammered in) hermeneutic). Moreover, because we anticipate these details, we furthermore fail to note the frail and hurt individual genuinely present with whom we may well identify. In this we thereby limit—even refuse—the pictorial gift that is on offer; and these latter facets are problems in addition to the knowledge oriented issues we have repeatedly stressed in the above. Through these shallow takings, these (en)forced understandings, we stop well short of "seeing!" what we could, we partake only of the little we give ourselves and not of the greater portion that has been set forth. It should be apparent what a disservice this is: a fresh world of phenomenology is there and ready to be had, but we are content to keep looping around the same tired old cul-de-sac.

Our final exhibit takes us forwards in time but backwards in sophistication. This is Heinrich Hofmann's "Christ in the Garden of Gethsemane" (1890),[42] and in it we see perhaps most clearly from all of the examples thus far what Falque is arguing in his "experiment" view and the associated church doctrine, as well as the significance such notions hold for those who associate themselves with what has come to be called "Christianity" in its long departure from the personhood of Yeshua. As Falque writes of the scriptural interpretation wherein Yeshua realizes what is to happen to him and assents to it: "What is at stake in taking on board 'suffering' is not simply making divine, but also making human: the nodal point and place of synthesis of all filiation."[43] Note that final term—*filiation*—this, I think, is the key here with its enunciation of paternity, of the father to son relationship (i.e. in Christian theology, of the one Father to the one Son bound into the Trinitarian sense of that relating). The highest of high Christologies, reflected in the below artwork, where Hofmann too has eschewed the supporting cast of the sleeping disciples, the "betrayer" and the soldiers with him en route to make their arrest, even the setting of the holy city where the tale's climax is meant to take place. We merely have Yeshua praying—eyes open—in a natural setting, clothed in flowing and, by the looks of them, quite luxurious and comfortable garments. He gazes at the heavens, a halo of light around the back of his upturned head, matched by a beckoning light from the sky that is breaking through the clouds. Here God/"God" is the Sun is the son/"Son", a straightforward symbolic line drawn through each that can leave no doubt as to the messaging intent of what is depicted, a painting that does not so much tell a story as it proclaims a public relations advert, the kind of art that can just as easily be displayed in a gift shop as it can behind or near to an altar, the type that generates income more than it does emotion. I am not sure how much "suffering" can be said to be being taken on here, but the "nodal point" Falque alludes to is clear enough, and with it the reading-in which the piece's title affirms allows a believer's mind to traverse directly to the narration in question; and in

---

42. Image (below) taken from "File: Christ in Gethsemane.jpg." Heinrich Hofmann, Public Domain, via Wikimedia Commons. Accessed April 21, 2022.

43. Falque, *The Guide to Gethsemane*, xxviii (from his "Opening: The Isenheim Altarpiece or 'The Taking on Board of Suffering'").

those Gospel accounts we of course *do* have suffering taken on: willingly, sacrificially, heroically. Hofmann gives us a "making divine," certainly, but the "making human" of the Falquean equation must come from the image-idea/idea-image we import. To my eyes, however, the portraiture itself does not call for that; it is far too exalted.

Figure 5: Heinrich Hofmann, "Christ in the Garden of Gethsemane" (1890)

There is no real pain to be found here, nor much anxiety, at most perhaps a kind of somberness—or earnestness—an acceptance of the (fore)known and/or the trusted to be (that which is becoming: the "to be-coming"). This is almost a caricature, really, a Yeshua hollowed out and with millennia of church doctrine poured in; so much so, in fact, that I hesitate even to use the name "Yeshua" and think rather the mythical "Jesus"—with all of its many amplified associations accreted and asserted—as a far more apposite fit. This is a full expression purely of the God/"God"-man a hair's breadth from his/"His" victorious resurrection and revelation of absolute divinity, a return to Perugino without even the necessity of consolation from an angelic visitor. We can find little to relate with here, aside perhaps from the famous prayer probably automatically recalled of "not my will, but your will" (e.g. Mark 14:36; Matthew 26:39, 42; Luke 22:42); although, by the tenets of high Christology, there may not be much need (or desire) for us to "relate" at all; rather one is to worship, to revere unquestioningly, and the figure of this work—if understood by the image-idea/idea-image orthodox teaching imparts—appears worthy of that. Nevertheless, I think it still fails Falque's "experiment" measure, and it does so due to the lack of a true mien of anxiety, that which is indeed the whole fulcrum of the Gethsemane narratives. On this Falque importantly queries: "Is Christ's anxiety in the face of his own death simply psychological? Or is it also, and more significantly, metaphysical?"[44] This is a question well worth asking, and so as we close our first viewing of these works let us dwell a moment on it.

Anxiety taken metaphysically intertwines with an earlier comment Falque makes, whereby he gestures towards the Christian faith structure as that spiritual (conceptual, attitudinal, comportment-al) vehicle wherein anxiety functions as a crucial methodology: "Throughout the Christian tradition anxiety points first of all to a narrow *passage* [again, Falque is using the French word for a nuanced emphasis: "journey"], as in childbirth, and not simply to a *wall* blocking the road ahead for modern man."[45] It is a crucible, a tool for making stronger. That may be so generally—thinking along developmental/training lines—but our doubt, however, is whether or not "anxiety" can be fully applied in an unadulterated phenomenological way in the confines of the specific Gethsemane context to the character of Yeshua as presented in the Gospels. We have argued that given the epistemological implications of a God/"God"-man comprehending (omniscience; and even if such were suppressed somehow a residual "knowing" would perforce remain) any "anxiety" would fall short of the mark of true *anxiety* (which surely—definitionally—must include some trembling for at least partially unknowns), but nevertheless that does not mean there cannot be lessons taken from this Garden scene for a consideration of anxiety in our own struggles with matters of the numinous.

Fortunately, we need not stop with the story as given. If our understanding is shifted, if we re-mould the received idea into an alternative and thereby allow for a new notion/event to be birthed from these image-ideas/idea-images (to be "seen!" from out of them), we might take much of value from these works and similar ones that have been passed down to us. Yeshua as the "Jesus" of legend does admittedly suit Gethsemane in a certain way since Gethsemane as an unfolding (and not merely as a place) is itself legendary (is a fiction), but the same fable may deliver for us more salutary lessons if the idea of Yeshua transforms in our mental approach (re-forms in our neuronal groupings) into what he was: Yeshua, a man who spent a life, a person who wrestled with the I-know-not-what; just as we do. In that otherwise-concept though, in our Christology so reduced there remains only "the anointed" in a very loose sense and "savior" only as "an indicator of a way,"[46] we find anxiety itself metamorphosing

---

44. Falque, *The Guide to Gethsemane*, 30.
45. Falque, *The Guide to Gethsemane*, 29; emphases in the original.
46. Etymologically *christos* as the Greek translation of the Hebrew *mashiyach* ("messiah"), both terms meaning "anointed" and referring to the pouring of oil (usually aromatic) over a person in an act

into something else: namely *angst,* and it is on that nuanced qualitative tweak where we will turn in a re-viewing of the afore-displayed works, a revisiting that enables the "lived facticity" (as Heidegger would have put it[47]) of Yeshua as Yeshua to bloom. By means of bridge spanning the old abstract of God/"God"-man whom we have been told to honor to the (not new, but underemphasized) man-man we would like to promote as *honorable,* allow me to offer what might appear to be an unrelated engraving, but only at first "glance." When seen/"seen!" through adjusted eyes the directness of this image-idea/idea-image ought to be transparent: William Blake's "Job Recounting his Experiences to his Daughters" (1825),[48] a force of pathos not to be outdone: Job, envisioned here after his long and manifold travails have at last come to their completion; Job the once-more father and householder; Job following the conclusion of the wager placed between the Accuser and the Almighty[49] regarding how this paragon of righteousness might react to unforetellabe testing; Job envisioned as weakly placing his arms in a posture—by Blake probably not done ironically—of semi-crucifixion; Job restored but yet defeated and exhausted, beaten and spent; Job the picture of undeniable "suffering, pain," of undeniably "teachably human":

---

of ritual elevation. Traditionally for Christians the association has usually been with a kind of kingship (symbolic of lordship, a rule or reign establishing), but for us perhaps we can rather think of it as an acclaiming—an enunciation—from one human to another, with respect for the clarity and depth of vision Yeshua demonstrated and gave to those around him, as best he could.

47. Heidegger, *The Phenomenology of Religious Life.*

48. Image (below) taken from "File: Job Recounting His Experiences to His Daughters LACMA M.48.5.2.21.jpg." Los Angeles County Museum of Art, Public Domain, via Wikimedia Commons. Accessed April 21, 2022.

49. Robert Alter, in his own translation and commentary on the text, gives us the following rendering of the tale: Job 1:6–12, "6And one day, the sons of God [Alter explains this phrasing in a footnote: "This celestial entourage is a literary vestige of the pre-monotheistic notion of a council of gods and is reflected in several of the canonical psalms (perhaps, most notably, in Psalm 82)"; for reference's sake, the first verse of that psalm reads thusly: "God stands in the divine assembly; among the divine beings He pronounces judgment"; *Tanakh* (NJPS)] came to stand in attendance before the LORD, and the Adversary [another footnote here: "The Hebrew is *hasatan,* and invariably uses the definite article [that is, *ha*] because the designation indicates a function, not a proper name . . . Only toward the very end of the biblical period would the term begin to drop the definite article and refer to a demonic figure."], too, came among them. 7And the LORD said to the Adversary, 'From where do you come?' And the Adversary answered the LORD and said, 'From roaming the earth and walking about in it.' 8And the LORD said to the Adversary, 'Have you paid heed to my servant Job, for there is none like him on earth, a blameless and upright man, who fears God and shuns evil?' 9 And the Adversary answered the LORD and said, 'Does Job fear God for nothing? 10Have You not hedged him about and his household and all that he has all around? The works of his hands You have blessed, and his flocks have spread over the land. 11And yet, reach out Your hand, pray, and strike all he has. Will he not curse You to Your face?' 12And the LORD said to the Adversary, 'Look, all that he has is in your hands. Only against him do not reach out your hand.' [This "against him" does happen later, by the way, when the Adversary returns and the God/"God" character gives permission for physical ailment, on the condition that Job's life is spared; see 2:6–7.] And the Adversary went out from before the LORD's presence." Alter, *The Wisdom Books,* 12–13.

Figure 6: William Blake, "Job Recounting his Experiences to his Daughters" (1825; 20th print)

As we have witnessed in our above explorations, due to the interplay of image-idea and idea-image it is impossible to approach a picture as a blank slate: some associations will always be present, and these are most typically culturally and historically bound. Thus neutrality is effectively blocked; biases in interpretation(s) are inevitable, and the (perhaps) sought ideal of objectivity is an illusion.[50] These assumptions of meaning we hold yield their inevitable notion/events and our lives bear witness to such, built and building from behind thickly distorting lenses—but there is a freedom to be found here, and once aware of these enactments we might liberalize and re-contextualize, breaking out new significations and hence novel applications. Through an understanding of one's inner workings an abstractum seedling may be planted that grows into another (an-other) initiatory stimulus when facing an image (or even a person): this is a fresh concept of the to-come, one aimed at a purposeful notion/event rather than merely arriving at a default, and it is one that is (or ought to be) chosen carefully, with—I offer—the wisdom of the trailblazers we have encountered in our

---

50. See Feyerabend, *Against Method*, for a solid analysis of this point; Polanyi, *The Tacit Dimension*, also makes a similar argument.

study above as aids on the way. The Christ is dead, long dead, buried and thoroughly rotted; long live the Christ. Let us find this "Christ" in the words and actions Yeshua spoke and performed in his own time, with an eye on what purport they held then (in the main as ethical and social, which we "saw!" through our selected parables), realizing that although naturally our present circumstances differ greatly from those of first century Palestine, that does not reduce nor nullify their effect and importance for any "kingdom" we might choose to pursue in our interpersonal relations and individualized undertakings. Yet we have introduced this enough; henceforth we commence with our re-viewing, our revisiting of the images already put on display, and as T.J. Clark has done for entirely different works and with entirely different goals,[51] in our going back and back may we find what these paintings speak to us today, tomorrow, the day after.

The first work we viewed in the preceding was Pietro Perugino's "Agony in the Garden" (1483–1493):

Figure 7: Pietro Perugino, "Agony in the Garden" (1483–1493); redux

51. Clark, *The Sight of Death*. Clark's book is essentially a diary of time spent with Nicolas Poussin's "Landscape with a Man Killed by a Snake" (likely date of 1648); although Clark began the project intending to study Poussin's "Landscape with a Calm" (1650–1651), he was simply too drawn to the snake picture to remain with the calm; a fitting comment, perhaps, on human nature.

158

Art and Interaction(s)

On another intercourse with this image, one born—as we will do for each of the proceeding—from a (notion/event) Yeshua taken not as savior but rather as sage, not as incarnated but rather as exclusively carnal, as a Jew and not as a Christian (and not even, moreover, as would-be founder of anything Christian), and certainly not as God/"God"-man but without doubt as man-who-sought-God/"God"; from this setting, what is related? We find a number of facets both striking and, frankly, rather dull. To begin, we might (or probably should) pay little heed to the background crowds which do not seem to be affecting our centered "main character" in any way (the Roman soldiers, Judas the Betrayer, the Temple authorities (seen on the left, most clearly signified by the figure with the long beard: a common trope for representing the "adversarial Jew")). They are of interest only graphically, and although we know them from the story of which they are meant to be involved (and we do keep the story: we are changing how we think Yeshua within it), they are bit players, and for that not particularly evocative.

Finding ourselves now before a Yeshua in the context and narrative that the artist has placed him in, we have our man kneeling on a large rock, foregrounded by three sleeping comrades and backgrounded by a natural scene of spare vegetation, a large body of water, and a sizable city constructed of stone amongst surrounding hills. We are aware that this is meant to be the Garden of Gethsemane, and we are knowledgeable too about the events that the Gospels claim took part there at this time; but for good measure we remind ourselves that the whole situation is poppycock, not history, and wherever Yeshua was when he was arrested it was not under these circumstances. (Scholars think it far more probable that he was taken either at the Temple or nearby it after the ruckus he caused there.[52]) Still, here is a portrait of Yeshua; his disciples—again, we know them to be "his disciples" because we recognize the given context even while attempting to comprehend it differently—have evidently been waiting on him for a long period and hence have fallen asleep while he tarries. Why it might be that Yeshua is portrayed as kneeling on a rock we do not know (artistic license?), but he appears to be experiencing a vision of an angel offering him a cup of something; what, and why? His face is passive in his gazing at (and almost beyond) the angel; his fingers in a relaxed and lightly enfolded gesture, hardly indicative of a man hard at prayer as we recall the Gospels have him. He certainly does not look troubled. There is neither anxiety, nor angst, nor much of anything here; it is just a person on a stone, possibly hallucinating (that face and that vague line of vision: is he on some kind of drug?).

---

52. The famous "Cleansing of the Temple" scene; here is Matthew's introduction of the event, from 21:12: "Then Jesus entered the temple and drove out all who were selling and buying in the temple, and he overturned the tables of the moneychangers and the seats of those who sold doves." *Thinline Bible with the Apocrypha* (NRSV). It should be noted that these people were providing services fully in accord with the sacrificial regulations as outlined in the Torah; Yeshua's attack on them was far more of a move against the standardized religious practices of priestly Judaism than it was a kind of anti-capitalist measure: this was an assault on the elite, not on economic exchange. For the ritual details concerning the types of actions and expectations involved in daily Temple function, along with many quite helpful explanations, see Plaut, gen. ed., *The Torah*.

We are cognizant of the story's setting, and we recognize that we want to try and rethink it instead with Yeshua as we have come to appreciate him, but we find that task almost impossible with the tools at hand. The painting, stripped of its Christianized overlays, is simply too *shallow*; it is entirely unsatisfying as an emblem of any kind of struggle, although clearly executed with a highly skillful technique. We do experience something in this re-facing; but it is predominantly disappointment.

The next work was Albrecht Dürer's woodcut relief of the same title, "Agony in the Garden" (1515):

Figure 8: Albrecht Dürer, "Agony in the Garden" (1515); redux

Here the approaching authorities and soldiers are barely visible—one has to squint or take out a magnifying glass—and even the disciples have been downplayed in their assignation to the far left of the frame, behind the (rather lovely and apparently windswept) tree. Of note, however, is the sword carried by one of them, whom only John's version (the much later written, and in many ways standout, of the canonical

Gospels with its differences in content and emphases) names as Simon Peter.[53] Nevertheless, all three men are again portrayed as at rest, though by the looks of things less comfortably so. They do hold our attention, but mostly as curiosities.

Far more important amidst the remarkable details of this work is, naturally, Yeshua. He is as well-dressed as Perugino has him—possibly even more so—but his countenance is altogether different with its evident worry. Yeshua is given as a person carrying a heavy mental weight, and the broodiness or meditative quality of his face strongly hints at one who is confronted by distressing unknowns. This altered reading-out from the work, it will be noted, fits our earlier criticisms quite well as it points towards a lack of omniscience: if there is, in and/or behind Dürer's effort, an affirmed (if somehow suppressed) certainty of resurrection and triumph in the Yeshuan figure's mind, then we do not find it reflected in the given expression.

For us this is a facet of great worth, for we have argued that the God/"God"-man omniscience that high Christologies affix are a striking point against the images, and indeed the entire Gethsemane scene (irrespective of its fictitiousness: the story of the Garden is ruined by having its "struggling" protagonist know in advance that he will be the ultimate winner). Yeshua is fretting, and this image allows us to read-in that he does not know what will happen—as we would not either—but that he has justifiable cause for concern since the Romans were none too subtle in how they dealt with people who had attracted a popular following. Yet in that we are made to think too on the courage Yeshua must have had: he knew his world—he lived it—yet he still kept, even sought, that very following, that role of teacher, rabbi, sage, because he deeply and genuinely believed in his (self-assigned) cause; would that each of us were so fortunate to have such a calling to live for![54] Yeshua—we can see/"see!"—felt that he had something to give and wanted to give it; results be what they may. Only naturally those potential consequences still caused him consternation; to this too we may well relate. In the fable of Gethsemane, in this image and the ideas it sparks, those "results" were coming to fruition—palpably, revealingly—and we might thereby take that shock of light inscribed around Yeshua's head not as being indicative of divinity (not as halo-esque) but rather as highlighting the distressed countenance. The ministerial good works Yeshua had been engaged in (by his own reckoning, although of course not

---

53. John 18:10: "Then Simon Peter, who had a sword, drew it, struck the high priest's slave, and cut off his right ear. The slave's name was Malchus."; the Synoptics read as follows: Matthew 26:51: "Suddenly, one of those with Jesus put his hand on his sword, drew it, and struck the slave of the high priest, cutting off his ear."; Mark 14:47: "But one of those who stood near drew his sword and struck the slave of the high priest, cutting off his ear."; Luke 22:49–50: "49When those who were around him saw what was coming, they asked, 'Lord, should we strike with the sword?' 50Then one of them struck the slave of the high priest and cut off his right ear." All quotations from *Thinline Bible with the Apocrypha* (NRSV).

54. In this regard Falque makes a quite astute remark: "[Christian] witness in our time takes the form of a humble recognition of a reason for *living* that could also be a reason for *dying*—when certainly other reasons, probably equally respectable, could also be worthwhile in their own way. Avowing meaninglessness [i.e. of life] evidently does not suppress the question of meaning: on the contrary, it innervates and exacerbates it." Falque, *The Guide to Gethsemane*, 27.

only by his own) were returning to haunt him, calling fate down onto his shoulders. Taken this way we might even have the *chutzpah* (a wonderfully appropriate (on so many levels) term of Yiddish derivation) to view the angel presented not as a heavenly servant but instead as a ghost, a specter of things past. (Never mind the look of comradely concern on the winged cup-bearer; cannot some ghosts be friendly? The reader will undoubtedly find examples (perhaps from popular culture) in no short supply.) This is a thoroughly intriguing re-interpretation, and what this work calls forth from us (altered reading-outs from variant image-ideas/idea-images) is beginning to demonstrate the possibilities of further pioneering notion/events.

Following Dürer was Carl Bloch's descriptively titled "An Angel Comforting Jesus before His Arrest in the Garden of Gethsemane" (1873):

Figure 9: Carl Bloch, "An Angel Comforting Jesus before His Arrest in the Garden of Gethsemane" (1873); redux

For this piece let us continue to take the angel in the wider reading-out inspired by our reflections on Dürer, but instead of thinking on this creature as a ghost we shall now simply label her/him "otherworldly"; that too though with the qualifying sense of a loose aetherealness rather than as entitative. In fact, on my own interaction with this image-idea/idea-image, I find the whole to be entirely otherworldly (in the standard sense); indeed, almost too so. As mentioned above, the pitch black background of the left-bound border yields a nearly "floating in space" feel to the artwork, and although natural setting elements are visible in the center right background (behind the prominent tree with its leaves (top left) so darkened they are visible merely as light reflectors), such lie in heavy shading. The eye is drawn again and again to the center with its robust interplay of color, but this is also underscored by shadow. Against all this fulsome dark our angel/alien/apparition shines radiantly in her/his white, and as indicated earlier I wish to use a non gender specifying pronoun for this being because I find the depiction so pleasantly either/or if one thinks along traditional (stereotypical) role definitions (or, perhaps more fittingly: either/or/both). The features are solid but soft, somber but concerned; the caress of one arm—the right—supportive and empowering; that of the other—just visible on the back of Yeshua's head—comforting, caring, compassionate. While taking the afore-listed qualities in "female/male" terms is admittedly diminishing, and again is merely reflective of received cultural ideas pertaining to the ought-tos of masculinity and femininity, we should remember that Bloch painted in an era when societal positions were more ensconced and less forgiving; and yet he still managed, I feel, to capture them beautifully in this kneeling emblem. The cumulative effect of the bright "other" and her/his placement within the contained narrative is so gratifying to an image-idea/idea-image of Yeshua as taken in a fully human manner that the addition of the wings to our solace-giver constitutes a great disconsolateness, forcing one to abandon what may have been a wonderfully down to earth and quite open hermeneutic.

Pushed in this direction, it is perhaps best to allow one's thoughts to carry over now to Yeshua himself, who in his positioning and posture—we immediately notice—is not engaging the angel/alien/apparition directly. He does appear to be leaning against the body of "his comforter" (in quotation marks/inverted double commas to maintain the nuance of a not necessarily embodiedness for this creature), but the manner in which he is resting on his own legs would perhaps be sufficient for self support. (Admittedly we would like to see his buttocks placed lower for this, as if he were resting on his heels, but I think there is nevertheless interpretative room for that being the case, at least with his right side if we imagine the foot angled upwards and hidden beneath his robe.) His gaze is downcast, hands folded in a loose gesture of prayer (that is, for how Western people tend to pray; Dürer's Yeshuan hands are actually closer to Asian styles), and again genuine worry is detailed by the setting of the brow and mouth.

Comprehending Yeshua as human, only human, on the image-idea/idea-image we prefer, this work now instigates a response of awe at the emotional depths to which this sage flung himself in the pursuit of his message; and in the place it got him to. He saw the world differently, he viewed (lived in) the *could-be* rather than the *is;* and suddenly, as he seeks solace in Gethsemane, he is confronted by an intuition of how very much that will cost him. In our return to this picture we are caused further to share the sympathy of the angel/alien/apparition, or possibly to go even "beyond" sympathy into empathy if we judge ourselves capable of genuinely understanding the factors at play. Before us is a crushed visionary, a person of uniquely grouped neurons (mental representative "maps"), who spoke and spoke of "the kingdom" he burned with, who never saw it realized—or anyway not to the degree attempted—and who has come to sense it imploding under the pressure of a powers-that-be wrecking ball. In this piece Bloch gives us a defeat; and we thank him for that, because our sought re-viewing starts from a concept (notion/event) of Yeshua as exemplary comrade, not as exalted "Christ." Yeshua the teacher could be (was) laid low—like any of us might—but Yeshua the God/"God"-man could never (fully, truly) be; and with that "never" comes the many interfering and (we argue) lessening notional concomitants, the blockages to any relating, and the deferral of responsibility for "kingdom" building from we today to a divinely wrought eschatological then which follows from such. Those are topics, however, for our following chapters.

Continuing with the present reacquainting, our next work is Nikolai Ge's "On the Mount of Olives" (1869–1880):

Figure 10: Nikolai Ge, "On the Mount of Olives" (1869–1880); redux

Here at last we are given Yeshua on his own; there are no supernatural elements to bestow gifts, no sleeping disciples to provide irritation, no approaching expedients of governance and politico-religious control. The work is not explicitly "garden" titled, but Gethsemane was (and is) at the foot of the Mount of Olives,[55] and we recall of the canonical "agony in the Garden" stories that Luke's account lists simply the Mount as location for the events (Luke 22:39), while John has the only slightly more defining "garden across the Kidron valley" (John 18:1; see also the discussion comparing the Gospels' Gethsemane accounts in the note at the start of this chapter).[56] It is clear that the locale is the same, and therefore too the familiarly associated fable and its details are brought to our minds by this artwork. What, though, does it communicate on this reacquainting? Here I think we find most clearly the angst alluded to earlier that Yeshua the sage gives us (the fully human, flesh-and-only-flesh man-man, no God/"God"-man); and by this I mean a psychological positing acting on a person with a much greater force than that associated with anxiety.[57] Again, there is no comforting "Christus Victor" knowledge for our Gethsemane Yeshua; he is facing a feeling of probable impending doom, and given the historical realities of (political) crime and punishment he likely recognized the form such would take if it indeed came, but certainness is not a part of his equation, and neither are any claimants being made by him (in his mind) to a "return to Heaven" thus pursuant "triumph." (In writing this way, incidentally, I am cognizant of the attributions apparently being leveled, and so for the sake of caution I note again that empirically none of this "really happened": as scholarly research has shown, the entire Gethsemane narration—framing and details—is a copy of the Davidic tale centered around his son Absalom's revolt (as found in 2 Samuel 15–17, and itself surely containing questionable details);[58] the point here is not the literal/historical one of "Yeshua felt this" or "Yeshua thought that," but rather the phenomenological one of "putting ourselves into the consciousness (i.e. the experienced mental awareness) of Yeshua in this (fictive) moment; if so, what does the art communicate? It is this "conscious of"[59] that is the binding and purpose of our study.)

---

55. Perhaps unsurprisingly, the tourism industry is now involved; see the article "Gethsemane," on *seetheholyland.net*. Accessed October 27, 2020.

56. Luke 22:39 reads: "He came out and went, as was his custom, to the Mount of Olives; and the disciples followed him."; with John 18:1 as: "After Jesus had spoken these words, he went out with his disciples across the Kidron valley to a place where there was a garden, which he and his disciples entered." *Thinline Bible with the Apocrypha* (NRSV).

57. These terms are arguably interchangeable, and indeed *Angst* in German is the ordinary word for "fear" or "anxiety" (we have Heidegger to thank for its entry into English in this way; for his analysis of the placement of the self within angst, see Heidegger, *Being and Time*, notably Division One Chapter 6; and for a broader discussion, see Sembera, *Rephrasing Heidegger*, especially Section 8 of Chapter 2), however I wish to draw a sharp line between their usages, at least in English. On my own thinking, "angst" carries an undertone of dissatisfaction or frustration that "anxiety" does not, although both words denote feelings of dread and negatively tinged future oriented concern (compare, for example, to "worry" or to "fret"; but of course there are layers to each of these). This differentiation will be further elucidated in the below.

58. Funk, ed., and the Jesus Seminar, trans. and comm., *The Acts of Jesus*, 150–1.

59. The very core of phenomenological methodology; see again Husserl, *The Essential Husserl*, and Smith, *Husserl*, for some starters.

Part 3 | Parables and Pictures

With that reminder, let us rejoin the journey. On this second viewing of Ge's "Mount" we are awakened to the thought that there is indeed no victory whatsoever, here or anywhere; and just as Bloch lent us a defeated Yeshua, Ge in turn grants a broken one. The "kingdom" call of a reformulated ethics and social structuring has fallen—it seems to him here in lonely forlorn (and thus to us in witness)—on unhearing ears; we understand a man gripped by a dream he desperately wanted to know as shared, one now—in Gethsemane—recognized as a "becoming" that is deeply tinged with the fear of a stillbirth. Here is one Jewish man pushing against the Israel he lived and knew in the way he lived and knew it, as the collective weight of his nation's history and its present standing pushed back. How many philosophers and sages have not been so emplaced? The "could be" against the horror of stasis: the frustration and utter despondence of it. Yeshua's face bespeaks a wearied almost-bewilderment; the dark, wintry forest behind him echoes it; one can nearly feel the approaching frost in the pale light of its weak sun. Ge's pictorial interpretation of the Garden is stripped down, its pathos bleak, and we are prompted to hear not the prayer which is recorded in the Gospels ("remove this cup" (Mark 14:36, Luke 22:42), or "let this cup pass" (Matthew 26:39)[60]), but rather its opposite: "may this cup come to be"; the cup of "kingdom" and not agony; a wish cried with the pain of insecurity that it would not/never could. Had everything been in vain? A ministry misspent? Might it not have been better to pass his days at the trade he inherited, the practicalities and small daily joys of regular work, family, place, belonging. It was too late now; and here, at the end, the realization dawned that whatever lay ahead (no omniscience), things had gone much too far. The die had been cast, Yeshua had placed his bet—how could he have not, given what burned within?—and he came up on the wrong side. If only. *Angst:* An apprehension of the unsettlingly, frustratingly *not*; a trembling at the consequences thereof; an unpinpointable existential displacement stretching far beyond agony or anxiety; an unutterable dismay. The message, and its proclaimant, as total failure; except that it—that message—it did survive; we are discussing it yet today. Is there then some hope for "the kingdom" after all? We wonder; and that we do so provides one last gem received from a re-viewing of Ge's portrait equipped with the alternative image-idea/idea-image we have offered: namely, the challenge to (at last) make "the kingdom" happen.

The final artwork in our series is Heinrich Hofmann's "Christ in the Garden of Gethsemane" (1890):

---

60. Wordings taken from *Thinline Bible with the Apocrypha* (NRSV).

ART AND INTERACTION(S)

Figure 11: Heinrich Hofmann, "Christ in the Garden of Gethsemane" (1890); redux

Once more this painting is solely of Yeshua, but it can hardly be said to be absent of supernatural elements. Although it is true that there is no angel to be found here, the none-too-nuanced dual symbolizing of the light from above breaking through the clouds and matched by a halo-like swathe of identically shaded glow around Yeshua's head effectively outdoes even the presence of a heavenly servant in its assignation of supernatural favor. This is not quite a proclamation of Yeshuan divinity per se, but it is very close to that, and taken in stride with the Gospel story its title references, the final effect is the same. Yeshua here is purely and solely the God/"God"-man, presented as somewhat leisurely at prayer, his outstretched arms lying comfortably (it appears) on a table-like rock, hands folded not exactly in prayer but more akin to a posture of rest. There is some concern evident in his expression—notice the set of the eyebrows especially—and his upward gaze does bespeak a certain call for help, but the triple layered clothing (a white undergarment can be seen just below the neckline) combined with a neat, polished appearance and mostly unperturbed visage do not really add up to the peripatetic vagabond "kingdom" dealer, champion of the poor, and would-be social reformer that our earlier examinations of the historical figure and the analyses of his parable teachings have brought us to accept. The notionally adjusted lenses we have been using in our re-examinations become blurred with this work, and its depiction of a nearly childlike and discounted image-idea/idea-image bereft of any theological (let alone philotheological) depth would be more at home, I think, in a fairytale than in an accounting of the man-man Yeshua. The mythos of the compounded substantive nature (fully human, fully divine) is heavy, too heavy, effectively prohibiting a comprehension of Yeshua and allowing only the figure of "Jesus."

In short, then, our re-viewing methodology designed to grant access to other reading-outs from these illustrations of a familiar Gospel story ground down by the same old (enforced) interpretations which have been read into them for centuries—travail in Gethsemane, a wish for the foreknown suffering to pass, an acceptance of salvific role, finally a submission to the holy plan of cross and resurrection—simply does not work with this piece. If we try to take Yeshua in the metaphysically reduced but ontically enhanced manner we have been arguing for, then we are left with the puzzling presence of an apparently well-heeled person fortuitously placed in a small ring of light in some kind of outdoors area (there is no vegetation to grant a "garden" feel to this picture, and the background land—in particular the middle right—is softened in hue, slightly smudged in effect); could this be the teacher we have heard about? The underclass outcast and toiler with the extant social order? He who spoke of a new way to relate to the Law and to one another? He who "has no place to lay his head" (Matthew 8:20, Luke 9:58[61]): no home, no set employment, no permanence nor stability? It hardly seems possible. Whoever this person is, he is not our man.

Hofmann's art naturally does work brilliantly for an intended purpose of presenting "Jesus the Son of God in Gethsemane with Full Knowledge of His Forthcoming Execution and then Arising from the Grave, having Once and for All Conquered Death and Hell," but, again, that is not our man. Rather, our *Jesus* is not, our *Yeshua* is; and our Yeshua is as he was: a peasant with a breathtaking idea of how the world might look if we thought and acted a bit differently. This has been our goal too, and in the preceding we have sought to engage these pictures through reformed eyes—via vision retrained by a re-reading and re-considering of some parables—and in that to let them do something entirely different to us. Hofmann, however, unfortunately takes us back to where we started with Perugino, and that is to the closed hermeneutics of the quotidian "Christ."

The Christ we want, the "Christ" who is dead—long may he live—cannot be seen ("seen!") from that vantage. Our "Christ," flesh rotted so far that nothing but pieces of utterances remain, taught a generosity towards others, a trust in one's life (in nature, in one's place in nature) within its unplanned (unplannable!) unfolding, and an equivalence of human value and worth. What he gave us, that left behind as legacy and mark, is "the kingdom": an abstraction, a kernel-shaped notion/event,

---

61. Matthew 8:20: "And Jesus said to him [that is, to a scribe who has just told Yeshua he will become a follower], 'Foxes have holes, and birds of the air have nests; but the Son of Man has nowhere to lay his head.'"; Luke 9:58: "And Jesus said to him [here the "him" is merely a "someone", described neither as "a scribe" nor as any social rank/occupation], 'Foxes have holes, and birds of the air have nests; but the Son of Man has nowhere to lay his head.'" *Thinline Bible with the Apocrypha* (NRSV).

one which encompasses an enormous potential for world reformation: in both the personalized "world" sense (Heideggerean) of one's perception from out of embedded circumstances, and (more so) in the generalized world (universal) sense of a shared social and physical environment. In this section we have sought to harness selected Yeshuan words and images—image-ideas/idea-images—in order to re-see ("see!") the entirety, supported by the new beginning of an elected conceptual approach (disregarding the received), and in that to also eliminate (as far as possible) the tired and shallow Christian triumphalist readings-in of the Garden narrative, recognizing that such has little or nothing to do with "the kingdom" we have studied. This last, the Passion Week-as-victory claims of an exaltation and a vanquishing via execution—the standard "atonement" understanding—will be the next target in our re-enfolding, our re-turn/(re)turn of Christianity to Yeshuan-Judaism: *a* Judaism (one amongst many). In the next division we shall seek to further strip this plastered surface and get to the core, starting from the same outset that Yeshua had in the (imagined) Gethsemane scene: Finitude, one's own end.

Part 4

TEMPORALITY: GOD/"GOD" HERE, "THE KINGDOM" NOW

Chapter 11

Afterliving

Preliminary: In this Part of our study I would like to think on death but/and life, on life as an ever-death, and from that conclusion the following one: that while life is death so too death is life; and there is no difference between. We shall look first at Yeshua in his context, the surrounding cultural ideas on death he dwelt amongst but more so the question of the afterlife in his ministry. Thereafter we will move to the phenomenon of death for us all, as known to us all: an analysis done from a personal perspective. With Yeshua's (possible) views in mind, as well as the companion thinking on our own mortal brevity, we shift again to the hermeneutical as per Yeshua's famed death, its subsequently assigned ontological meaning and some alternatives thereto: ramifications in myth and symbol. Finally we will contemplate what to do with a thoroughly dead Yeshua and his never-was/already-is "kingdom" message, that which is "spread out upon the earth"[1] yet always "to come."[2] Our efforts may not prove comfortable for all readers, but we will try to remain open and—with grace—hopeful.

How might Yeshua have considered death? Did the afterlife ring for him? *Was* there an afterlife for him? If so, how much of an emphasis may he have given to the postmortem, and would such have tinged the firmness or laxness with which he held his own being while he breathed, walked, talked? We might wish for a Yeshuan equivalent to Marcus Aurelius' famed *Meditations*,[3] but lacking anything even remotely close we will have to make do as we can. I would like therefore, here at the outset, to emphasize how much of the following is speculation and conjecture, a tossing of hermeneutical dice to see how they land. Perhaps we shall have some luck.

1. Meyer, trans. and intro., *The Gospel of Thomas*, Logion (Saying) 113, 63; Funk and the Jesus Seminar, *The Gospel of Jesus*, 67 (their fifteenth chapter, verse seven).
2. Caputo, *The Weakness of God*.
3. Aurelius, *Meditations*.

Part 4 | Temporality: God/"God" Here, "the Kingdom" Now

We do know that the belief in bodily resurrection for the righteous (viz. with regard to fidelity in ritual observation, apparently often thought about in "end of history" terms rather than immediately; it is unclear if this was *only* for the righteous or could be further extended) was a common and largely accepted Pharisaical concept in first century Judaism(s)—although this was heavily contested by the Sadducees[4]—and that it had been so since at least the time of the book of Daniel.[5] (This notion was obviously to become of enormous significance to Yeshuan-Judaism as it was later reformulated therein, and we will examine the twists that the apostle Paul and others put onto the idea in Chapter 13 below.) However, the form of this "bodily resurrection" as likely accepted at the time is distinct from the supposedly same belief that we might be familiar with in our own era, especially if comprehended from a contemporary Christian point of view. To understand how we will turn to the pages of the deuterocanonical text of Second Maccabees, where it is outlined intriguingly and subtly, but almost beneath the surface, as it were.

The collection of the four (possibly five) Maccabean books are an admixture of historical and literary homage to various Jewish struggles during the long years of Greek rule that occurred after the conquests of Alexander the Great, when the Middle East and North African regions were divided into competing Greek kingdoms. On the whole these documents tell the story of an ongoing Maccabee family-led revolt, overseen by a series of brothers across a number of years;[6] the section that concerns us most in the present study is the seventh chapter of Second Maccabees (dated to the

---

4. The immortality of the soul was also denied by this group, whose members were essentially composed of the upper classes (positions held by both lineage and wealth); see "Sadducee," *Encyclopædia Britannica*. Accessed March 19, 2020.

5. The idea in Hebrew is *t'chiyat hameitim* and it has a long and contentious history within Judaism: it involves souls being reunited with dead bodies and eventually came to be linked directly to the Messianic Age and the rebuilding of the Temple. Naturally Yeshua would have thought quite differently on this (the Temple of course stood in his time, but it was nevertheless an era of some messianic expectations, as we have detailed), but if he recited the Amidah prayer then he may have been influenced by the notion; that prayer was formulated in the first century BCE and so only slightly preceded Yeshua's birth; see "Jewish Resurrection of the Dead," *My Jewish Learning*. Accessed September 15, 2021. The Amidah (in one modern version) contains the following: "You give life to the dead; great is your saving power. / Your lovingkindness sustains the living, Your great mercies give life to the dead. You support the falling, heal the ailing, free the fettered. You keep Your faith with those who sleep in the dust. /Faithful are you in giving life to the dead." Harlow, ed. and trans., *Siddur Sim Shalom*, 107. Caputo also discusses this notion in his *Cross and Cosmos*. There is some debate on the dating of Daniel, largely differing between more strictly orthodox groups on the one hand and less traditional readers on the other (the narrative portion of the text is related to the sixth century BCE Babylonian exile), but the scholarly consensus seems to be for a composition between the fourth to second centuries for the first half of the book (the non-apocalyptic chapters), and then around the middle of the second century BCE for the latter half (chapters seven through twelve), making that part contemporary with Second Maccabees, which we will look at in more detail. See the introduction to Daniel by Wills in Berlin and Brettler, eds., *The Jewish Study Bible*, 1640; and the entry "Daniel, Book of," in *New World Encyclopedia*. Accessed December 21, 2020; Ehrman's summative post "A Resurrection for Tortured Jews (Second Maccabees)" gives this timeline as well: *The Bart Ehrman Blog*. Accessed December 16, 2020.

6. For an overview, see: Toy, Barton, Jacobs, and Abrahams, "Maccabees, Books of:," *Jewish Encyclopedia*; and also "2 Maccabees," *New World Encyclopedia*. Both sites accessed December 21, 2020.

late first century BCE[7]), wherein seven brothers (not the aforementioned leaders) and their mother are cruelly tortured and executed for refusing to apostatize and violate Jewish Law. It is through the depiction of the characters and their proclamations whereby we are able to piece together a picture of resurrection that might well have influenced Yeshua in his own thoughts (though again this is merely my hypothesis), one that directly connects martyrdom with revivification, and that latter both bodily yet in a dimension far more limited than how the afterlife is taken by many today.

To better approach Second Maccabees and the abstractional shift it makes in comprehending life and death from a historical Jewish cultural context (I am considering the relationship this text may have played with *t'chiyat hameitim* (see the note above), either as reflective of that notion's early developments and/or even as influential on them), that is to really appreciate the force of the *bodily* resurrection viewpoint that emerged, we will first need to revisit Kugel's important work on ancient Hebrew ideascapes. From the perspectives of our modern world, and with the weight of the traditions we have received bearing down on us, we will be accustomed to taking a somewhat Cartesian, somewhat wandering *atman*, interpretation of the soul wherein while it inhabits the body it is not really inclusively a *part of* the physical: rather it is *connected to* the physical. (In addition to Descartes we can probably blame Paul himself for this; but more on that in the forthcoming.) The soul is what "lives forever," and after we die our soul will find its way either to Heaven or to Hell, where it (or "me", if one takes "soul" to equal "self") will receive a new "Heavenly body" (or "Hellish body," though oddly enough one never hears of such put so explicitly despite the logic of the scheme demanding it) that will maintain its particular existence eternally. May it be a good one! Which, naturally, is the basis of the entire church's trade-off mechanism; but not, as we will explore, of the Yeshuan-Judaic one. Nevertheless, it is with this structuring that we are well acquainted, and from it we may find ourselves reading-in to Second Maccabees what is not there; hence, to try and find what is actually there, we must re-think the soul conception itself since our ideas are not what Yeshua and his contemporaries would have borne in their minds. Kugel gives us the following:

> In the Hebrew Bible, the soul is not really the hypothetical entity that this word conjures up in English. . . . The most common word for soul, *nefesh*, also used to mean "throat" or "neck" in an early stage of Hebrew. It is what the breath and all nourishment travel through once they are inside the body, and thus the word also came to mean, only slightly metaphorically, "appetite" or "desire." More generally, however, *nefesh* designates a person's mind or self, that inner part of a human being that one cannot see from the outside. Another word for soul is *neshamah*, which comes from the common Hebrew root meaning "to breathe" and thus seems to be analogous to words like "spirit," "psyche," *anima, dusha,* and *atman,* all of which derive from words for "wind"

---

7. Toy, Barton, Jacobs, and Abrahams, "Maccabees, Books of:," *Jewish Encyclopedia*. Accessed December 21, 2020.

or "breath" in Indo-European languages. In all these cases, the soul is what keeps a person going, animates the body from the inside, and thus in some sense is the very source of our vitality.[8]

The soul then, in the parameters of these historical and cultural confines, might be thought (by us now) as a nomenclature for a kind of sustaining life-force that, despite the etymological connection with abstracts such as those represented by references to a person's "mind" or "self," is not a strictly individual affair since, as Kugel continues:

> Although the soul is the place of a person's innermost being, it is not always said to be identical with the person who owns it. On the contrary, the soul is commonly conceived to come from, or in some formulations even to belong to, God.... Thus, the soul is "given to" or "put into" or "breathed into" a person by God at birth, only to be "gathered back" or "returned" to Him when the person dies.[9]

Again, the connection with *atman* here I find quite fitting, because on this view the issue is one of the soul's "return" to God/"God", and in that—one would think—its recollection or *re-absorption* into that from whence it came; to Semitic peoples this was perhaps taken as a (regretted) simple end, to Subcontinental peoples instead a (welcomed) liberation or release.[10] In either sense, the soul as an autonomous and uniquely associated quality of a specific physical form is very much a finite appendage (or affixation), it is a battery that runs out and/or is recycled upon death. Depending on one's interpretation, the soul could arguably continue as soul (or spirit or psyche, et cetera) even if recollected or re-absorbed by/into the divine, but its connection with X meat-sack named Sarah or Yakob or Sindhuja is clearly limited. This is the held and widely accepted conceptual antecedent to what Daniel and especially Second Maccabees changed within Judaism (more accurately: within many parts of existing Judaisms); or, given that nothing happens in a vacuum—that every "new" is birthed from out of its embedded confines—strongly guided in a particular direction that which had been slowly emerging (i.e. Daniel and Second Maccabees were reflective of, and influential on, a societal-notional shifting), one whose details we are now prepared to engage.

The seventh chapter of Second Maccabees, as remarked, tells a tale of breathtaking courage amidst shocking horror, and it is through what some of the brothers in the story say to their torturers as proclamations of defiance that we gain hints of the underlying beliefs, the abstracts which must have been culturally common enough to find narrative expression in the manner they did: that is, without the author presuming a

---

8. Kugel, *The God of Old*, 165.
9. Kugel, *The God of Old*, 166.
10. On Vedic conceptions of the *atman* and its wanderings, one cannot go wrong with the classic compilation and translation by Müller, *The Thirteen Principal Upanishads*.

need to include explanatory asides or addendums. The first quotation (of five, all from the same chapter[11]) we will examine is from the ninth verse, which reads: "And when he [the second of the seven brothers] was at his last breath, he said, 'You accursed wretch [in reference to the Greek Seleucid ruler Antiochus IV Epiphanes (reigned 175–164 BCE), who had tried to eliminate Jewish distinctiveness in favor of Hellenic acculturation], you dismiss us from this present life, but the King of the universe will raise us up to an everlasting renewal of life, because we have died for his laws.'"[12]

The final clauses here are where the most impactful nuances are to be found, I think, and especially in the dependent conjunction of the last one. There is initially the "dismiss[al of] us from this present life"—physical death, of course—followed by the definitive "will raise us up"—no question about it—into not only *another* life but an "everlasting renewal of life"; this now requires a slight pause. The operative term here, to me, is "renewal," and since Second Maccabees was written in Greek[13] it might be helpful to consult the original, which literally reads as: "into age-long/eternal renewed life us will raise up/resurrect."[14] The New Revised Standard Version's (cited above) "raise us up to an everlasting renewal of life" seems a very good English fit;[15] and there is that "renewed/renewal."[16] I find this significant in light of later developments in resurrection thinking (following Paul, with Neoplatonist colorations) that would come to focus on delicacies such as "spiritual bodies" (explored in Chapter 3 above); such are not on offer here. Rather this is a far more straightforward "return to" or "renewal of," namely, a repeat, re-start, a do-over, a round two. This is not the "everlasting life" of a fluorescently glowing soul-person walking streets of gold outside treasure filled mansions such as we might fantasize about, it is a same-me-in-the-same-flesh, and living once more in presumably much the same way (without, naturally, all the Antiochus IV nastiness). This conclusion is reinforced by the second quotation.

Verse eleven in the English translation we are using is given as, "and [the third brother] said nobly, 'I got these [i.e. his hands and tongue, about to be cut off] from

---

11. In this I am largely following Ehrman, "A Resurrection for Tortured Jews (Second Maccabees)," *The Bart Ehrman Blog*. Accessed December 16, 2020. Please note though that he does not include statements from the brothers' mother, as I have here.

12. *Thinline Bible with the Apocrypha* (NRSV).

13. See again: Toy, Barton, Jacobs, and Abrahams, "Maccabees, Books of:," *Jewish Encyclopedia*; and "2 Maccabees," *New World Encyclopedia*. Both accessed December 21, 2020

14. Lanier and Ross, eds., *Septuaginta, vol. 1*, 1593. A version of this book and chapter in the Greek and with clickable translations is also available online at: "2 Maccabees 7," *Kata Biblon*. Note that the Septuagint uses Koiné Greek, which was the form of the language during the historical period in question (bridging Ancient and Medieval-Modern); since Second Maccabees was written in this Greek it is quite at home in the Septuagint collection, which is mostly otherwise Greek translations of the Hebrew originals; see "Septuagint," *New World Encyclopedia*. Both sites accessed December 22, 2020.

15. By way of comparison, the New Living Translation version reads instead: " . . . the King of the world will raise us up again to live forever . . . "; *Catholic Holy Bible* (NLT).

16. The term used is *anabiosin* (root: *anabiosis*), and my lexicon lists *anabioo* as "come to life again"; see Danker, rev. and ed., *A Greek-English Lexicon of the New Testament and Other Early Christian Literature*, 59.

Heaven, and because of his laws I disdain them, and from him I hope to get them back again.'"[17] Thus another linkage is asserted between a renewal of (return to) one's specific physical form and adherence to Jewish Law, and this is moreover done in the hope (belief) not of a *new* pair of hands and *new* tongue but of a *repetition* ("get them back") of the selfsame hands and tongue which at the time of his speaking were still current parts of the brother's overall biological frame. Indeed, there is not even a desire for an improvement expressed—no wish for super hands or an impervious tongue or the like—simply what he has redux (evidently considered as a gift "from Heaven": a positive body image indeed!). Then in verse fourteen we learn the limits of this resurrection program: "When he [the fourth brother] was near death, he said, 'One cannot but choose to die at the hands of mortals and to cherish the hope God gives of being raised again by him. But for you [the address is still to Antiochus IV Epiphanes] there will be no resurrection to life!'"[18] This is quite interesting; resurrection is not only bodily in an apparently regular physical sense—albeit "age-long" or "eternal"—it is also seemingly reserved only for the deserving, qualified by dint of specific religious practice. There is a type of in-group (denominational) trade-off going on here: martyrdom rewarded with resurrection; but the extent of such is left open. Would all observant Jews qualify under this conception, or only martyrs?

In verse twenty-three the mother of the brothers states, "Therefore the Creator of the world, who shaped the beginning of humankind and devised the origin of all things, will in his mercy give life and breath back to you again [note the "back to you": a *renewal*], since you now forget yourselves for the sake of his laws."[19] The emphasis in this might appear to be on legal observation (although only arguably so, the "forget yourselves" is quite ambiguous and could be interpreted as implying "suffering for"), and if that reading is taken—one would presume—then resurrection would be available to all whom are sufficiently pious; however, in thereafter counseling her final son in verse twenty-nine to also "prove worthy of your brothers," she tells him to "Accept death, so that in God's mercy I may get you back again along with your brothers."[20] This seems to tilt the conceptual balance more firmly towards martyrdom as precursor or necessity for the bodily repetitious resurrection scheme being affirmed ("so that" implying cause-effect dependency). It is difficult to judge firmly one way or the other though since the text on its face is not explicitly clear, but we might conclude from the context and from our analyses thus far that culturally (or rather subculturally as not every element of society accepted this tenet; for example, we have remarked that the Sadducees rejected such) it may have been a case of comprehending martyrdom as a sure route to a return to life, while perhaps also diligent practice could get one there

---

17. *Thinline Bible with the Apocrypha* (NRSV).
18. *Thinline Bible with the Apocrypha* (NRSV).
19. *Thinline Bible with the Apocrypha* (NRSV).
20. *Thinline Bible with the Apocrypha* (NRSV).

too. The history of faith, in its broad sweep, would come to favor the more lenient of these views, and naturally not only in regards to Judaism(s).

There is one final subtlety to take note of, and it may be quite surprising from a modern perspective (our contemporary biases): as Ehrman points out, in Second Maccabees there is no mention of an afterlife punishment for the wicked, or even for a postmortem for them at all (I take it that death-as-finality itself was considered retribution enough); and that the book, like Daniel, was written during a period of persecution (he adds that this was the same persecution, exhibiting support for the position that assigns a later compositional dating for Daniel).[21] What is presented is a repeated physical—in the body one is now—and eternal (or "age-long": the Greek term used in Second Maccabees means both[22]) life after one's initial death for at least martyrs but possibly also for every person who demonstrates a sufficient faithfulness on the one hand, versus said initial death as the abrupt, complete, and permanent ending on the other. The extremity of the compensatory plan far outweighs that of the punitive; in Christianity (as opposed to Yeshuan-Judaism) this would of course change greatly and move in the direction of a more balanced decree (forever-great or forever-gruesome), but I do not think that transition was sought for the purpose of arriving at a "balance," as we will consider in the following. Taken together, these clues point to a document probably produced with the intention of encouraging steadfastness—no matter what—in one's religious practice for the sake of the rewards to be enjoyed, and the absence of any comparable associated chastisement hints at either a fairly magnanimous outlook on the part of the victims of oppression (all things considered), or the possibility that a sense of true powerlessness—which might prompt calls for one's "enemies" to suffer more—had not (yet) sunk in. This latter will be revisited shortly.

Yeshua may well have had this perspective on death and bodily resurrection as a divine reward for service; perhaps not in a strictly legalistic interpretation of "service" since his views on observance were evidently wider than those of the professional priestly class and analogously minded scholars, but as we pointed out in the above he did demonstrate a number of approximations to the Pharisaical approach,[23] and we even suggested that he might reasonably be considered to have been a sort of "closeted" (or unrealized, non-admitted) Pharisee/"Pharisee." If Yeshua did truly believe that his public message and ministry were either in line with God's/"God's" wishes (as he comprehended them), or—more boldly—as actually coming from God/"God",

---

21. Ehrman, "A Resurrection for Tortured Jews (Second Maccabees)," *The Bart Ehrman Blog*. Accessed December 16, 2020.

22. Lanier and Ross, eds., *Septuaginta, vol. 1*.

23. See Chapter 3; to recap, the Pharisees acknowledged the Oral Law as being valid, sought to use reason and personal conscience as behavioral guides, and held general beliefs that came to be common in Yeshuan and early church circles: namely, worship was neither Temple dependent nor called for animal offerings (prayer and study were utilized), a messianic hope was promoted, angels and demons were affirmed to be existent, and bodily resurrection was accepted; see "Pharisee," *Encyclopædia Britannica*; and Kohler, "Pharisees," *Jewish Encyclopedia*. Both websites accessed March 18, 2020.

perhaps he would have reasoned that death was a small price to pay, and one that would anyway be followed by a reinstatement. Such would be encouraging notions to carry, and the centuries before and after Yeshua are not lacking in figures that clung to the self-professed "rightness" of whatever cause they championed even to the point of execution or assassination. While we cannot know with even slight certainty how the historical Yeshua (as opposed to the narrative Yeshua of the biblical accounts) might have thought about his own death, we do know that these ideas were widespread at the time he lived, that they were common especially amongst the poorer elements of society (Yeshua's own socioeconomic background, and the "popular masses" for whom and to whom the Pharisees labored), that they gained traction during periods of oppression (be it by Greeks, Romans, or others), and that even very many decades before Yeshua lived their presentation in a text (Second Maccabees) was not felt to warrant explanation: every reader and/or hearer already knew about resurrection and what such entailed. On the grounds of this evidence I think it is entirely reasonable to suppose that Yeshua likely—even probably—held the same or very similar.

If so, his teachings can be approached in a way that takes them as aligned with the divine in the eyes of their proclaimant (Yeshua's self-understanding in regards to his didactics), as being potent and pertinent and consequential enough to risk being killed for (while he was comforted—and the threat lessened—by an assured resurrection), yet still not as being necessarily bound to any kind of infallible foreknowing (as we studied in the previous chapter with our time in Gethsemane). What we have, then, is a highly self-motivated and self-assured Yeshua, and in no way does this view require the God/"God"-man conceptuality which later came to be pinned on him. What we have is a human "savior" (read: "guide") that has almost nothing to do with soteriology and very much to do with ethics and sociality. In short, we have a Jewish teacher being quite Jewish, we have Yeshuan-Judaism, as we have been attempting to argue—and to discover—all along. Naturally such assertions require a return to the man's words, and so we move next to search for hints of death and the afterlife in what Yeshua could have said, might have said, or may possibly have said, depending—of course—on the text (the "con"/text) examined.

Readers will be familiar with the many pronouncements in the New Testament Gospels that purport to be from Yeshua and that concern themselves with such afterlife projections as "treasures in Heaven" (e.g. Matthew 6:20 and 19:21; Mark 10:21; Luke 12:33) or "weeping and gnashing of teeth" (e.g. Matthew 8:12; Luke 13:28); additionally the "Last Judgment" held at "the end of the age" (or "on that day") might come to mind (e.g. Matthew 7:13–23; Luke 13:23–28; or the "Sheep and the Goats" portion of Matthew 25:31–46, wherein the concluding verse includes a reference to both "eternal punishment" and "eternal life"). I would like to offer, and henceforth examine, the thesis that all such are equally as fictitious as the Gethsemane tale, the manger and Magi at birth, the walking on the water, and the many other storytelling (propaganda) myths that were placed onto Yeshuan-Judaism by Christianity in the early church's redirection and transformation of the movement. I will admit that this is surely an unoriginal claim, but for that is nevertheless an equivalently important one; with a request for patience then we shall spin this hermeneutical wheel again—and maybe we can do so in a unique way.

My argument is thus: the speculation of Yeshua having had a Second Maccabees-type understanding of personal death and resurrection (for the righteous) appears to be well grounded, or at least highly possible, and this view—it should be noted—is absent of any penal dimension. Moreover Yeshua's teachings, as we have appreciated time and again in the foregoing, were heavily focused on "the kingdom" as he envisioned it, and on the realization thereof: these are ethical, social, behavioral, moral, and perspectival matters, deeply rooted in the "here and now," this present existence: they are forcefully *mortem* and not postmortem. Situationally, socio-historically, Yeshua lived and died a peasant's life around the years of the first third of the first century CE, in a Roman occupied Palestine that was largely peaceful (by comparative standards), and some decades before the First Jewish-Roman War (or First Jewish Revolt; 66–73 CE). It was an era of Roman discrimination against their Palestinian subjects more than one of persecution (the truly severe events—culminating with the siege of Jerusalem and the leveling of the Temple—were yet to unfold), a time of vast differences in living conditions between the rich and the poor, a period of a Hellenized Roman globalization, universalization, cross-cultural interactions, goods and ideas moving (mostly) freely and widely across the Mediterranean basin; under these circumstances Yeshua proclaimed his message and engaged in his ministry. This original movement, the grounding conceptual layer of the edifice we term "Christianity" today (which is to say: Yeshuan-Judaism before it was turned into something else), I propose, lacks the retaliatory ethos that would emerge partly (or mostly) as a result of the changing political climate in the years after Yeshua's execution.

The altered notions we are acquainted with at present—quite far from this foundation—are an outcome, I think, of the increasing intensity of conflict between initially the Jewish communities in Palestine and their Roman rulers, and then between the Yeshuan-Jews with their Gentile compatriots against the more mainstream Judaisms. What I suspect occurred on the individual ideational and perspectival level within the Yeshuan-Judaic grouping after Yeshua himself—the great hope—was so easily and summarily killed and quieted (well against the typical "liberator"-type Jewish messianic expectations[24]) was an ever-deepening *ressentiment* in the Nietzschean sense, a placement of one's own pain at personal failure or (complex of) inferiority onto an external enemy or rival, whether or not said "enemies" and/or "rivals" took themselves

---

24. Although again, as outlined in Chapter 3 above, such views were not uniform, and the discovery of a first century BCE stone engraving describing a messiah who physically suffers and then resurrects after three days is so compelling we must not let the weight of our received interpretations cause us to forget it; see Bronner, "Ancient Tablet Ignites Debate on Messiah and Resurrection," *The New York Times*. Accessed January 29, 2020; and Boyarin, *The Jewish Gospels*.

to be in those roles.[25] This was a natural psychological process among the oppressed or those who thought of themselves as "oppressed," and it seems quite rational to conjecture that an acceleration of such would have taken place along the parallel lines alluded to as that which developed into "the church" sought to distinguish itself from a version of rabbinic Judaism that was coalescing and becoming dominant amidst increasingly earnest re-organizational struggles following the Roman destruction of the Temple in 70 CE.[26] Heaven as a treasure-filled place of reward, and its opposite of Hell as a torture-filled place of punishment, were not issues for Yeshua and are not parts of Yeshuan-Judaism; but each very clearly became of enormous concern to the church with regards to its position under Roman governance and in respect to its relationship of previous peerage with ex-coreligionists: to those post-Yeshua (post-execution) but pre-church believers who took themselves to be under the constraints of both Rome and priestly tradition/Law, this *ressentiment* further came to mean not merely a deferral of hurt but a vengeance-victory: God/"God" doing to the "enemy/rival" in the next life what one cannot hope to do to them in this. Hence, I suggest, the felt need (and likely in an unaware, unrecognized form) to further emphasize a presumed afterlife, and especially as punitive. For evidence of this a return to the scriptural but non-canonical Yeshuan texts we have examined in the above should (hopefully) suffice.

It will be recalled that *The Gospel of Jesus* is a reconstruction of the most likely actually stated words of Yeshua along with some bare narrative framing (inclusive of John the Baptizer (or Baptist)) as put together by the scholarly consortium The Jesus Seminar; it is not an extant text per se but rather a stripped down collection of (highest) probabilities as ascertained by historico-critical, linguistic, and literary analyses. We therefore place this compilation at the start of a timeline of a proposed conceptual *ressentiment* creep, as our bottom or "zero" rank from which to judge. We do this on the simple basis that if they are in fact the nearest we can come to the genuine utterances of Yeshua himself then they are the bar against which everything else ought to be measured. In the text—if the Jesus Seminar did its work well (and from an academic perspective it seems quite robust even if not impervious to criticism)—we do not have what the author of Mark, for instance, claims Yeshua said; rather we have what Yeshua really said (or as near as we can get anyway; one degree nearer at the least). Next in our line is *The Gospel of Thomas,* which has been dated to the middle of the first century (or possibly later),[27] and hence is historically close to the years of Yeshua's lifetime. This is an actual document that can be (and is) read and studied. Thereafter we put the so-called "Lost Gospel" of Q, which is a suppositionally re-assembled text based on the shared features of Matthew and Luke (see Chapter 9 above); since this "book" is

---

25. Nietzsche introduces this in his *On the Genealogy of Morals* (1887).

26. Boyarin, *Border Lines,* discusses in great—and very intriguing—detail how the two movements of what became rabbinic Judaism and what became Christianity established their own identities at least partly in response to the other.

27. Barnstone and Meyers, eds., *The Gnostic Bible,* 43.

one by inference only and no physical copy has (yet) been discovered it is hard to date, but given that the authors of Matthew and Luke apparently both made use of it in their compositions (if the "Q hypothesis" is correct), a scope of the 50s-90s CE is common, with some scholars favoring the earlier years therein.[28] Q might be contemporary with *Thomas* or even a little earlier than it, but since we have *Thomas* yet do not have Q I wish to give more weight to *Thomas* in our explorations; this is admittedly merely a decision taken on my part, and I could well be wrong to do so. Finally are the canonical Gospels: Mark at around 70 CE and after the Temple's destruction, Matthew about 85 CE, Luke roughly 90 CE, and John near the end of the first century.[29] Hence our timeline: *The Gospel of Jesus* → *The Gospel of Thomas* → Q (→ the canonical Gospels, which will not be examined for reasons detailed shortly).

Our methodology will be to search out the proffered increasing appearance (or display) of *ressentiment* as evidenced by references to a polarized (reward/punish) afterlife and/or divine judgment by Yeshua/"Yeshua" from this trio of non-canonical texts/"texts," following the order just listed (and for clarity: the first double quotation marks/inverted commas signify that which was likely spoken (Yeshua) versus words afterwards put into his mouth ("Yeshua"); the second set (texts/"texts") of double quotation marks/inverted commas allow for *The Gospel of Jesus*' reconstructed status and Q's uniquely hypothesized *and* reconstructed status). We will not delve into the canonical texts themselves due to how well-known such already are, including the widespread understanding of their afterlife content; rather we will simply look first through the contents of *The Gospel of Jesus*, then *The Gospel of Thomas*, and finally Q in our effort to determine what afterlife "evidence" may be gleaned therefrom, citing the remarks as we find them and making some brief additional comments when called for. With luck our case should become fairly clear.

What is most noteworthy in this endeavor about *The Gospel of Jesus* is its impossibility: there is nary a syllable in the entirety about Heaven, Hell, the judgment, "on that day" (as in: the day of final divine sentencing of souls), nor even the Hebrew Bible's shadowy term *Sheol* (roughly like Hades: a place of quietude and darkness but not punishment). Yeshua has nothing to say about what awaits after death and very much to say about how one ought to spend one's time in life. If *The Gospel of Jesus* is indeed an accurate depiction of the most likely instructions and wisdom that he imparted to his followers and wider listeners, then the earthly (even *earthy*: very much

---

28. Borg's preface in *The Lost Gospel Q* gives a date of "in the 50s of the first century," making it concurrent with Paul's letters (and with *The Gospel of Thomas* if its earlier compositional dating is correct); see Powelson and Riegert, trans., footnotes, and eds., *The Lost Gospel Q,* 13.

29. Funk and the Jesus Seminar, *The Gospel of Jesus,* 111–13. Incidentally, the New Testament's finale—that is, the Book of Revelations (surely the apotheosis of a *ressentiment* trend)—is thought to have been written around 96 CE; see White, "Understanding the Book of Revelation," *PBS: Frontline.* Some scholars contend there were multiple authors for the book, and that its parts were composed and collected over the last quarter of the first century; on this see The Editors of Encyclopædia Britannica, "Revelation to John: New Testament," *Encyclopædia Britannica.* Both sites accessed December 24, 2020.

Part 4 | Temporality: God/"God" Here, "the Kingdom" Now

an everyday "dirt under the fingernails" type of ethos pervades) behavioral content of "the kingdom" which we explored in our previous section through a study of select parables was more or less the whole of it. Yeshua was interested in comportment: me towards you, you towards me, both of us towards God. There is, though, one saying that might apply to our efforts here, from the second chapter (as Funk and his associates divided their collection):

> *The Gospel of Jesus* 2:29–33:
>
> *On anxieties:* ²⁹He used to say to his disciples, "That's why I tell you: Don't fret about life—what you're going to eat—or about your body—what you're going to wear. ³⁰Remember, there is more to living than food and clothing. ³¹Think about the crows: they don't plant or harvest, they don't have storerooms or barns. Yet God feeds them. You're worth a lot more than the birds! ³²Can any of you add an hour to life by fretting about it? ³³So if you can't do a little thing like that, why worry about the rest?"³⁰

If such daily necessities are not to be considered as cause for concern, one might infer, then surely something even further out of reach like the afterlife would not as well. Our baseline of comparison for Yeshua's overarching message on death and what follows it then—these most probably authentic of his varied teachings, taken together—is therefore *nothing at all*. Yeshua's efforts do not appear to be soteriological, and if there were elements along those lines then they were not primary. We should note that this is not a *rejection* of the afterlife—Yeshua, we have conjectured, might well have accepted the resurrection-as-righteous-reward conceptual package—but neither is it justificatory for perceiving postmortem mechanism(s) to be motivational for one's conduct at present; nor indeed for beliefs to which one adheres. The disciple frets: What is going to become of me? Yeshua's reply: Do not worry! (In that retort we can almost hear an additional ring of "Who knows!")

Moving now to *The Gospel of Thomas*, there are two sayings which we can apply to our quest: fifty-one and fifty-seven. The first reads as follows:

> *Thomas,* Saying 51: ¹His [Yeshua's] followers said to him, "When will the rest for the dead take place, and when will the new world come?"
>
> ²He said to them, "What you look for has come, but you do not know it."³¹

If these were Yeshua's words and not later implantations, they are a wonderfully clear mismatch between the apocalyptic and re-creation/replacement oriented expectations of his audience and Yeshua's own focus on the now-moment. One wonders: Was the response here about "has come" in reference to "the rest for the dead," or rather to "the new world"? In the open-endedness that query faces we have a delightful

---

30. Funk and the Jesus Seminar, *The Gospel of Jesus,* 19.
31. Meyer, trans. and intro., *The Gospel of Thomas,* 41.

puzzle (and very fitting for the general tone of *Thomas*, in this reader's opinion); one in which, however we determine an answer, it yet throws us off balance. These words and thoughts are compelling, and they are on topic for our search, but nevertheless there is no evidence of otherworldly-directed *ressentiment* to be discovered in this saying; either in the followers' question or in Yeshua's answer. The dead will "rest": the implication might be for the "good dead," for those who passed away in beneficent favor and standing with God/"God" and the community, or it might be for all the dead, everywhere and regardless: each interpretation seems possible if the text is taken merely as written. Still, while we do not (and cannot) know definitively, given the socio-historical circumstances of first century conditions as we have outlined them, it strikes me that the former comprehension is the more likely of this pairing. Once more, however, the ultimate Yeshuan answer seems to be along those same lines: Do not worry about it.

The second saying we will quote from *Thomas* is both a little more direct and quite a bit more centered on reward/punishment:

> *Thomas,* Saying 57: ¹Jesus said, "The father's kingdom is like a person who had [good³²] seed. ²His enemy came at night and sowed weeds among the good seed. ³The person did not let them pull up the weeds, but said to them, 'No, or you might go to pull up the weeds and pull up the wheat along with them.' ⁴For on the day of the harvest the weeds will be conspicuous and will be pulled up and burned."³³

Although on reflection it does appear possible to take this saying in more ways than an outright reference to a divine verdict (it could, for example—and in this following the general "kingdom" ethos of inclusion—be an appeal to communal acceptance and a tolerance of any and every member), the assertion of a forthcoming "final judgment" ("on the day of the harvest") does indicate at least a leaning towards an apocalyptic understanding, and probably in that as constituting some form of a once-and-for-all definitiveness (the whole population of the summative dead plus those currently yet alive). Add to that the "pulled up and burned" (as well, really, of the pejorative use of "weeds") and a punitive aspect comes clearly into view; one that is indeed guaranteed to occur in the future, thereby bearing the double hallmarks of a *ressentiment* and an accompanying comeuppance/revenge outlook. There is, though, nothing *eternal* about this, no endless torment in an unchanging Hell. This lack is significant. If *Thomas* was in fact composed during the mid-first century and not later on, then its nearly absent (but not quite) *ressentiment* may reflect a social situation of increasing tension between one party (the Yeshuans) and at least one other (here referred to as "the weeds"). Thinking historico-politically, this probably makes the most sense in the context of the early church's efforts to distinguish itself from the

---

32. This is Meyer's insert in his role as translator.
33. Meyer, trans. and intro., *The Gospel of Thomas*, 43.

Part 4 | Temporality: God/"God" Here, "the Kingdom" Now

other Judaisms; and moreover of the remaining need at this juncture, two decades or more after Yeshua's death, to *effortfully* so distinguish; from which we can deduce that Yeshuan-Judaism was still sufficiently Jewish that it was not obvious to every observer (whether outsider or—intriguingly—even insider) where a line might be drawn.[34]

Q, for its part, contains six sayings that relate to an afterlife and/or judgment, some of which can be grouped together. The first two, sayings thirty-one and forty-one, both deal with condemnation of the wicked, but do not therewith explicitly describe a penalty on the level of an eternal Hell, although punitive measures are still invoked. The imagery used in each nevertheless implies such a "Hell," making them somewhat intermediary; both will be quoted together:

> Q31: [Here Yeshua is instructing the disciples that while they are engaged in itinerant preaching if a town does not welcome them they are to wipe off its dust from their feet as they depart.] I tell you, on that day Sodom and Gomorrah will be better off than that town.
>
> Beware, Chorazin! Take heed, Bethsaida! If Tyre and Sidon had seen the miracles performed in your midst, they would have changed their ways long ago, sitting in sackcloth and ashes. It will not go as hard with Tyre and Sidon at the judgment as with you. As for you, Capernaum, do you think you will be exalted to the heavens? No, you shall go crashing down among the dead![35]

> Q41: [Yeshua is speaking] The Queen of Sheba traveled from the ends of the earth to hear the wisdom of Solomon. Today, something greater than Solomon is here. The people of Nineveh heard the preaching of Jonah and changed their ways. But now, something greater than Jonah is here.
>
> At the judgment, both the Queen of Sheba and the Ninevites will condemn this generation.[36]

In these "the judgment" and punishment for a failure to repent are the common themes, with "crashing down among the dead" listed outright and the referencing of Sodom and Gomorrah (both of which were eliminated by fire; see Genesis 18:16–19:29) hinting further at painful destruction. It should again be noticed, however, that there is nothing ongoing about these chastisements: they are one-time events occurring "on that day." There are two other points of interest, moreover, and the first of which does hint at a longer-term perspective: that is that the historical cities and personages evoked will also be present at "the judgment," whenever it may take place. Are these then to be raised up from a death slumber for that purpose? Having already been punished to yet be punished once more? Are these dead now in a kind of purgatory

---

34. Again, for an account of the fascinating history of division and identitarian struggles during these centuries amongst the Judaism(s) and what emerged as Christianity, see once more Boyarin, *Border Lines*.
35. Powelson and Riegert, trans., footnotes, and eds., *The Lost Gospel Q*, 65.
36. Powelson and Riegert, trans., footnotes, and eds., *The Lost Gospel Q*, 75.

(perchance a *Sheol*) state, with or without awareness of current conditions? Are they already being further chastised in some untold manner during the meantime between an initial physical annihilation and the coming "judgment"? We do not know, and the text gives no clues.

The second further facet is the (attributed, probably) use of "something" by Yeshua two times in Saying 41; the first to compare himself (presumably; or did he mean his ministry?) to Solomon, and the second to Jonah. Solomon of course was the great king, Jonah the reluctant prophet; these are very diverse allusions, and it is hard to know what to make of either, particularly the usage of "some*thing*" rather than "some*one*." The opaqueness of the lines hinders much genuine application, but the assertion of being Solomon-esque certainly matches with later Christological claims, while that of being Jonah-esque is probably more in line with an earlier Christology that had not yet attained the same stratospheric theological heights. Nevertheless, these assignations do not seem fitting as being empirically Yeshuan when held against "the kingdom" proclaimant whom we have come to know: my sense (and it is little more—but also little less—than that) is that the entire saying lacks authenticity; in any case both of these Q citations are further evidence of a growing *ressentiment*.

The next two Q sayings we will examine deal with those who consider themselves morally virtuous but in fact are not; or anyway are not by the ascertainments of the Q author(s) (and/or possibly Yeshua, if the words are his). In each of these it seems a reasonable assumption to understand therein a more forceful distinction being asserted by the Yeshuan group as over and against their (ex-)fellow Jews. If Q, like *Thomas,* is a mid-first century product, then again this makes sense; if however Q has (or proves to have) a later dating, then these may further be read in light of a desire by the Yeshuans to not only proclaim themselves as separate from other Jews but to do so with the expediency called for in the face of Roman wrath during or after the Jewish Revolt of 66–73 CE (as mentioned above; a kind of "it was not us but them, we are innocent" public relations maneuver). The sayings below are forty-four and sixty-four:

> Q44: [Yeshua is speaking about religious leaders who emphasize the Law but essentially "do nothing to help," as it were] That's why the Wisdom of God said, "I will send them prophets and messengers. Some they will kill, others they will persecute. This generation will have to answer for the blood of every prophet shed since the beginning of the world, from Abel to Zechariah."[37]

> Q64: [Yeshua] I predict that people will come from east and west, and north and south to sit with Abraham, Isaac and Jacob at a great banquet in the realm of heaven. Those who think the realm of God belongs to them will be thrown out into the dark where they will cry tears of bitter regret.[38]

---

37. Powelson and Riegert, trans., footnotes, and eds., *The Lost Gospel Q,* 78.
38. Powelson and Riegert, trans., footnotes, and eds., *The Lost Gospel Q,* 98.

Part 4 | Temporality: God/"God" Here, "the Kingdom" Now

In the first instance we again have a pointing towards condemnation and an unspecified punishment ("will have to answer for"), whereas in the second there is the far more detailed "thrown out into the dark" with its "tears of bitter regret." While such are possibly more in line with the imagery we today hold regarding what happens to those on the "wrong side" of the future Heavenly soul sifting, the canonical Gospel parallels based on Q are even more explicit with regards to the last saying: and frighteningly so. We list them here for the reader's benefit:

> Matthew 8:11–12: [Yeshua] ¹¹I tell you, many will come from east and west and will eat with Abraham and Isaac and Jacob in the kingdom of heaven, ¹²while the heirs of the kingdom will be thrown into the outer darkness, where there will be weeping and gnashing of teeth.[39]

> Luke 13:28–29: [Yeshua] ²⁸There will be weeping and gnashing of teeth when you see Abraham and Isaac and Jacob and all the prophets in the kingdom of God, and you yourselves thrown out. ²⁹Then people will come from east and west, from north and south, and will eat in the kingdom of God.[40]

Each of these biblical portions is a good example, I think, of the *ressentiment* we are claiming, and given the more firmly confirmed later dating of both Matthew and Luke, the increasing degree of such is also hereby well illustrated.

Similarly to the immediately above Q sixty-four is Q fifty-six, in which Yeshua is telling a parable of a manager of an estate who is put in charge by the owner while he goes away on a trip. In it we again find discipline being meted out for moral failure, but the castigation is not (once more) of an eternal sort, and is also not nearly as harsh as that described by the Gospel accounts:

> Q56: [Yeshua] But if the manager says to himself, "The owner is not coming back for a long time," and begins abusing the workers and feasting and getting drunk, the owner may return unexpectedly. Instead of receiving a reward, the manager will be cut off and will share the fate of the unfaithful.[41]

Note that the punishment described is (only) being "cut off" and "shar[ing] the fate of the unfaithful"; if Yeshua did say this, and if he did think in terms of a Second Maccabees format, then this "fate" might simply be physical (regular old) death without a bodily resurrection as reward. Again, for comparison here are how Matthew and Luke have the same ascribed verbalization:

---

39. *Thinline Bible with the Apocrypha* (NRSV).
40. *Thinline Bible with the Apocrypha* (NRSV).
41. Powelson and Riegert, trans., footnotes, and eds., *The Lost Gospel Q*, 90.

Matthew 24:51: [Yeshua] He [i.e. the owner] will cut him [i.e. the manager] in pieces and put him with the hypocrites, where there will be weeping and gnashing of teeth.[42]

Luke 12:46: [Yeshua] the master of that slave will come on a day when he does not expect him and at an hour that he does not know, and will cut him in pieces, and put him with the unfaithful.[43]

In Q then we find a preponderance of negative messages about a coming judgment, hints—but not direct assertions—of an afterlife, and insinuations that postmortem sentencing is something to be feared, and thus (one would think) an objective for which one ought to orient one's life. Again, we must highlight how far we have come from the Yeshua of "the kingdom" and *The Gospel of Jesus*. Moreover, if Q is indeed roughly a mid-first century creation, then we have traveled that vast notional distance in a very short time (and in a very bad direction!). Much did take place in Palestine between the occasion of Yeshua's death and the decades that followed, in which the Yeshuan community began coalescing around an idea of itself and thereby also increasingly splitting from the other Judaisms, and such events of course include the political developments associated with a shared Roman occupation. As mentioned, *ressentiment* is probably a natural psychological reaction to external pressures, or at least so for a particular mindset or environmental (situational) framing, and I am not trying to cast blame in making the assertion of its presence and growth. I do, however, find this all very un-Yeshuan, and (as especially the remaining segments of our study will explore) detrimental to those of us who find provocative kernels in "the kingdom" message and wish to both live more caringly ourselves and to see our societies better reflect the ideals—like justice, fairness, generosity, forgiveness—that are promoted by, and from within, Yeshua's would be/is "kingdom."

The final Q saying that concerns itself with the hereafter, or rather might so concern itself, is not of a negative nature. It references Heaven, but does so in a way that may be purely metaphorical and not necessarily as a destination, whether understood temporally or eternally. This is numbered fifty-four, and however one thinks on such issues as "Heaven," and whatever one's personal "treasure" consists of, this is a piece of generally good (and positively familiar) advice, requiring—for our purposes at least—no further commentary or critique:

---

42. *Thinline Bible with the Apocrypha* (NRSV); the full reference is verses forty-five to fifty-one. For scholarly fairness I should point out that a footnote to this version further gives "cut him off" as an alternate reading to "cut him in pieces." The New Living Translation (*Catholic Holy Bible* (NLT)) has only "cut the servant to pieces" with no variant.

43. *Thinline Bible with the Apocrypha* (NRSV); full reference verses forty-two to forty-six. Here again a footnote indicates "Or *cut him off*," while the New Living Translation states "cut the servant in pieces" and once more gives no other reading; *Catholic Holy Bible* (NLT).

Part 4 | Temporality: God/"God" Here, "the Kingdom" Now

> Q54: [Yeshua] Store your riches in heaven where moths and rust are powerless and thieves cannot break in. Wherever your treasure is, your heart will also be.[44]

May it be with peace. In attempting, then, our analysis of Yeshua's historical world (and further, "world" in the Heideggerean sense) we have tentatively concluded that he could have (likely did have?) taken a view of death that associated itself with the Second Maccabean perspective of a bodily resurrection as reward for piety, which might or might not have extended beyond those suffering martyrdom. This understanding was a physical conceptualization, and it differed greatly from the "eternal soul in Heaven or in Hell" notion that is prevalent in our own era (ideationally that is, regardless of one's verification or rejection of such). Thinking that Yeshua did accept this revivificational position, it would have been an encouraging one in the face of the dangers ranged against him by virtue of the insurrectionary potential of "the kingdom" teachings he was spreading; it might even have been motivational, as we will explore below.

We also argued, however, that in the decades following Yeshua's execution the core nature of "the kingdom" program as originally espoused was transformed through a combination of mounting social pressures and (likely) political considerations, and these not mainly from outsiders but at the hands of Yeshua's own self-proclaimed disciples and evangelists, conducted via a process of (unrecognized) *ressentiment* that advanced as the years did. Moreover, with the community officialdom, hierarchy, administrative apparatuses, and a burgeoning system of orthodoxy—from "the church" to "*The Church*"—came Neoplatonic abstractions absorbed in from non-Semitic sources, and thence too the accompanying emergence of a posited immortal and individualized self-soul bound for an ever-reward or an ever-punishment; an historical unfolding which Caputo has summarized succinctly.[45] As the church cemented all such within itself deeper and deeper over centuries of debate and decisions, the dogmatism of these perspectives only gained in strength, as we are well aware from the heritage we have received. Our question now, in light of this conceptual legacy and its still long modern shadow, is how ought we—inheritors perhaps against our will—to think about our own deaths set upon the background of a culturally lingering tease (or tug) of an afterlife? How might we brave the brute fact of biological death, confronted in the tearing down of antecedent and likely unacknowledged "belief residuum"? What should we keep from these millennia between Yeshua and ourselves, and what should we let go?

---

44. Powelson and Riegert, trans., footnotes, and eds., *The Lost Gospel Q*, 88.
45. Caputo, *Cross and Cosmos*; see Part 1, and especially Chapter 9.

Chapter 12

(Honestly) Facing Finitude

YESHUA MIGHT HAVE KNOWN he was at the center of a risky venture. His world was replete with the violent suppression of perceived threats to existing imperial authorities, and within the contemporary context of John the Baptizer (Baptist) and other acclaimed or self-claimed apocalyptic prophets the air was already heavy with frightening consequences when he first set out on his own ministry.[1] He almost would have *had* to think about death, and probably often; if in these ruminations he took comfort from a belief in a future physical restoration he would not have been alone, neither then nor now. (Although, as compared with how we might imagine a resurrected form, the "shape" would be different.) Death was perhaps more visibly present in the everyday for Yeshua than it is for us, yet we all face it and all find ourselves thinking on it, however often or infrequently, and in this we merely carry out a longstanding reflective tradition: almost from philosophy's "official" commencement[2] death has been a topic of interest. Epicurus (341–270 BCE), for example, in his "Letter to Menoeceus," issued this famous refutation to the common intuition that death is a harm with the words:

> Death, therefore, the most awful of evils, is nothing to us, seeing that, when we are, death is not come, and when death is come, we are not. It is nothing, then, either to the living or to the dead, for with the living it is not and the dead exist no longer.[3]

However logical this may be though, it is a viewpoint that feels somehow unnatural, one not easy to arrive at; perhaps this counter-intuitiveness is what drives us in the opposite direction, towards the hope/belief/yearning of the "more" offered for

---

1. Crossan, *Jesus*, emphasizes the apocalyptic milieu of the Palestinian environment at this time.

2. That is, from a Western tradition perspective (broadly, Graeco-Roman into European and then today's Continental and Analytic divisions). Cavarero has argued that this is a peculiarly masculine obsession and that a more feminine philosophical outlook would focus itself instead on birth (creation)/becoming; see her *In Spite of Plato*.

3. Quoted in Rosenbaum, "How to Be Dead and Not Care," *American Philosophical Quarterly*, 217–25 (218).

Part 4 | Temporality: God/"God" Here, "the Kingdom" Now

instance by a Second Maccabees, or a self-soul, or some other version of a "life again." This compulsion, this inner burn, is of course thoroughly connected with modern approaches to the figure of Yeshua himself, assigned—to the exclusion of nearly everything else—as he has been with soteriological import by the church's teachings. In the next chapter we shall consider this view of Yeshua as a death-for-life substitutive tradeoff, but prior to that in this chapter let us instead pull back our investigatory lens and contemplate more widely on death *in totum*, on the sheer inescapability of it, whether stripped of meaning or not, and this as situated from within the arguments of important twentieth and twenty-first century thinkers. We will try to find an alternative way to look at death in order to better prepare ourselves for a reconsideration of what has been asserted regarding Yeshua's death, and with our recently proffered conjecture on what Yeshua might have thought himself as a potential bridging point between. In this our focus will be strictly personal—i.e. *my death:* one's own inevitable future demise—theoretically, perspectivally, and then finally ethically.

Many, many years after both Epicurus and Yeshua, Sigmund Freud would observe that our respect for the dead often exceeds truth (I read this as indicating such phrases as, e.g., "He was a good man, beloved by all . . . "), despite the deceased's no longer needing such.[4] This superfluity, we might add, can also run counter to the actual needs of the living who may bear grievances against the departed and be offended at the laudatory way he is being eulogized. Freud succinctly summarized the default position that we who live tend to have towards death with the following: "We have shown an unmistakable tendency to put death aside, to eliminate it from life," and a little further on in the same text, "We cannot, indeed, imagine our own death; whenever we try to do so we find that we survive ourselves as spectators. The school of psychoanalysis could thus assert that at bottom no one believes in his own death."[5] This purported ungraspability is a contention that we will return to; the attitude here described is the same one which Heidegger wished to challenge in his notion of being-toward-death, an idea—a platform—upon which we shall pause to pirouette.

Heidegger was concerned with the individual in the midst of the social, the self in the world (and "world") into which she is "thrown" at birth, incorporating the embedded constitutive aspects we have studied: those historical, socioeconomic, biological, cultural, linguistic, et cetera, details over which none of us have any control. In the automatic (automaton-like) and unreflective mode in which we tend to operate from within this setting, death is something indeterminate and "out there" in the future: *and therefore of no real threat.* As Heidegger put it, "'One dies' spreads the opinion that death, so to speak, strikes the they."[6] He adds that, "Everydayness stops

---

4. Kaufmann, "Existentialism and Death," *Chicago Review,* 75–93 (82–3).

5. Freud, "Our Attitude Towards Death," in *Reflections on War and Death,* 7–12 (7). Available online and accessed January 13, 2021.

6. I.e. "they" as in the anonymous "one" or "every/anybody"; in this case with the nuance—likely unnoticed by the subject herself—of always being about "someone else"; Heidegger, *Being and Time,* 243.

with this ambiguous acknowledgement of the 'certainty' of death—in order to weaken the certainty by covering dying over still more and alleviating its own [i.e. the self's] thrownness into death."[7]

Essentially Heidegger is asserting that death, in the manner in which it is normally considered in our day-to-day lives, is a fact that is recognized intellectually if called upon but not something that is ever really felt. We might compare this to how many of us associate with the sun's so-called movement: Yes we *know* (in this historical epoch) that the sun is stationary and it is the Earth which rotates and revolves, but phenomenologically it really does seem to us as if the sun goes up and comes down, and indeed it is based on this latter notion—and not the concept of solar implacability—that we direct our lives. Thus it is, Heidegger thinks, that death is ultimately something ignored: we neither expect it as we should, nor make any attempts to mentally draw close to it. In this accusation of a widespread neglect of death he does echo Freud (and many others), yet Heidegger goes further and stresses how such a willful avoidance is to our detriment. For a more authentic life, in order to distinguish oneself from the "they" who surround and to better and more fully engage in one's own being, death must be faced as a possibility.

Herein the analysis becomes more problematic: this term "possibility," in Heidegger's usage, is an area of no small contention, while also being of vast importance to his broader being-toward-death, and so we will need to dwell on it for a moment and attempt to understand—or at least find a response to—what it is that Heidegger may be arguing. Taken on its surface, the word would appear to indicate that for Heidegger death becomes a project when it is purposely accepted, when it is faced up to, embraced, planned (in a way) and, so to speak, *built* authentically. Paul Edwards has written that while this sense of "task" or "act" is the typical reading of Heidegger, and in fairness is based on Heidegger's own initial use of "possibility" in the very same work, it is in fact wrong—and the fault for so many thinkers mistaking the term's implications lies with Heidegger himself since he suddenly shifts the way he employs the word and, Edwards accuses, he probably does so intentionally to be vague and hence (thereby) appear to be arguing something deeper than he actually is arguing.[8] Edwards' claim is that in writing of death as a possibility Heidegger is not writing of the death-moment or a (potentially extended) period of literally dying, but rather of deadness as such, and that not as the state of having already passed (as if something could be placed in to compose a post-mortem "state" as such), but rather as the nullity of every state. "Possibility" really means that death allows no actualization of anything, thus saving us from mistakenly hoisting any content into or onto the state of death (the condition of it). If Edwards is right in his assertion, then Heidegger's engagement of the word essentially runs counter to the term's very definition.

---

7. Heidegger, *Being and Time*, 245.
8. Edwards, "Heidegger and Death as 'Possibility,'" *Mind*, 548–66.

Part 4 | Temporality: God/"God" Here, "the Kingdom" Now

If there is a task or act involved here, it would be undertaken regarding *dying*, which is to say the path to death—whether long or short (and here we might recall the Gethsemane images of Chapter 10, regardless of the fictitiousness of the event(s) depicted)—but even on that Edwards thinks Heidegger's conclusions are unwarranted. He writes, "It is not necessarily nonsense and it may in certain cases be true that a death-producing event is a task and a capital possibility;[9] and the same holds for 'dying'. As universal propositions, however, these statements are quite certainly false."[10] Jean-Paul Sartre also made a similar critique of Heidegger's "possibility" as a project of some kind—which, again, is how most readers have taken it and how Heidegger himself certainly appears to be using the word for much of his analysis—when he pointed out that in death nothing at all is realizable, and hence it is not a possibility but rather "the nihilation of all my possibilities."[11] Edwards thinks Heidegger comes to realize this only at the end of his discussion on death and therefore as a kind of corrective abruptly makes the move to (mis)employ the term in the (new) sense of "annihilation":

> What are we to make of this conclusion and the way in which Heidegger arrived at it? Primarily two things—first, if one agrees, as I do, that there is no survival, Heidegger is quite right in describing death as *total* absence, and, second, that his use of the word "possibility" is fantastically misleading.[12]

Edwards summarizes that, "Heidegger is *not wrong, but perverse*. He uses language which is almost certain to be misunderstood and the misuse, as I have indicated, is not completely unintentional."[13]

Heidegger's prose is certainly often overladen, and while I sympathize with Edwards and find his distinctions between a period of dying, a death moment, and deadness as a state to be highly necessary and very helpful, I think that Heidegger might (*might*, it is often difficult to really be sure of anything when reading Heidegger) in fact be indicating that it is the facing-up-to that is the possibility or task rather than anything else, which if so would then be about an attitudinal adjustment rather than a condition. It is true that in his discussion of the "*possibility of the impossibility of existence*" in Section 53 of *Being and Time*,[14] the topic does seem to be about annihilation—deadness per se—but the same extended analysis also states that "anticipation does not evade the impossibility of bypassing death, as does inauthentic

---

9. Edwards states that he considers "capital possibility" to be a better translation than the more standard "distinctive possibility" for Heidegger's original German of *ausgezeichnete Möglichkeit*.

10. Edwards, "Heidegger and Death as 'Possibility,'" *Mind*, 548–66 (554).

11. Sartre, *Being and Nothingness*, 537; Kaufmann, "Existentialism and Death," *Chicago Review*, 75–93 (86).

12. Edwards, "Heidegger and Death as 'Possibility,'" *Mind*, 548–66 (557); emphasis in the original.

13. Edwards, "Heidegger and Death as 'Possibility,'" *Mind*, 548–66 (562); emphasis in the original.

14. Heidegger, *Being and Time*, 251; see especially the second paragraph of the page listed. Emphasis in the original.

(Honestly) Facing Finitude

being-toward-death, but *frees* itself *for* it" (i.e. the attitude allows itself to recognize the unavoidability of death), and because anticipation discloses all possibilities, one is thereby granted (or takes?) "the possibility of existing as a whole *potentiality of being.*"[15] On my understanding (and I may well be wrong), this is emphasizing the responsibility inherent in working towards and achieving a relationship with one's own coming death as opposed to the default "they" position as described above. If one can establish an authentic looking-to one's death then it attains a "certainty" that is "more primordial than any certainty related to beings encountered in the world or to formal objects, for it is certain of being-in-the-world."[16] One's death finds its place for one (or perhaps that could be phrased vice-versa: one finds one's place with (for/in relation to) death), and that is centrally located.

On this note we might return our thoughts to the first century and to Yeshua, whom we have speculated likely would have thought on his own death given the context of his obviously dangerous (self-assigned) mission amidst the very visible results of what happened to teachers like himself who gained a large enough following for the Romans to notice: assuming that Yeshua did indeed hold to a Second Maccabees-type physical resurrection as divine reward for (at least) martyrs—and that he further would have foreseen himself as falling into that category—then although we today might consider such an expectation (or even the more reduced version of "expectation" as "hope") to be fantasy,[17] it would nevertheless qualify as "authentic" on the grounds being argued for. It is not, of course, authentic in an annihilatory manner, and for that Heidegger would probably find fault or grounds for comment were he to have thought on it, but if this was Yeshua's considered and determined comportment towards his personal upcoming death (whenever he might have thought it possible; near or far), then it nevertheless meets the criteria we have been examining. In the next chapter we will once more find reason to contemplate Yeshua's facing-towards his death, but at this juncture I think it pertinent to highlight that there is nothing in this of prescience, as we argued earlier, and certainly not of a foreknowledge (foregone conclusion) along the lines of a guaranteed resurrection and heavenly ascent in the guise of God/"God"-man raised, such as the narratives of the canonical Gospel accounts would have it. The Second Maccabees physical resurrection that (we have speculated) Yeshua may have expected/hoped for would be that: an expectation, a hope, and therefore—however fervently believed—not a *knowing* upon which an equal grounding might be formed. It is a matter of degree. I know that gravity, when functioning normally (as it has every second of my life thus far), will ensure that my footsteps help propel me along, whereas I expect that I will get where I am walking to, and hope that I do not trip along the way.

15. Heidegger, *Being and Time*, 253; emphases in the original.
16. Heidegger, *Being and Time*, 253–4.
17. Or we might not, we might rather cling to such or to similar dearly; I write here only from one perspective, subject to change as everything is, and intend no assertions nor avouchments of absolutes.

Part 4 | Temporality: God/"God" Here, "the Kingdom" Now

Yeshua's mindset, as we have been exploring it, conceivably could have been thus: a) "My 'kingdom' message is paramount and must be shared, despite the real risk of official persecution it may engender for me should the authorities deem myself a threat as they did for John and the others"; b) "Said persecution could take the form of execution"; c) "Nevertheless, I have faith and trust in my Father; should I be killed for his sake then he will restore my body to life"; d) "In that I find the strength to run these dangers for the sake of the ministry God has given me." Such would make sense, it would fit within the regular workings of human psychology, and it would match the conceptual framework and socio-historical embedded elements detailed in the preceding. There is a slightly darker (potential) nuance here as well though, and that is that if all of the above were indeed the case, then it is possible that an idealized view of martyrdom—and its subsequent reward—may have given rise to a "wanting" to die but not a *wanting* to die: that line between the "hidden in the mental background, sensed but not seen," and the acknowledged, admitted, and accepted. This too would fall within the confines of what we recognize as the workings of the human mind, and it again demonstrates the power of the image-idea/idea-image and the staggering abeyance of an unsprung notion/event. To even begin to publicly preach, after all, requires a particular kind of ego, a form of self-regarding or self-lauding, and the grander one's following becomes—we might think—the more one ascertains oneself to be both worthy of it and even of further recognition; of the kind, perhaps, granted to heroes. For a dominant culture these would likely be the conquerors, for an oppressed people they would be the unbending martyrs, those whose victory came in ceding nothing, whatever the cost. We know on which side the Palestinian Jewish population of the first century lay.

Let us come back to our own facing-towards though, to our humbler positions and efforts to understand what this being-toward-death might be about. On it, John Llewelyn reminds that Heidegger is expressly focused in *Being and Time* on "concern" or "care," and that this care a self has about itself and its world cannot segregate amongst or between time lines: past, present, and future must all be considered together.[18] The interpretation we offered above of one's *approach* being the object of analysis here (Heidegger's, Yeshua's, ours, whomever's) reaffirms taking the trouble-laden word "possibility" in its usual sense, and moreover allows us—if it is correct—to read Heidegger as treating the term consistently and without insinuating any verbal subterfuge on his part. Again, this reading may be mistaken and is probably not altogether original in its conclusions, but it does at least correspond well with how other commentators have understood Heidegger (for what that might be worth). Yet still, this hardly settles much, and indeed now raises a further aspect, leading both out of and deeper into our general roundabout on "possibility": Is one's personal death actually truly faceable? Comprehensible? Acceptable to a sufficiently meaningful degree?

---

18. Llewelyn, "Review: *Heidegger on Death: A Critical Evaluation* by Paul Edwards," *The Philosophical Quarterly*, 388.

(Honestly) Facing Finitude

Could Yeshua have thought—truly, fully—what we guessed he might have? Can we? Earlier we noted that Freud thought contrarily, and he is not alone in casting doubt on the human ability to come to terms with finiteness.

As remarked, death is not typically a topic that we (the "they") bear in mind in the midst of daily affairs and must-do activities, of the seemingly incessant miscellanea. Heidegger is quite apposite in his investigation, I think, when he insists that death is "covered over" for most of us most of the time, that it is not felt, and even if so certainly not as it applies to oneself and one's future. An aphorism of E.M. Cioran puts the everyday (every person) perspective thusly:

> Deep inside, each man feels—and believes—himself to be immortal, even if he knows he will perish the next moment. We can understand everything, admit everything, *realize* everything, except our death, even when we ponder it unremittingly and even when we are resigned to it.[19]

Simon Critchley too emphasizes the terribly difficult conditions we live under wherein while we must come to terms with our limitedness, nothing in our environments is particularly conducive to helping with that, and he cites approvingly what he regards as Stanley Cavell's central insight of "*the need for an acceptance of human finitude as that which cannot be overcome,*" neither in a redemptive sense along the lines of a religious understanding nor in a willed and willful victorious sense such as a Nietzschean "superman" (*Übermensch*) might imply.[20] It is, he states, a "radical ungraspability" as we find ourselves mired in an "inability to lay hold of death and make of it a work and to make that work the basis for an affirmation of life."[21]

From common experience this might seem true enough, but one problem that we ought to recognize here is that the talk of death's "ungraspability" or "mystery" or "inadmissibility" et cetera, clouds over the simple fact that *death* is not an object of knowledge at all, and neither is it something we could "lay hold of" nor "make of it a work"—the work we do is on our *thoughts* (our attitudes) in relation to it, not on it itself. This distinction is crucial. The lack of capability in this regard, additionally, is not due to some inner quality of death per se, but rather to its absence, to its utter nullity. On the epistemic side, Richard Cohen writes that "death is recalcitrant to knowledge regarding its nature. It is not enough to say that one knows nothing and can know nothing about what death is."[22] Hence to label death as a "mystery" or to claim its "ungraspability" carries the (surely unintended) subtlety of a hidden continuity of some manner with one's life, wherefore a concept such as "knowledge" or "work on" might apply (i.e. have something upon which to "know" or to "work on"). Here again I think the issue revolves around a failure to distinguish dying from death; the former

---

19. Cioran, *The Trouble With Being Born*, 159; emphasis in the original.
20. Critchley, *Very Little . . . Almost Nothing*, 157; emphasis in the original.
21. Critchley, *Very Little . . . Almost Nothing*, 31.
22. Cohen, "Levinas," *International Journal for Philosophy of Religion*, 21–39 (29).

does relate epistemologically to life, the latter does not—except as the brute fact of that to which we are headed: a destination of utter naught. The entirety of what we can "know" about that finality is merely that it will occur; it is otherwise—and must be—*contentless*. We might have expectations or hopes (à la our presumptions about Yeshua's possible attitudinal approach), but again such are not "knowings": the robustness involved is many shades reduced. Similarly, the whole of what we may "work on" regarding death is that period which *precedes it;* in other words: one's life, itself, in its duration and the fullness of which is a dying when death as the end is confirmed.

Heidegger was right, I think, to advise against the penchant to "paint" into death a substance of some kind,[23] to imagine that death were a thing that might be comprehended or created. Emptiness does not sit still long enough to be reflected upon—emptiness does not sit at all, it is no object—and it needs no hands to labor over it. Whatever language we may try to use to outline or define that which we cannot fathom will be wide of the mark precisely because it is so indescribable: only silence will do; and that too has its flaws. A thousand points might be proclaimed about dying and each be correct; but death is not dying. In that decisive differentiation death can be seen to not only be unknowable, unworkable, but *inapplicable:* as annihilation death is not "this" nor "that" as if it had relatable characteristics, and it only "is" in the sense of "not." An attitude to *it* (it itself) cannot be formed because it "is not" "anything" whatsoever; yet a turning-towards the fact that death is what we inevitably face and will one day reach (or attain?) *is* something that is formable, and this, we find, is our "possibility," it is our task and our challenge. In this, and surely we can add "in this authentically" (i.e. in Heideggerean vernacular), every moment of life is dying, and hence the manner in which we shape ourselves in that relation will clearly affect both one's being towards oneself as well as one's being towards others. The phrasing in that previous clause, incidentally, is intentionally meant to evoke the same being-toward-death that we have been considering, for it is the intersection of self-death-others that will make up the remainder of this chapter, and then—as remarked—we will revisit more thoroughly what these ruminations might mean for us having attuned ourselves to our own deaths: possibilities in the activity of a re-relating to Yeshua, to his death as it has been related and as it more probably was, to his "kingdom" teachings and to the value they hold, and of course to the many rippling aftereffects of each.

Facing finitude: Boost or balm?

Death then—Yeshua's, yours, mine—is not a topic for analysis; it is not even a topic at all. It is a fact, a brute one, a datum connected to the biology of life; nothing more and nothing less. Taking death in this way would allow a de-romanticization, a de-fetishization (or at least go a long way in that direction), a danger to which many

---

23. Heidegger, *Being and Time,* especially Sections 50–53; Edwards, "Heidegger and Death as 'Possibility,'" *Mind,* 548–66.

(Honestly) Facing Finitude

thinkers past and present appear prone, perhaps induced by a stance that takes death as a "mystery," a beyond that somehow transcends, and thereby fall victim to the temptation to "conflate death with an alternative sort of life"—as Harry Silverstein put it when discussing the Epicurean "no subject" challenge which was quoted in this chapter's opening[24]—or in other words, to foisting a content into the void.[25] Another aphorism of Cioran's should suffice to exemplify this trend:

> Life is nothing; death, everything. Yet there *is* nothing which is death, independent of life. It is precisely this absence of autonomous, distinct reality which makes death universal; it has no realm of its own, it is omnipresent, like everything which lacks identity, limit and bearing: an indecent infinitude.[26]

The closing "indecent infinitude" has a wondrous, poetic ring, an expression evocative of some awe, and while it fogs and distorts the view we seek of death in its affixation of quality even while claiming its lack, the pairing does still point in a helpful direction: the absence of a "realm" and an "identity," while the limitlessness and bearinglessness also identified by Cioran might better be put as simply inapplicable, and thence remove them from any listing. Since we cannot think about death, since there is nothing in death to think about (acknowledged here even by Cioran), we focus instead on seeking an approach to dying: on the undeniable of, the unavoidable to, which leads only unto a final not-(...). For those who have embraced dying in life this felt finitude has often been taken as an impetus, but I think it can also be applied as a salve. First we will examine what some notable writers have had to remark on that more common prior facet (impetus), wondering about Yeshua's possible thoughts in regards while simultaneously considering our own, before then moving on to the latter (salve) and applying the same reflective methods.

To regard one's (lifespan) circumscription as an incentive for X action or goal is to understand only too well the givens of brevity, and therefore to stoke the fire, pour on fuel, redouble one's efforts in striving for whatever objective/desire/pursuit: that attainment which one has ascertained as being both meaningful and meaning-making: the very "stuff" of life (note as well how such is authentic in the manner we have been attending to; an inauthenticity would rather entail a more passive allowing, a trait which would not fit with "impetus"). This is taking a decision and bending all one's might towards it, embracing one's internal alarm clock[27] in the quest to accom-

---

24. Silverstein, "The Evil of Death," *The Journal of Philosophy*, 401–24 (406). This reminds us too of Cavarero's charge that such is a peculiarly male fascination, and has been since (Western) philosophy's inception; Cavarero, *In Spite of Plato*. By this I am certain she does not intend an *exclusively* male obsession, merely a *predominantly* male one.

25. "Void" importantly and not "abyss," which would carry a nuance of space and therefore something that might be engaged, filled, and/or interacted with in some manner. As always, we must take great care with our terminology.

26. Cioran, *The Trouble With Being Born*, 152; emphasis in the original.

27. A device, we are only too aware, which typically does not alert us as to how much time remains before it rings.

Part 4 | Temporality: God/"God" Here, "the Kingdom" Now

plish that sought while one yet can. There are many potentially resulting attitudinal permutations of this perspective, but for our purposes studying (and briefly applying) just three will suffice; for each we will start by offering a representative citation which can then be prodded and poked.

The first comes from Walter Kaufmann and elicits what we might call "the marathon" view of death. He writes that:

> . . . once I have succeeded in achieving—in the face of death, in a race with death—a project that is truly mine and not something that anybody else might have done as well, if not better, then the picture changes: I have won the race and in a sense have triumphed over death.[28]

This is a call to taking one's life as an exercise in accomplishing, to train hard for the grueling forty-two kilometers one finds at birth, to strap on running shoes as soon as one can, and then to pump one's legs as hard as physically possible until the finish line has been reached. If one can do that, Kaufmann argues, everything else falls by the wayside. Moreover, upon the completion of one's central, defining undertaking and the accompanying accolades (either stemming from oneself in recognition and/or (if one is lucky) from others), any extra time spent is purely a bonus, in many ways irrelevant. Kaufmann goes so far in this as to state that what happened to two famous Friedriches—Hölderlin and Nietzsche—in their later years (madness and vegetation, respectively) does not really matter since their works had by then been done. Death may come at any moment; one is ready and satisfied, satiated and full.

Some issues that come to mind regarding this being-towards is that first and foremost there is hardly any guarantee of being able to actually do what one sets out to attempt. In the messy and complex real world of the practical far too many extenuating circumstances will be involved: do chance's dice fall in your favor, or against? Might the obstacles encountered be overcome, or will they prove insurmountable? Are there enough controllable elements? How large a role does luck play? Additionally, no matter how much effort one makes, there is always the possibility that one has chosen poorly and is pursuing something either beyond one's ken or so dependent on other factors as to be highly unrealistic and therefore unlikely. Furthermore Nietzsche, at least, considered himself to be in the very midst of his life's great work—his revaluation of all values—when he succumbed to the disease that left him comatose and eventually killed him. From his own point of view his meaning-making project was far from finished.[29] A final counter is that presumably few of us would be prone to taking the months or years following the closure of a long term task very positively if such were thought of merely as an "extra," as "icing on the cake": a nice addition

---

28. Kaufmann, "Existentialism and Death," *Chicago Review*, 75–93 (91).

29. What is particularly odd is that Kaufmann, having written about Nietzsche's personal history in the introduction to an earlier collection of translations and commentaries on the philosopher's work, surely knew this and yet included him as an example in his argument; see Nietzsche, *The Portable Nietzsche*, 1–19.

to one's time, but not a necessary part. This calls to mind a biography of the novelist Kurt Vonnegut written by Charles J. Shields in which the last fifteen years of the great cynic's life are filed into a chapter titled simply "Waiting to Die, 1992–2007."[30] Idling away the days until a welcome death arrives does not seem to match the accomplisher-as-conqueror image that Kaufmann means to conjure.[31] Still, this is nevertheless a viable attitude which one might form with respect to one's passing, and it does respond to the call of finitude.

On these grounds it is hard to judge whether Yeshua should be viewed as a failure or a success, as someone who "won" Kaufmann's "race with death" or who lost it. On the one hand, Yeshua did build up a ministry and movement to the extent that both it and his teachings (however thereafter misshapen) flourished astoundingly long after his own passing and thus must definitively count as a project that (at least in its beginning) was truly his; but on the other hand—like Nietzsche—he was halted in the very midst of it. Were we to take the God/"God"-man view of Yeshua, the high Christology wherein he was the pure and sole divinity instantiated in fleshly form while yet retaining full omnipotence and omniscience, and who—as purpose and in fulfillment of a (self-)given redemptive mission—refrained from using the powers available to him and instead willingly proceeded to death with an absolute prescience of each eventuality and ultimate outcome, then we might easily conclude that Yeshua had achieved in this Kaufmannesque manner; the problem being, of course, that we have since the very start of our study effortfully sought to reject this comprehending. Our journey has been one of (perhaps painful) reassessment, of seeking to find the actual Yeshuanism ("kingdom," "way," et cetera) that has always been a Judaism, both more and less a portion of the great Hebrew heritage bequeathed by history and tradition. We have come too far to now simply shrug and say he knew it all along and thus "won the race." Honesty, and integrity in the search, rather calls on us to admit that Yeshua probably finished poorly in this particular marathon, but—we hasten to add—such hardly matters in light of the arguments we have already made against Kaufmann's call: that for anyone at any time taking a being-toward-death stance of this sort—while certainly possible—would not on the whole be very beneficial.

Similarly to Kaufmann's position is that of Steven Luper, who finds life's meaning—and thereby the relation to its ending—as indistinguishable from success: in place of Kaufmann's "marathon" we have only "the finish line." The quotation we will take from him is this:

> Your life has meaning just if, and to the extent that, you achieve the aims that you devote to it freely and competently . . . These achievements are *the* meaning of your life.[32]

30. Shields, *And So It Goes*.

31. Even so, this "welcome death" is a notion that we will return to in a more positive vein in what follows; adjusted from how such might seem here, of course.

32. Luper, "Life's Meaning," in *The Cambridge Companion to Life and Death*, 198–212 (198); emphasis

Part 4 | Temporality: God/"God" Here, "the Kingdom" Now

Here again what one is able to do in life is what matters, only now it appears to be the *entirety* of what matters: a frightening thought, as will become clear in the below. On what such "freely and competently devoted" aims might consist of, in an earlier work Luper argued that meaning is connected to desire fulfillment, and that desires must be unconditional in order to be strong enough to compel one to go on living (and thereby, of course, striving for their realization).[33] While admittedly this position is not a direct comment on finitude (mortality) per se, it is evident that based on reasoning along these lines Luper would consider a death reached without the attainment of one's goals as indicative of a life which lacked meaning (and possibly also purpose), hence it therefore seems plausible to infer that on Luper's conceptual framework the meeting of one's chosen objectives would indeed qualify as justifying the antecedent life as spent—however so spent—inclusive, of course, of said life's necessary ending. This is not to assert that Luper would take the fact of death as a positive (my sense is he would not because (if for no other reason) it interrupts the projects one has underway), nor that he might think of the time following an achievement as the kind of "surplus" we saw with Kaufmann;[34] rather I wish merely to highlight that for this perspective too death can be satisfactorily met only if one can read into the existence prior to the death moment an affirming/affirmative "proof" of some kind. To admit to—or, perhaps better, to "satisfy"—finitude appears to first require "achieving" a meaning.

In response to this we might again point to the highly contingent nature of goal attainment, and to the somewhat chilling consequences this outlook has for those of us who spend year after year in pursuit of that which, try as we might, remains outside our grasp. Luper would have to count our lives as meaningless by his conceptualization, and it is more than conceivable to think our deaths might be so labeled as well; deemed a fair finality to failure? Yet how does one *fail* at living? The suggestion is close to being offensive. Not meeting an objective attempted might be called a defeat, but could an entire period of biological vitality be? Even if, on these merits, the life in question were considered "meaningless"? There is furthermore the issue of Luper's connection between unconditional desires (and the fulfillment thereof) and being: I do not know many—or any—people that would state they are keeping themselves alive due to their held restriction-free wishes. In my experience—certainly personally for myself, but for many others I would think—most of us carry on living more or less because we do not die, picking up now this, now that as important along the way; and while there are no doubt certain things people might say they live *for*, that is a separate issue from the compulsion *to live* itself. I do not need to be compelled to go on living,

---

in the original.

33. Luper, *The Philosophy of Death*, 77.

34. Luper does not differentiate between a "great aim" (à la Kaufmann) from the everyday notion of more general "aims"; on my understanding his focus is on the continual movement between the making and meeting of ambitions instead of on a single overarching pursuit (perhaps more akin to a series of personal projects).

I simply do; and then in the midst of that I create or find what I direct my energy towards. Might I discover meaning therein? I may, or I may take it from elsewhere, but Luper's "to the extent that" addendum to the assertion that life is only meaningful through verifiable successes appears particularly cruel when we remember the hard realities of an unpredictable world and the subsequent lack of a guarantee of anything within an existential situation as heavily conditioned as a human animal's.

In fairness, we must admit once more—we must remember—that Luper's argumentative stance is not strictly an attitude to the fact of human finiteness; it is not a being-toward-death, at least not completely. However, given its conjunction of *the* (i.e. sole) meaning in a life—every one of which is capped only by an ending—with goal attainment, the implications involved in taking such a view severely limit how one could potentially perceive one's future death opposite either the meaningfulness or the meaninglessness of one's present life (which is also the period of one's dying). Death, as was argued, *is* nothing—it "is" annihilation—and what therefore matters is the dying, that way and route to death, that which coincides exactly with one's living in a perfect overlap of each moment, every breath (the body's sustenance) constitutes one more movement towards the permanent cessation of one's breathing. This is the central importance of being-toward-death, of confronting and accepting finitude. If we are bound to understand this period of living-dying as one long potential failure, or as maintained merely by a string of (restriction free) desires, then we are left with little "possibility" and quite a bit of "covering over" (i.e. not actually facing death for the chasing after of "success" and/or cravings); or, in other words, what we would have is a focus (an obsession) with what-I-want (now/soon) instead of the appreciation of limitedness and the (mental) working through thereof. An acknowledged finality is still a motivator for action on Luper's account, but it is a glossed over and hidden one, and in that disputably insufficient.

With Luper's view as well our judgments regarding any potential (speculated) Yeshuan being-toward-death split widely on the same Christological axis. On the traditional high Christology, his death was not merely a goal fulfillment, it was the entire purpose and point of his being. By that telling, Yeshua (in keeping with this conceptual package let us shift to calling him "Jesus") was born—of a virgin, and with the many other overtly and nebulously Hebraic-Semitic narrational and Graeco-Roman mythological elements—for the single twinned purpose of preaching himself as savior and then becoming the same via execution/propitiation of divine (self-)bloodlust. His objective was death: and not a natural one either; hence the telling we have would be for Luper supremely successful, an absolute attainment of "the aims that you devote to it [i.e. one's life] freely and competently."[35] "Jesus" was born to die; not in the way that you and I are born to die because we each do die, but actually born *to* die, for that express aspiration and none other. Facing this, we might think (conveniently forgetting the Gethsemane tales) that any being-toward would be easy for "Jesus": it was

---

35. Luper, "Life's Meaning," in *The Cambridge Companion to Life and Death*, 198–212 (198).

Part 4 | Temporality: God/"God" Here, "the Kingdom" Now

after all his *raison d'être*. Supposedly through this death, moreover, X, Y, and Z have been claimed by the church (and this almost in defiance of Yeshua's "kingdom" message, as we have tried to show); but such were the results, they were the consequences of the "act" of dying (of getting killed), and not therefore falling within the same category of directness. By this understanding "Jesus" had the single telos of having himself murdered, which once done would lead to this and that (other Xs, Ys, and Zs) in the metaphysical realm as connected eventualities, as effects or—perhaps most clearly—as aftereffects of the originary (passively) becoming dead. Although on the orthodox doctrine these were *intended* aftereffects—foreknown with the prescience we rejected in Chapter 10 when examining our selected artworks—they nevertheless remain definitionally on that secondary level, as opposed to the primary one of a straightforwardly sought endpoint.

This though is well-known, and we need not belabor the point any further, particularly since what is of far more interest to us is how Yeshua's being-toward-death might have been for him in the absence of any God/"God"-man assumptions. For that, Yeshua could still have taken this "achievementism," as it were, positively all the same when thinking about his life (naturally I mean the kind of reflections that take place in maturity) in that he could have ascertained himself as having reached the Luperean meaning-making qualifiers listed above via the visible realization of his "kingdom" message's promulgation and its presumably (at a minimum) medium- to long-term abiding. His public ministry was his life's "devoted aim," and even with Luper's (horrid) supplemental of "to the extent that" a positive turn could be taken in light of the followers and disciples he could daily see around himself (whether or not he deemed them to have "gotten it," they were unmistakably present nevertheless). On this we must take note that in rejecting the God/"God"-man perspective, we have to accordingly admit that Yeshua could not have pre-envisioned how any of it might have played out years and years hence, but naturally none of us can either; and at any rate a broad enough consideration of history indicates how nothing on this Earth could truly be "successful" if by that we mean infinitely lasting (let us not forget that our Sun will eventually expand and burn this whole beautiful planet to a state less than cinders[36]). Yeshua, if he were a Luper man, could have been pleased at the end, but then I doubt he would have agreed with an accounting on these terms when I remember the parables he told and the selfless, self-disregarding contents of his advice. For us too I think we should leave Luper by the proverbial wayside: the entire "success"-contingency of this being-toward is dreadful really, disheartening, and ultimately inhuman(e); or anyway that is how this "failure" of a creature finds it.

Sartre provides our closing illustrative example on human finiteness and a potential (and intriguing) attitude in relation to it, a further being-toward which, following

---

36. Although not for quite some time (at least by the way we count); see Wendel, "When Will the Sun Die?" *Space.com*. Accessed January 20, 2020.

(Honestly) Facing Finitude

our previous samples, we might wish to call "finding the right running shoes" approach. He states:

> . . . human reality would remain finite even if it were immortal, because it *makes* itself finite by choosing itself as human. To be finite, in fact, is to choose oneself—that is, to make known to oneself what one is by projecting oneself toward one possible to the exclusion of others. The very act of freedom is therefore the assumption and creation of finitude.[37]

In this "making itself" selection and pursuit are once more paramount, and interestingly Sartre places finitude as reflective of choice rather than as a straightforward, pure fact; of nature or otherwise. Were humanity blessed (or cursed, take your pick[38]) with immortality, finitude would yet remain an essential element since the exercise of freely deciding entails limitation—this over that—and in such acts recognizes the fragmentary nature involved: by A it is clear that I remove B from the picture. Self-fashioning, the path through life that one sets out on and subsequently ever-renews/reforms within Sartre's asserted "assumption and creation of finitude," is of necessity a reduction; but it is a willed and purposive one, and in that there is none (or anyway little) of the "turning away" against which Heidegger argued. This is rather an approach to life made with eyes wide open to the eventualities that pertain, which of course includes death (*"even if"* immortal—Sartre is not imagining an alternative world of immortals, he is emphasizing the very known mortality we face). Paraphrasing, this position strikes me as being readable thusly: I will die but now I choose, and in that I make my being, and furthermore make known to myself this created creaturehood. As with Sartre's oeuvre generally the openness of human existence and the insistence on actively grasping that openness are what are paramount.

Amongst the attitudes to finitude that discover in it a stimulus to exist fully while one yet does, this is perhaps the least objectionable in that it promotes the *pursuit* of goals and not the attainment thereof. Win or lose, Sartre seems to be saying, what is crucial is to play the game: and in that the game one favors while following the manner which one determines (i.e. throw out the rulebook if it does not suit you). There is, though, a nuance here in relation to personal circumscription that I think is slightly misleading when it comes to life perceived as a continuous dying. To write, as Sartre does, that choice ("The very act of freedom") is an "assumption and creation of finitude" is to use the term "finitude" in a way that is more akin to a narrowing or a limitation of breadth, a whittling down of options, rather than in the temporal sense of length in which we usually think when we reflect on the ultimate end of our lives at the moment of our death (if we are fortunate to have the space for such a meditation,

---

37. Sartre, *Being and Nothingness*, 545–546; emphasis in the original.

38. I am reminded of how in *The Silmarillion* Tolkien presents the elves as thoroughly surprised by the strange gift of mortality that the Creator gave to the human race, and yet I think the Creator got it right: our thanks for mortality! See Chapter 12 "Of Men" in the third section "Quenta Silmarillion"—and relatedly the creation account "Ainulindalë," which forms the first section—in Tolkien, *The Silmarillion*.

that is). I agree with Sartre that self-making and the seeking of that which one actively decides on—stressing too that "success," attainment, achievement, et cetera, have nothing to do with this—are the pillars of a view on finitude that both apprehends and accedes to its inevitability, but to me an emphasis on brevity is more apposite than one on self-applied constriction, and that is so because while we can understand the form in which our choices reduce even while they construct, we cannot come to terms with our utter exit thereby. That is, Sartre's view as espoused here helps us better comprehend limitedness as a condition *within* life rather than limitedness as a condition *of* life. It is, perhaps, a matter of emphasis; Sartre's on empowerment, ours on facticity. In a being-towards, I think, the latter is preferable. I will die: all consciousness, all perception, all emotion, action, the entirety of this world-soaked entity, will fully and unfailingly cease: that is the reality I must look to, and not only the situational contours within such while they yet experientially proceed.

On the whole, this is a being-toward-death of some merit, acknowledging the centrality of choice and the constricting of resulting options thereby, but in that as well the embarking on a continual journey of self-making and self-asserting. Applying this to Yeshua, it does appear to fit well with what we have come to know of the historical man; and that regardless of the form of Christology—or, indeed, of the full rejection thereof—which one might take. Yeshua's pursuance of a rabbinical and nomadic lifestyle was clearly a decision made in an awareness of the instabilities and restrictions such would bring (once more, these could easily be known without any manner of divine omniscience involved; they might be better known, in fact, on absolutely mortal terms since then they would be felt without any reassuring notion of latent power whereby one could "turn these stones into bread"; e.g. Matthew 4:3 and Luke 4:3[39]); such hazards were part of the point for him, an element of his "kingdom" ethos to trust entirely in God's goodness and providence (as in—again from Matthew and Luke—the "birds of the air" and "lilies of the field" passages of 6:25–31 for the former, 12:22–28 for the latter;[40] additionally, the non-canonical books we have used as sources for

---

39. These verses, taken from the story of Jesus' temptation after a forty-day fast in the wilderness (note the purposive name usage: Jesus' and *not* Yeshua's: I cannot find this anything but fictitious; yet instructive all the same, as many a good story are), read thusly: Matthew 4:3: "The tempter came and said to him, 'If you are the Son of God, command these stones to become loaves of bread.'"; Luke 4:3: "The devil said to him, 'If you are the Son of God, command this stone to become a loaf of bread.'"; *Thinline Bible with the Apocrypha* (NRSV).

40. Matthew 6:25–31: "25[Yeshua] 'Therefore I tell you, do not worry about your life, what you will eat or what you will drink, [a footnote reads: "Other ancient authorities lack *or what you will drink*"] or about your body, what you will wear. Is not life more than food, and the body more than clothing? 26Look at the birds of the air; they neither sow nor reap nor gather into barns, and yet your heavenly Father feeds them. Are you not of more value than they? 27And can any of you by worrying add a single hour to your span of life? [another footnote reads: "Or *add one cubit to your height*"] 28And why do you worry about clothing? Consider the lilies of the field, how they grow; they neither toil nor spin, 29yet I tell you, even Solomon in all his glory was not clothed like one of these. 30But if God so clothes the grass of the field, which is alive today and tomorrow is thrown into the oven, will he not much more clothe you—you of little faith? 31Therefore do not worry, saying, "What will we eat?" or "What will we drink?" or "What will we wear?"'"; Luke 12:22–28: "22He [Yeshua] said to his disciples, 'Therefore I tell you, do

"kingdom" teachings also contain near perfect parallels to these sections[41]). Yeshua would undoubtedly have been aware, moreover, of the life-threatening dangers that these determinations brought, especially if we recall from Chapter 2 that he was likely acquainted with, and indeed studied under, John the Baptizer (Baptist), whom himself was executed for politically expedient reasons. While it is a given that on balance we cannot do much more than guess about what kind of being-towards Yeshua may have personally attitudinally held (although we can, I think, conjecture that he did have some formulation of one, given his circumstances and certain awareness of the risks he ran, as mentioned) Sartre's "right running shoes" would probably suit him, as a "pair" of this sort might for us; and all the more so, as suggested, if we further

---

not worry about your life, what you will eat, or about your body, what you will wear. 23For life is more than food, and the body more than clothing. 24Consider the ravens: they neither sow nor reap, they have neither storehouse nor barn, and yet God feeds them. Of how much more value are you than the birds! 25And can any of you by worrying add a single hour to your span of life? [a footnote here reads: "Or *add a cubit to your stature*"] 26If then you are not able to do so small a thing as that, why do you worry about the rest? 27Consider the lilies, how they grow: they neither toil nor spin; [another footnote reads: "Other ancient authorities read *Consider the lilies; they neither spin nor weave*"] yet I tell you, even Solomon in all his glory was not clothed like one of these. 28But if God so clothes the grass of the field, which is alive today and tomorrow is thrown into the oven, how much more will he clothe you—you of little faith!'"; *Thinline Bible with the Apocrypha* (NRSV).

41. The parallels are: *The Gospel of Jesus* 2:29–35: "29He [Yeshua] used to say to his disciples, 'That's why I tell you: Don't fret about life—what you're going to eat—or about your body—what you're going to wear. 30Remember, there is more to living than food and clothing. 31Think about the crows: they don't plant or harvest, they don't have storerooms or barns. Yet God feeds them. You're worth a lot more than the birds! 32Can any of you add an hour to life by fretting about it? 33So if you can't do a little thing like that, why worry about the rest? 34Think about how the wild lilies grow: they don't slave and they never spin. Yet let me tell you, even Solomon at the height of his glory was never decked out like one of them. 35If God dresses up the grass in the field, which is here today and tomorrow is tossed into an oven, it is surely more likely that God cares for you, you who don't take anything for granted!'" Funk and the Jesus Seminar, *The Gospel of Jesus*, 19–20; and *The Lost Gospel Q* Sayings 51–52: Q51: "Jesus spoke to his disciples: 'Don't be anxious about your life. Don't worry about getting enough food or having clothes to wear. Life means more than food and the body is more than clothing. Look at the ravens. They don't plant seeds or gather a harvest. They have neither storehouses nor barns. Yet God feeds them. Aren't you more important than birds? Can any of you, for all your worrying, add a single moment to your life? If worry can't change the smallest thing, then why be anxious about the rest?'"; Q52: "[Yeshua's words] Look at the lilies that grow wild in the fields. They don't weave clothes for themselves. But I tell you, even King Solomon in all his splendor was not dressed as beautifully as these flowers. If that is how God clothes the grasses, which are green today and burned in the sun tomorrow, how much more will God provide for you. How little faith you have!" Powelson and Riegert, trans., footnotes, and eds., *The Lost Gospel Q*, 85–6; and finally *The Gospel of Thomas* Saying 36 (quoted first from the Coptic, of which we have the entire document): "Jesus said, 'Do not worry, from morning to evening and from evening to morning, about what you will wear.'"; (and from the Greek, of which we have only fragments, with the angle brackets indicating the translator's insertions): "1<Jesus says, 'Do not worry>, from morning <to nightfall nor> from evening <to> morning, either <about> your <food>, what <you will> eat, <or> about <your robe>, what clothing you <will> wear. 2<You are much> better than the lilies, which do not card or <spin>. 3And since you have one article of clothing, what < . . . > you < . . . >? 4Who might add to your stature? That is the one who will give you your clothing." Meyer, trans. and intro., *The Gospel of Thomas*, 37 and 73, respectively. As mentioned in the main text, the evidential preponderance of this sentiment makes the whole rather confidently indicative of an actual Yeshuan teaching instead of a later insertion by authors whose books were to become canonized.

tweak the nuance of the stressed limitedness in the direction of being a condition *of* life rather than a condition *within* life. That small notional move, it was argued, could provide a better grounding for an authentic facing-up-to of our inevitable brevity.

Thus for confronting finitude and finding in it an incentive to act, let us now turn to finitude as balm. Albert Camus remarks that, "We get into the habit of living before acquiring the habit of thinking. In that race which daily hastens us towards death, the body maintains its irreparable lead"[42]—a wry way of asserting that we simply do not think; the same "covered over" more eloquently put (befitting of Camus, naturally). Indeed, this does seem to be our lot, our "default setting" as it were; for as mentioned in the preceding considerations on Luper's argumentative stance, most of us live only because we are born, we do not exert much reflection on it, each day presents its own challenges and demands, and we find ourselves either meeting them or not. Thereafter the next. The years glide by, sickness and frailty present themselves if an accident or tragedy does not do so first, and we realize suddenly—much too late—that this fact we most sought to avoid will no longer be ignored: I will die, I have been dying—all of *this* has been a dying—and I am dying even now, this very second. Mortality, ineluctability, inescapability. Heidegger urges us to face this and find a way with its possibility(ies), Kaufmann to create a life's (worthy) work, Luper to succeed in one's devotions, Sartre to choose and to pursue. I would like to add "welcome" to our list.

To "welcome" death is a phrase that could easily be read in a manner which I do not intend here: I am not advocating suicide by this, nor a reckless courting of danger,[43] but neither am I necessarily staking a position against either of those; at least not yet: we will consider the important role of the other in one's death below. Instead, by evoking this coinage in the way I am, I wish to present death as a balm, as an alternative to the attitudes of both one's personal death as ignored—as a (mere) fact always about "them" (what we might call the "standard" approach)—and as a prompting (pushing) motivator along the lines of the three positions described thus far. In attempting this, I ask the reader to allow me first a simple background outline, a marking of boundaries with a few preliminary and minimal comments: We find ourselves alive, none of us choosing either to be born nor the manner and conditions into which we were born, every aspect of our being comes to us in our developmental years as a *fait accompli*, and we remain powerless to do anything but be buffeted and shaped—stamped and moulded—by these forces. By the time we are finally cognitively developed enough to start to think for ourselves we have already been so acculturated and "educated" that we are effectively programmed, made into automatons, ready to be slotted into the existing socioeconomic structures dominant wherever and whenever we chanced to

---

42. Camus, *The Myth of Sisyphus*, 6.

43. My thoughts on suicide are often in flux (I can understand it, have trouble endorsing it, but similarly cannot deem it as purely negative when I think of the whole human condition and the weight of tragedy and pain which many carry), but an earlier argument was presented within a wider context in Oberg, "Reconsidering Euthanasia," *Journal of International Philosophy*, 297–305.

have been "thrown," as Heidegger evocatively described the embedded conditionality of we human animals. John Lennon perhaps phrased it better though: "When they've tortured and scared you for twenty-odd years /Then they expect you to pick a career."[44] Our understanding is limited, our reach miniscule.

None of this, of course, is new nor especially revelatory, we know it already but—very much like death—mostly fail to *feel it* in the midst of our day-to-days. What I wish to therefore highlight about this fact of our contextualization is that the act of living is never chosen and, given the biological imperatives and conditioned perceptions that form large parts of that situatedness, recognizing suicide as an option and purposely not taking it does not of itself impart any responsibility: it does not mean that one "embraces life" simply because one does not immediately end it. If that were the case then everyone breathing would be living authentically and Heidegger could have saved himself the trouble of penning *Being and Time* and his host of other works, really. Camus' "one truly serious philosophical problem"[45] of self-murder (the question of whether to commit it or not) is a provocative statement, but it is also a fairly empty one because again we—or she or you or he or I—typically go on living simply because we go on living. The challenge is to confront existence and then to have it out with this beast, to come to some kind of conclusion, something measured, something forged with the materials to hand: to "authenticize" as Heidegger urged in his way, and as Sartre did as well (and Kaufmann, on a generous reading of his "life's work" approach).

Yet if we are clear sighted enough we may nevertheless still arrive at the judgment that even filling up a life to its brim with meaning-making activities and objectives will ultimately end in the same ignominious manner, that sooner or later every legacy fades (if we are even fortunate enough to have generated one), and that the best response might therefore be to let go: to live, perhaps, without ever asking for *more*. This is not necessarily to make life into that shirt one received on a birthday past—a nice enough gift, but not something wanted—but neither is it to cling to life in the way that a "marathon," "finish line," or "right running shoes" set of principles could evoke. Rather, one confronts finitude, strives to accept it, sets X in the meantime, and then ever-prepares for cessation, secure in the ideational framing that if one's X is done or not done, if it is a "success" or a "failure," the whole matters little. It is only the doing, and when the end does come one smiles; there is nothing else for it. This is welcome, this is balm.

Could Yeshua have thought thusly? It is an intriguing query. He had his ministry, he was seemingly entirely devoted to the dissemination of his "kingdom" message, but absent the substitute-sacrifice telos of a high (traditional, orthodox) Christology his aims probably went no further than to keep at what he was at: preaching and dispatching adherents to do the same. We have reasoned that he would almost certainly have

---

44. Lennon, "Working Class Hero," *John Lennon/Plastic Ono Band*.
45. Camus, *The Myth of Sisyphus*, 1.

been aware, and accepting of, the perils before him; could that mean in turn that he took a "welcome" to death, or at any rate did not hold so tightly to life that he would trade his mission (his own "task X") for more of it, for surviving longer?

I suspect that Yeshua, who appears to have found daily basics enjoyable and not merely agreeable (that is, if we take the accusations leveled against him as accurate—or as at least partially accurate—e.g. of the "glutton" and "drunkard" sort as found in Matthew 11:19 and Luke 7:34, and then again supported by our non-canonical sources[46]), might not have taken finitude as a balm per se: he could very well have wanted more of life—as much as he could get—but, importantly, that "as much as he could get" would be contingent on a format of living *without* any changes to that which he was about in life. His being-towards would not then, I wager (and again, this is merely my own speculating based on our study thus far and some considerations done over the years heretofore) involve opening the door to death (a "welcome")—despite essentially doing even more than that via purposefully attaining a public following which he could easily predict the authorities would have understood as threatening to them; unless, on the other hand, he did at least on some preconscious level "desire" (but not *desire*) martyrdom for the resurrectional reward we think he likely believed would be his—but neither would it involve slamming the door shut and bolting the lock. In Yeshua's mind, let us propose, death would come when it would, and although his actions courted it (and he was cognizant of this) they did not constitute a forceful "yes"—but then neither a flat "no"—his focus was on the present within his being-towards, on the time between the undertaking of his teaching and whenever it might

---

46. Yeshua is speaking to a large audience in these verses, praising John the Baptizer (Baptist), but also complaining somewhat about the treatment he has received from particular segments of society: Matthew 11:19: "the Son of Man came eating and drinking, and they say, 'Look, a glutton and a drunkard, a friend of tax collectors and sinners!' Yet wisdom is vindicated by her deeds. [a footnote adds: "Other ancient authorities read *children*"].'; Luke 7:34: "the Son of Man has come eating and drinking, and you say, 'Look, a glutton and a drunkard, a friend of tax collectors and sinners!'" *Thinline Bible with the Apocrypha* (NRSV). The New Living Translation is a little more direct in how Yeshua describes his own behavior: Matthew 11:19: "The Son of Man, on the other hand, feasts and drinks, and you say, 'He's a glutton and a drunkard, and a friend of tax collectors and other sinners!' But wisdom is shown to be right by its results." In this version Luke 7:34 reads exactly the same as Matthew but without the final sentence on wisdom (which composes the next verse (although worded as "But wisdom is shown to be right by the lives of those who follow it. [with a footnote: "Or *But wisdom is justified by all her children.*"]"). The "wisdom" sentiment, incidentally, is also found in Luke 7:35 in *Thinline Bible with the Apocrypha* (NRSV).) *Catholic Holy Bible* (NLT). For the non-canonical parallels, Funk and the Jesus Seminar, *The Gospel of Jesus*, 47 (9:4–5) reads: "4This mother's son [i.e. "the Son of Man" in traditional usage] appeared on the scene both eating and drinking, and you say, 'There's a glutton and a drunk, a crony of toll collectors and sinners!' 5Indeed, wisdom is vindicated by all her children."; and Powelson and Riegert, trans., footnotes, and eds., *The Lost Gospel Q*, 60 (Q26, in its latter portion following an indictment of "this generation" and a reference to the Baptizer) has: "Now the son of man comes, eating and drinking, and you say, 'Just look at him, a glutton and a drunkard, a friend of tax collectors and outcasts.' But Wisdom is being proven right by all her children." *The Gospel of Thomas*, however, does not contain an equivalent saying to this.

end/be stopped. In these now-moments he determined himself as one vocationally engaged in (what he comprehended as) "my Father's business."[47]

Burning with his "kingdom" message as he was, Yeshua was maybe possessed of a drive that not each of us could admit to having. Possibly rather for the more ordinary folk we represent—although of course this would vary widely and naturally too depend a great deal on circumstances—we need not necessarily have a reason to go on (we merely do), but neither need we have a reason to stop going on. This being so, or in probability so, we may wish to form a being-toward-death which is wise to the thin overlap, the layering, in "welcome" and "balm": we could take the joys which we find or form or discover during life, but in that we could yet maintain an approach to unquestionable human limitedness that is preparatory for the release and the finality of death, of an end. We could welcome what we see coming, we could take it as balm. Achieving an approach like this would require effort, and thus we would have to ready ourselves attitudinally (conceptually) such that finitude becomes a part of us: we learn to neither cover over death nor to run from it, and we come to find solace in the absolute *stop* without feeling any need to seek or rush that which is anyway already en route. In short, we keep our minds on death; and we live. This is admittedly something of a stroll through a graveyard, and it may appear rather bleak to many, but it remains a way open to us, one more option: a single being-towards amongst others. On it however we do well to recall that we are not alone, and by walking the path we perforce affect those around. That extension is the aspect which must shape our final deliberation.

My death and you: Whose loss?

In a discussion of facing one's own personal death, as ours has been thus far in this chapter, it is perhaps only to be expected that the focus would remain individuated and internal, particularly from within the wider phenomenological methodology that our study has employed (and will continue to use until the end). We have sought to temper this somewhat through the inclusion of meditations on what Yeshua may have thought about his coming death in view of the other aspects regarding the man and his message which we have covered, but that has necessarily been about "him"; and with a "he" like Yeshua—who casts such a vast shadow over history: and whether we

---

47. I refer here to the story of the child Jesus (again, clearly not our historical Yeshua) when he was discovered in the Temple by his parents Mary and Joseph, who had been earnestly scouring the crowds for him having been separated during the Pesach (Passover) festivities, and his responding to their scolding for not remaining close by with the following (from Luke 2:49): "He [Jesus] said to them [his parents], 'Why were you searching for me? Did you not know that I must be in my Father's house?' [a footnote reads "Or *be about my Father's interests?*"]" *Thinline Bible with the Apocrypha* (NRSV); the New Living Translation adds an interesting nuance with its "need to," see Luke 2:49 there: "[the boy Jesus] 'But why did you need to search?' he asked. 'Didn't you know that I must be in my Father's house?' [a footnote reads "Or '*Didn't you realize that I should be involved with my Father's affairs?*'"]" *Catholic Holy Bible* (NLT).

take that casting as justified or not, it is a simple and bare fact of our epoch—obfuscating clouds remain a threat. Hence we shall hereafter attempt a bit of revelatory light through a reflection on my-death-me done in direct conjunction with your-life-sans-me: or in other words, to stretch this navel-gazing beyond the casket we have been picturing ourselves within. Let us think the relation on both sides of the box's lid.

To begin, we might consider that while value has its roots in the present—in what is now a part of our lives; be it material, conceptual, desirous, et cetera in form—it is nevertheless directed towards the future if its valuation is really to stick, something which Samuel Scheffler has astutely pointed out.[48] In this our own tomorrows are of course limited, sometimes even truncated, and it is with regards to this in which we have analyzed the above potential attitudinal postures. Hidden—or "covered"—in any being-toward-death, moreover, is that aspect of the other in whom we may (selfishly, self-centeredly) see or hope for a continuation of our being beyond the confines of one's transitory meat-sack, and this mostly by route of descendants and/or personal legacy. Such concerns are not typically strictly "me-oriented" though, and indeed it is probably more often the case that they are only slightly "I"-focused since the human standard is not merely to care for oneself—that is instead the hallmark of a clinically psychopathic personality—rather to be deeply preoccupied with and for the sake of those to whom one is related and/or whom are dependent upon one, in any specific form or another. This facet of our being is as much a part of the embeddedness earlier remarked on as the historical, familial, genetic, climatic, geographic, economic, societal, et cetera, et cetera inheritances are. At birth we fall (are "thrown") into a world that is nothing if not thoroughly interconnected; we and all those around us. Given this, we each find "a dual value investment between self and community that seems inevitable, an inextricability of self from community,"[49] and if we therefore attempt to work out a way of dying—a constant within life: living is a dying, as argued—that takes into its consideration only the "self" of a "me"—a singularity, as if one might exist outside situational bonds—then we find ourselves confined in what Edith Stein called "the prison of our individuality," a place where "Others become riddles for us, or still worse, we remodel them into our image and so falsify historical truth."[50] Aside, though, from simply caring for those close to one, to being perhaps worried about their welfare after one has died, how might an ethics of the other fit into this picture? How could an approach to finitude, to the fact of death, affect the way in which we situate ourselves with those who surround while we are yet still here?

In thinking on this we find Emmanuel Levinas writing that significance in life stems from an "authority" that pertains to one even after death, meaningfully tied in with the sociality that each self both contributes to and receives from, that this indeed

---

48. Scheffler, *Death and the Afterlife*.

49. Apologies once more on the self(!) reference; Oberg, "Prescience and an Early Death," *Think*, 34–42 (36).

50. Stein, *On the Problem of Empathy*, 116.

is "an obligation that death does not absolve."[51] Cohen connects this idea further with the (general) notion of justice which most of us inherently tend to hold to one degree or another, and asserts that however we may term such an "authoritative" concept (e.g. as "justice," "authority," "God," "the transcendent," "the supernatural"), it is from out of its "imperative force [that] death and mortality make sense."[52] We will comment on this shortly, but first a further clarificatory note on the topic of futurity and Levinas' ethical considerations vis-à-vis finitude is called for: Levinas emphasizes that death is always a to-come, something that none of us can ever "catch up to," and thus any kind of being-toward-death simply cannot (on his view) be subjectively integrated.[53] This perspective does take death as annihilation, but also with the caveat that we are unable to understand it.[54]

In reacting to these thoughts against the notional background of the differing being-towards we have examined, we will probably find the future orientation of valuing (as far as others are concerned) to be a valid aspect of human existence; such appears undeniable whenever we place the self in any kind of context. Stein is therefore right, I think, that if we limit our reasoning to only this "me" (regarding death, but indeed not only on death; Stein's own concerns were elsewhere in the essay cited), then we lose—we distort—a great deal; in my judgment Levinas and Cohen too are also correct to emphasize the care for others we (usually) exhibit, but—and here I do object—*not in the way they have*. My death will reduce not only me to nothing, but also—for me—everything that does now and has ever related to me; and this not merely perspectivally but crucially phenomenologically (that is, if one rejects the kind of afterlife same-self-as-now conceptions which we have). Whatever "obligation" I might incur cannot last beyond my death, and to assume that any could is to make the same imparting-into-death (the *im*-placement, *re*-moving, *in*-serting) mistake that Heidegger warns against; and that whatever we make of the "I" itself. Nothing whatsoever regarding my post mortem state can touch me during life because there *is* no state to be had there, it *is* nothing, "I" am thence nothing, every care and concern today about what might happen to my family tomorrow will cease with the stoppage of my physical functioning. The "authority" or "force" is that abbreviated. I cannot "catch up to" death, yes, but such is an irrelevancy because death is not a *thing* to "catch up to"—again, it is nothing—*no thing*—at all, it is not a state but the *absence of all states*, all statehood, all (in our Heideggerean vein) "possibilities" of state-ness/conditionality. Death is "nothing" not in the sense of "empty" as if it were a container that might have a filling but currently does not; rather, death is "nothing" as in "non-,"

---

51. Levinas, *Time and the Other and Additional Essays*, 114; quoted in Cohen, "Levinas," *International Journal for Philosophy of Religion*, 21–39 (37).

52. Cohen, "Levinas," *International Journal for Philosophy of Religion*, 21–39 (37).

53. Levinas, *Time and the Other and Additional Essays*; Cohen, "Levinas," *International Journal for Philosophy of Religion*, 21–39 (31).

54. Levinas, *Time and the Other and Additional Essays*.

as in void, as in null: not a romantic "infinite blank" as Cioran might have put it, but a plain old boring "blank," an electrical wire cut, charge lost. Our failure to grasp the absoluteness of annihilation is the source I think of these abstracted confusions and persistent inadequacies regarding potentially appropriate attitudes towards finiteness.

Yet still the real issue is not death but *dying*, and we certainly can "catch up to" that because we already are—right now we have each lost (perhaps a good) part of our lives in reading this, I am sorry to say. We must disagree too, moreover, with Cohen's declaration that death and mortality only make sense in the face of an ongoing justice (i.e. ongoing as in "(t)hereafter," although certainly this is not limited to—and I surely do not think Cohen means to imply—abstractions such as Heaven/Hell), but not because justice is to be discounted or that notions of it are excessively temporal, rather due to the lack of any "making sense" being a consideration. Humans die, exactly as every living entity does: why need the process "make sense" in a rational or a justificatory way, as if existence had to be exculpated? The quest to come to (personal) terms with this condition is absolutely laudatory, but efforts to "explain" it are not; and, upon reflection, we might find such offerings to be more often than not demeaning, offensive even (e.g. "She died for the greater good of X"; or, worse, "God took her from us so that God/we might achieve X" (this is not our God/"God")). Nevertheless, in moving through these thoughts we have found that what remains in an approach to death as either motivator or balm is the other—our existences' "you"s—and that whether we choose to adopt a being-toward-death which takes it as a means for promoting action (motivator), or as a comforting feature of cosmological facticity (balm); those who surround us now will yet figure importantly into each. We will therefore try to move deeper into this "how"—from both perspectives of motivator and balm—before concluding with a few additional musings on what a "kingdom" viewpoint (Yeshuan-thinking) might consist in if it were applied to this topic of "my-death-and-the-other."

In this effort to come to terms with personal finitude, to establish and maintain—continuously, in the midst of our day-to-day suchnesses, thises and thats—an attitude towards death and its annihilative quality, we are of course in and will always remain amongst many others and interwoven elements, embedded factors which Lisa Guenther stresses includes geniture itself as a part of what is bequeathed. Our lives are, she writes, "stretching along between birth and death";[55] which might seem obvious enough, but she adds the somewhat provocative thought that however others respond to our death after it has occurred forms an additional "leftover" which "helps constitute the intersubjective meaning of my own death in ways that I cannot control or choose, but which nevertheless form[s] an important aspect of my Being-with-others."[56] We are aware of such while alive (acknowledgedly or not), and so it behooves us too to be cognizant of—and vigilant towards—these facets as we shape, keep, and/or shift the approach to death that we ever-choose to take. It may be that after death we are

55. Guenther, "Being-From-Others," *Hypatia*, 99–118 (105).
56. Guenther, "Being-From-Others," *Hypatia*, 99–118 (113).

(Honestly) Facing Finitude

very soon forgotten, it may be that our absence is even celebrated, yet regardless there will be a temporary portion that resides, as it were, "of" us although we ourselves have ceased. There is that signification in which one's own "I," once posited in a living other, can never be fully removed. An allegory for the metaphysics here might be the memory that remains; the "photo on the family shelf." In the midst of this thickness of being the lives of those others—and for other others—carries on, and the cyclical, entwined structures involved have ramifications worth considering. Due to this plaiting, Adriana Cavarero has argued that "individual death in its dramatic, centripetal meaning is immediately relegated to the background, as something that in the larger scheme of things belongs to the primitive phenomenon of life."[57] This is an alternative from the preceding (purely self-)focus, supported by ethical lines of reasoning: going from *a life* to (human, at any rate) *life tout court*.

Yet even so, I doubt that experientially, phenomenologically, a relegation of this magnitude would make much of an impact on an individual as far as one's personal death is concerned—it may become a comforting part of a being-towards, but only if one were to seek to erase or to extravagantly minimize one's sense of individuality could such become a primary attitudinal comportment—yet there is nevertheless a noteworthy theoretical nuance in play here. If we do not happen to be living (and so dying) during a time of total planetary apocalypse, we will strongly think that life, as a system, will continue beyond our ceasing, that however extended or briefly the others with whom we have shared our time remember our having been, the fabric of our subsistence with theirs and within our environs will bear some kind of contributory mark. For our selves (personal being-hoods) annihilation will be complete, but for our "were-heres" there is a footprint of sorts; at least for a (cosmically speaking short) while. If we find in death a motivator, such notions might encourage us in the manner and constructing of those project(s) undertaken; or, on the other hand, if we find in death a balm it might provide a further layer of psychological rest: one's inescapable ending welcomed still the more in the warmth of its having formed an allotment inside the great wheel of birth-growth-decay-death-birth that characterizes this inhabited universe. In this thinking the other remains central: not in the as-separable manner that many in the Western lineage have traditionally argued for, but instead as crucial in an alterity partially constitutive of self. While we must confront our own deaths, coming to terms with our own limitedness, we do so amongst *we*—always and everywhere—and therefore this constituted "we" of you-me-situatedness must naturally contribute to any facing of finiteness, any being-toward-death, in whatever form adopted: as motivator, as welcome, or as something else.

Thus for us today, thus for background; in closing this chapter we shall once more cast our minds into the first century, to "the kingdom" and its call, and we will wonder—or rather "best guess": a small attempt at an uncovering—what a Yeshuan outlook along these lines might consist of. Such would not necessarily be bound to

---

57. Cavarero, *In Spite of Plato*, 113–114.

PART 4 | TEMPORALITY: GOD/"GOD" HERE, "THE KINGDOM" NOW

one historical epoch, of course—we are not asserting that Yeshua's words were only for the first century, far from it—but for perspective's sake we will need to bear with our musings the world (and "world") from which they were begot. On that "begot," maternal delivery is indeed a fitting image (image-idea/idea-image) here since our contemplations will center on some rather mysterious (purportedly) Yeshuan statements regarding family.

Turning again to our trio of non-canonical texts we gather some small evidence. The below quotations have been taken from the scholarly vetted words of *The Gospel of Jesus*, the academically (critically) reconstructed so-called "Lost Gospel" of Q, and the serendipitously discovered *Gospel of Thomas*; our reasons for turning to these pages remain the same: namely, that each predates the canonical Gospels and that although we cannot definitively proclaim full authenticity of them as "the very words" of Yeshua, they do represent the best we can do if we wish to attain a historically closer dating to actual potential utterances by Yeshua himself, and moreover if we desire (as we do) to "clear the air" of the redactions and insertions that occurred in the processes of building up an orthodoxy: since these texts are not in the authorized scriptures they are, possibly, able to be thought of as "untouched" (or rather more accurately: far less "touched up").[58] Firstly, then, are the sayings in which Yeshua is given to describe whom he considers to be his "true family":

> *The Gospel of Jesus* 11:5–9:
> *True relatives:* [5]Then his mother and his brothers arrive. While still outside, they send in and ask for him. [6]A crowd was sitting around him, and they say to him, "Look, your mother and your brothers and sisters are outside looking for you."
> [7]In response he says to them: "My mother and brothers—who ever are they?"
> [8]And looking right at those seated around him in a circle, he says, "Here are my mother and my brothers. [9]Whoever does God's will, that's my brother and sister and mother!"[59]
>
> *Thomas*, Saying 99: [1]The followers said to him, "Your brothers and your mother are standing outside."

---

58. A reminder: *Thomas* and Q have both been placed between 50–70 CE (roughly; some scholars date one or the other later), with the first of the canonical Gospels—Mark—at 70–80 CE (again roughly, but more consensus here); see once more Funk and the Jesus Seminar, *The Gospel of Jesus* (a convenient listing is given on page 117); Powelson and Riegert, trans., footnotes, and eds., *The Lost Gospel Q*; Barnstone and Meyer, eds., *The Gnostic Gospel*; Funk, ed., and the Jesus Seminar, trans. and comm., *The Acts of Jesus*; and Levine and Brettler, eds., *The Jewish Annotated New Testament*.

59. Funk and the Jesus Seminar, *The Gospel of Jesus*, 55. Again, and just as a refresher, the chapter and verses here are according to the unique organization of this reconstructed account of Yeshua's words and actions (which in this case also includes a bit on John the Baptizer (Baptist) at the beginning).

²He said to them, "Those here who do the will of my father are my brothers and my mother. ³They are the ones who will enter my father's kingdom."⁶⁰

In both of these statements Yeshua identifies his familial relations as consisting of those who do God's/"God's" will rather than as those who are actually related to him through the biological channels of blood and genetics. Considering the centrality of one's family members to one's life, livelihood, and identity—and in antiquity even more so than when compared with our times—this rejection of convention and the natural order is striking. Q does not in fact have a direct parallel here, but it does contain a related sentiment, one also echoed in *Thomas*: namely, the below (with the angle brackets in the latter indicating an insertion by the translator):

> Q40: As Jesus was speaking, a woman in the crowd raised her voice and said, "Blessed is the womb that gave birth to you and the breasts that nursed you."
>
> He replied, "Blessed rather are those who hear the word of God and observe it."[61]

> *Thomas*, Saying 79: ¹A woman in the crowd said, "Blessings on the womb that bore you and the breasts that fed you."
>
> ²He said to <her>, "Blessings on those who have heard the word of the father and have truly kept it. ³For there will be days when you will say, 'Blessings on the womb that has not conceived and the breasts that have not given milk.'"[62]

Although in each of these Yeshua is not denying his mother per se, he is emphasizing that what he considers to be paramount is not the human-human relation between a parent and child, but rather the human-divine relation, and that as concerns obedience by one to the other (the lower to the higher). It is interesting to note the apocalyptic tone in *Thomas* that is missing in Q ("For there will be days . . . "), which need not necessarily be indicative of any kind of "final judgment" scenario—such might merely refer to troubled times of fully human and/or environmental making—but is nevertheless still somewhat ominous. That is, however, another matter from the one which occupies us at present.

Continuing on we have three sets of sayings where Yeshua further downplays family groupings as institutions worthy of cohesion and allegiance, culminating in what are, I think, incredibly stunning declarations on how one ought to gauge oneself emotionally towards one's birth order, and that specifically vis-à-vis himself and his (self-perceived) mission and movement. Organizationally we will place first those sayings which indicate intrafamilial conflict; secondly those which seek to break ancestral ties; and finally, those which forcefully sunder living bonds. For the initial and

---

60. Meyer, trans. and intro., *The Gospel of Thomas*, 59.
61. Powelson and Riegert, trans., footnotes, and eds., *The Lost Gospel Q*, 74.
62. Meyer, trans. and intro., *The Gospel of Thomas*, 55.

Part 4 | Temporality: God/"God" Here, "the Kingdom" Now

the final *Thomas* portions in these sets we will also include alternative translations (by Leloup, as above) due to some intriguing differences, particularly in the closing sentence of Saying 16, where Leloup adds a Greek word that appears just so, untranslated, in this otherwise Coptic book—*monakhos*—from which our words related to the monkhood and being a monk derive. In all cases the angle brackets below once more indicate an insertion by the translator, whereas the square brackets contain my own additions for the sake of clarity:

1. Intrafamilial conflict:

> Q57: [Yeshua] "Do you suppose that I am here to bring peace? No, I have come to bring the sword of division. My message will divide father and son, mother and daughter, mother-in-law and daughter-in-law.
>
> Those who prefer their father or mother to me are not deserving. Nor are those who prefer their sons and daughters.
>
> Unless you carry your own cross and follow me, you are not worthy."[63]

> *Thomas*, Saying 16: ¹Jesus said, "Perhaps people think that I have come to impose peace upon the world. ²They do not know that I have come to impose conflicts upon the earth: fire, sword, war. ³For there will be five in a house: There will be three against two and two against three, father against son and son against father, ⁴and they will stand alone."[64]

> *Thomas* (Leloup), Saying 16: Yeshua said:
> People may think that I have come to bring peace to the world.
> They do not know that I have come to sow division upon the earth: fire, sword, war.
> When there are five in a house, three will be against two and two against three; father against son and son against father.
> And they will stand, and they will be alone and simple <*monakhos*>.[65]

2. Breaking ancestral ties:

> *The Gospel of Jesus* 3:13–14
> *Let the dead bury the dead*: ¹³To another he said, "Follow me."
> But he [the other] said, "First, let me go and bury my father."
> ¹⁴Jesus said to him, "Leave it to the dead to bury their own dead; but you, go out and announce God's imperial rule [i.e. "the kingdom"]."[66]

---

63. Powelson and Riegert, trans., footnotes, and eds., *The Lost Gospel Q*, 91.
64. Meyer, trans. and intro., *The Gospel of Thomas*, 29.
65. Leloup, trans., intro. and comm., *The Gospel of Thomas*, 15.
66. Funk and the Jesus Seminar, *The Gospel of Jesus*, 23.

(Honestly) Facing Finitude

Q27: As they walked along the road, they met a man who said to Jesus, "I will follow you wherever you go." Jesus answered, "Foxes have dens and birds have nests, but the son of man has nowhere to rest his head."

To another he said, "Follow me." But that person replied, "Let me go and bury my father first." Jesus answered, "Let the dead bury their dead. Your duty is to go and spread the news of the realm of God [i.e. "the kingdom"]."

Another person said, "I will follow you, but first let me go and say goodbye to my family." Jesus said to him, "No one who puts a hand to the plough and continues to look at what was left behind is suited for the realm of God."[67]

(This saying from Q actually contains three elements which each deserve our attention; here the "breaking ancestral ties" part is of course the middle section, the "sundering living bonds" the closing portion, and then the famous "no home" feeling-outlook given in the opening (foxes and birds) which we will comment on separately in what follows. Next, however, we list the other "sundering" quotations which can be found.)

3. Sundering living bonds:

The Gospel of Jesus 11:10–11:

Hating father and mother: [10]Once when hordes of people were traveling with him, he turned and addressed them: [11]"If any of you comes to me and does not hate your own father and mother and wife and children and brothers and sisters—yes, even your own life—you're no disciple of mine."[68]

Q69: [Yeshua] "If you love your father and mother, or your son and daughter, more than me, you cannot follow me. Unless you take up your cross and let go of all you possess [by implication one's family surely seems to be included here; but as a "possession"?], you cannot truly follow me."[69]

Thomas, Saying 101: [1]"Whoever does not hate <father> and mother as I do cannot be a <follower> of me, [2]and whoever does <not> love <father and> mother as I do cannot be a <follower of> me. [3]For my mother <gave me falsehood>, but my true <mother> gave me life."[70]

Thomas (Leloup), Saying 101: Yeshua said:
Whoever does not hate their father and mother
as I do
cannot become my disciple.
And whoever does not love their father and mother

---

67. Powelson and Riegert, trans., footnotes, and eds., *The Lost Gospel Q*, 61.
68. Funk and the Jesus Seminar, *The Gospel of Jesus*, 55.
69. Powelson and Riegert, trans., footnotes, and eds., *The Lost Gospel Q*, 104.
70. Meyer, trans. and intro., *The Gospel of Thomas*, 59.

PART 4 | TEMPORALITY: GOD/"GOD" HERE, "THE KINGDOM" NOW

as I do
cannot become my disciple.
For my mother made me to die,
but my true mother gave me Life.[71]

What Yeshua appears to be doing with these statements is the incorporation into his "kingdom" ministry of a complete restructuring of social connections, and this is not, on the face of things, merely for his closest confidants either, lest we be deceived by the presence of such terms as "disciple"; rather that word should be applied broadly, as is evident from the generally stated "division" within a family that his message will bring, or in that he makes these remarks to those who have approached him quite probably for the first time instead of specifically towards his inner core (if he indeed had such a select cadre, or if he considered those who may have thought of themselves as "select" in the same manner in which they judged their own relationships with him). The associations that Yeshua stresses are grounded ideationally, ideologically, they are the "sisterhood and brotherhood of the Party" in a way not unlike how certain cults (religious and political) have been known to encourage their membership to sever all communications and dealings with biological family members and then to adopt fellow adherents in that way instead. This is quite frightening, and it is very disturbing to find Yeshua—by accounts a man of peace, surely—uttering these sentences. Yet here we have them, from the oldest sources, and multiply accounted for across texts whose authors could not have collaborated nor had access to one another's works. Such details give much weight to the (at least partial, if not full) authenticity of these orations, and so we must do something with them.

I think the key here is once more Second Maccabees and its conception of (physical) resurrection as a divinely bestowed reward for martyrdom (and/or possibly religious fidelity). We have speculated that Yeshua quite likely embraced this view himself, yet I do not think that Yeshua was trying to construct the type of cult-like pyramidal hierarchy with himself on top which may come to mind for us by such comparisons (i.e. "I am martyr, I am hero, God/'God' will raise me to lead you again"); instead he was giving voice to an ethos that oriented itself towards a particular freedom from the world, which is to indicate a perspective of non-attachment, and that this was indeed representative of a peculiar being-toward-death that adjoined both individual attunement and a place for the other within that personal comportment. *The Gospel of Jesus* 11:11 passage cited above is particularly revealing in this regard ("If any of you comes to me and does not hate your own father and mother and wife and children and brothers and sisters—yes, *even your own life*—you're no disciple of mine."; emphasis added[72]). Allow me to briefly expound on this, returning to the "no home" feeling-

---

71. Leloup, trans., intro., and comm., *The Gospel of Thomas*, 51.

72. Matthew and Luke each also contain a parallel here: Matthew 10:37: "'Whoever loves father or mother more than me is not worthy of me; and whoever loves son or daughter more than me is not worthy of me'": note as well the softening involved, such as that seen in Q69: going from "hate" (*Gospel*

(Honestly) Facing Finitude

outlook we glimpsed above in Q27 for further support. That same expression is also repeated in both *The Gospel of Jesus* and in *Thomas*:

> *The Gospel of Jesus* 3:11–12:
> *Foxes have dens*: [11]As they were going along the road, someone said to him, "I'll follow you wherever you go."
> [12]And Jesus said to him, "Foxes have dens, and birds of the sky have nests; but this mother's child [i.e. the nuanced and hard to precisely render "son of man"] has nowhere to rest his head."[73]

> *Thomas*, Saying 86: [1]Jesus said, "<Foxes have> their dens and birds have their nests, [2]but the child of humankind [this is again the "son of man": Leloup gives the capitalized "Son of Man" here; see his p. 47] has no place to lay his head and rest."[74]

I take these as a reinforcing of the lightness or "looseness" that Yeshua is recommending his followers adopt towards life, to considering themselves to be without a "home"; probably not so much in the concrete sense of a determined building and location, but instead with the undertone centered on the human relationships that such almost always involves; in other words, a stable and settled commitment for which one may be willing to sacrifice ideals for the sake of holding onto. He directs those who would join his "kingdom" way of being to absolutely cut away everything that might prevent them from orienting the entirety of their existences to God/"God" and the complete surrendering to the "will" of the divinity: and presumably further by that latter ("will") signifying too a faithfulness to the instructions on how one ought to conduct oneself as rendered by the surrounding Jewish culture and lifestyle in which Yeshua lived and died, and which his own program never repudiated, merely modified (and this, we will remember, was hardly uncommon in first century Palestine; Yeshua was one amongst many sages and Jewish associations that offered competing interpretations from out of commonly received and accepted foundations). In the Yeshuan viewpoint presented then, we can glimpse a being-towards that is more than capable of welcoming death—a bodily resurrection *will* follow (the strength of faith)—and one where what matters are not the current circumstances themselves, but the remaking of those circumstances into "the kingdom."

This is part and parcel of a widespread alacrity to categorically let go of everything in one's situation in order to better "obey"/follow God/"God" as said God/"God" was

---

of Jesus, *Gospel of Thomas*) to "love more than," which naturally includes the possibility of loving each, only internally (perspectivally) ranking that love differently; and also Luke 14:26: "'Whoever comes to me and does not hate father and mother, wife and children, brothers and sisters, yes, and even life itself, cannot be my disciple.'" This is much closer to *The Gospel of Jesus* and *The Gospel of Thomas* versions quoted here; both New Testament verses from *Thinline Bible with the Apocrypha* (NRSV).

73. Funk and the Jesus Seminar, *The Gospel of Jesus*, 23.
74. Meyer, trans. and intro., *The Gospel of Thomas*, 55.

Part 4 | Temporality: God/"God" Here, "the Kingdom" Now

understood in the embedded notional and practical meanings within which Yeshua and his compatriots found themselves "thrown" at birth: these are the image-ideas/idea-images wherein they dwelt. Yeshua's various adjustments of those established norms, moreover, could well have been readily accepted by (be acceptable to) the underprivileged citizenry who came to listen to him, the same set of social classes to which he himself belonged (Chapter 2). In the face of the daily hardships they endured—the nearness of death included—he promoted a "welcome" to individual demise, a preparing, an almost rushing-towards that was conceptually underpinned by the promise of another life via a corporeal resurrection here on earth (at least for martyrs, maybe for the faithful generally; the reader will recall from the previous chapter that the abstracts of a fully envisioned Heaven and Hell were many years distant from this historical period (the vagary of *Sheol* notwithstanding)). Nothing, Yeshua seems to be insisting, is to be grasped so tightly that one might not be free to release it: Not what one's family members think; not one's obligations to those who have gone before; not the duties and complications one has with relations now; not even the life one is living: be always prepared to sacrifice the entirety. This is a being-toward-death that does take into account the other (albeit, one might think, only negatively), and while the ethics of a comportment like this certainly appear to be arguable from many standpoints, it is nevertheless thoroughly developed and coherent within its theoretical framework. It also ties in directly with the re-examination we will make of our own received and traditional "atonement" interpretation, and the "sacrifice" ideas related to it, concerning Yeshua's execution: points which will form the topic of our next chapter.

Chapter 13

Sacrificial Nonsense

THUS DEATH IS RIGHT there, faced and accepted, "welcomed" in a being-towards filled with a faith/belief abstraction (i.e. in a "resurrection") that reduces, or possibly eliminates, any natural fear of it. (While also, oddly, simultaneously forms an ongoing threat/fear/worry of abandonment on the part of those who might rely on the person offering this jovial handshake to demise). We think—we have supposed and conjectured—that Yeshua's own being-toward-death was along these very lines; and maybe not just "along" but quite close in fact. We considered the reasons offered above to presume that he held a Second Maccabees-type version of physical restoration—or anyway at least a positing that was (very) similar to it—to be strong and tenable; even robust. From this combination, we offer, it is realistic to understand Yeshua as someone willing to die for his cause; but—pushing on our proffered—that "cause" was not the received (orthodox) one of an atonement economy, of a this-for-that in which God/"God" was so offended by we its/her/his creatures that a self-manifestation and self-destruction were required to propitiate God's/"God's" self-felt (self-produced?) affront. When looked at from enough notional and emotional distance the whole scheme is somewhat ridiculous really, and if we were not so used to it the acceptability of such would surely be dismissed out of hand. God/"God" was sufficiently angered/disturbed/exasperated with us humans that God/"God" needed to become a "human-God/'God'" compound in order that other (regular) humans might murder said compound to thereby achieve satisfaction for the same compound's (or at least the divine essence within the compound's) sense of retributive justice? There is admittedly much of mystery in this universe, but the preceding proposition strikes as a tale told badly.

Nevertheless, as a story with a moral and a purpose it does do something to us, we must recognize that, and moreover the historically achieved deep-seated familiarity strengthens this. In the below we will therefore seek to determine *what else* the crucifixion by itself—the scene of it, minus the appended "child sacrifice" part—might do if only the underlying conceptual framework were removed and/or shifted. Hence, allow me to propose the following guidelines for our query: 1) Yeshua genuinely accepted a physical resurrection as a reward for martyrdom, and maybe also for "only" religious fidelity; 2) Yeshua also held a concept of sin and forgiveness (return and redemption), one that was probably generally in line with his heritage's teaching on the matter but was understood by him more pacifically; 3) Yeshua was aware of the dangers to his person that he ran by proclaiming the message he did in the manner and places undertaken; and finally, 4) Yeshua all the same judged his message ("the kingdom") to be worth the risk, and he was willing to die for this (self-appointed) cause (likely buoyed mentally by Point 1 above with its restorative promise). Together these elements give us a Yeshua who may have, in some ways, "welcomed" the cross, but not—crucially—a Yeshua who saw his death as universally soteriological, nor even probably as history changing. He might have expected that his voice would echo louder for its having been silenced publicly and violently by the authorities against and about whom he wished reform, but we cannot assume he would have imagined his words to carry across the continents and the centuries in the way they have. Yet *they have,* they have; and that is something truly remarkable. Let us therefore spend some moments gazing anew at that body hanged, and we will see what happens.

On the outer and the inner rest our re-wondering of the crucifixion, on the outer and the inner of what happens experientially as we look upon its reproduction, its creative depictions. This is the same "what happens" that we earlier argued hinges phenomenologically on the ideational taken in relation to this image-idea/idea-image, on an "intentional inexistent"[1] that nevertheless is filled with enough realist force to bury itself so deeply in the psyche that it aborts every other potential interpretation, that it premeditatedly (preconceivedly, *pre-conceive-ably*) disgorges that which otherwise might have been. In the traditions we have collectively received regarding this particular execution, our intuitions are tilted towards a quick movement into transactional thoughts and feelings, and that whether we believe them to be true or not, necessary or not, applicable or not. We are each so ensconced in the standardized plotline that any other point of view is precluded prior to its very possibility, and that is so even if we are not and have never been Christian: the "readings" are there and are culturally, socially unavoidable. If we have other allegiances, or perhaps no allegiances, we might think "The Christians say this was . . . ," but then nevertheless we end at the same destination. The conceptual structuring has simply been erected too concretely into Western—and now global—culture, our enclosures have been brought too near, our gardens too overrun; yet like any stubborn weed this teaching too can be drawn out and pulled up by its roots; if so, what may be left? What happens if we reason and then extend an interpretation which states Yeshua's execution as not inevitable but still one that he chose to accept (should it indeed come to that, he may have thought)? What if nothing whatsoever were spiritually required for redemption (not for theirs then

---

1. Lycan, *Consciousness and Experience,* 152–3; see also Chapters 5 and 6 above, and additionally "The Idea and Its Reality" portion (found on pages 219–24) of Oberg, "Bloodying God," in *Image, Phenomenon, and Imagination in the Phenomenology of Religious Experience,* 209–28.

nor for ours now; not for anyone's any time), but yet this comportment of a "sacrifice/ release" was still a mark of adherence to "the kingdom"? What if—even to a believer— there was no need for "sin" in the offending sense of the term and no holy judgment against which "atonement" were thereby called for? What if we allowed ourselves to think a sacrificially avoidant perception of divinity, one which demands nothing in any sense of a "sacrifice": be it of a form of nonhuman animal, human animal, financial, durational, vocational, et cetera?

To commence on this exploration we will need to recall some of the results of the analyses of Chapter 11 above, wherein we concluded that the oldest and most reliable records available indicate a Yeshuan outlook that contained divine recompense for righteousness (namely, corporeal resurrection), but did not additionally have a corollary punishment antipode that ran in parallel with it. Rather "the kingdom" and its benefits were about this present existence and the better living of it, with the *ressentiment*-style ethos that arose within the ranks of Yeshuan-Judaism as it was on its way to becoming Christianity being a result of (a reaction to) the experienced shifting political realities of the time. We examined as our baseline the thoroughly scholarly vetted words of *The Gospel of Jesus* and found absolutely nothing punitive whatsoever; next we turned to *The Gospel of Thomas* and discovered merely a reference to "the day of harvest" on which "the weeds . . . will be pulled up and burned" (Saying 57,[2] where "the kingdom" is being compared to a person sowing seeds in a field and an enemy tries to ruin the crop); and thereafter we re-opened the Q document—which is possibly contemporaneous with *Thomas*, but possibly also of slightly later origin—and found six sayings of more or less directness: some about reward/rebuke in this life, and some about the same in an afterlife. Q, we recall, was fundamental to the crafting and/ or redacting of the Gospels of Matthew and Luke (at least, so it has been theorized and fairly strongly supported by the academic community even if not actually "proven"), and then there, finally, in the canonical books is where we most clearly recognize truly strong emphases on matters of "Heaven" and "Hell" with their connected ideologies. This progression should not surprise us.

Therefore, in order to further deepen our understanding of and support for a purportedly more devaluing (that is, in taking it far less centrally than what we may glean from the canonical presentations) Yeshuan perspective with regards to "sin" and the consequentially resulting human-divine/human-human relating that matches with the outlook, we will initially situate ourselves via representative biblical phrasings of non-judgment from above conjoined with remission (indeed, that and more) from below through a reading of Matthew 5:45b and Luke 6:32–36. Taking these chronologically later accounts of Yeshua (and quite certainly ones with additions appended: "words put in the mouth of" type phrasings) backwards, we will then look again to our trio of *The Gospel of Jesus*, *The Gospel of Thomas*, and Q for similar sentiments and instructional teachings, hoping therefrom to reformulate the

2. Taken from Meyer, trans. and intro., *The Gospel of Thomas*, 43.

antecedent conceptualities of "sin" and "redemption" lying behind Yeshua's approach to the realities (to the real dangers) of his (potential) crucifixion and its (potential) reverberations. If Yeshua thought otherwise of his death than how we have been told to believe he did (that is, if the man himself did not comprehend his personage as "atoning sacrifice"; and furthermore, if—we radically offer—he did not even consider redemption to be necessary), then how might we today respond to the crucifixion? This, I think, is a question of vast importance to our overall project; and to much that is beyond it. In this effort we seek to remake the eventualities of that famous execution event: that is, to reconstruct it as an *Event* in the philosophical sense but one with far different associations of meaning; and thenceforth a refashioning of the intuitive reactions we may have, or could have, to a viewing of the crucifixion when it is presented visually in works of art and/or emotionally in evocative language which spurs one to reflection or recollection. Here, then, is the Matthean selection:

> Matthew 5:45b [Yeshua is speaking about loving one's enemies]: "for he [i.e. God/"God"] makes his sun rise on the evil and on the good, and sends rain on the righteous and on the unrighteous."[3]

Contextually the canonical point in this very well-known portion is that we ought to do good to everyone, for God/"God" is good to everyone. The standard hermeneutic for this verse has been so instilled in us that we tend to equate it with the so-called Golden Rule and/or the storied "on one foot" dictum of Hillel,[4] but the implications here are actually much more far-reaching, and indeed somewhat revolutionary. As Robert J. Miller has stressed, for an agricultural society such as that of Palestine both before the first century and for some time after (indeed, the same holds even in our era, although to a lesser extent), rainfall was a lifeline and thus considered to be a benediction from the controlling divine forces, be they Israel's or another nation's

---

3. *Thinline Bible with the Apocrypha* (NRSV).

4. E.g. Matthew 7:12: "In everything do to others as you would have them do to you; for this is the law and the prophets."; or Luke 6:31: "Do to others as you would have them do to you." *Thinline Bible with the Apocrypha* (NRSV). Although there has been an unfortunate trend to think this originated with Yeshua, the ethos stems from the Jewish notion of non-retribution (or at most an equal retribution, which as we discussed above was a strongly reductive sentiment in a historical period wherein vengeance typically involved going far further than what was done to oneself or to one's family and/or friends) and equal treatment within the community; e.g. Leviticus 19:18: "You shall not take vengeance or bear a grudge against your countrymen. Love your fellow as yourself: I am the LORD."; or again 19:34: "The stranger who resides with you shall be to you as one of your citizens; you shall love him as yourself, for you were strangers in the land of Egypt: I the LORD am your God."; the most straightforward "equal measure" teaching can be found in the "eye for eye" formula of Exodus 21:24; *Tanakh* (NJPS). Hillel's statement, and it is quite a wonderful nugget, is as follows: "Once there was a gentile who came before Shammai, and said to him: 'Convert me on the condition that you teach me the whole Torah while I stand on one foot.' Shammai pushed him aside with the measuring stick he was holding. The same fellow came before Hillel, and Hillel converted him, saying: 'That which is despicable to you, do not do to your fellow, this is the whole of the Torah, and the rest is commentary, go and learn it.'"; from the Babylonian Talmud, *Shabbat* 31a (internal quotation marks added), see "Quotes on Judaism & Israel," *Jewish Virtual Library*. Accessed March 17, 2021.

Sacrificial Nonsense

(with the prophets sometimes battling it out—as it were—over the weather).[5] There was moreover, and specifically with respect to (but not *exclusively* with; although for our purposes we focus on) Jewish society at the time of Yeshua (and again, before and after) a prevailing notion that proper behavior generated extraneous benefits while improper actions resulted in cursing and demerits. Yet what do we find asserted here? That everyone gets gifted, no matter what; and that equally. Of course we know this to be true, we recognize that the world is not "fair"—and how it grates!—but then to go yet further, as Yeshua does, and to proclaim that God/"God" actively blesses the wicked just like God/"God" does for the righteous: one can see ("see!") how such cuts across the grain and must have been quite shocking to his original listeners, unsettling of the presumed norms and conventional understandings (the prior existence of Qohelet/Ecclesiastes notwithstanding).

The Gospel of Luke's extended version is in the same narrative setting (Yeshua on loving enemies) but without the sun/rain metaphor, and as will be shown in the following the Q account incorporates both; but if Q did in fact provide the basis (or a partial basis) for these two Gospels then such makes eminent sense. The Luke text is:

> Luke 6:32–36: "[32]If you love those who love you, what credit is that to you? For even sinners love those who love them. [33]If you do good to those who do good to you, what credit is that to you? For even sinners do the same. [34]If you lend to those from whom you hope to receive, what credit is that to you? Even sinners lend to sinners, to receive as much again. [35]But love your enemies, do good, and lend, expecting nothing in return [a footnote states: "Other ancient authorities read *despairing of no one*"]. Your reward will be great, and you will be children of the Most High; for he is kind to the ungrateful and the wicked [that conjunctive *for* is potent, and through it the same sun/rain avouchment]. [36]Be merciful, just as your Father is merciful."[6]

Once more the challenge is to treat all alike irrespective of the other's behavior and how one might judge such (righteous/unrighteous), and with the non-Matthean addition of doing so without any expectations for oneself.[7] Thus we are to be magnanimous, but this does not mean that there are not distinctions and divisions being drawn here amongst what amounts to a categorizing of people (the good, the bad, the ugly?[8]), and although Yeshua (in)famously was very willing to consort with those whom his society deemed to be "sinners," he himself still appears to have accepted that

---

5. Miller, "Free Rain," *The Fourth R*, 3–6 and 20 (see especially pages 4–6).

6. *Thinline Bible with the Apocrypha* (NRSV).

7. For more context, here is a fuller section from the highlighted Matthew verse, 5:44–45: "[44]But I [Yeshua] say to you, Love your enemies and pray for those who persecute you, [45]so that you may be children of your Father in heaven; for he makes his sun rise on the evil and on the good, and sends rain on the righteous and on the unrighteous." *Thinline Bible with the Apocrypha* (NRSV).

8. Thank you Sergio Leone, Clint Eastwood, Lee Van Cleef, and Eli Wallach. "The Good, the Bad and the Ugly," *IMDb*. Accessed March 18, 2021.

grouping as such, as the multiple "sinners" enunciated in this passage would naturally require an antecedent notion of "sin" by the speaker, with those who habitually commit it thereby further becoming "sinners"; yet nevertheless, what is being claimed as the result? Essentially nothing: there is no difference, no comeuppance, no punishment for "the bad"; rather quite the opposite. The deeper enjoining Yeshua is hinting at then is not to give in order to get, but to give because it makes one more excellent; but here is where things get hazy, where our sight ("seeing!") goes grey. Luke 6:35, for example, has "Your reward will be great": that certainly indicates an expectation; but it is possible that this phrasing was an insertion by a (shall we say squeamish?) later writer/editor and not a purely Yeshuan framing, as a comparison with the (almost certainly) authentic words—as ascertained by the many scholars of the Jesus Seminar who vetted the sayings—of the non-canonical *Gospel of Jesus* shows:

> *The Gospel of Jesus* 7:5:
> *Sun and rain:* Jesus said, "God causes the sun to rise on both the bad and the good, and sends rain on both the just and the unjust. As you know, God is generous to the ungrateful and the wicked."[9]

There it ends, as with the Gospel of Matthew, with neither boon nor bane affixed, with no consequences whatsoever aside from the beneficence of God/"God". We do note however the buttressing that the terms "ungrateful" and "wicked" provide, signifying again that Yeshua did think there were differentiations to be made between types of actions and actors, but evidently not enough such that they automatically—at least—guaranteed later realizations (or manifestations) in the form of pluses and minuses within a person's daily life. "Sin" but sans consequences? Let us continue reading and pondering on this, for the lines blur again—and then again—with additional readings from Q and *The Gospel of Thomas*.

In Q we also have mention of a "reward," but the closest *Thomas* parallel to any of the above indicates only that one ought to give (and that merely financially) without further commenting on "love," "bless," "do good," et cetera. At this juncture, taken overall, we have a presentation of loving and giving without expecting a return from those to whom one serves, but possibly with expecting (or at least anticipating or hoping for) a bonus from God/"God"; and, in either case, with an objective in so doing of thereby becoming more exceptional oneself. However this is considered, there is no punishment for the "categorically bad," or for "being bad," and that strikes me as a crucial difference, one which reflects strongly on any "redemption" ethics we may read into the terms (or have drilled into us by others) as they stand. Firstly then the aligning Q portion, and immediately thereafter that of *Thomas* (with the bent brackets again indicating insertions by the translator):

> Q16 [Yeshua is speaking]: "Treat people as you would like them to treat you.

---

9. Funk and the Jesus Seminar, *The Gospel of Jesus*, 39.

If you love those who love you, what credit is that to you? Even sinners do the same. If you do good only to those who do good to you, what merit is there in that? Even sinners do that. And if you lend to those from whom you hope to receive, what reward is there in that? Even sinners lend to sinners.

Instead, love your enemies and do good, expecting nothing in return. You will have a great reward, and you will be children of your Father in heaven. He makes the sun rise on the bad and the good. He sends rain to fall on both the just and the unjust."[10]

Thomas, Saying 95: [1]<Jesus said>, "If you have money, do not lend it at interest. [2]Rather, give <it> to someone from whom you will not get it back."[11]

There is "sin" and there are "sinners," but God/"God" blesses all equally and freely; that much appears to be repeated with sufficient force that it can be accepted as part of Yeshua's own outlook. Yet we are still somewhat adrift on the "doing good" variable: What is the "why" in it? Would "the kingdom" ethos admit of a concealed "for me" internal to the motivation one has to do for others? Wishing for a recompense—or at least an acknowledgement—seems entirely natural, and might simply be a facet of human biology; should such therefore be fought, or meekly be accepted? Do not the results of social welfare anyway matter more than whatever potential hopes for oneself the performer of the beneficial acts might have? To move towards solving—or at least to coming closer to such—this dilemma on righteousness for its own sake versus for the purpose of benefit (now? later on?), it might help to examine who in Yeshua's viewpoint qualified as belonging to the "category" of "sinner"; and the answer to that is of course "everyone." As will be obvious, this is hardly an original Yeshuan notion; and since the idea is so thoroughly attested in many multiple biblical sources (from both the Hebrew Bible and the New Testament),[12] we will skip over the received texts and go straight to our non-canonical sources. "All have sinned": but so what? This is where things start to get interesting, for Yeshua puts yet another spin (in addition to the non-retributive "sun and rain for everyone" already examined) on comprehending

---

10. Powelson and Riegert, trans., footnotes, and eds., *The Lost Gospel Q,* 49.

11. Meyer, trans. and intro., *The Gospel of Thomas,* 57; Leloup's version of Thomas Saying 95 adds a "never" which in its finality casts an interesting nuance on the whole, I think: "Yeshua said: /If you have money, /do not lend it with interest, /but give it to the one /who will never pay you back." Leloup, trans., intro., and comm., *The Gospel of Thomas,* 49. There is another Thomas logion somewhat akin in spirit to that expressed in Saying 95, namely number twenty-five, which reads: Thomas, Saying 25: "[1]Jesus said, 'Love your brother like your soul, [2]protect that person like the pupil of your eye.'"; Meyer, trans. and intro., *The Gospel of Thomas,* 33. This is even less directly connected with the above linear of Matthew—Luke—*Gospel of Jesus*—Q I think, but one can still find in it a common refrain of "give."

12. See, for example, "27 Bible Verses about All Have Sinned," *Knowing Jesus.* Accessed March 18, 2021. In citing this reference I do not mean to endorse the website nor its clearly biased purposes, I simply wish to give some indication of how widespread this assumption would have been within Yeshua's cultural milieu and in the years that followed, and how easy it is for us today to come upon information like this. Again, what is compelling is not that Yeshua thought there were "sin" and "sinners," but the conclusions and extensions he drew therefrom.

Part 4 | Temporality: God/"God" Here, "the Kingdom" Now

"sin"; not so much with regard to what constitutes it, but rather with the relativity thereof. This is the point which will provide a bridge for our proposal that Yeshua did not conceive of "redemption" as being necessary; although the path to that (initial) destination will be somewhat winding.

Below then are our non-canonical representative samples on "all have sinned" as spoken by (as attributed to) Yeshua; and the reader will no doubt immediately recognize each of them: the sliver/speck and timber/plank of respective "faulty carpentry" jargon, and the very heartwarming and humbling "first stone" story:

> *The Gospel of Jesus* 13:11–12:
>
> *Sliver and timber:* [11]Jesus said, "You see the sliver in your friend's eye, but don't see the timber in your own eye. [12]When you take the timber out of your own eye, then you will see well enough to remove the sliver from your friend's eye."[13]
>
> Q20: "Why do you notice the speck of sawdust in your brother's eye and not the wooden plank in your own? How can you say to your brother, 'Let me take out the sawdust from your eye,' when you cannot see the plank in your own?
>
> Hypocrite! Remove the plank from your own eye first; then you will see clearly enough to remove the sawdust from your brother's eye."[14]
>
> *Thomas,* Saying 26: [1]Jesus said, "You see the speck that is in your brother's eye, but you do not see the beam that is in your own eye. [2]When you take the beam out of your own eye, then you will see clearly to take the speck out of your brother's eye."[15]
>
> *The Gospel of Jesus* 7:20–30:
>
> *The first stone:* [20]The scholars and members of the purity party bring him a woman who was caught committing adultery. They make her stand there in front of everybody, [21]and they address Jesus, "Teacher, this woman was caught in the act of adultery. [22]In the Law Moses commanded us to stone women like this. What do you say?" [23](They said this to trap him, so they would have something to accuse him of.)
>
> [24]Jesus stooped down and began drawing on the ground with his finger. [25]When they insisted on an answer, he stood up and replied, "Whoever in this crowd has never committed a sin should go ahead and throw the first stone at her." [26]Once again he squatted down and continued writing on the ground.

---

13. Funk and the Jesus Seminar, *The Gospel of Jesus,* 63.

14. Powelson and Riegert, trans., footnotes, and eds., *The Lost Gospel Q,* 53.

15. Meyer, trans. and intro., *The Gospel of Thomas,* 33. Matthew 7:3–5 and Luke 6:41–42 have the canonical versions of these pronouncements, which are essentially the same as each other and as the sources here. It is somewhat interesting to me that only Q has the emphatic "hypocrite," which is also picked up by the Matthew and Luke relatings.

> ²⁷His audience began to drift away, one by one—the elders were the first to go—until Jesus was the only one left, with the woman there in front of him.
>
> ²⁸Jesus stood up and said to her, "Woman, where is everybody? Hasn't anyone condemned you?"
>
> ²⁹She replied, "No one, sir."
>
> ³⁰"I don't condemn you, either," Jesus said. "You're free to go, but from now on no more sinning."[16]

Please allow me two side comments on this last citation before moving into our main thesis on the above in full: The first remark is to note the very unfortunate misogynistic nature of the entire section, even including gender label as a form of address ("Woman, where is . . . "), which does mar the beauty of the whole somewhat for modern readers. In this however we ought to remember that appraisements which find direct fault with the expressive character itself are essentially anachronistic, and that although lesser treatment of one half of society by another half such as that being demonstrated here was commonplace to the level of being taken for granted (a presumed "just the way of the world") does not justify such, the historical facts of the matter should prevent us, I think, from being overly zealous purely about the textual style today (while we must still remain on guard lest the inherent sexism be taken and applied anew). In reading this we can perhaps instead be glad that things have changed, and additionally do our best to help continue trends towards further equality. My second aside is simply this: The humility that comes with age! How lovely that the elders lead the way in this group retreat.

Moving now to what I would like to proffer as a conceptual re-reading (re-imagining) of a Yeshuan perspective on "sin" and the required responses to it (if any, and if so then what), if the immediately above is taken together with the groundwork we have laid through earlier chapters of our study, then cumulatively we might discover in our findings a notional five-pointed "package" which entails and results in: 1) An acceptance that indeed yes, "all have sinned" and "all are sinners" but—and this is the typically provocative Yeshuan twist—2) *My sin is always greater than yours*. Again, Yeshua did certainly appear to take "sin" as a given (and thus for him there would be no mental scare quotes/double inverted commas; I, on the other hand, use them because I do not accept "sin" as a valid theological concept under its modern associations; but that discussion will have to momentarily be paused); yet, and as just mentioned with

---

16. Funk and the Jesus Seminar, *The Gospel of Jesus*, 41 and 43. This can be found in John 8:3-11; there the "scholars and members of the purity party" are listed as "scribes and the Pharisees," and additionally a footnote following verse eleven reads: "The most ancient authorities lack 7.53–8.11; other authorities add the passage here or after 7.36 or after 21.25 or after Luke 21.38, with variations of text; some mark the passage as doubtful."; see *Thinline Bible with the Apocrypha* (NRSV). Thus, once again, there is much we cannot claim definitively, and we must admit that absolutes are probably impossible with everything in any endeavor to reach as far back as we are attempting; but then again, our purposes at present are primarily phenomenological in light of variant hermeneutics. That the scholars of the Jesus Seminar ranked these verses as very likely authentic does carry weight, I think, and moreover it certainly seems to fit with the general "kingdom" message.

Part 4 | Temporality: God/"God" Here, "the Kingdom" Now

regards to the prejudiced presentation of the "first stone" story, that was most likely a matter of historico-cultural reality: it was "in the air" for people of the place and time, even "the very air they breathed." Of course Yeshua's is not an empirical assertion, and objectivity or a third person point of view are entirely irrelevant to the emphasis I think he wished to aver; rather within "kingdom" thinking, "I" am always more "sinful" than "you"; I have always "missed the mark"[17] more than you, my plank will ever be bulkier than your speck, and I absolutely have no right to be throwing stones. Naturally this extends to my obligation not to condemn you, but then—yet more compellingly—3) God/"God" *does not condemn either*: and, for clarity, I would like to strongly stress that I am not making this claim from a reading which understands Yeshua as divine or as the dogmatic God/"God"-man compound in the preceding "first stone" story (e.g. as some have read the closing comment of "I don't condemn you, either" to indicate something along the lines of "Not even I, God incarnate, condemn you either") or other similar canonical relatings, but rather by the deep significance of the "sun and rain" expression, by the matter-of-factness of it, by the pure unambiguous character of the daily demonstrations of the blessings of God/"God" as delivered in the natural world indiscriminately to every living creature.[18]

Henceforth lies the first of our own two (appended) radical conjectures, tiny oblations poured out for the reader's thought: 4) Since one should not judge another—and should a reason be needed not to, then the quality of everyone being at fault ("me" more than "you," always) ought to suffice—and since God/"God" does not differentiate amongst "categories" of people following "sinner/righteous" delineations in demonstrating love and care but instead gives freely to all, then in the continuous act of this giving God/"God" might be interpreted as not even judging *whatsoever* (note that this goes beyond "not condemning") and thus, if that is the case, then *there exists no judgment*, although there nevertheless are—and quite perforce in that—causes and effects. Yeshua, I think, was trying to impart to his listeners that God/"God" is purely love and only loves, but all the same such does not change the abrasive force of one's (me/you/we, and probably often) "missing the mark" ("sin"), and thereby too whatever consequences might result in this intertwined and twisted planet of ours.

Let us take this further. If God/"God" does not judge in this life (negative things may happen, but then positive as well; neither, however, should be taken as "divine signs" of favor or disfavor) then one's actions cannot logically be done for the sake of reward or recompense (there are simply no guarantees, no strict good = blessings, bad = cursings formulae to be calculated), although—lo!—blessings anyway: comforting

---

17. As the Hebrew meaning indicates; this etymology tends to be well-known but is easy to forget I think when the word is used in English, likely due to its heavily (over)burdened "atonement" associations via the very same received understandings of the crucifixion event which we wish to counter in the present chapter (and in what follows).

18. In that for the human and nonhuman as well, we might add. To those who would wish to retort that the world is not purely "good" I would gently indicate that such was not Yeshua's point, although admittedly it too is indeed a matter of course.

sunshine and life-giving rain. Fine and well, perhaps—and thank you, God/"God"—but there is yet more. Recall from Chapter 11 that Yeshua himself did not focus on any afterlife, that the records we have of him supposedly doing so are most probably later insertions and additions, and that while we did conclude he almost surely personally embraced a Second Maccabees-style belief in physical resurrection as prize (reward) for martyrdom,[19] what seemed to matter most to him in his "kingdom" message was the better/otherwise living of this life amidst the dust and dirt of the moment. These aspects indicate a minimizing and/or full erasure of postmortem issues; not only as matters for concern but as matters *tout court*. We ought to forget about such. "Erase those worries!" we are told (paraphrasing), "God/'God' will provide."[20] Therefore, connecting these many dots (walking the path, taking the bend), we suggest conclusively our final "packaged" point: 5) *There is no need for redemption in Yeshuan thought because "sin" is universal and God/"God" does not adjudicate, not at present and not in any fantasy "hereafter."* This being the case, it follows that Yeshua could not have conceived of his death—whenever and however he thought it might occur[21]—as being remitting or as located anywhere within an economy of atonement for, again, any such was simply not necessary. We are everyone sinners, we are everyone already forgiven, we are everyone preemptively "redeemed": Always.

We have dwelt on Yeshua's potential being-toward-death, his general outlook and attitude towards it; we are led to ask now how that might have taken him in regards to what he surely knew to be the physically endangering vocation he set himself upon. Conjunctively, we wish to reflect on what we today may take the crucifixion setting as an event/Event to mean, or to gesture at, in the absence of any appended abstract of absolution. I think, as has been multiply hinted at, that death for Yeshua was quite reductively a risk he was willing to take (although he may have only guessed at it as one possible form of punishment; others such as public flogging, imprisonment, et cetera might well have occurred to him too), bolstered by a self-perceived assurance of a postmortem physical resurrection here on Earth. For him, once more, spreading "the kingdom" ethos and working to find it realized were worth any dangers courted. If we accept that and shift to meditate on our own place (seeking application of these

19. Possibly also for religious fidelity; contrary to the preceding in the text above, this is obviously a "good = blessing" reward example, the important difference however hangs on this cause-effect relation being *between* lives (pre- and post-resurrection) and not *within* a life.

20. The birds of the air, the flowers of the field: a staple "kingdom" teaching; see again Funk and the Jesus Seminar, *The Gospel of Jesus*, 19–20 (2:29–35); Powelson and Riegert, trans., footnotes, and eds., *The Lost Gospel Q*, 85–6 (Q51–52); Meyer, trans. and intro., *The Gospel of Thomas*, 37 and 73 (Saying 36 from the Coptic and Greek sources, respectively); and for a canonical version Matthew 6:25–34; *Thinline Bible with the Apocrypha* (NRSV).

21. Recalling from our Garden of Gethsemane discussion in Chapter 10 that we have removed omniscience and even prescience from our consideration of the Yeshuan narratives (and too that those very Garden stories themselves are fictitious), yet even so Yeshua could well have had—and probably did have—a premonition or intuition that he was likely to come to some form of official censure due to his ministry. In thinking thus then our own reactions to viewing the Gethsemane images changed too, a finding which will apply to this chapter as well when we try to (re)look at the embodied cross.

altered notions), what may be more resonating for us are the eventualities to be realized hermeneutically from this particular execution when it is comprehended as a totally fortuitous happening, as a pure effect of the multifarious historical factors which came together just so, just then, and thence—towards further operation—what that could mean for our long sought after (our continued labors to see/"see!," to "resurrect!") new/old Yeshuan-Judaism.

This is captivating, for if we might have a Christianity without Yeshua as flesh destined for a substitutional offertory slaughter, one where not even—and especially—Yeshua understood himself that way, then countless applicatory possibilities and innumerable comprehensions of the man and his teachings spring forth. As we did in the preceding with our visit to the Garden of Gethsemane, let us here attempt a fresh approach to the image-idea/idea-image of Yeshua's execution, one which has been won via the altered anterior conceptual space we have been working towards. Through now thinking on Yeshua's death as exterior to "sin" and "redemption," wherein there is neither atoning act nor even a need for one, we find differing intuitions presenting themselves in tandem, making themselves felt. For the remainder of this chapter, then, I ask the reader to hold in mind an image of the embodied cross against the arguments presented (a kind of reactionary litmus test; probing the balance of the conceptual and the pictorial halves), a sign which, while admittedly handed down to us with many additional non-historic accretions, is nevertheless representative of an occurrence we can have much empirical confidence in (quite unlike Gethsemane). This naturally entails a returning to our earlier phenomenological methodology of symbol-response, although in a slightly compressed manner. As a final preparation for the creative task of trying to think what Yeshua may have thought, we ought also to shake free our ingrained presumption (either in a narrative sense ("in the story the character knew") or in a more literal sense ("Yeshua the historical personage knew")) that he simply was aware of and accepted that he would be tortured and crucified, and that such was necessary for his perforce mission. For this "shaking free" then, here is another brief logion from *The Gospel of Thomas* to push us towards a right(-ly refracted) frame of mind: The words could well be authentic,[22] but they might not be; on that we again apply our Husserlean "brackets" and pay attention instead to what happens internally (concept and picture; intuitions, emotions) as we read:

> *Thomas,* Saying 98: Jesus said, "The father's kingdom is like a person who wanted to put someone powerful to death.

---

22. There is a parallel in *The Gospel of Jesus* but not one in Q. *The Gospel's* (listed as 12:39–41 on their numbering scheme) reads: "*The assassin:* 39Jesus would say, 'The Father's imperial rule [i.e. "the kingdom"; Funk and the Seminar members sometimes use differing terminology where we have remained with one phrasing for the sake of simplicity and clarity] is like a person who wanted to kill someone powerful. 40While still at home he drew his sword and thrust it into the wall to find out whether his hand would go in. 41Then he killed the powerful one.'" It will be clear how very similar to *Thomas* this is (nearly identical), and *Thomas* is moreover given as the scholars' source in their considerations. See Funk and the Jesus Seminar, *The Gospel of Jesus,* 61.

> While at home he drew his sword and thrust it into the wall to find out whether his hand would go in.
>
> Then he killed the powerful one."[23]

It is possibly disturbing to imagine Yeshua making a simile like this, it certainly does not fit with the received view of him; yet just like the "powerful man" in this selection the "Jesus" figure of over-familiarity must be killed, and it will take some effort to achieve that. Unnerved, therefore—and aiming for still more unnerving—we continue. A recap: Our Yeshua is a teacher, a wandering sage with a program for being-in-the-world that consumes him to the point he has devoted his entire occupation to spreading it through public preaching; he is a social reformer, a rabbi of sorts, an almost-something-like-a-Pharisee; his only "magic" is verbal, he has no prescience about future events beyond what any of us might have, and though he knows the risks he is taking he does not (probably from his point of view *cannot*) cease nor even slacken in his undertaking. He is headed towards death but may merely have little more than an intimation of such; anyway he guesses *something* will befall him, his luck will run out, his time will come. Mentally, attitudinally, he is ready, thinking that should it lead to *that*, well then, God/"God" will resurrect him and he will live to walk and speak once more. Any consequences would be for him and him alone; his (possible) execution is self-understood as carrying the meaning of martyrdom, but he would not also have appended a redemptive/salvific posit to that since he was convinced any such was entirely unnecessary: God/"God" blesses all and judges none.

This Yeshua is quite alternate from the character the church has presented to us these long centuries, but yet still—as with that God/"God"-man compound version—ours finds his end at the cross. It was a sacrifice, we think, but not a substitute; at least not on Yeshua's comprehension, although that latter significance and the outgrowths thereof were obviously to be read into it (and my goodness with what gusto!). To further and finally jog these shifted ideas then another visual and notional image might help at this point (image-idea/idea-image), and thus below is placed El Greco's famous "Christ on the Cross, in a Landscape with Horsemen";[24] with it, moreover, I would like to make the challenge that we gaze on the work and, whatever we may have heard or been taught regarding it, see nothing there but a purely mortal man—a remarkable, unique, entirely human person—being killed by colonial authorities who were seeking to put down the agitation this public sage had been stirring; that is, that we "see!" it in this way, and then thereafter perceive what occurs within from a viewing such as the suggested, supported by the abstractional outline of the above. The art piece:

---

23. Meyer, trans. and intro., *The Gospel of Thomas*, 59.

24. Retrieved from: "File: El Greco—Christ on the Cross, in a Landscape with Horsemen—1610–14.jpg." El Greco, Public Domain, via Wikimedia Commons. Accessed April 21, 2022.

Part 4 | Temporality: God/"God" Here, "the Kingdom" Now

Figure 12: El Greco, "Christ on the Cross, in a Landscape with Horsemen" (1610–1614)

Here a dying man; nothing more, but neither nothing less. Contemplatively, these thoughts and feelings maintained in observance, we draw out the implications—deeper into this spiraling whirl—to inspect what sort of Yeshuan-Judaism we may discover through the freedom achieved from a jettisoning of the "atonement" interpretation which forms the cornerstone of what we call Christianity. Tracing the links: If there is no requirement for redemption, we can go one better than even Yeshua and completely drop "sin" in its modern usage altogether (hence my repeated placing of quotation marks/inverted double commas, as mentioned). We may wish to maintain an idea of "sin" in its originary sense of "missing the mark" or failure to be/do what one could/ought, but that is very different from the associations of profound internally assessed guilt, despair, and dependence on an underserved grace to offset the affront leveled against a judging divinity that "sin" as a loaded word carries today. The nuances and repercussions between what it once meant but now means are so wide, in fact, that I find another term altogether is called for; but I do not wish to offer one since I think it preferable to focus instead on doing away with "sin" entirely while keeping only the motivation to realize that one has not lived up to what one might, and therefore—as in everything—to try, try again. No sin/"sin," no atonement, no substitutional human sacrifice: redemption as always already because never has been needed. Yeshua could have reasoned there might be a cross for him, but he did not *know* and most probably did not want it even if he was willing to risk it (but in that accepted risk we find astonishingly exemplary courage and passion: "kingdom" living, surely). What form of a phenomenology of the crucifixion are we constructing with these premises?

In answer we firstly need to summarize the metaphysical grounding our heretofore "weak" theology[25] has sought to establish, starting with a recapitulation of what Keller taught with her extraordinarily beneficial highlighting of the initial Genesis creation account:[26] God/"God" was not singly present prior to the creative act, but was alongside the pre-existing materials (*equally* pre-existing? of course we do not (cannot) know . . .) used to forge the heavens and the earth,[27] not first generating the raw materials by itself,[28] and certainly not conjuring up both the ingredients and the finished product in one fell sorcerer's swoop. This resulting reduction in the "what" of creation makes the claims to omnipotence presumably demonstrated by the narrative problematic because one is compelled to conclude that God/"God" was not able to do just *anything* in God's/"God's" construction (transparently God/"God" was confined materially and *had* to work with what was *already available:* an ipso facto limiting). As

---

25. A thousand thanks again to Caputo for his wonderful works: Caputo, *The Weakness of God*; Caputo, *The Folly of God*; Caputo, *Hermeneutics*; Caputo, *Cross and Cosmos*; and of course many more.

26. Indeed, other Semitic creation myths too, not only the fine Hebrew one we use today.

27. Keller, *Face of the Deep*; and for more on the ancients' imaginative thoughtscape, horizons, and "worlds" in the phenomenological senses see again Kugel, *The God of Old*. It is worth re-emphasizing the import of the words (even in translation) and noting the nuances invoked: Genesis 1:1–2: "In the beginning when God created the heavens and the earth, the earth was a formless void and darkness covered the face of the deep, while a wind from God swept over the face of the waters." *Thinline Bible with the Apocrypha* (NRSV). Again, the presentation is of extant and uncreated: 1) the *earth* as formless, 2) the *deep*, and 3) the *waters*. This is not the pure vacuum of contemporary popular imagination (which we have of course been trained to picture through the repetitious drilling of now-traditional (but not *then* traditional when the text in question was written, nor even when it was edited and redacted) "official" interpretation. For further support, there is additionally the wording of the first century BCE deutero-canonical text (probably first written in Greek) *The Wisdom of Solomon,* which reads at 11:17 thusly: "For your all-powerful hand, /which created the world out of formless matter, /did not lack the means to send upon them a multitude of bears, or bold lions [the context is on punishment for the wicked]"; *Thinline Bible with the Apocrypha* (NRSV). This is important: "out of *formless matter*" (emphasis added) and *not* out of "nothing"; the held image of the author(s) seems still to be that of the Genesis author(s)/editor(s), thus reinforcing the incredibly longstanding perseverance of this creational concept which—we remind the reader—did not transform into the present *ex nihilo* version until the late second century CE (roughly between two hundred to three hundred years after *The Wisdom of Solomon* was penned), and was only then offered as a response to a contemporary theological controversy; on that see Caputo, *The Weakness of God,* especially 75–83. A brief overview on *The Wisdom of Solomon* can be found at: Harrington, "Wisdom of Solomon," *Oxford Bibliographies*. Accessed June 09, 2022.

28. I use the pronoun "it" here to avoid attaching a gender to the divine, but "themselves" would also be possible to accommodate the same gender based concerns, and then there the technically plural form would have the accompanying advantage of invoking the Trinity, which given our context would be quite appropriate I feel. I should add though that by mentioning such I do not mean to endorse the Trinity concept per se (although again technically, the Trinity is nevertheless orthodoxly singular).

also singled out in Chapter 9, we recall that for the ancients the process did seem to have required a number of attempts before it was right (or—and this bears repeating as well—not "right" so much as "good enough"), although how long it took and how many times it had to be redone is anyone's guess.

If, therefore, God/"God" did not create out of nothing, if God/"God" even made mistakes along the way and needed to conduct said creation over again in part or in whole while the act remained a work in progress, then these facets together give way to a further necessary diminution in our conceiving of the divine: that of omniscience (with its accompanying perfect foresight: an omniscient manufacturer would not need to re-do a product). God/"God" was therefore limited in *usage* and in *know-how*. Taking this deeper yet, if both omnipotence and omniscience (are allowed to) fall away, then conclusively any number of other things might happen that God did not/has not fore-allowed (pre-permitted), and hence God's/"God's" will might not be done and God/"God" might not be able to prevent such; God/"God" might even be disconcerted by such. Furthermore, if extant creation remains still as a work underway—as it would appear to given the non-static nature of the observable and unobservable alike, at least from our linear perspective—then the entirety becomes comprehensively transformed and whole worlds—*the* world—open up to incredible possibilities; we human animals suddenly find ourselves in the bizarre position (to many modernly conditioned minds) of being co-creators due to our behaviors clearly contributing towards the shaping and moulding, the transfiguring and (re)building of the very "this and that" upon which we tread.[29] (I note that for a significant portion of contemporarily practicing rabbinic Jews this understanding will be anything but bizarre: the concept of *tikkun olam* as "world repair" is essentially thus; yielding for our study, of course, one more pillar for the Yeshuan-Judaism which is *a* Judaism amongst other Judaisms.)

In progressing, as we must, care is called for in maintaining these propositions: omnipotence has become (astounding) potence, but not *omni;* omniscience has become (astounding) nous, but not *omni;* omnipresence, however, *has not been touched.* (This proves seminal for the revisionary theology which I would like to meditate upon in a future work; as does, we can hint at now, a more extensive move away from thinking God/"God" as a being with X attributes (such as omnipotence, omniscience) and towards the thinking of an existential-experiential—but yet total: our only "omni"—pervasiveness.) In the present, however, ours is not to soar those lofty skies, and so let

---

29. The effects an interpretation such as this would have on the issue of theodicy will not go unnoticed, and the responsibility for the ill we do subsequently rightly (I think) can be seen ("seen!") as resting squarely and only on our own shoulders. The ill that strikes at us, moreover, is probably best taken as one more aspect of this sticky, messy, intertwined world of probabilities which we inhabit. Nothing is perfect, yes? I am again grateful to Caputo's books for stimulating such deductive thoughts, and for the ethical calls made. The state of the planet (socially, politically, environmentally, et cetera) as our own fault might seem obvious enough, but that so many do not (wish not to) admit to that belies any claimed transparency.

us keep our feet on this earth and our eyes on that set of wooden beams, embodied now by a very mortal, very broken personage. With the preceding taken conjointly, what might such imply for Yeshua and his crucifixion? Starting with the sheer fact of it, with the hung man, we remember that on the accepted, taught, and "correct" understanding of an executed Yeshua as trade-off, as the flesh and blood donation needed to propitiate an omnipotent and omniscient divinity, Yeshua could easily have "come down" from the cross as the Gospel stories (quite slanderously) tell us the spectators and Jewish religious authorities taunted him to do,[30] yet that he refrained in order to fulfill his sacred mission. On this point Caputo, who also champions a "lowered" theopoetics (as he would no doubt label it) similar to the one we are considering and will expand on, writes:

> On my accounting, Jesus was being crucified, not holding back; he was nailed there and being executed very much against his will and the will of God. He never heard of Christianity's novel idea that he was redeeming the world with his blood. His approach to evil was forgiveness, not paying off a debt due the Father [Caputo uses the traditional male terminology], or the devil, with suffering or with anything else.[31]

Yeshua might not (one would think almost certainly *did not*) have wanted to die, at least not in that way and not at that point in his ministry and life, however willing he may have been to risk it. He simply did. He got killed, he got stuck up on a raised beam and left to slowly and painfully breathe his last while carrion birds circled overhead, dogs yelped below, and those who loved him and were unafraid (or disregarding) enough of the patrolling soldiers onsite to unashamedly weep and wail: for him, and for their own felt loss. In this, Yeshua may have chosen to submit himself to the treatment received and thus been somewhat participatory; the Gospel of John gives us a Yeshuan trial scene before the Roman governor Pontius Pilate wherein he does not deny what he is charged with;[32] assuming there is at least some degree of historical

---

30. See e.g. Mark 15:29–30 and Matthew 27:41–43; Mark: "29Those who passed by derided [a footnote reads: "Or *blasphemed*"] him [i.e. Yeshua], shaking their heads and saying, 'Aha! You who would destroy the temple and build it in three days [a reference to an earlier recorded Markan prophecy from (put into the mouth of) Yeshua in 14:58], 30save yourself, and come down from the cross!'"; Matthew: "41In the same way [i.e. like those crucified nearby to Yeshua are related to have remarked in verse forty] the chief priests also, along with the scribes and elders, were mocking him, saying, 42'He saved others; he cannot save himself [a footnote reads: "Or *is he unable to save himself?*"]. He is the King of Israel; let him come down from the cross now, and we will believe in him. 43He trusts in God; let God deliver him now, if he wants to; for he said, "I am God's Son."'" *Thinline Bible with the Apocrypha* (NRSV).

31. Caputo, *The Weakness of God*, 44.

32. Relayed in John 18:28–40, which is too long to quote here in full but includes the following important verses: "35Pilate replied, 'I am not a Jew, am I? Your own nation and the chief priests have handed you over to me. What have you done?' 36Jesus answered, 'My kingdom is not from this world. If my kingdom were from this world, my followers would be fighting to keep me from being handed over to the Jews. [... "handed over to the Jews": my goodness this is something coming in the context of all we have worked towards in establishing Yeshuan-Judaism ...] But as it is, my kingdom is not from here.' 37Pilate asked him, 'So you are a king?' Jesus answered, 'You say that I am a king. For this I was born,

basis in that (although given John's polemical character by that point in the canonized narrative there probably is very little, if any) we might find Yeshua fully recognizing what could happen to him but accepting the events he perceived unfolding as befitting of the vision espoused in his "kingdom" teachings. Perhaps in that he thereby aimed to fashion an event/Event through his martyrdom (i.e. in the historically-puncturing sense, although of course Yeshua would not have internalized it in those academically situated terms; he also would likely have been reassured regarding any potential for death via his self-presumed Second Maccabees style resurrection). Whatever the case there may have been, what we can know did occur with empirical certitude is that collectively Christianity as a system has taken hold of this execution image and flipped it into a strange and almost masochistic debit card payment. Minds today—as Christians or not, the interpretation has permeated global culture—have been trained to understand (once more, whether agreed to or not) something in the crucifixion that was unimaginable to every reasoning, feeling person prior to Saint Paul's introduction of the offense-exchange abstract: a notion that thereafter took on a reality (a realism) that became so thickly rooted it has blotted out all others and resulted in the binary of either full acceptance or complete rejection. This is tragic, a gross mutation of the already unjust.

In closing we shall think a little more about Saint Paul and this idea cum image-idea/idea-image he left us, one which (unfortunately, to my mind at least) we have turned into a fortress. As an apostle of the early church and as a foundational theologian for it, Paul interjected into Yeshua's message a telos, arguably apocalyptic in nature, that included within it an overlay of the hermeneutic of the sacrificial scapegoat, the offering required to carry the sins of the people into the wilderness,[33] thus turning

---

and for this I came into the world, to testify to the truth. Everyone who belongs to the truth listens to my voice.'" *Thinline Bible with the Apocrypha* (NRSV).

33. I refer here to the procedure described in Leviticus 16:21–22: "21Aaron shall lay both his hands upon the head of the live goat and confess over it all the iniquities and transgressions of the Israelites, whatever their sins, putting them on the head of the goat; and it shall be sent off to the wilderness through a designated [a footnote here reads: "*Meaning of Heb. 'itti uncertain.*"] man. 22Thus the goat shall carry on it all their iniquities to an inaccessible region; and the goat shall be set free in the wilderness." *Tanakh* (NJPS). Other animals were sacrificed directly as part of the Yom Kippur (Day of Atonement) rituals, described in detail in the whole of Leviticus 16. As an aside, it might be commented upon that the usage of "it" regarding this goat helps to contribute, I think, to the very unfortunate (and far too widespread and ingrained) perspective of comprehending nonhuman animals as objects/tools despite the obvious presence of gender in these creatures, a trait easily recognizable and especially so in mammals. Why not call the goat a she or he? Merely that pronoun shift could have profound effects on our thinking and resultant ethical behaviors. (As might, considering the above, a regular pronoun shift when referencing the divine.) That the animal is here (and manifestly in sacrificial structures generally) a "tool" is beyond doubt. To return to the broader point, see e.g. Paul's phrasing in Romans 3:25: "whom [i.e. "Christ Jesus"; from the end of the previous verse] God put forward as a sacrifice of atonement by his blood, effective through faith." *Thinline Bible with the Apocrypha* (NRSV). John 1:29 also makes a straightforward link with this imagery (via the words of John the Baptizer (Baptist)), but since scholars date the writing of that Gospel as much later than Paul's epistles (composed in the late first to early second centuries as compared with Paul's work done in the mid-first century, as we have discussed), Paul can be understood to take the foundational role.

Yeshua's execution into a cipher which the crucified man himself could not have imagined and—if our argument has held—would have been nowhere near his mind during his intense suffering. Boyarin makes a very solid case for understanding Paul as being driven by a form of dualist thinking that involved a primary "lower" literal layer and a secondary "higher" allegorical layer (hence, e.g. cosmically: material or transcendent; and e.g. anthropologically: flesh or spirit; importantly here the material or flesh levels are not "bad," they are simply "not as good").[34] In taking Paul to have been engaged in viewing the world and its occurrences around him through conceptual lenses like these, we might apply it to his imposed offense-exchange reading of the crucifixion as such being the allegorical level of Yeshua's death, wherein would then be found the spiritual import, meaning, and—crucially—transformative power. The act (by which I mean to indicate the sense of it as a thing assented to ("allowing oneself to be killed") rather than the passive "being killed") became for Paul the gateway whereby the old means of Law on the literal level were superseded by the new means of Law conducted spiritually: in faith and "life in Christ." Again, this—so Boyarin argues and I agree—is neither a denigration of Law nor flesh per se, but is a promotion of the "new alternative" Paul believes to be available because of what Yeshua's dying in the way he did supposedly accomplished on that "higher" level.[35] Naturally for any of this to work one has to accept a great deal of preceding abstractions, primary amongst which would be an acquiescence to "sin" as applicable; but Paul of course did just that, and so for him the pieces fit together beautifully. For us, it is a jumbled mess.

If we were to place Yeshua's "kingdom" message, after all, onto the ontological planes Paul seems to have dwelt in, we would need to acknowledge how intensely "literal" and "lower" it would be. His was a ministry focused on the very present time of everydayness, and on having trust simply and fully therein (e.g. such as a comportment of taking each day as a gift, of asking/allowing God/"God" to do what God/"God" wills through and amongst us, of purposefully avoiding plans and contingencies to make space for divine movement(s): in short, "the kingdom" not as a "where?" but as a "how?"[36]), with neither a pursued telos nor—so we have attempted to put forth—any requirement for redemption (despite Yeshua too acceding to "sin" in a phenomenal way). In "the kingdom" framing, what was being offered was the practical and ethical choice of either being in the world through standardized associations of power (authorities, hierarchies, relations, et cetera), or of being in the world through the connections of powerlessness, of (in some ways) severance,[37] of giving

---

34. Boyarin, *A Radical Jew*, see especially Chapter 3.

35. Boyarin, *A Radical Jew*, see again Chapter 3.

36. Caputo, *The Weakness of God*; particularly the "nearness" section on 167–8, and to a lesser degree (being more action focused) the remarks on Derrida and "adieu" on 265–9.

37. Recalling the consequences of following him which we found Yeshua to be asserting in Chapter 12, namely: 1) Intrafamilial conflict, 2) Breaking ancestral ties, and 3) Sundering living bonds; what we ought to make of those and how we ought to respond I wish to leave open to the reader.

and forgiving, of resting and not worrying, of taking what comes as it comes. Caputo summarizes the whole as:

> The kingdom is not describing physical transformations of entities but the *existential transformability of our lives,* having to do with the most powerful and transfiguring figures of self-transformation, in which we and all things are made new. It has to do with the *call* that the kingdom issues, the call to be of a new mind, a new heart.[38]

This is a living-now, and naturally so is Paul's; it is only that while Paul of course too supports "the kingdom" message, his accounting of its "living-now" entails so much more happening on symbolic and notional realms when compared with Yeshua's pragmatic, dirt-beneath-one's-fingernails version. What is somewhat ironic, and mostly overlooked, is that this same Pauline offense-exchange comprehending with its parallel column of a vengeful and demanding deity (completely against the figure Yeshua taught to love and trust) was nevertheless not even Paul's central stance; his emphasis appears to have primarily been on the results thereof which were mentioned in our "gateway" remarks: Namely that for Paul, in Yeshua as the Christ, in the form of his demise and the "fact" of his physical resurrection (something which Paul firmly embraced as documentary), a new order had been initiated that established a way of being "higher" than that taught by the strictly physical application of the Law (both as received in the holy writings of Torah and the Oral Torah traditions) and that was stripped of its ethnic and genealogical dimensions.[39]

What is so striking then is that we should nevertheless have inherited this other (side) view as our main one, this concept of the scapegoat as exchange, as propitiation, this hermeneutics of transaction and a gory butchering that buys off a tyrant: a crushed, ground-down innocent whose literal blood allegorically soaks up and dissipates the Creator's wrath. Surely this is an anti-Christ-ian (i.e. non-Yeshuan) means

---

38. Caputo, *The Weakness of God,* 206; emphases in the original.

39. Caputo, *The Weakness of God,* particularly Chapter 2; and Boyarin, *A Radical Jew,* notably in Chapters 1 and 5. Boyarin emphasizes how for Paul outward markings especially (such as, most centrally, circumcision) had become absolutely no longer applicable. For an example (with some comments from me) of this "new order" view, yet one that still contains possible elements of the atonement view visible within it, see e.g. 2 Corinthians 5:14–17: "For the love of Christ urges us on, because we are convinced that one has died for all; therefore all have died. ["All" have already died; an interesting nuance here of an act done: dead and therefore re-birthed or to be re-birthed.] And he died for all, so that those who live might live no longer for themselves, but for him who died and was raised for them. [If one were so inclined one could read "atonement" into the "he died for all" here, but this is not a necessary understanding, I think.] From now on, therefore, we regard no one from a human point of view; even though we once knew Christ from a human point of view, we know him no longer in that way. So if anyone is in Christ, there is a new creation: everything old has passed away; see, everything has become new! ["No one" is seen from a human point of view, especially not Yeshua we might think; everyone "in" Christ is a "new creation"; these are intriguing concepts and point to transformative ethics and ontologies, but aside from highlighting the apparent vanguard position Yeshua is given here as the first "new human" in a sense—transhuman in a twist on modern jargon, perhaps—we unfortunately cannot expound further without carrying ourselves too far off topic.]" *Thinline Bible with the Apocrypha* (NRSV).

of taking the content of "the kingdom" message and its mission. How is it that we have kept this frankly offensive abstractional set (to sensibilities, but not least as well with respect to any serious effort at an understanding of the transcendent) as our core structuring framework? Looking once more at El Greco's painting above it should be clear how utterly betraying to Yeshua and his sagely-rabbinic efforts it is to feel nothing but the mind-numbing guilt of "for my sins" by that scene instead of a challenge to perceive and interact with the world and others in the liberating way Yeshua taught and lived: even to the extent that he abandoned himself to easily predictable and equally terrifying outcomes in order to get his point across. Can we re-train our intuitions to see/"see!" "the kingdom" beckoning to us from out of—and beyond—the embodied cross, to take Yeshua as an exemplar rather than a "God/'God'-man," or are we so psychologically broken that we are irreparably drawn to a provoked guilt, to the offense-exchange with its demanding regal divinity that is Pauline and not Yeshuan? Perhaps more than anything we have merely heard the story too many times and thus stopped thinking about it.

A further query confronts: If indeed the oft alleged historical reason of a desire to strategically separate the institutions of synagogue and church during the decades following Yeshua's death as what came to be called Christianity emerged from the surrounding religio-cultural milieu was a/the causal agent at work, then again why the prominence for this (sub)reading of Paul? What appeal would an "atonement" interpretation have over Paul's own evidently preferred understanding of a Yeshuan crucifixion-resurrection pairing as "gateway" to a universalized soteriology which was based more ideologically than it was ritually? Would that not have been sufficient for the forging of a "new covenant"? (Even if we disagree with it, the option is there to be recognized.) Or better yet: Why not another comprehending of Yeshua, his "kingdom" ministry, and the lived possibilities towards such altogether? Why must we ever come back to the common experience of pain, to the Buddhist *dukkha* of life[40]—suffering yes, but also dissatisfaction, foundational disappointment, even a certain *je ne sais pas*—and the temptation of finding relief through a projection of inescapable hurt onto a convenient victim in lieu? Is the received orthodox bundle that has been promulgated these long centuries by church officialdom at its core little better than a release valve?

One shudders to ask the question, but it is hardly an original one. Nietzsche—with typically brilliant color—put this same transactional hermeneutic as Western culture's "stroke of genius," an act of outrageous self-violence done in the name of love, the germ of a collective sense of (bloodthirsty) justice that led to the confused and confusing power games played out on the geopolitical world stage ever since.[41] "An

---

40. This is a nuanced concept but one cannot really go wrong by addressing the source: The Buddha, *The Dhammapada*.

41. Nietzsche, *On the Genealogy of Morals*. For the full discussion, see the "*Second Essay*: 'Guilt,' 'Bad Conscience,' and the Like", 57–96.

PART 4 | TEMPORALITY: GOD/"GOD" HERE, "THE KINGDOM" NOW

eye for an eye" taken out of all context of equal retribution; or instead—reading away from Nietzsche, launching out from off of him—we might call it something like a faux apprehension, a pensive and forced half smile at the finiteness and willfully ignored limitations we know to mark ourselves, a kind of wink at the almost-acknowledged self-deception involved in an embrace of suffering and mortality while simultaneously pushing away both and erecting a symbol of a dying God/"God" in order to make of it a figure of eternal life. The *ressentiment* we ruminated on in Chapter 11 echoes here. We are weak, cannot face death, and therefore have constantly presented this "for us" as token of a yearned-for immortality. While we do feel guilty with these maneuverings, we have nevertheless greedily taken what was proffered: a self-manufactured balm, an ingenious means of twisting (tricking) against the grave. It is well time to stop, for we can do better; Yeshua's memory and his message deserves very, very much more.

The next chapter, a last division within this Part 4, will seek to provide a brief summary of the journey we have attempted heretofore, and—if we can—also build a bridge to the philotheology I wish to struggle towards in the close to our study. As a first step in this direction of "could," of what different ideational associations might lead to when Yeshua, "the kingdom," and Yeshuan-Judaism are beheld anew, a final logion from *The Gospel of Thomas* on how delicate any sought balancing may prove (the bent brackets indicate translator's inserts):

> *Thomas,* Saying 97: [1]Jesus said, "The <father's> kingdom is like a woman who was carrying a <jar> full of meal. [2]While she was walking along <a> distant road, the handle of the jar broke and the meal spilled behind her <along> the road. [3]She did not know it; she had not noticed a problem. [4]When she reached her house, she put the jar down and discovered that it was empty."[42]

---

42. Meyer, trans. and intro., *The Gospel of Thomas,* 59. Again, I think we should try not to be distracted by the gendered language in the above; the text was after all born of its historical moment, a detail which in no way precludes its ability to teach.

Chapter 14

DEATH IS/WAS BIRTH

WHAT TO DO WITH a dead Yeshua? How ought we to gaze on this spark that lit a flame which has burned now for two millennia? The man is manifestly dead, in the conditioned "state of" sense explicated above (our parsing of death/dying/dead), and even if one thinks him miraculously revived à la Christian doctrine it is not Yeshua whom one mentally and emotionally approaches but "Christ": i.e. a figure transitioned from God/"God"-man to "plain and simple" God/"God" (taking the official Trinitarian line); or, if one prefers, from God/"God" to God/"God"-man and then back again to God/"God". Thus even the New Testament does not assert a "new life" (or way of life, an orientation of one's existence) in *Yeshua* but rather one in *Christ,* as 2 Corinthians 5:17 puts it: "So if anyone is in Christ, there is a new creation; everything old has passed away; see, everything has become new!"[1] Having ceased genuine physicality Yeshua has become an abstraction, an image-idea/idea-image, an encoding and term loaded with far more associative details than the grammatical standing as a proper noun typically implies. This we have suggested in the foregoing: that Yeshua *is not* (the corpse has long since decomposed), but "Yeshua" *is* and "lives": that is, as long as he is remembered; but in this way too the Buddha "lives," Ramakrishna "lives," Muhammad "lives," Zoroaster "lives," Lao Tzu "lives," and of course let us not leave out Abraham, Sarah, Jacob, Moses, and Ruth (while apologizing for the many we must nevertheless cut from our abbreviated list). On our historico-critical view we wish to go no further; but note how very far we are going.

Taking then this "living Christ" (the image-idea/idea-image) into a symbology of the phenomenologically felt, and from there to the possibilities for a being-towards, I would like to briefly offer in the below that we consider as genuinely "resurrectional" (resurrection-capable) what this figuration has to offer. This is not a call for a new life *in* Christ, because again Yeshua the human who became labeled "Christ" has died and remains—as you and I will—very much non-existent; instead this is a gesture for a new life *of* Christ (Yeshuan-Judaism), one wherein Yeshua as notional stand-in for

---

1. *Thinline Bible with the Apocrypha* (NRSV).

Part 4 | Temporality: God/"God" Here, "the Kingdom" Now

"the kingdom" abides as a convenient shorthand for that message's "could be," for the challenge to re- and co-create with God/"God" this shared human substance. Can we learn (re-tooling intuitive reactions) to see/"see!" Yeshua and/or those connected icons such as the crucifix or empty cross with minds attuned to "the kingdom" in place of an atonement hermeneutic (whether accepted or not)? If we can, I think, we honor his legacy and make of his life a truer applicatory witness than that which the church has promulgated in his name; this would, moreover, be thus for those outside the edifices of orthodoxy as well as those within. Hence, a short review.

Throughout the preceding (and especially in Chapters 9 and 11–13) we have encountered "the kingdom" and its simultaneous "is now"/"may become," its claimed ontological position as already "spread out upon the earth" (*The Gospel of Thomas*, Saying 113)[2] while yet still needing to be made (and by us), and—I would like to append—in that surely continually maintained and renewed as well. What did this vision of our/another world consist of? For ease of reference and recall a truncated listing of the main points follows, taken from the scholarly vetted non-canonical and, to a lesser extent given the political realities which have informed our critical judgments, parallel canonical sources that have been deemed most likely authentic:

- In "the kingdom" there is a reversal of expectations, of the accepted defaults of society (e.g. of the "last-first, first-last" sort); important here is that the "top" (the "first") willingly reduce themselves towards the "bottom" (the "last"): the analogy we gave was of the social pyramid flattening itself into a rectangle, even a line.

- "The kingdom," as remarked, is already present and universal: it is now and is for everyone, based on an individual and direct, unmediated relation between us and the divine, between us and one another; therefore in "creating" this "kingdom" we are bringing what is extant (although unseen/un-"seen!") into the open.

- "Kingdom" behavior is marked by "absurd" generosity, reflecting God/"God" who gives endlessly and equally of God's/"God's" love, mercy, and grace, whatever we may deem the recipient's qualities to be.

- Connected with this munificence is the requirement to re-work priorities both personal and communal towards social parity without expectations of reward, especially such as those of an afterlife or other telos beyond this Earth.

- Somewhat disturbingly, those who have are asserted to be given more, and those who do not have to end up with still less. This ethos may fit better with the wider Yeshuan program if it is taken as being an assertion regarding knowledge, but it could admittedly be about the material; conclusions appear open.

- From Keller's revealing of the thought-world of the historical period Yeshua lived in, we determined the deeper spiritual heritage under consideration to be

---

2. Meyer, trans. and intro., *The Gospel of Thomas*, 63; Leloup, trans., intro., and comm., *The Gospel of Thomas,* 57, has "spread out over the whole earth."

instructing us that God/"God" might not be omnipotent nor omniscient, but that in creation God/"God" works *with* nature (and not *over* nature) and thence (here "the kingdom" part) with individuals and groups in each beneficent "making."

- This last aspect is reflected in the interconnectedness of every iota of the world, of how despite our each being tiny "mustard seeds" in/of "the kingdom" (which again is "here-now"/"yet-to-be") what we do has far-reaching and vast effects of which we are almost entirely unaware; nevertheless the results are there, and they are thoroughly interwoven.

- "The kingdom" is action focused, not belief focused.

- We are to share and distribute material goods freely and without regard for need or determinations of what is "fair"; once more in reflection of God/"God" who blesses the "righteous" and "unrighteous" alike with "sun" and "rain." In this we rely on God's/"God's" providence and have honest concern and fraternity irrespective of class, gender, or ethnicity; "the kingdom" is not "just" (justice) as we usually assign it, but in the end all will be well.

- "The kingdom" is present oriented, a living-now, and it does not emphasize an afterlife or reward; if there is any such it seemingly is comprised of a promised physical resurrection for martyrdom, although possibly also for faith fidelity.[3] There are no concepts of hell, damnation, or judgment. Death is not to be feared (and, we added, may even be "welcomed" in one's acceptance); enjoy life while it lasts with thanks and trust in God's/"God's" gift of it.

- "Sin" exists, but there is no need for redemption; moreover, "my" "sin" is always greater than "your" "sin" in "kingdom" thinking (perspectivally, bearing no relation to empirical realities).[4]

- We should be loose and homeless in/with the world, grasping nothing so tightly that it cannot be released (non-attachment); this extends to one's family and social ties.[5]

- Connected with the immediately above, some consequences Yeshua warns may come of following his "kingdom" ideology are: 1) intrafamilial conflict, 2) breaking ancestral ties, and 3) sundering living bonds. While on the surface these are perhaps deleterious, they indicate an exhaustive acceptance of persons that again overturns existing hierarchical rankings and assumptions and establishes in their

---

3. I, for one, feel free to dismiss this aspect of "resurrection" as an historical relic and understand death to be entirely annihilatory. Then too though I take this mortality with thanks for myself and with memory and honor for others.

4. "Sin" as a divine affront can be left aside as well in my view, for the reasons discussed above, while the "mine more than yours" and the originary meaning of "missing the mark" appear worth keeping.

5. The first here (non-attachment) is a widespread ethos and fairly easy to agree with (less so of course to actually practice!); the second I find highly tenuous, bordering on (if not outrightly) unethical.

place *ideational* ties.[6] (In this, incidentally, I think we can find the root for what later became the radical outreach efforts of some early Yeshuan-Jews to the many other groupings in the wider Graeco-Roman cultural sphere.)

In reading through our compiled list we are struck by how very ethically centered it is, with little of what might be termed a theology to be found. From Yeshua's various "Father" statements it would appear that he held to a more or less "standard" first century Jewish viewpoint of God/"God" as a distinct supernatural being, world creator, and interactive agent within human history, albeit with the important (and quite remarkable) caveats that we have noticed, perhaps most surprisingly in the casting of God/"God" as non-judging in a retributive sense. We are still to strive for the prescribed lifestyle the Law expounds (although perhaps in a looser sense), but in such to have trust in the goodness of the divine and the soil upon which we dwell, and to understand that God/"God" is loving, merciful, caring, and will provide for what we need.

The "kingdom" vision espoused is moreover vast, embracing, gritty and almost dirty in its sheer earthiness, it is far more of Martin Buber's "I-Thou" or Levinas' "face" than of the confessional and institutional orders we have come to associate with Yeshua's claims and ministry.[7] We are to turn towards God/"God", to look after one another with neither social distinction nor indeed with what would appear to be logic (give, give, and give we are told, whether the other needs it or not), and incredibly, considering the socio-political climate of the time and place, all this may extend (or be extendable) across the Jew/Gentile divide. At least, that is what the final point with its trio of relationship cause and effects appears to indicate, and we would hardly be the first to assert this as it is one of the centerpieces of Paul's writing, stressed perhaps most succinctly in Romans 2:11: "For God shows no partiality."[8] (The Greek there is even more interesting: "For [there] is not partiality with God"; which if translated more literally could read: "For there is not favoritism according to God."[9]) Yeshua is telling us that what we do and how we interact matters a great deal, whether we understand the nuances involved or not, whether we perceive any results or not; we are not to judge, not to worry, not to grasp, and to trust: it is exceedingly simple and excessively difficult amidst the busyness and bustle of our communities geared to always promote self-interest and structured to have us think in those terms alone. "The kingdom" is the to-be of today, the finally-come of tomorrow.

---

6. The degree of advantage or positivity to such ties is also highly debatable, I think (much against, but also much for): nevertheless, at the least it might surely be stated that while an exhaustive acceptance is most welcome, the place of lineage and the senses of belonging and identity that familial networks can grant also carry clear benefits for the human psyche. This is an interesting point that needs far more discussion than can be spared for it here, although some further remarks are made in the below.

7. Martin Buber, *I and Thou*; Levinas, *Totality and Infinity*.

8. *Thinline Bible with the Apocrypha* (NRSV).

9. *The New Greek/English Interlinear New Testament*; final rendering done by the author. Boyarin, *A Radical Jew,* is quite explicit on this notion's importance for Paul; see especially Chapter 6.

Death Is/Was Birth

This conceptual assemblage, this way-of-being, is not, however, without its risks to self, and aside from the rather prosaic complaints that could be made about possibly being taken advantage of by unscrupulous others (Yeshua would no doubt laugh such off), there are the more serious issues regarding the psychology of identity, belonging, community, and place, as noted. Each of our definitional (defining) selves are composites of a great number of factors very far out of our control, naturally including the results of the genetic lottery which express themselves in our persons, but so too the lineages and traditions to which we are heirs and—if we so choose—guardians and bearers (indeed, considering cultural influences on the self during its formative years there is a significant degree to which we cannot help being—at a minimum—bearers of these strains, if nothing else).[10] An existential re-orientation of the kind that Yeshua seems to be proposing is therefore an entirely revolutionary one, and it is little wonder that we find in the received narratives encounters between Yeshua and those who would otherwise like to follow him but discover themselves unable to (for instance) "let the dead bury their own dead."[11] In this stance and its repercussions we can perhaps glimpse a hint of the motivating forces behind both some Yeshuan-Jews' desire to break with their fellow Jews but non-Yeshuan-Jews, and that of some non-Yeshuan-Jews to enforce a schism (an expulsion or "excommunication") between their (sub)communities' memberships as the differences grew more pronounced. I acknowledge that this is merely speculation on my part, but if Yeshua were only half as provocative as the picture we have of him indicates, then surely it is at least possible that a portion of his adherents would have attempted to present themselves and their new understandings of human-divine and human-human interrelating using similarly bold techniques and strategies, and such could well have been sundering. That may even have been the point for some: a daring to be thrown out, and then to build, to begin something "different."

Whatever the case or cases was or were, systemic Christianity arose and staked its position in the world; ours now is the less radical task of admitting that this Christianity which we know contemporarily is based on tenets altogether non-Yeshuan (the "God/'God'-man" and "atonement" devices in particular), and thus to re-fold (a more genuine) Yeshuan-ism into its proper place within Judaism(s), itself perforce understood more broadly than we are probably accustomed to thinking it from a twenty-first century perspective wherein the familiar is taken for the whole and the ever-was (which any cursory glance at Judaism's history would quickly cure us of). I contend that the first four Parts of our study have provided the necessary grounding for a serious consideration of the argument for return (a historico-critical Yeshua and a more thoroughly certifiable "kingdom" message highlight the person and ministry

---

10. I make a full argument for selfhood and identity in Oberg, *Blurred*; Chapter 2 is particularly relevant to this aspect.

11. Funk and the Jesus Seminar, *The Gospel of Jesus*, 23 (3:13–14); Powelson and Riegert, trans., footnotes, and eds., *The Lost Gospel Q*, 61 (Q27); both are quoted in Chapter 12 above.

Part 4 | Temporality: God/"God" Here, "the Kingdom" Now

as Jewish-reformative rather than as "Christian"-establishing), yet what remains is to move from this "not" into the "and so": Christianity is *not* Yeshuan, and what is Yeshuan fits better philosophically, phenomenologically, and theologically as a form of Judaism(s); *and so* what do we want to think of God/"God" in light of that? This too is a hazardous venture, and it may take great courage on our part to attempt a re-forging of the inner and the outer along these deeply identitarian and notional lines; the worldviews in which we are currently embedded might prove resistant, perhaps resiliently so, perhaps threateningly so.

Yet we shall try. If Yeshua is allowed to become a code or a marker ("Yeshua"), then let us reorient it; a symbol, after all, "lives" anew each time it is created and re-created, shaped, moulded, formed. Cavarero, we remember, has argued that Western philosophy has heretofore been an overly masculine exercise obsessed with death and oblivion, of facing (or running from) the abyss;[12] "atonement" fixations of Christ hanged with their guilt, damnation, and thirst for absolution and immortality, each lines up unsettlingly well with this assertion. In gratitude, then, we shall take her analysis as a *bon mot* and attempt to follow her lead into a more "birthing" mode of reflection; "the kingdom," we think, seems to cry for precisely this (the challenge to fashion, to find/realize). In the proceeding final Part 5 of our endeavor we will therefore seek a fresh philotheology that positions our "worlds" metaphysically into a peace-making and a re-making, one where "the kingdom" elements of Christianity might be allowed to melt (return) into a purer Yeshuan-Judaism, and where the great re-awakening and re-acquainting that our quasi-Pharisee wandering peasant sage called for is heard with ears attuned to finitude, to "today," to the other as ever-concern in this here-now—all we have—and with eyes that "see!" redemption has always already been because never was needed. "Salvation" thus springs from within to the ceaselessly constructed without. Yeshua is dead, true Yeshuan-Judaism has yet to be born. It is up to us to confront this, to decide; and we are asked *to do:* may we prepare our hands.

---

12. Cavarero, *In Spite of Plato*. In her book Cavarero seeks to "rewrite" this through fresh examinations of some feminine figures chosen from Greek mythic traditions.

Part 5

A Peace-Making, a Re-Making

Chapter 15

Endless Construction

"But the necessity for a renewal of theology, whether Jewish or Christian, should not occlude the riches of its past."

EMMANUEL FALQUE[1]

IN THIS FINAL CHAPTER to our study we shall seek to attempt a double, and doubly open ended, quasi-(faux)conclusion: The first will be to try and re-consider Judaism as such away from how we might think we know it (a small undertaking to rid ourselves of preconceptions: external or internal), to attempt to raise the question of what it does or may involve to be/"be" Jewish/"Jewish," as stemming from our analyses heretofore through which we came to understand that to follow Yeshua and/or conceive value in "the kingdom" is not "Christian" but is (a version of) Judaism, it is Yeshuan-Judaic. What might this mean for persons of various identitarian/desiring identitarian commitments? Secondly it will be to wonder what a was-Christianity become Yeshuan-Judaism based on the set of thirteen loose "kingdom" takeaways (described in the previous chapter) might consist of and/or be like in functional terms (the "look" we try to "see!"); this will entail both positives and negatives and take the form of a commentary. Thus, in closing, we shall endeavor one more try at both theory and practice.

This initial portion focuses on the former, and the latter can thence hopefully be read in light of it. Herein we ask the following: If "Jesus" (the figure) is and always has been nothing but an inflated icon (an idol), and if Yeshua (the personage) is no more—but yet no less—than a dead Jew, what is to be made of aspects of belonging for those who wish them (to one extent or another), for those who may want to align/associate with the God/"God" of Israel while not, perhaps, already actually being Jewish (by birth or by conversion) in the modern understanding of that term? In other words, for those who might find a full ritual re-attuning, or the ethnic, genealogic, and socio-cultural implications of the commonplace comprehension of "Jewish" (potentially overly narrow) to be obstacles too daunting to overcome; what for them? Could

---

1. Falque, *The Guide to Gethsemane*, 52.

such nevertheless become more authentically Yeshuan-Judaic in their self-perceived modes of being-in-the-world, and if so of what may that consist?

To answer we would do well to remember the note of "today" on which Chapter 14 ended, the focus on the "here-now" as all that we have; which indeed we think is a perspective Yeshua himself shared, and if he did expect a resurrection as/if a martyr, even then such would be tied to the dusty roadways of his home: a corporeal once-more rather than some form of a spectrally disembodied "spirit in Heaven" like how many in the present century imagine. Thus, on either side of our wondering (about being/"being" Jewish/"Jewish" through birth or conversion), this is a matter of Earthly existence; and if we are then to further perpend—if we are allowed to further comment—in regards to a group of people who might audaciously be claimed "a" people, then let us do so with nothing hidden and with no offense meant: let us speak Israel and discover what may be learned from her "yes" to "today," to "here-now"; and only thereafter to attempt some applications of the Yeshuanism we have carefully extracted heretofore. If our goal is to fit an adjustable (one size for all) "kingdom" message within what might be termed "degrees" of Judaism(s) (and recalling that we have already argued for a melted down and/or re-enfolded Christianity put back into Judaism(s)), then we begin with an eye to the exceedingly general, from there into the scriptural, return again to the (slightly) more familiar past, and lastly examine the situation from an experiential and individual point of view, making no claims to what it might "mean" definitively for person X or Y as far as the labels go ("Jewish," "Christian," "Yeshuan," et cetera). Those decisions are anyway clearly out of our hands—we are neither qualified nor prepared to make them—so instead we simply ponder, and we try to think a *being-as* within an *otherwise*.

Historically and culturally the Jewish people must surely be a group who live—exuberantly, forcefully, proclamatory, leaving a wonderfully beneficent shade on this world far out of proportion to number or size; and, as John Oesterreicher has emphasized, the Jewish nation as a *nation* is celebrated within this ethno-communal framework by the Hebrew phrase *Am Yisrael chai*: "The people of Israel lives."[2] Her continuation, naturally not only in the sense of statehood but importantly in that sense, is itself an ongoing miracle: her presence on this Earth an indication of hope, trust, joy in the face of come what may; she is a "being" who thrives against the odds, a "yes" as absolute as any torch-bearing Prometheus might carry down from a mountain hermitage to we townsfolk going about our unsuspecting business on the flatlands below.[3] Israel as a geographic entity initially was not, her existence merely a promise,

---

2. Oesterreicher, *The Rediscovery of Judaism*, 24.

3. I intend here a Nietzschean allusion, of course: were the Prometheus of myth to break free of his punishing chains he might well appear as Zarathustra, and clearly Nietzsche imagined both himself and his character in that way. The message, moreover, would anyway be the same; see Nietzsche, *Thus Spake Zarathustra* (the edition cited is an unabridged republication of the original printing done by the Macmillan Company of New York (1911)). Nietzsche worked on the text in parts from 1883–1885, but the book was not published in full until after his death in 1900; see the introductory note on pages vi–vii.

Part 5 | A Peace-Making, a Re-Making

then she was, was not again, was again, for long centuries was not once more, was, was not, was, and is, *is yet*. During one of those more ancient stretches of "was not" (the Babylonian captivity, circa 598/7–538 BCE[4]) the prophet Ezekiel lived and wrote, and amongst the many famous images and imaginings he left us we have the so-called Valley of Dry Bones of chapter thirty-seven. The whole vision covers verses one through fourteen, but here we quote only a part—the opening ten verses—for reasons that will (if we are successful) better align with our objectives, which differ from the prophet's original ones. The text, as taken from the Tanakh:

> Ezekiel 37:1–10: [1]The hand of the LORD came upon me. He took me out by the spirit of the LORD and set me down in the valley. It was full of bones. [2]He led me all around them; there were very many of them spread over the valley, and they were very dry. [3]He said to me, "O mortal, can these bones live again?" I replied, "O Lord GOD, only You know." [4]And He said to me, "Prophesy over these bones and say to them: O dry bones, hear the word of the LORD! [5]Thus said the Lord GOD to these bones: I will cause breath to enter you and you shall live again. [6]I will lay sinews upon you, and cover you with flesh, and form skin over you. And I will put breath into you, and you shall live again. And you shall know that I am the LORD!"
>
> [7]I prophesied as I had been commanded. And while I was prophesying, suddenly there was a sound of rattling, and the bones came together, bone to matching bone. [8]I looked, and there were sinews on them, and flesh had grown, and skin had formed over them; but there was no breath in them. [9]Then He said to me, "Prophesy to the breath, prophesy, O mortal! Say to the breath: Thus said the Lord GOD: Come, O breath, from the four winds, and breathe into these slain, that they may live again." [10]I prophesied as He commanded me. The breath entered them, and they came to life and stood up on their feet, a vast multitude.[5]

Prior to thinking—to *plumbing*—the symbolic potential of this passage (that is, what may be *read into* it, which we will quite openly do since, as mentioned, ours is not the purpose of the author, and neither does our undertaking need affiliate itself with his, nor moreover with the long centuries of interpretations on this and the following biblical texts: instead we attempt the task of a fresh, *unshadowed* hermeneutics), I would like to draw our attention to two odd phrasings which may be easy to overlook. Both are, in fact, of the same oddity, and both are uses of one tense where another is to be expected; indeed, where another is even to be found depending on the translation. In verses four and nine Ezekiel is told[6] to prophesy "over these bones"

See also the general introduction by Kaufmann in Nietzsche, *The Portable Nietzsche*, 1–19.

4. Editors of the Encyclopædia Britannica, "Babylonian Captivity," *Encyclopædia Britannica*. Accessed April 22, 2020.

5. *Tanakh* (NJPS).

6. We could attitudinally frame it as either "commanded" or "requested," I suppose, and our

and "to the breath", then he is given the content of what is to be stated, in each case with the same prefatory remark: "Thus said the Lord GOD" (verses five and nine), with what follows of course being the prophesy itself. "Thus *said*", and thereafter "I *will* cause" and "*Come*, O breath"; why the past tense in the attributive introduction? Why not "Thus *says*"?

That, the reader will note, is actually how the translators who produced the New Revised Standard Version of the Bible have it; the relevant verse sections there read as: "⁵Thus says the Lord GOD to these bones: I will cause breath to enter you, and you shall live", and "⁹... Thus says the Lord GOD: Come from the four winds, O breath, and breathe upon these slain, that they may live."⁷ This usage of "says" makes much more logical sense within the future direction under deliberation in this passage—what God/"God" will do—and more grammatical sense as well considering the following verbs (although perhaps the New Revised Standard Version's "breathe upon" of verse nine is less attractive than the Tanakh's "breathe into" due to the latter's more positive evocation of a life force *entering*), but precisely the illogic and non-grammaticalness of the former give us pause. The translators of the Tanakh make no (punning: *valley of dry*) bones about—are really quite proud of—their fidelity to the Hebrew that the scriptures were written in, the sacrosanct and treasured literary heritage, no "yod" (or "yud": the smallest Hebrew letter) of which was ever (purposefully) allowed to be misplaced throughout the venerable tradition. Might there then be a half-buried lesson at work? Perhaps the answer lies in the divine issuance: God/"God" has willed such and such, decided upon X and instructed (or, let us take the softer road, *asked* rather than *commanded*) its prophet to announce the *fait accompli*. God/"God" does not speak without also having acted; its word is deed and whatnot. These nuances bear dwelling upon, are deserving of whatever time is given them—possibly more—and so let us now shift, with this same mental bearing, to the more straightforward theme of resurrection (resuscitation) as found here.

The prophesy itself is addressed to those Israelites forcibly living abroad in Babylon, and is in regards to the fulfillment of their longed-for return to their ancestral land, as verses eleven through fourteen (the closing of the vision) state explicitly; we have previously truncated these verses to give weight to the contemporary application we wish to make, but for the sake of clarity and forthrightness can cite them now:

> Ezekiel 37:11-14: ¹¹And He said to me, "O mortal, these bones are the whole House of Israel. They say, 'Our bones are dried up, our hope is gone; we are doomed.' ¹²Prophesy, therefore, and say to them: Thus said [note: *said* once more] the Lord GOD: I am going to open your graves and lift you out of the graves, O My people, and bring you to the land of Israel. ¹³You shall know, O My people, that I am the LORD, when I have opened your graves and lifted you

---

inclination one way or the other would probably speak volumes about personal theological and hermeneutical leanings; the Hebrew term is rendered into English simply as "said."

7. Ezekiel 37:5 and 9b, as taken from *Thinline Bible with the Apocrypha* (NRSV).

out of your graves. ¹⁴I will put My breath into you and you shall live again, and I will set you upon your own soil. Then you shall know that I the LORD have spoken and have acted"—declares [interestingly not *declared*] the LORD.⁸

Thus a declaration of certain restoration, a renewal of hope, an urge to trust and wait, to have faith (how very Yeshuan!); surely this is a message that need not be historically nor ethno-specifically bound, and hence I repeat the reason for choosing to cut this portion initially. In most matters, when approached from a scholarly point of view, context is perforce everything (or at least is extremely important), but in the present we wish to be *in the present,* and this calls for a perspective that leans deeper in the direction of a more fully human—shall we put it—rather than an academic one; or the straitjacketed version of "academic," at any rate. We need not overly confine ourselves when looking to this type of literature to find in it a morsel for sustenance, a piece of heavenly manna (punning again); such is the allure and reach of the world's collective scriptures; and again we think Yeshua would probably nod in agreement.

Yet is this though the "world's collective"? Does it not instead belong primarily, perhaps exclusively, to the Jewish people as an ethno-communal grouping, and hence potentially excluding ("would-be" or "are") Yeshuans? No doubt there are many who would argue so, and possibly even some within extant Christian traditions and denominations, whose own sacred compendiums are of course composed of the Hebrew Bible plus what are, in effect, a number of appendices (with no offense nor denigration of said documents intended). Yet I think the numinous urge and the quest for transcendence that each world faith displays is sufficiently panhuman to justify the determination of applicability found for anyone in *any one* of what we have generously received from our species' forebears: every text is "world collective," and although beauty may be in the eye of the beholder it is more so in the heart.

Let us return to our bones. Dried and scattered, bereft of any semblance of life, nary a drop of blood—that spark of energizing biological fire—to be located anywhere. Dead: absolutely. What is the procedure of regeneration for this sad lot? Seemingly nothing internal; the bones are first fitted together by an unseen outside power, and then sinews, flesh, skin grow over them by layer, before finally being animated by a summoned breath of life (recalling, incidentally, the "first man" Adam's invigoration in the second of the Genesis creation accounts).⁹ The direct contextual allegory here is the contemporary assemblage of Israeli political abductees in Babylon, but we will not hesitate (we will make *no bones about;* why not re-apply our earlier pun?) to stretch this line the very distance to those now concerned: and each of us is now concerned. As I write this a worldwide pandemic has gripped rich and poor alike in

---

8. *Tanakh* (NJPS).

9. Genesis 2:7: "the LORD God formed man from the dust of the earth. He blew into his nostrils the breath of life, and man became a living being." The first creation account, in the previous chapter, simply has (Genesis 1:27): "And God created man in His image, in the image of God He created him; male and female He created them"; *Tanakh* (NJPS).

a manner not seen for over a century.[10] Humanity—literally the current whole of humanity—lives under a plague the final end of which is neither entirely predictable nor preparable; uncertainty has suddenly turned the daily life of every one of us on its head, and it seemingly happened overnight. Absolutely it feels that way. Like Israel in her Babylonian exile many of us sit and wait, wearied, wondering. Verse eleven informs us that Ezekiel's fellows declared their hope gone, but we today, having by necessity become aware of more of her history, know that the Jewish nation—as a nation—are the people who live, who declare "yes"; and how could that be in the absence of hope? To hope is to "yes" in the adverbal usage of the noun; can we join in this, not only in relation to immediate needs and worries, but in general? May we "be" "Israel" in this way? While or while not also "being" "Yeshuan"? What might such mean? Could it even mean anything? These questions drive us in contemplating a "yes" wherein was-Christianity is/has become a Judaism(s), and the role or place of Yeshuanism therein.

What we are asking, therefore, is whether or not there is a separable attitudinal level of or to Judaism(s) as a way-of-being that might be made distinct from its obvious—and obviously centrally important—hereditary and ethno-cultural level which some Yeshuans may feel more comfortable with when coming to terms with the Yeshua of history and the needed adjustments to approach called for by the reduced (eliminated?) Christology we have presented in the above. Firstly then, to help engage our thinking, let us spell out the currently standardized and regularly accepted accounts of full and established (as it were) membership in the people Israel. By tradition, that is, by Jewish religious law, belonging concentrates on matrilineal descent: one must have a Jewish mother (i.e. with traceable Semitic lineage and the added expressed convictions of the religion and covenant as delivered through Moses (note that there have been/are other Semitic peoples)).[11] Fathers are naturally wonderful and to be welcomed, but strictly the affixation here rests with the other procreational side. If one converts into Judaism, therefore, one is adopted as the "daughter" or "son" of Abraham and Sarah (*bat/ben Avraham v'Sara*), the foundational biblical forebears, and thus attains the "proper genetics" (to put it somewhat crudely and loosely). Yet this might seem tenuous at best and dogmatic at worst—I imagine many an Orthodox/non-Orthodox argument has been centered around such—what, after all, is to become of a child who has grown up in a practicing Jewish home where only the father fit this bill while the mother was otherwise (i.e. a "Gentile")? Does that child need to go through the whole conversion process? Some authorities would indeed require just that, others would be more embracing, perhaps easing or eliminating anything of

---

10. Specifically the coronavirus, or COVID-19 in the more technical appellation, pandemic; my hope—prayer—is that by the time of publication it too will have passed. Words cannot do justice to the suffering of this (and much else).

11. On this and a great deal more, see the very accessible (the delightful) introductory book by Kahn-Harris, *Judaism*.

the sort for continued communal enrollment. That though is perhaps the real key to the entirety: this notion and quality of *community*.

We who may not have been born into that Tribe which unites the many types of Judaisms as *a* community-so-considered might still take and learn much from the parameters laid down within the tradition, and it is in that reduced (redacted?) sense that I wish to argue for the possibility of a "being Israel" which would assist/enable dry bones to resurrect in a Yeshuan-Judaism for those who wish it, absent the additional ritual and lifestyle details of Judaism(s) which many would-be/are Yeshuans may not also desire, while for those who do a more correct accession into mainline Judaism(s) as practiced today is of course always possible.[12] What I mean here is that if we take (was-)Christianity as really one of multiple Judaisms—the result of our re-enfolding project—then the questions of what this Yeshuan-Judaism might look like, as well as its relation to other Judaisms, present themselves. In some ways, moreover—at least as far as our objectives are concerned—the strictly definitional aspect as delineated within Judaism(s) at present (and aware that this too travels along—as everything does—an ever-evolving routeway) is neither applicable nor inapplicable: the identitarian label we are considering is mostly intended as an internal aid towards the adoption of a certain conceptual framework provided by the lineage so symbolized (the vastness of it; including of course Yeshua and his teachings). What, then, might be involved in "being" "Israel" in this additional or alternative manner that is perhaps not for everyone a "conversion" but is a form of adoption? Two criteria seem to me best fitted for this: 1) an acceptance of "complete monotheism," which need not necessarily be mainstream theist: it could instead indicate mystery, call, force, event, transcendence, et cetera (even the Neoplatonist aethereal and removed One of a philosopher like Plotinus;[13] the cruciality here is that of an otherwise-than), and 2) a "wrestling with" God/"God", a not-sure-but-will-keep-trying approach to the other/Other, to the question and the unknown, to the importantly *unknowable* within the experience of human functioning in its many forms.[14]

---

12. The Reform movement perhaps has the most experience with "outsiders" in this regard; see the questions and answers page on the conversion process here: "Choosing Judaism," *ReformJudaism.org*. Reconstructionist Judaism may also interest readers wishing to engage, or simply to learn, more: "Reconstructionism," *Reconstructing Judaism*. The other major non-Orthodox grouping is Conservative Judaism, and an introduction to its approach on converting can be found here: "Conversion to Judaism," *The Rabbinical Assembly*. All three websites accessed June 17, 2021.

13. Hadot, *Plotinus, or The Simplicity of Vision*; O'Meara, *Plotinus*.

14. Hence, with regards to the other two dominant monotheistic faith lines in our present trajectory, not the sort of Christianity that is necessarily connected to "God/'God'-man" type comprehensions (i.e. the regular and non re-enfolded Christianity, as opposed to the Yeshuan-Judaism we have been attempting to argue for) because I think the historical Islamic critique of this kind of orthodox Christianity as being an essentially polytheistic religion holds; but not Islam either since it is grounded within an attitude of "submission" rather than "struggle" (which is not something negative in and of itself; it is merely not the point here), as its very name makes abundantly clear (the literal English rendering of this Arabic noun is just that: submission); see the very informative introduction in *The Qur'an* by Abdel-Haleem. Purely on the term's translation, see the "History and Etymology" portion of the entry in the

We will take these in turn. On the first criteria, I think, is the readiness to accede to the event(/Event)—as it has become known in philosophical circles—to the breakthrough of what Heidegger termed Being, or ground, or clearing, or the uncovered/revealed,[15] to the delicate and epistemologically nearly empty pre-formed (pre-enunciated, pre-figured) intuition we have of a *something,* that which rests (or lurks) foundationally, undergirding while simultaneously flowing through life and the cosmos, as Paul Tillich's exposition of God/"God" conceived as the "ground of being" does.[16] To put this very simply, it is an embrace of the "I have no idea." Expressed in that way we admit that it hardly seems like a worthy philosophical concept,[17] yet as with much that appears shallow initially there is a great depth here. The history of institutional religion, and much of its professional and/or scholarly cohort theology, has been one of an ongoing attempt to pin down and encircle—to square in and categorize—the numinous such that it[18] might be more readily grasped by our limited intellectual capacity. This trend might have reached its zenith, or its limit, in so-called negative theology (describing by not describing, indicating only what the transcendent is not), a system with roots in ancient Hindu schools of thought where the Ultimate Reality is put simply as *neti, neti:* not this, not this.[19] Yet whatever the case, Heidegger was not indicating the divine (although we are here willing to gloss his Being with an other/Other that might be "divine"), but he was nevertheless engaged in what is essentially the similar move of pointing to the (and to the importance of) I-know-not-what; which is of course something of a shrug, but yet a gesture. This acceptance and openness to the acknowledged impossibility of ever arriving at a pre-assigned meaning, a solidity, an endpoint, is our first necessity to think "Jewishly" in

---

Merriam-Webster online dictionary: "Islam," *Merriam-Webster.* Accessed April 28, 2020. Lest this be mistaken for what it is not: What we are trying to offer by these remarks is another way of understanding, not criticism.

15. Heidegger, *Being and Time.*

16. This is Tillich's striking pan*en*theism (and not *pan*theism): God/"God" in everything and everything in God/"God"; *Dynamics of Faith.* Note that Tillich did not use our quotation marks/double inverted commas, and also that the terminology "panentheism" was evidently coined by Hartshorne to describe his own views; see the preface by the editors in Kane and Phillips, eds., *Hartshorne,* ix.

17. That we can put it that way may indicate just how opaquely and exaggeratedly Heidegger wrote; some would go further and criticize his style as highfalutin, although perhaps even *bloated* would be an appropriate description . . . This does not take away from the thinker's brilliance though, nor does it touch on his horrid personal views and politics; much has been published on these latter aspects, but Nancy, *The Banality of Heidegger,* is a recent and interesting take.

18. Strictly "it," as will no doubt have been noticed (and as was referred to earlier regarding the gendering of the divine in thought and communication). In my view, we ought to stringently forego both masculinizing and feminizing pronouns in our referencing, and I humbly ask the reader to keep in mind too that the abstraction we are seeking to develop can or cannot (either way) be thought of in a being-ness or creaturely-type figuration; we might—sooner or later—have to learn to take God/"God" as an existence without existentiality (I hope to explore this much more in a future work). Such could be akin to, but even vaguer than (or further beyond), Heidegger's splicing of "existentiell" and "existential"; see again his *Being and Time,* especially Sections 54 and 62.

19. Müller, trans., *The Thirteen Principal Upanishads.*

PART 5 | A PEACE-MAKING, A RE-MAKING

the manner we wish to argue for, and it is naturally strongly connected to our second (but more on that in a moment). At its core this mental attuning might best be termed a tenuous ever-discovery, a comfort in the void, a friendly association with unsettledness, a stroll along the edge. Who knows? No one. Thank God/"God" for that!

Our second criterion, as mentioned, takes the first's mental framing but does not leave it there. Rather, a kind of application is made, a practice that could be (not without irony) depicted as acting on the unactable, as a fool's errand, as purposely waging a losing battle; but never ceasing to wage. This is the "wrestling with," the ever-try/seek/search, and it is conducted without the hope of an answer but within the hope of a hope: that last clause will—I sincerely hope(!)—make more sense as we proceed. To meditate more thoroughly on this, then, to seek to clear it up, we will begin by visiting the notion's scriptural source: the famous story of our/"our" Jewish/"Jewish" patriarch's extra-human grappling match as related in Genesis 32:25–29, commented on very briefly in a note to Chapter 3. We now quote the passage in full, first from the Tanakh and thereafter, for comparison, from the New Revised Standard Version (whose verse numbering again differs slightly). Thus from the Tanakh, with some comments inserted in brackets for clarification and use in our later discussion:

> Genesis 32:25–29: [25]Jacob was left alone. And a man wrestled with him until the break of dawn. [26]When he [this is the wrestling partner, note that there is no capitalization of this "he" pronoun throughout, hinting that this participant might not be—but might be, as below—God/"God"] saw that he had not prevailed against him, he wrenched Jacob's hip at its socket, so that the socket of his hip was strained as he wrestled with him. [27]Then he [again, the partner] said, "Let me go, for dawn is breaking." But he [Jacob now] answered, "I will not let you go, unless you bless me." [28]Said the other, "What is your name?" He replied, "Jacob." [Another hint this is not God/"God", who surely would have known; unless the question were rhetorical?] [29]Said he, "Your name shall no longer be Jacob, but Israel, for you have striven with beings divine and human, and have prevailed." [*Divine and human!* A designation that this partner is both at once? Or a reference to this occurrence and to other ones? Moreover, why the plural "beings"? A footnote at this point reads: "*Or 'God* (Elohim, *connected with the second part of "Israel") and men.*"; note that this term—Elohim—is grammatically plural but can be used for singular reference, and elsewhere in the scriptures it is almost always translated as here, as single divinity.][20]

There are many fascinating levels at work in this passage, foremost amongst them the entirely open question of the identity of the wrestling partner and the suddenness—and apparent pointlessness—of the assault itself. ("And a man wrestled with him": to what end or for what purpose? No justification is provided.) To start with, we might ascertain that the combatant here is an angel or "intermediary" creature

20. *Tanakh* (NJPS).

between *homo sapiens* on the low end of the spectrum and the singular God/"God" on the highest. What is puzzling about that view, though, is the *el* marker in the awarded nomenclature of *Israel*: it is an indication of divinity—Jacob's striving with—and as remarked it is typically used throughout Hebrew scripture to refer to *the* Divinity, that is, to God/"God" proper. A further complication is one that Kugel has pointed out, that at this period in the Hebraic narrational and theo-cultural development there were a great many theophany stories wherein God/"God" would appear out of nowhere in a form very much like any one of us, and only after some interaction did the recipient of divine attention realize (in a kind of enlightenment moment) whom they were dealing with.[21] In that context the intended meaning of the above could well be that the partner *is* God/"God". Or, on the other hand (and perhaps just as conceptually easily), another superhuman "personage" of a third sort (neither an angel nor God/"God"; if "personhood" can be applied absent its anthropomorphic implications, that is); but again that *el* would seem to support the former reading.[22] Why the text does not indicate this directly no one living today can really know, and we are probably best served in reminding ourselves that its original author almost certainly did not know either, and might not even have thought much about it. The tale is a founding one about a "forefather" (a real historical figure? an historico-cultural placeholder?) who was so strong as to "wrestle" (struggle) with God/"God", never to give up, not to win but neither to lose, to ask for (to demand) a blessing, and in return to receive a transformation. This is inspirational, and its telling and centrality within Jewish mythology gives us a very good example of the manner and degree of notional affirmation/orientation that we wish to advance in our task of moving into a "being" "Israel" in (partial?) thinking and feeling, in our progression towards describing what a Yeshuan-Judaism need have as criterion.

Here is how the New Revised Standard Version has the same (although notice that the verses are instead numbered twenty-four through twenty-eight):

> Genesis 32:24-28: [24]Jacob was left alone; and a man wrestled with him until daybreak. [25]When the man saw that he did not prevail against Jacob, he struck him on the hip socket; and Jacob's hip was put out of joint as he wrestled with him. [26]Then he said, "Let me go, for the day is breaking." But Jacob said, "I will not let you go, unless you bless me." [27]So he said to him, "What is your name?" And he said, "Jacob." [28]Then the man said, "You shall no longer be called Jacob, but Israel [a footnote reads: "That is *The one who strives with God* or *God strives*"], for you have striven with God and with humans [another footnote: "Or *with divine and human beings*"], and have prevailed."[23]

---

21. Kugel, *The God of Old*, see Chapters 2 and 3, and especially pages 24 and 44-5.

22. It has even been suggested that this episode may represent Jacob struggling internally with the psychological implications of his pending reunion with his brother Esau; for one example of this, see Molen, "The Identity of Jacob's Opponent," *Dialogue*, 187-200.

23. *Thinline Bible with the Apocrypha* (NRSV).

Part 5 | A Peace-Making, a Re-Making

In this translation the signals of who is speaking when are somewhat clearer, but what is most pronounced as compared with the Tanakh's wording is that the naming act (of "Israel") is much more straightforwardly connected with God/"God" in the referenced striving (in the text and especially in the first alternate reading in the footnote): "with God and with humans" does not leave the space for as many individualized comprehensions as "beings divine and human" does.[24] On the whole this rendering appears to reduce the possibility of taking the apparitional partner in the lesser "angel" or "intermediary" sense (e.g. pushing a reading of "you strove now with God/'God' but have also striven with humans at other times and hence this name change"), but a definitive conclusion remains out of reach. Yet such is after all precisely our point: there is not now, and additionally can never be, a definitive conclusion to any of this. We are arguing that opacity as a positive. The tradition has handed down to us this tale as "Jacob wrestling with God/'God,'" and the lived ramifications which flow (which are allowed to flow) from taking on such notionally (image-idea/idea-image) are significant and potentially wide ranging. We do not know, cannot know, but we keep at it: "wrestling," struggling, striving.

Caputo, in his championing of what he has labeled a "weak theology" or a "theology of the event" (or "the unconditional"),[25] recently offered such as a type of post-religion religiousness (or a postmodern faith) that he thinks is more in keeping with where we culturally find ourselves: increasingly at odds with belief in the form of a pure faith but nevertheless maintaining that intuition which Heidegger bespoke above.[26] This "theology" is the transcendent understood as the *unforeseen* rather than—or more than—the *unseen*. For Caputo, God/"God" is far more of a symbol than anything else, and therefore it is part of, or is indicative of, an event/the unconditional (for example, in the works cited he often frames this as something happening: "in the name (of) God"), and hence too as a token of the future as being beneficent (i.e. hope): "The name of God is a nickname for hope, for hope against hope. The future is always better, not because it is, but because that is our hope."[27] To Caputo the constituent sense of awe evoked by freeing oneself for mystery in the way we have been considering need not come from a spiritual direction, but could also be had via a study of modern physics (astro-, quantum) and what is being revealed about our cosmos in those sources.

In responding to this I would add that from my own perspective, and contrary to Caputo's view, since the disciplines of the empirical sciences are based on

---

24. Again, how conjunctive is the Tanakh's "and"? Does it split the "beings" in two, or combine them somehow (a mixing)? The New Revised Standard Version's second footnote's listing of "with divine and human beings" appears to suggest a clearer division, and interesting as well is the other alternate reading in the initial footnote of "God strives," placing the emphasis on the opposite half of the equation, as it were.

25. Perhaps most directly see Caputo, *The Weakness of God;* but also Caputo, *The Folly of God.*

26. Caputo, *Hermeneutics,* Chapter 10.

27. Caputo, *Hermeneutics,* 320.

methodologies and presumptions of ultimate discoverability (in other words, in "end results"; however remote and/or tentative such might be at times, confidences are nevertheless developed: e.g. very few today doubt that gravity is an active force), I think rather we ought also to move beyond the version of "mystique" even of a field such as theoretical physics, and thus find ourselves more fully in a comfort and a homebuilding simplicity with and within a flat "I do not know." We can additionally give God/"God" as well more substance than the whisper of the event's to-come while still—delicately—taking care to keep it hinged on the fractional breadth of air between existence and existentiality, and far, far removed from the self-reflecting impositions and attributive lists that many interpreters have pushed onto the numinous. The phenomenology of religious experiences appears to offer some support along these lines, and structurally this matches better with our "wrestling." Thus, while we do not have, and can never have, any hope in attaining an "answer" to this—to life, circumscribed and overwhelming as it so often is when we pay enough attention—we yet do already have, and can continue to have, hope in hope: in the hope of having hope. That is, we may if our two proposed criteria are indeed sufficient and are met, if we 1) open ourselves to (the possibility of) an (mono-)other/Other, and 2) continually strive for, struggle with, seek after that unknowable. This is what we have called "being" "Israel," becoming "Jewishly attuned" as applied to the Yeshuan-Judaic attitudinal bearing (although I think one might drop the Yeshuan aspect here and still remain within the general composure). Where might an approach/stance/"hope" like this take us? What kind of practicalities and ethics could it produce?

Let us pause to notice how life-affirming this Jewish/"Jewish" comportment can be. This is a challenge; and I will admit that I have sometimes found this thing "existence" to be quite onerous, that I have often kept going merely because I did not stop rather than out of a desire for more or longer. Certainly the wish for longevity has been far from my mind: quite the opposite. Out of this decidedly non-Judaic point of view have sprung probably too many meditations on death (the reader will no doubt roll her eyes; and rightly so!), and from them the conclusion I arrived at was the need for a constant and active engagement with one's personal passing: the "welcome" being-toward-death outlined in Chapter 12. To add then to my shameless self-quoting, here is a brief statement of the mentality preceding those analyses; the contrast with what we have been considering in the immediately above will be obvious:

> What is it to not wish to be alive but to also not wish (strongly enough) for death such that one makes the very large extra step to suicide? To think and feel this way might result in a life experienced as a passing of the time, as a kind of bizarre purgatory, a sentence being served, neither an acceptance (life!) nor a release (suicide). To such an individual I offer this attitudinal "welcome": finitude as balm.[28]

---

28. Oberg, "Approaches to Finitude," *Journal of Applied Ethics and Philosophy*, 8–17 (14).

Part 5 | A Peace-Making, a Re-Making

This is a simple weariness at being, and it is not uncommon. Emina Melonic, in a review of a new biography on the poet Sylvia Plath, writes that, "A few days before she [Plath] took her own life [on February 11, 1963], she expressed both mental and physical fatigue to Barnhouse [Ruth Tiffany Barnhouse, Plath's therapist at the time]," and "According to Rollyson [Carl Rollyson, the biographer] Plath's 'last surviving words revealed her distracted thinking: "I am incapable of being myself and loving myself. Now the babies are crying, I must take them out to tea.""'[29] A feeling of alienation within the flesh one is (body = mind = body); busyness and the "musts" of tedium as release; Plath was thirty years-old when she died, leaving behind two children. She would have identified with the "blight man was born for" in the penultimate line of Gerard Manley Hopkins' poem "Spring and Fall,"[30] and too with finitude as balm, its promise of an end as a welcome—a grateful—signal granting solace to one's steps on the path, prodded from behind as we are, finding ourselves at the (possibly merciless) mercy of these multiply embedded circumstances of birth. That—birth—of course carries us back: We who were not graced enough to have been born into that Tribe (ethno-communal) which bequeathed this positivity of/in existence; for us, what are the options? Some will wish for conversion, some will wish for the Yeshuan route, some will wish for another (mainline God/"God"-man Christian? Stoic? Buddhist? Hindu? Muslim? Atheist humanist? Scientific materialist? Shaman spiritualist? there are thousands). If death is anyway annihilative then each of these must be deemed valid, although perhaps not equal in beneficence; a few final words on our boiled down Jewish/"Jewish" perspective.

In the *haftarah* supplementary reading to the weekly Torah portion called *B'har* (covering Leviticus 25:1–26:2; the *haftarah* is from Jeremiah 32:6–27), the prophet (a contemporary of Ezekiel) is currently under imprisonment as a traitor for counseling surrender to the Babylonian army again besieging Jerusalem in 588 BCE.[31] Nevertheless, he makes the necessary legal and financial arrangements through his secretary to purchase a plot of land on his cousin's behalf, paying the full price while the city and nation are struck by starvation, disease, and utter frailty perched on the edge of collapse before overwhelming enemy forces; and he does this from the confines of his

---

29. Melonic, "Done It Again," *The New Criterion*. Accessed May 08, 2020. The reviewed biography is: Rollyson, *The Last Days of Sylvia Plath*.

30. The poem can be found here: Hopkins, "Spring and Fall," *Poetry Foundation*. Accessed September 03, 2021. In its entirety it reads: "*to a young child* / Margaret, are you grieving /Over Goldengrove unleaving? /Leaves like the things of man, you /With your fresh thoughts care for, can you? /Ah! as the heart grows older /It will come to such sights colder /By and by, nor spare a sigh /Though worlds of wanwood leafmeal lie; /And yet you will weep and know why. /Now no matter, child, the name: /Sorrow's springs are the same. /Nor mouth had, no nor mind, expressed /What heart heard of, ghost guessed: / It is the blight man was born for, /It is Margaret you mourn for." The website lists the source as: *Gerard Manley Hopkins: Poems and Prose* (Penguin Classics, 1985).

31. This was the second of two conquests, within which several waves of deportation and exile took place; see once more the article: Editors of the Encyclopædia Britannica, "Babylonian Captivity," *Encyclopædia Britannica*. Accessed April 22, 2020.

own punitive prison cell.[32] There could be few more forceful pictures of firm (of obstinate) hope than this. Disaster may now be at hand but there will be a return: the land and people will grow afresh; the generations to come will indeed come; continuation and renewal are a surety. We might marvel at this; Yehsuan-Judaism, I think, would suggest that we marvel *with* it.

The world is a difficult mess any way one looks at it: continued existence requires affirmation and something bad could arrive as easily as not; one never knows, one never *can* know.[33] Yet we can hope in hope, particularly if we are also able to fully aver—to unabashedly embrace—our first criterion's transcendence, wonder, and mystery, supplemented by the tenacity of our second facet. This conceptual device signals an unreservedness that is perhaps less fragile to life's vicissitudes, while also retaining a core optimism of "Who knows? These bones might yet live again." Thus we find ourselves in Ezekiel's valley, confronting the possibility—I would not put it as a promise, not quite—of reinstatement and regeneration: of the form returning, then the sinews, skin, a smile; and no stimulating external force is necessary. We will therefore end our study with some offerings on what a Yeshuan being-in-the-world may (at least partially, incompletely) entail and imply, drawn from the listing of core teachings which were gathered in our foregoing chapter. Using this compilation we shall unrestrainedly critique—mere remarks—one by one, and the reader is asked to take these as nothing more than thoughts from myself.

"The kingdom" in thirteen bullet points, with comments

Rather than repeat the full summative set of "kingdom" facets together as was done in Chapter 14, below we present them one by one (slightly reworded for better overall flow) and with responses given to each. We will have more to say on certain areas than on others, and no doubt there is much more that could be said on everything than we will prove capable of indicating; my desire is only to spark a dialogue that ideally remains unfettered and ongoing. If we accept the argument for re-enfolding Christianity back into Judaism(s), based on the necessarily reduced Christology that results from a historico-critical study of the personage Yeshua, and if we further strip down and weed out the voluminous words that were later placed into his mouth instead of what (likely) genuinely proceeded from it, we come finally to that which (within the parameters of high probabilities) actually did form the "kingdom" message. What then is that? What are we left with, and what does it mean for us today? Moreover, along with our theoretical constructs of image-idea/idea-image and notion/event, what might—if anything—be done henceforward with these "kingdom" concepts

---

32. See the introductory comments, text, and notes in Plaut, gen. ed., *The Torah*, 861–3.

33. Caputo stresses this unevenness of the event in his "weak theology" as well; see his works referenced here, especially Caputo, *The Folly of God*, and Caputo, *The Weakness of God*. I owe very much to his provocative treatments, and must be forthright in my gratitude.

in a living phenomenological and applied approach? Any answers must naturally be individual, be personal and pending, but we will attempt (strive for!) some few possibilities. To begin:

- In "the kingdom" there is a reversal of expectations, of the accepted defaults of society (e.g. of the "last-first, first-last" sort); important here is that the "top" (the "first") willingly reduce themselves towards the "bottom" (the "last").

What seems to be taught here is an embrace of a deep equality in the general treatment of others, one that ignores the social markers of class, gender, ethnicity, social position, and even age. Although one might expect a typically uncontentious ethos such as "respect the elders" to remain, evidently this too would be included amidst all age groups (no ranking), and the same elders would be required to debase themselves as a part of this. Such might either be a form of social upheaval, or perhaps a kind of universal humility. Caution, however, appears to be called for since "equality" can slide easily enough into what amounts to a mutual disrespect, and also because a sustainable flattening of the sort described has historically proved impossible the few times it has been attempted, for example, in communist situations, or even in the early church if Paul's letter to the Ephesians and its listing of "some would be apostles, some prophets, some evangelists, some pastors and teachers" (4:11)[34] is indicative of a hierarchy and not merely an outlining of possible roles. We might add as well that even if, charitably, we grant Paul the benefit of the doubt and think he intended purely to differentiate occupations and not statuses, nevertheless human nature being what it is a stacked system inevitably developed.

Paul in fact appears to demonstrate this himself—perhaps without noticing—in his frequent insistence on introducing himself as an apostle in the salutatory openings of his letters, for instance Galatians 1:1, Romans 1:1, 1 Corinthians 1:1, and 1 Timothy 1:1 (which read, respectively, "Paul, an apostle—sent neither by human commission nor from human authorities, but through Jesus Christ and God the Father"; "Paul, a servant [a footnote reads: "Gk *slave*"] of Jesus Christ, called to be an apostle, set apart for the gospel of God"; "Paul, called to be an apostle of Christ Jesus by the will of God"; "Paul, an apostle of Christ Jesus by the command of God our Savior and of Christ Jesus our hope"); and then the further interesting addendum of sorts later on in 1 Timothy 2:7: "For this [the "this" here is what Paul takes to be God's/"God's" program of salvation] I was appointed a herald and an apostle (I am telling the truth [a footnote has: "Other ancient authorities add *in Christ*"], I am not lying)."[35] If these are not meant to establish credentials then I do not know what is, and if credentials are to be established then surely there is an underlying mentality of both their necessity and desirability, and hence too of an applicable worthiness that could only be established through a negative comparison—i.e. not having the proper credentials—and

---

34. *Thinline Bible with the Apocrypha* (NRSV).
35. All quotations taken from *Thinline Bible with the Apocrypha* (NRSV).

thus making one "better" (the having) and the other "worse" (the not having): in other words, establishing a system of ranking which produces a hierarchy.

Reinhold Niebuhr observed that the ethics Yeshua espouses are set purely vertically (that is, only on the human-divine axis), and that while such might help to inform a social ethic one cannot be directly taken therefrom.[36] This conclusion is arguable—one might try to copy or re-apply the attitude of the vertical in a horizontal direction, for instance—but it is an intriguing suggestion. Perhaps we might also suspect that only Yeshua himself was really able to live up to the ideals he taught; as Roy W. Hoover put it: "Jesus [Hoover is concerned with the historical Yeshua but uses the traditional narrative-associated "Jesus"] dined and fraternized with anyone who would give the idea of God's reign [that is, "the kingdom" message] the time of day, and was mocked as a drunkard and glutton for it."[37] Was Yeshua truly nonplussed by such digs at his person? If so, that would be a laudatory example of magnanimity, and of a non-discriminating "one of us" gesturing. One final caveat that I feel must be added to this last aspect though is that someone else was always paying for Yeshua's eating and drinking; does this then point towards or away from a position of social equality? Inevitabilities once more.

- "The kingdom" is already present and universal: it is now and is for everyone, based on an individual and direct, unmediated relation between a person and the divine, between a person and another; therefore in "creating" this "kingdom" we are bringing what is extant (although unseen/un-"seen!") into the open.

The difficulty in this, I judge, lies in the latter portion wherein one needs to perform a kind of mental gymnastics in order to balance the dual abstracts of now/to-be; this is not a criticism however, for I think that just such notional acuity is an advantageous requirement of any faith that would also be a *thinking* (as any "good faith" would, in my view on spirituality as taken broadly). The prior part here deals with an elimination or ignoring of institutional authorities (specifically for Yeshua the professional Temple priesthood, but of course this easily extends out) in favor of autonomized religiosity, and this is both attained easily enough (particularly if one has a *thinking faith*) and is typically beneficial to the manner of de-ritualized and somewhat mystery-oriented approaches that Yeshua apparently favored, witnessed by his looser attitude towards Jewish Law as it was observed during his epoch. The effectuating of the hidden yet existent though, that entails a veracity of purpose and a willingness to resolutely maintain one's focus on what might be done at any given moment in order to "kingdom live," and thereby make an internal potential (evidently universally held) into an external reality (effortfully produced).

This Yeshuan viewpoint on an individual's place and purpose—within "the kingdom," but also generally in the facet of human-divine interrelating—might be

---

36. Niebuhr, *An Interpretation of Christian Ethics*.
37. Hoover with Miller, "The Historical Jesus Is Not History," *The Fourth R*, 5–10 and 20 (10).

Part 5 | A Peace-Making, a Re-Making

contrasted with how the church later came to consider both its place (as institutional and authoritative) and its members' lifestyles as essentially a *telling* and a *following*; we will quote the famous theologian Karl Barth as an example here but the trend, I think, is not limited to Protestant circles:

> The essence of the Church is the event in which God's Word and revelation in Jesus Christ, and the office of Jesus Christ as God's ordained Prophet, Priest, and King, is accomplished to the extent that it becomes a *Word* which is directed toward, reaches, and touches certain men [*sic*]. In this event, these men [*sic*.] are touched in such a way that with their human existence they give an answer corresponding to this word. In this event they receive the freedom to make an accounting with their whole being for the truth revealed in Jesus Christ, for His giving of Himself for their and the whole world's sins, for His Lordship as the Resurrected. In short, they receive the freedom to follow Him and in this sense to be "Christians."[38]

It should be clear how un-(almost anti-)Yeshuan this is, with the necessity of a passive reception of a particular notional set by a select (predestined? it almost appears so . . .) group of people who only thereafter are enabled to properly "be Christians" and demonstrate what is asserted to be the truth of the church: and that as established, definitive, and unchangeable (i.e. the referenced incarnation and atonement accounting). In fairness it could, nevertheless, be argued that the "already here" Yeshuan angle is indeed being presented since on this understanding "Jesus" has come and gone (and hence "left his trace" as it were), but this is neither individual and direct (the church mediates) nor is it "kingdom" aimed in the ethical-relational sense (tinges of elitism); although again arguably it may be so in a belief sense based on the stated positioning of this group as living exemplars of specific ideas (note, however, that the ideas being proclaimed are not those of Yeshua's "kingdom," as we discovered in our analysis of the atonement (sacrificial economy) abstract; see Chapter 13 above).

- "Kingdom" behavior is marked by "absurd" generosity, reflecting God/"God" who gives endlessly and equally of God's/"God's" love, mercy, and grace, whatever we may deem the recipient's qualities to be.

If Yeshua did consider his ministry and message of greater importance than his own life, and therefore "allowed" (i.e. did not fight against nor run from) himself to be crucified, that would surely be tremendously generous. However, there might have been more involved (or maybe not), as we will ruminate on shortly; for the moment, we highlight merely that for a person today to seek to be Yeshuan this "kingdom" point would involve an openness and purposeful benevolence demonstrated to everyone in one's surroundings. Quite naturally such precludes allowing oneself to dwell on—let alone enact—feelings/plans of resentment and/or revenge. As the giving of

---

38. Barth, *God Here and Now*, 78.

God/"God" being addressed is exemplified via emotional measures the focus is probably in those regards, but not exclusively as our next summative point will indicate.

Stretching this out a little further, we might comprehend this as an inclusivity that is not bound by any in-group/out-group criteria, if such items are taken (as they unfortunately usually are) to relate to merit. Everyone is worthy of receiving one's full giving of care, comfort, time, regardless of any of the details related to each donee, and moreover this is to be performed in a manner which goes far beyond what may be socially accepted or called-for. Give and do not ask, is the teaching here. (Which is not, of course, a purely or originally Yeshuan ethos, but it does seem to have been especially stressed by him.)

- Connected with the preceding call for a generalized munificence is the requirement to re-work priorities both personal and communal towards social parity, and this without expectations of reward, such as an afterlife or other telos beyond this Earth.

Here I think is where the monetary details (possibly) not highlighted in the previous statement come foremost into play, and that because of the nuanced shifting from what one does (one's generous behavior) to how one adjudicates (one's priorities) appertaining to the community and with a purpose directed towards equality. We noted above that a true flattening of the lines between persons is most likely impossible given human nature—that hierarchies of one sort or another will always develop—but it may prove easier to coax the economics than it does instinctual mindsets: programs could naturally always be developed, and the early church itself evidently attempted something of a communal living, if the account in The Acts of the Apostles can be taken as at least partially historically accurate (4:34–35: "[34]There was not a needy person among them [the believers], for as many as owned lands or houses sold them and brought the proceeds of what was sold. [35]They laid it at the apostles' feet, and it was distributed to each as any had need."[39]). While this could—if it really occurred—have been ordered based on eschatological expectations (e.g. Yeshua would soon return from Heaven and history would be brought to an end), that is not a necessary interpretation; and regardless Yeshua's "kingdom" indeed seems to call for precisely the sort of giving and care that an arrangement like a commune could provide (although once more not necessarily; different organizations might achieve the same result).

A doubt does come to mind at this juncture, however, for if our speculation that Yeshua held a Second Maccabees type of belief in resurrection as reward for martyrdom (and possibly also for religious fidelity) is correct—and the evidence did appear reasonable, possibly even robust—then that would be exactly an expectation of reward, and furthermore one in an afterlife version, albeit an "afterlife" lived on this Earth according to the contours of the concept (a corporeal restitution rather than a spiritualized (ghostly) "essence" being transported). Moreover, if Yeshua was not

39. *Thinline Bible with the Apocrypha* (NRSV).

only willing to die for his message but actually courted death for the sake of becoming a martyr—which, once more, is certainly not absolute but is conceivable—then there would again be a telos present; but this too would not be connected with any "beyond". The case is a consternating one; yet regardless, what is pertinent for us is not whatever particular psychological orientation Yeshua might have held during his lifetime but instead the exhortations towards equality and justice directed towards the building of an improved society for all: something we noted is a very Jewish concern.[40]

- Somewhat disturbingly, those who have are asserted to be given more, and those who do not have are said to end up with even less. However, this tenet may fit better within "the kingdom" if it is taken as a statement on knowledge, although it could be read as being about material goods; conclusions appear variable.

As remarked, this is a difficult fit, yet it was included in our description of "kingdom" details due to its presence in the most reliable texts. There is also, indeed, the evidence for authenticity provided by the mere fact of its unpleasantness and quality as an oddity; this is exactly the sort of uncomfortable leftover that a later redactor or commentator would be most likely to edit out entirely or at least to dilute in some manner. The reader will recall from Chapter 9 that this aspect is placed in the context of the Parable of the Talents (or coins/money) in Q81, *The Gospel of Jesus* 4:36-38, and Matthew 25:28-29,[41] wherein it serves to illustrate the bonus for the "faithful servant" and the censure for the "wicked servant"; hence any provocation is removed by a simple alignment of good act = reward, with bad act = punishment. However, it also appears as a standalone sentiment in *Thomas* Saying 41 and *The Gospel of Jesus* 4:22-23,[42] and there in the form of a very straightforward "more to the haves, less to

---

40. See again "Tikkun Olam," *My Jewish Learning*. Accessed July 15, 2020.

41. Given here for convenience, respectively: Powelson and Riegert, trans., footnotes, and eds., *The Lost Gospel Q*, 117 (Q81): "[The rich man, here a nobleman who has been made a king in another land and thereafter returned, is speaking] Turning to the others, he said, 'Take the silver coins from him and give them to the fellow who turned ten coins into one hundred.' /'But sir!' they protested. 'He already has a hundred coins.' /'Yes,' the king replied, 'and to the person who has something, more will be given and that person will have an abundance. The person who has nothing of real value will lose even what he thinks he has.'"; Funk and the Jesus Seminar, *The Gospel of Jesus*, 31 (4:36-8): "*Money in trust:* 36But his master replied to him [the final servant, who only buried the money he was given], 'You incompetent and timid slave! So you knew that I reap where I didn't sow and gather where I didn't scatter, did you? 37Then you should have taken my money to the bankers. Then when I returned I would have received my capital with interest. 38So take the money away from this fellow and give it to the one who has the greatest sum.'"; Matthew 25:28-29: "[The rich man, having returned from his journey and learned how his last servant buried the money entrusted to him and therefore earned nothing extra by making profitable financial use of it, is speaking here] 28'So take the talent [i.e. a coin] from him, and give it to the one with ten talents. 29For to all those who have, more will be given, and they will have an abundance; but from those who have nothing, even what they have will be taken away.'" *The Go-Anywhere Thinline Bible with the Apocrypha* (NRSV).

42. Again respectively: Meyer, trans. and intro., *The Gospel of Thomas*, 37 (Saying 41): "1Jesus said, 'Whoever has something in hand will be given more, 2and whoever has nothing will be deprived of even the little that person has.'"; Funk and the Jesus Seminar, *The Gospel of Jesus*, 29 (4:22-23): "*Have and have not:* 22Jesus used to say: 'Those who have something in hand will be given more, 23and those who have

the have-nots." If the purpose is in regards to materiality, it appears not only unjust but also in direct opposition to that which was considered immediately above on the centrality of working for more equal societies. Although it is perhaps unfair to expect total coherence from Yeshua given that his was an orally based and inveterate ministry and thus might have produced small differences at any number of points or places, we can at least think he would have maintained a steady general ethos (which, on all other points, does seem the case). What was suggested as a possibility then was the other mention in Matthew about more/less—namely 13:10–12—which explicitly states the "secrets of the kingdom of heaven" (verse eleven)[43] to be the topic at hand, and therefore the issue is one of knowledge: those who already know will learn more; those who do not know will become more ignorant.

That this "secrets" reference comes from Matthew (written circa 85 CE) makes me a little dubious; that it fairly neatly does away with the discomfort involved more doubtful yet. Even so, and in a way against my "better skepticism" as it were, I cannot imagine Yeshua to be referring to actual products being forcibly removed from the poor. His was a message of complete trust in divine providence, and in (as just examined) warm and open generosity of both heart and hand. The singular statements we have of this (i.e. the non-parable embedded versions) could be fragments, or merely the remembered shock ending of the originary stories; and Yeshua could indeed have told his closest followers that they would learn more than the "them" of his general audiences who came and went: that, in fact, would only be rational. Although I disagree entirely with his conclusion, from Thomas Aquinas' take on Yeshua's default superior knowledge about the Christian faith (i.e. for Aquinas: the faith of Christ in himself) and therefore Yeshua's actual non-faith on the topic (he *knew* and thus did not need to *believe*; that is, for Aquinas' "Jesus" it was a certainty), a parallel may be drawn. Brian Davies summarizes this as, "Christ, he [Aquinas] says, was 'the first and original teacher of the faith [i.e. of Christ as simultaneously fully human and divine: from *Summa Theologiae* 3a.7.7]'. With this point in mind, he denies that Christ had faith. His position is that, in teaching his own divinity, Christ was speaking from knowledge."[44] A *knowing* is more certain than a *believing* on this perspective (wonderful epistemological arguments could be made here on all sorts of sides); and if that thought is followed, then those who possess the knowledge will come to have more via (perhaps) the superior grounding and starting position, whereas those who do not possess the knowledge will lose even what little they (think they) know, either (perhaps) through their own doubts and equivocating, or through the need to take

---

nothing will be deprived of even the little they have.'"

43. Here is the section: Matthew 13:10–12: "10Then the disciples came and asked him, 'Why do you speak to them [i.e. Yeshua's general audiences] in parables?' 11He answered, 'To you it has been given to know the secrets of the kingdom of heaven, but to them it has not been given. 12For to those who have, more will be given, and they will have an abundance; but from those who have nothing, even what they have will be taken away.'" *Thinline Bible with the Apocrypha* (NRSV).

44. Davies, *The Thought of Thomas Aquinas*, 298–9.

Part 5 | A Peace-Making, a Re-Making

the effort and time to search things out. Again, if we accept the knowing > believing stance (which I do not on the face of it since I think the terms need a fuller defining than the vulgar usage grants), then too within the context of the parable the meaning works when the "money" (talents or coins) is understood metaphorically.

- From Keller's revealing of the thought-world of the historical period Yeshua lived in, we determined the heritage to have presented God/"God" as working *with* nature (and not *over* nature) in the act of Creation, and therefore Yeshua's "kingdom" might well have pictured God/"God" cooperating with individuals and groups in each beneficent "making."

I think that the ramifications of understanding God/"God" as non-omnipotent and non-omniscient (as the reconsideration of Genesis 1:1–2 necessarily led to; see our analysis in Chapter 9) cannot be overstated. Yeshua and his contemporaries most likely held to a view of Creation wherein God/"God" used what was there to be used (i.e. not *ex nihilo*), and perhaps also they held that God/"God" might have needed to perform the Creative act a few times before being satisfied with it. Even if so, we should take care to realize that this would not have reduced God's/"God's" power nor magnificence nor sovereignty for them; yet it does still—very importantly—establish a God/"God" that works *with,* and one can only work with what is to be had, to be offered. Depending on our choices, the favorable might not come about, the ill might prevail; of course this also fits with Yeshua's Judaic, and general first century, background covenantal patterns of thought: indeed, the entire ancient world's sacrificial/religious edifices were built on *do ut des:* a plea of tit for tat. Give to God/"God" that God/"God" might give; give to God/"God" that God/"God" might *be able to* give? To an ancient mind probably not the latter, but the potential does seem present; perhaps it was merely unacknowledged, haunting thoughts like a specter. (What is interesting about Yeshua is his partial break with this in insisting that God/"God" blesses all regardless; considered shortly below.)

What, then, might be drawn from this? Firstly is the God/"God" who cannot, and secondly is the onus (but also privilege) of human responsibility. It is up to us. God/"God" may wish for X, Y, or Z, but it simply is incapable of doing such on its own. God/"God" not only wants to work with us, it *needs* to; else the thing will not come to pass. For a Yeshuan this could mean that while "the kingdom" is already "here," it must be brought out (as above): it is always both "here-now" *and* "yet-to-be"; and this "bringing" (birthing, producing) is surely continuous as situations shift and new demands become called for, new transformations made necessary. Once more, this is all very Jewish:[45] but then so was Yeshua, and so is Yeshuanism, whatever its later heralds might have turned it into.

---

45. "Tikkun Olam," *My Jewish Learning.* Accessed July 15, 2020.

- Every iota of the world is interconnected, and despite our each being tiny "mustard seeds" in/of "the kingdom" what we do has far-reaching and vast effects, of which we are almost entirely unaware; nevertheless the results are there, and they are thoroughly interwoven.

This is quite heartening. "The kingdom" already *is* but still must be *made;* we do what we can—in trust—and although we may or may not see any benefits eventuate, nevertheless they are there: as we work the world does get better. To think such naturally calls for a degree of faith, and if we similarly have hope we might find help on the way. The "seed" of each "kingdom" act grows in unobservable (although we might "see!") and unpredictable ways, establishing altered realities which establish "shelter for birds", "branches" for the healing "nests" of others.[46] To an endeavoring Yeshuan this is an exhortation to keep going, to stay with it; and surely in that it is an ethic which anyone concerned for the welfare of the world and of others can agree with.

- "The kingdom" is action focused, not belief focused.

Would that this remained so! When examining Yeshua and his calls for "now" and "do," one cannot help but think of James 2:14: "What good is it, my brothers and sisters [a footnote reads: "Gk *brothers*"; I should add that the word here, *adelphoi* (root: *adelphos*), is generally used in scripture to mean "fellow community member"], if you say you have faith but do not have works? Can faith save you?"[47] These were of course not Yeshua's words, but we can certainly imagine him saying them. In conjunction, furthermore, with the above Aquinean premise that knowledge is greater than belief this becomes more interesting still, and one wonders what might have been if the church had historically taken a more Peter-James developmental line than the Pauline path it actually trod. Boyarin, as described in the preceding, has given us a thoroughly instructive account of the historical pressures that pushed both early Christianity (was-Yeshuan-Judaism) and rabbinic Judaism to emphasize adhering to a set of proper beliefs as definitional for the achievement of in-group acceptance;[48] but while Judaism was later able to mostly move away from this Christianity has—somewhat strangely to my mind—kept its rigid dogma. In the modern Christian case these nuances are used as well to distinguish amongst denominations, and sometimes in

---

46. The well-known Parable of the Mustard Seed, which I think need not be quoted again; but for interested readers the references are: Matthew 13:31–32; Mark 4:30–32; Luke 13:18–19; *Thinline Bible with the Apocrypha* (NRSV); Funk and the Jesus Seminar, *The Gospel of Jesus,* 17 (2:19–20); Powelson and Riegert, trans., footnotes, and eds., *The Lost Gospel Q,* 95 (Q61); Meyer, trans. and intro., *The Gospel of Thomas,* 31 (Saying 20); and Leloup, trans., intro. and comm., *The Gospel of Thomas,* 17 (where "shelter" is rendered as "rest"). See once more Chapter 9 above.

47. *Thinline Bible with the Apocrypha* (NRSV); on the Greek term cross-reference: *The New Greek/English Interlinear New Testament.*

48. Essentially each group felt the need to push off from the other; the socio-political tumultuousness of first century Palestine should also be kept in mind here. Boyarin, *Border Lines;* and see Chapter 3 above.

quite a minute manner. Regardless, a Yeshuan—it would seem—acts; and if "salvation" is even needed in Yeshuan-Judaism (which we think it is not: *even if it were* is my emphasis here) it is not in the way the church has taught everyone to assume (see the below). "The kingdom" must be effortfully established, and no amount of "officially approved thinking" could attain that. While it is admittedly true that beliefs can/do motivate behaviors, I suspect Yeshua would have found such a splitting of hairs irritating and retorted to "just do."

- We are to share and distribute material goods freely and without regard for need or determinations of what is "fair"; once more in reflection of God/"God" who blesses the "righteous" and "unrighteous" alike with "sun" and "rain." In this we rely on God's/"God's" providence and have honest concern and fraternity irrespective of class, gender, or ethnicity; "the kingdom" is not "justice" as we usually assign it.

Here again we find Yeshuan-Judaism's concern with social welfare, its "world repair" (as, once more, remains central today in Judaism[49]), and intriguingly its sidestepping of the then traditional and thoroughly ensconced *do ut des* (Latin: "I give that you may give") approach towards both human-divine and human-human relatings. God/"God" blesses everyone and does not punish; as should we. In conjunction with the generosity stressed in our third point we might worry that a Yeshuan being-in-the-world could lead to excessive fervor and, in "overdoing it," result in one's own loss. Yeshua, however, appears to offer perfect trust as the remedy to that (how practical a solution this proves is, I think, open to debate, however beautiful the sentiment may be). God/"God" *will* provide; only wait. As a mendicant teacher Yeshua himself relied on the generosity of others, and so a cynic might find his calls to give and distribute easy to make if one owns little oneself and is accustomed to freely receiving, but the challenge is justified all the same because if we imagine a world in which everyone is far less obsessed with "me" and "mine" we can only determine it as better than the one we are already familiar with. As we have stressed, "the kingdom" not only *is,* but *could be.*

This facet of an open redistribution is further unique in its disregard for the "fairness" associated with economic positioning. Although it is true that for Yeshua's historical time the gesture away from an ethnically oriented charity was generally something new in itself, to add to that a willful ignoring of social rank is remarkable. In essence, the Yeshuan position is not only to give to the poor but to the rich too; we may well ask what the purpose is in that. If conjoined with the general arc of the heretofore, however, it is at least conceivable—and probably very supportable—to take the lesson as directed both at supplying for the real material needs of those around one and for the cultivation of an attitude that is benevolent in all situations unattached from one's own embedded (default) circumstances (continued below) and the natural

49. "Tikkun Olam," *My Jewish Learning.* Accessed July 15, 2020.

tendency to worry about the future. Perhaps the common thread throughout this whole listing is simply that: "Give."

- "The kingdom" is present oriented, a living-now, and it does not emphasize an afterlife or reward; if there is any such it seemingly is comprised of a promised physical resurrection for martyrdom, possibly also for faith fidelity. There are no concepts of hell, damnation, or judgment. Life is to be enjoyed while it lasts, with thanks and trust in God's/"God's" gift of it.

We have considered Yeshua's likely Second Maccabees style idea of a corporeal return as divinely ordained recompense for martyrdom, but as remarked in the footnote to this point in the previous chapter we should feel free to dismiss this as an historical relic the way we have disregarded resurrection generally. Death is an end, and we may "welcome" it or we may not (in Chapter 12 we examined a number of approaches to one's own death, as well as some related ethical matters between one's death and others), but with it comes a cessation of selfhood.[50] That, however, is not the crux of this "kingdom" perspective; rather it is that *even if* there is a "something else," what is paramount for us today is that "today," taken moment by moment and in gratitude. Yeshua might have accepted his own death—he might have expected it, and hence his refusal to cede ground in the contours of his ministry, forcing the issue (daring the authorities)—only (or largely) because he deemed himself virtually guaranteed to be brought back; we cannot know and moreover this does not concern us. What does matter in trying to ascertain what "kingdom" being may consist of is the very important difference here between Yeshuanism (as a Judaism(s)) and the manner in which the church came to instruct its congregants, even as historically early as when the latter Gospel books were written.[51] The Christians came to place death absolutely centrally—the entire atonement message is aimed at a safe getaway into Heaven—whereas Yeshua, like any good Zennist,[52] instructed his followers to

---

50. I realize of course that beliefs on this vary widely, but to borrow from Aquinas again, a belief is not knowledge; at any rate, the manner in which I delineate the self contains bodily elements which would preclude any continuation of the same self postmortem; see Oberg, *Blurred* (especially Chapter 2: "Laying the Groundwork"), for a full argument and definitional parameters. At a minimum I may note here that I do not find a mind/body dualism to hold any defendable conceptual water: mind is a function of body and thus mind equals body. There might be some interesting theological implications of this worth exploring (particularly if one were to stretch the metaphysics of experience).

51. In Chapter 11 we examined the lack of evidence for an afterlife message—and especially in connection with any punishment—in the earliest and most reliable texts (i.e. *The Gospel of Thomas*, Q, and the reconstructions presented in *The Gospel of Jesus*), which probably hail from the middle of the first century or slightly later and precede the non-Markan books (Mark about 70 CE) by a few decades; on those, Matthew carries a composition of roughly 85 CE, Luke at around 90 CE, and John near the end of that century (it is not uncommon to see dates in the early second century for its final form, however); for some overviews and summaries, see Funk and the Jesus Seminar, *The Gospel of Jesus*, 111–12.

52. There are many wonderful Zen primers; here are a few (starting with my favorite): Alan Watts, *The Way of Zen*; Seung Sahn (priestly name), *Ten Gates*; Paul Reps, compiler, *Zen Flesh, Zen Bones*; and on Zen meditation specifically, Thich Nhat Hanh, *The Miracle of Mindfulness*.

keep their minds in now and (slightly apart from the Zennists) their deeds aimed at "kingdom" construction for the betterment of this existence, inclusive of material anxieties. A large part of enjoying life is, after all, connected with the physical thuses and suches of which Yeshua often spoke.

- "Sin" exists, but there is no need for redemption; moreover, "my" "sin" is always greater than "your" "sin" in "kingdom" thinking (perspectivally, bearing no relation to empirical realities).

As was mentioned in the note on the first listing of these "kingdom" points in the previous chapter, I cannot agree with "sin" as a valid concept when understood in the mode of divine affront in which it is held in much (primarily Western) religious discourse, both in our present era and in the time of Yeshua's. This topic was discussed at some length as well in Chapter 13 and need not be repeated here, but I would like to highlight two nuances that may prove helpful. The first is that although "sin" was measured as a wrongdoing towards God/"God" and/or others in the Judaism(s) of first century Palestine, its etymology is closer to "not doing what one ought to have done" than it is to the implications of English words like transgression, rebellion, disobedience, offense, et cetera.[53] This is the image that Yeshua would have had in mind, but he still seems to have accepted it as something necessarily done *against* the divine (we might think of this as a behavior committed despite being told not to), rather than the softer taking of it as something more akin to "would have been better to" (e.g. such as a misplayed move in a game of chess (of which I make many!)). The second nuance I find worth enunciating is that in biblical thinking there were two forms of this: the accidental and the purposive, with the latter naturally being deemed worse than the former (and hence traditionally requiring different measures for absolution).[54]

What I find worthwhile here is the gentler "should have" as recognized by measuring the deed (thought, word, et cetera) against an established code or system of teaching or the like. This need not, of course, be religiously based,[55] but it often is; whatever the source such can prove useful guides for daily praxis: along both the human-human axis and the human-divine axis, if one is so inclined to include it. From a purely Yeshuan perspective then (and certainly the Judaic element is strong here), there are these failings of ours, necessarily damaging and in need of restitution, although that may only involve a confession of fault and a determination to do better; from a modified Yeshuan perspective (as I would have it; and I remind the reader that

---

53. For an explanation of the Hebrew term and English meaning, see: Benner, "Definition of Hebrew Words: Sin," *Ancient Hebrew Research Center*. Accessed September 10, 2021.

54. For a conservative—but detailed and explanatory—article on this, see the former Chief Rabbi of the United Kingdom Jonathan Sacks' website, where he has given us this: "Vayikra (5771)—The Dimensions of Sin," *Jonathan Sacks*. Accessed September 10, 2021. (Note that 5771 is the year according to the traditional Jewish calendar's counting system (late 2010 to late 2011).)

55. The Ancient Greeks' Virtue Ethics comes to mind here; for an introduction see Russell, ed., *The Cambridge Companion to Virtue Ethics*.

I am nothing but an engaged thinker), there are these failings of ours, but we need go no further with them than to acknowledge error, adjust ourselves, and make amends socially when applicable. I would not compile a list of debts owed to God/"God", and—this is fascinating—Yeshua might not have either, even if he did not analyze out the final results of the "no need for redemption" stance.

Recall the "kingdom" aspects of God/"God" freely blessing all, the non-emphasis on an afterlife (indeed the absence of any; except perhaps for resurrection as reward for martyrdom (maybe also fidelity, as noted)), and the lack of a punitive dimension in Yeshua's overall message. Taken together, what we have is a "sin" that is better thought of as an internal nudge to improve (essentially, a conscience) in areas that may concern others or that may only be between one and God/"God" (as in the "missing the mark" form of "should have" and not the "affront" version). Thus "sin" becomes an instructor on the way, assisting us as we walk and seek a constructive "path of life."[56] Moreover, since to Yeshua "my" "sin" is always more than "yours" a sense of humility can always be kept in the attitudinal tweaking involved, graciously ignoring the externalities: e.g. although "your" killing someone is quite obviously a greater wrong than "my" cheating on a test at school, "I" do not consider it that way. From a practical point of view we must expect that the law would still punish "you" much more severely than "me," but "the kingdom" is not always the most practical of places, and Yeshua's concerns were anyway not in those quarters.

- We should be loose and homeless in/with the world, grasping nothing so tightly that it cannot be released (non-attachment); this extends to one's family and social ties.

We also placed a footnote to this in its first presentation in our earlier chapter, commenting on how the orientation of non-attachment is a common one amongst the world's teachers and heritages, and that whatever one's allegiances to creed or situation it is an idea that can usually be concurred with. One never knows, after all; time flows on and what is here today is gone tomorrow; to insist on static circumstances and positions of ownership is folly most evident. From the Buddha to Epictetus to the *Bhagavad Gita* to Boethius to the "mindfulness guru" in a shopping mall we can gather this advice: and it is excellent, there is no doubt about that. What is less advantageous—bordering, as noted, on the unethical in my view—is the extension of this comportment towards the others in one's life. My sense is that in espousing "the kingdom," Yeshua was aiming in this portion of it to promote one's relationship with God/"God"—direct, without intercessors—as uppermost and hence everything else becomes a distant second to it; our final "kingdom" point below will further explore this facet and its (possibly) "darker" side. The historical sketches we laid out in our

---

56. To "stray from the path" is also a meaning of the Hebrew term used to designate "sin"; see again Benner, "Definition of Hebrew Words: Sin," *Ancient Hebrew Research Center.* Accessed September 10, 2021.

Part 5 | A Peace-Making, a Re-Making

opening chapters left us with a Yeshua who apparently did not get married nor procreate (or anyway we can find no evidence of such; which is not of course definitive proof of a lack of romance or anything else, simply that while we do not know he probably kept himself a bachelor); as everyone who does have children knows, a young one is the most astounding treasure imaginable—beyond imagination—and absolutely should be treated as such: valued and cared for endlessly. I would argue for similar, although naturally shifted, considerations towards one's parents, siblings, other family members, friends, colleagues, acquaintances, et cetera; really any person in one's everyday deserves a "non-loose grasping" in the senses of honor, respect, and value. Yeshua counseled us to be willing to walk away from them. In fairness, we could hold this Yeshuan viewpoint while still rendering honor, respect, and value during our times together with these others, and circumstances will no doubt call for "letting go" as people naturally depart from us or we from them (changing jobs, moving homes), but realizing those potentialities is many shades apart from cultivating a mindset of detachment to one's familial and extended networks, and I think it is also many shades warmer and more humane.[57]

- Connected with the previous point, some consequences Yeshua warns may come of following his "kingdom" ideology are: 1) intrafamilial conflict, 2) breaking ancestral ties, and 3) sundering living bonds. While on the surface these are perhaps deleterious, they indicate an exhaustive acceptance of persons that again overturns existing hierarchical rankings and assumptions and establishes in their place *ideational* ties.

This final facet of "the kingdom" (according to our listing) emphasizes similar notions of relational lassitude as the one before it. Here, however, the results of the mental and behavioral detachment from one's biological and cultural embedded elements are spelled out fairly clearly: a Yeshuan adherent risks alienating and/or losing family, cannot (i.e. is not to: outrightly should not, by the teaching's edicts) honor the lineage of which one is a member over those personally chosen ties, and then once more the divorce from those currently in one's social circles is expounded. What is put in their place—most interestingly and, as this idea was to develop, somewhat hypocritically—are bonds of a purely abstracted conceptual nature: in the early days a follower (weakest ideational bonds), then a Yeshuan community member (stronger ideational bonds; and note that these first two both entailed still being Jewish), and then in the later stages a "Christian" (strongest ideational bonds).

This last element of in-group association as established by the proclaimed personal accession to a particular notional package, and then the insistence (which grew

---

57. I would make similar arguments against these sentiments in Buddhism, for those who are wondering; see again The Buddha, *The Dhammapada;* Hagen, *Buddhism;* and also for another modern take but with different emphases than Hagen offers, Tilakaratne, *Theravada Buddhism.*

and grew[58]) on pledged fealty to an ever-narrowing set of dogma and hermeneutics, clearly did bring conflict of all sorts; and it not only set Yeshuans against their families, neighbors, and other Jews generally, but too Yeshuans against Yeshuans in a series of disputes that lasted centuries and finally required the intervention of the Roman Emperor to bring to an end; although even so many issues remained boiling beneath the lid, as it were.[59] It did also, however, achieve a new form of identitarian psychology, and this is an eventuality that has had very far-reaching effects in world history, particularly in Western nations. No longer were the defaults of one's birth to matter completely for who one was—belonging ceased to be fully given and moved towards being taken—henceforth "I" became largely a choice. (The foundation this laid for political movements based on the segregated individual are as clear as day.) When the dust settled in the early church anyone of any background could become a Yeshuan, and converts were actively sought anywhere and everywhere. It was the dawning of the Missionary Age, and it was the birth of a comportment that has mostly stayed firmly entrenched in each corner of the church, regardless of denomination or the divides between Catholic, Orthodox, and Protestant circles (as each emerged). This was obviously hugely advantageous for Yeshuan-Judaism from socio-political and economic angles, but let us remain a moment on the psychological.

It is probably not difficult to concede that it is indeed a wonderful development for a group to accept everyone in such a way, without prejudice (at least initially) and likely with some measure of tolerance as well (again, at least initially). The danger, however, lies in the idea that it is possible for one to completely dissociate from the conditions of one's birth, and moreover that it is healthy to do so. The whole must be taken in context of course, and the church came to believe and to teach that the internal embrace of specific abstractions were necessary for each person's soul (accepted as a given reality) to escape from eternal punishment and enter into eternal bliss—whatever we might think of these notions, if one is devoted to them then they perforce become extraordinarily motivating—and thus in a sense the compulsion to "join us" and "start life anew" has a certain innocence; but it is also recklessly naïve. A person can convert, and conversion can be a wonderful and enriching, meaning-giving and purpose-creating experience; but a person cannot rid themselves of the cognitive functioning of the vast array of influences bequeathed from the settings of those originary forces which produced and raised them through infancy and childhood: elements which include not only biological ties but the reaches of the socio-cultural, linguistic, epochal, geographic, climatic, economic, formative chance encounters, educational moulding, et cetera, et cetera. To avoid what might be an easy misreading here, let me state outright that this is not an argument against the possibilities and merits of

---

58. Boyarin, *Border Lines;* and not only for Christians: as mentioned, in these years rabbinic Judaism too reacted to the Christian "challenge" ("crisis"?) by demanding allegiance to its own set of doctrines.

59. Editors of Encyclopædia Britannica, "First Council of Nicaea," *Encyclopædia Britannica*. Accessed January 20, 2020.

conversion, nor is it a denial of the bonds betwixt people that are so formed, rather it is to emphasize the extraordinary degree to which we, each of us, are conglomerations, constellations of the uncontrolled and galaxies of those unchosen factors that were sedimented into our brains' areas of automatic judging and reacting and which created our intuitive systems.[60] These mechanisms were outlined at some length in Chapter 5 in our consideration of the notion/event, and therefore here we need merely glance at a few of the potential consequences of this last "kingdom" condition.

To link oneself to others through little more than commonly held ideas (details of culture and language would in most cases likely apply as well, if only partially), and to accept as given that those ideas might lead to one (at an extreme) severing family ties—including ancestrally—in favor of a commitment to said ideas, and that the same consequence may result pertaining to non-family members within one's social circles as well, amounts to an attempt to ignore the cumulative biological and historical patterns that resulted in one's existence in the first place. Again, I do not wish by this highlighting of cognitive matters to denigrate conversion or claim that these risks will of necessity eventuate; I simply hope to illumine the hidden perils of this kind of all-or-nothing approach which Yeshua appears to advocate. Changing or altering one's religious commitments (ideational associations; often too ritual, ethical, and social) can be—and frequently are—transformative, but the new does not (cannot) replace the birth-embedded, and it is psychologically unhealthy to adjudicate it as so, let alone to promote it. Thinking this through within our present context: If a person is born and raised in a Christian family and wishes to remain Christian then naturally these ills are not likely to be realized; if a person later in life decides to become a Christian and has the support of their non-Christian family in doing that, likewise things will probably remain generally fine.[61] It is understandable, though, how such may not; and if not Yeshua seems to advise favoring the notional above all else in life. Are we able to concur? Circumstances can be extremely difficult, but my own feeling is that each person should attempt to work towards some kind of balancing of one's "fate" (the birth-default) and the affirmations one decides to pronounce, to effortlessly minimize conflict, honor one's ancestors regardless (overall at least, if not in every detail), and never to purposefully sunder the whole of what one's heritage has bequeathed.

The reader will note how in this last example we have terminologically slipped from Yeshuan-Judaism into Christianity, but I would contend that this serves to articulate what empirically occurred: that which was Yeshuan-Judaism, as it became reformulated into the something-else of Christianity, took this final "kingdom" element and increasingly emphasized it, as was implied by our comment on the Missionary Age and as a glance at church history very quickly confirms. If, however, Yeshua is

---

60. This extends to the self and its formation; again, a full argument and alternative self-theory can be found in Oberg, *Blurred*.

61. Not only in the Christian case, of course, other religions have tenets like these; but our topic at hand is on Yeshua's legacy.

not the God/"God"-man of myth, then his stresses here and elsewhere may be freely considered, downplayed, or abandoned. The beauty of a Yeshuanism that is understood as a Judaism and has naught to do with (and no need for) any soteriology is that nothing is forced, we take and leave as we see fit: yes or no, more or less, now or then, this "kingdom" point or that; may God/"God" help.

"The kingdom" then, as with the entirety of Yeshuan-Judaism, is best understood as an option, or rather as a complex set of possible ways to relate to this essentially Jewish way of comprehending the world and our place in it, and that whether we decide to be/"be" Jewish/"Jewish" or not, whether we appropriate Yeshuan ideals or not, and if we do then to what extent. Everything is possible; how much is "seen!"? In a careful study of the Czech philosopher Jan Patočka's work that extends it into theological dimensions, Martin Koci writes that: "In Patočka's opinion, faith is a particular mode of thinking and of living in openness to the future . . . faith is something to be thought about, that faith is thinking."[62] We have attempted to think anew the Yeshuan faith, to re-think it as what it was and hence to re-understand where it belongs. In order to do so we began with a situating that was based in historico-critical studies and that yielded a very human Yeshua, and hence our insistence on calling him by his Aramaic name and not the later appellation of "Jesus" with all of its burdening associations. This "new" Yeshua presented an entirely other image of the man as man, as one man, as a person who lived and struggled and died in the midst of circumstances he did not choose and could not control: exactly as with us. He did exercise the decisions available to him, and surely with a courage and effect beyond what most of us manage, first evidently in following John the Baptizer (Baptist), then later on his own as he apparently abandoned the eschatology of his former teacher and established a unique ministry and message, travelling ceaselessly to speak it, making it his career. This is a Yeshua that did indeed take himself as an important pedagogue with something to offer to his whole society, but not as someone who was founding a new religion, let alone as an equal to the God/"God" of the entire universe. The de-Christologizing so entailed was further set within the confines of a first century Palestine rife with messianic fervor and no shortage of spiritual leaders, even including the astonishing archaeological evidence from a stone at least decades before Yeshua's time that described a physically suffering savior who rose from the dead after three days (see Chapter 3): resurrection choked the conceptual air; but it was not always "resurrection" in the way we assume such now, as our analysis of the role Pauline thought and imagery played in the development of how attestations regarding Yeshua came to be comprehended helped show. The picture changed incontestably, and with it the whole grounding, hence we next turned our attention to the notion/event and image-idea/idea-image.

From this bracing of methodological approaches we considered how ideas give rise to experienced realities, how the concepts we intellectually accept (with awareness

62. Koci, *Thinking Faith after Christianity*, 13–14.

or those we have taken on to the depth at which they have become intuitive biases) act to create the happenings in our lives, and then—cyclically—feed back into the reinforcement of the same, or instead form pressures towards adjusting the underlying abstracts. The "notion/event" is written with a slash rather than a dash because the two are ever-linked in a dance of cause and effect and cause and . . . on and on and on as lived experiences accrete, are processed, and remain. Similarly for the pictures we hold—both literally (physical images) and mentally (perceptual amalgamations)—and the reactions we have and perform to these images as well both go into and come from antecedent abstractions. What we see is hardly ever "seen!" and what is "seen!" could well be a comprehensional breakthrough of what is ocularly being seen. Beholder is beheld; and vice versa. As an exploratory example of these processes within historical Christianity—especially as witnessed in the movement away from root Yeshuan-Judaism—we took Japan's Hidden Christians as a case study for the phenomenology of the icon and analyzed what conclusions might initially be drawn from such.

Gaining a new perspective on the power of the image-idea/idea-image therefrom (and ascertaining firsthand the potency of the notion/event too in the remarkable syncretism with Japan's extant religions that took place), we then experimented with what a new phenomenology of the embodied cross (i.e. a new idea placed into the image) might result in if the core meaning-generating conceptualization were moved away from what the church has traditionally taught a believer ought to feel in response to the crucifix and instead into what may be felt from a "kingdom" based viewing of the same. Perhaps to our surprise we discovered that even for those who are not followers of any sort of Christianity—either in its modern day or in its "truer" Yeshuan-Judaic variety—there is still a great deal in the crucifix that can engage one at an emotional level and elicit powerful reactions, and this even if the (historico-critically accurate) perspective is taken of Yeshua as neither foreknowing his execution (while probably able to guess at the possibility of) nor indeed desiring it: although we may not find "sacrifice" there we do find *surrender,* and this is breathtaking. That presentation was not enough, however, and we soon recognized that further detailed work on what exactly "the kingdom" might/could be was required, and so we moved to a textual investigation of some select parables and related scriptures, relying on what are deemed by scholars to be the earliest and most reliable works. Sifting out the wheat from the chaff, as it were,[63] we started to piece together some key points of what Yeshua took

---

63. I could not resist this wink at the Gospels; for the reader's convenience: Matthew 3:12: "His [this is John the Baptizer (Baptist) speaking about the "one who is more powerful than I [who] is coming after me" (verse 11)] winnowing fork is in his hand, and he will clear his threshing floor and will gather his wheat into the granary; but the chaff he will burn with unquenchable fire."; Luke 3:17 "His [again, John the Baptizer is speaking about the "coming one"] winnowing fork is in his hand, to clear his threshing floor and to gather his wheat into his granary; but the chaff he will burn with unquenchable fire." *Thinline Bible with the Apocrypha* (NRSV). Powelson and Riegert, trans., footnotes, and eds., *The Lost Gospel Q,* 37 (Q4) includes this sentiment, and may have been the source for the canonical verses: "John the Baptist said, 'I baptize you with water, but someone more powerful than me is coming. I am not fit

his "kingdom" living to encompass, aspects which were returned to again and again in the remainder of our study.

This took us once more into the image and its phenomenology, and that through a more literally visual angle, namely, that which confronts from the frame: these were the Gethsemane artworks: foundations and reactive birthings. While scholars consider the Garden of Gethsemane scene itself to be pure fiction as an event, as a notion/event it clearly is not that; this raises interesting queries. What is the "truth" of something like the Gethsemane narrative? If the entire episode was simply made up to illustrate a desired doctrinal position, then what might be taken from it for us if we do not accept said doctrine? These facets are intriguing and arguable from a number of perspectives, and in our research we selected some representative art pieces purporting to illustrate this aspect or that of the tale, approaching them in a serial phenomenological analysis that started first from the God/"God"-man Christology point of view and then from a historico-critical stance. What was especially revelatory in this was what we noted taking place when we removed the possibility of Yeshua having a perfect prescience of his death and guaranteed resurrection (the God/"God"-man correlates). Even taking the Garden story as fictive and its character as stripped of foreknowledge, the images themselves were yet able to move us when we apprehended them as depicting a simply human man in the midst of a personal trauma (*angst*); and this difference, we think, is due to the functioning of the image/idea-idea/image (and its connection with the notion/event). This process was instructive. The experiences we arrive at within our environments—through whatever means, including purely internal ones—are cognized through antecedently posited notional "lenses," and thereafter circle back to further inform understandings ("polish" or "bend" the "lenses") of those same antecedents (possibly building more) in interactions but also *perceptions:* individualized senses of/within a being-in-the-world. Naturally such extends to any relationship (or its absence) we might determine ourselves as having with the divine.

The question of "being" having been raised, we explored the afterlife in a Yeshuan context, again taking the most authenticated documents as our foundation, and discovered (quite apart from how the Gospels present things) that for Yeshua such was essentially of no matter. We proposed that he very well might have committed himself to a Second Maccabees form of self-regarding with respect to his own future martyrdom should such eventuate (probably considered by him as at least a possibility given what was happening in his socio-political surroundings), and assumed therefore that

---

to untie his sandals. He will baptize you with holy spirit and fire. His pitchfork is in his hand, ready to thresh the grain. He will gather the wheat in his granary; but the chaff he will burn in a fire that never goes out.'" It is unclear to me whether this is meant in a "final judgment" sense or in a more regular punitive sense; if the former then this would contrast with our considerations of how Yeshua presented the afterlife in the textual sources (see Chapter 11; but again, this is John the Baptizer speaking). Interestingly, the other Synoptic Gospel of Mark has no parallel to this, although it does have the Baptizer "preparing the way" (Mark 1:1–8; *Thinline Bible with the Apocrypha* (NRSV)); and similarly Funk and the Jesus Seminar, *The Gospel of Jesus,* 11 and 13 (their 1:1–16) does not include this verse in its *"A voice in the wilderness"* section on the Baptizer (page twelve lists the source material).

he would be corporeally resurrected as reward for his diligence, but this is not the resurrection tale that the Gospels narrate. We should emphasize how significant this is: If Yeshua did not teach (much) about any presumed afterlife, and if he did not himself seem to consider it worth a great deal of focus (other than, perhaps, a fervent belief—and thence comfort—in physical reinstatement as recompense for righteousness), then the resulting ideational package is far more in line with a typically Judaic concern with appropriate living now than it is with the mainline Christian orientation towards a "then." Once more we realize that Yeshuanism is Yeshuan-Judaism; it is not Christianity. Furthermore, we took the entire notion of any kind of postmortem "continue" as entirely irrelevant; in our facing of/up to finitude we arrived just there: the end, death as annihilation.

This remains a somewhat radical position, and after reviewing how some other thinkers have struggled with it we offered instead "welcome": the being-towards-death that takes it as a balm, as a brute fact that must be confronted and acknowledged, admitted, embraced. There is nothing else for it given the manner of creature we are; but this is not a negative and death is nothing to be feared. I will die; everything I do and am will (quickly) fade and be forgotten; the human fate is thus and it is quite liberating. We work for the betterment of today with a mind for children, grandchildren perhaps. We can do no more. We try, and we hope. Within this, therefore, the astonishing surrender that was Yeshua's crucifixion, his willingness to give himself for his cause, is remarkable even if not singular within history. It must be admitted that if Yeshua did—as we suspect—cleave to a Second Maccabees style expectation of receiving a corporeal resurrection once he had taken that ultimate step, then this would have been both comfort and stimulus to him; but many ideas can motivate, whether fanciful or not. What is important here, I think, is the nature of the path that he took in giving himself, in that sacrifice which has so tragically been turned into something else entirely.

Prior to our conclusion that was the final major topic we analyzed: the possible meaning of Yeshua's execution and the baleful nature of what has been read into it. If Yeshua did seek martyrdom—and there is certainly no guarantee of that—it still would not entail the atonement economy we have heard about these many centuries now (and such would clearly fail to apply all the more if Yeshua's death was indeed something that happened *to* him and was thus quite apart from what he desired). That interpretation of Yeshua's life and ministry does much damage to—and no promotion of—the "kingdom" message as we uncovered it in previous chapters. Rather than presenting God/"God" as demanding propitiation, Yeshua taught that it blesses the good and bad alike ("sun" and "rain" for everyone). We reasoned that although Yeshua did probably consider "sin" as conceptually existent and applicable, he did not thereby connect it with any particular punishment; and absolutely not with eternal torment if we take the most reliable accounts as giving us a truer picture of Yeshuan-Judaism than those yielded by the later written Gospel accounts. This led to our reconsiderations of the abstract "sin" and its place within "the kingdom" overall. Perchance most salient there is that if our dissection of the relevant aspects is correct then redemption is entirely unnecessary (with acquiescence to the idea "sin" or without it) in any kind of metaphysical sense because it *already is:* we are preemptively forgiven. We may wish to correct ourselves, to right our own paths, but we need neither worry about nor fear any kind of extremely painful and unending torture resulting from our missteps taken on the way. Let us note again how very Jewish this is;[64] Yeshuan-Judaism: Christianity (as we know it today) is not Yeshuanism, and Yeshuanism is a Judaism. However that may be, Yeshua did die, he was killed, but his death was no ending (here we are, two millennia later!), and so we had to query: If the atonement economy view can be (very rightly) abandoned, then the Yeshuan legacy that most firmly remains is the message, the nuanced tweaking of the social, the ethical, the perspectival encapsulating that was/is "the kingdom." Yet beyond the title, what is it? Yeshua lived and died a Jew; it is as simple as that. His ministry was never intended to create a new religion based on himself; and the one that did end up being established "in the name of" him (as it were: a *reading-in* par excellence) is not even his. Where then does that leave those who find worth in his words—whatever they were, as best they can be ascertained—today? For those attracted to Yeshuanism, to Yeshuan-Judaism, what choices are available? What may be pursued?

The question remains, and it is unanswerable in any kind of definitive manner: God/"God" be thanked! Since Yeshuanism is a Judaism, conversion to one of the Judaisms of our time is naturally one possibility; yet there may be some who would not desire such but would still like to live "more Yeshuan." To those the alternative of "being Jewish" (as opposed to *being Jewish:* we earlier spliced this as be/"be" Jewish/"Jewish") is another. In either case the ethno-communal importance of the Jewish people as *a people* must surely be respected, its heritage and place honored (*Am Yisrael chai:* "The people of Israel lives," as we opened this chapter.) Given the conditions of embeddedness we find ourselves in at birth, there is probably little to be done initially but to start from—and perhaps to remain on; one may determine it best to remain on—one's inherited and pre-established paths, but each is worthy and can offer solid guidance; the more so the more open and reflective we are, seeking always an approach which is learned and stretched and personalized through sincerity and devotion. This is the "wrestling with" that is such a core part of (any) Judaism, taken either in its fuller and more proper meaning or in the reduced "Jewish" potentiality we offered in the dual positions of firstly an acceptance of some form of complete monotheism (albeit not necessarily "theist" in the "being" sense of the term; a call, force, mystery, event, transcendence, or an otherwise-than would also fit), and secondly the never-"winning"

---

64. Related to the splicing of "sin" in its Hebrew meaning (see again Benner, "Definition of Hebrew Words: Sin," *Ancient Hebrew Research Center.* Accessed September 10, 2021), is *teshuvah* ("repentance"): the "returning" to the "right/better path" from which one has gone astray via recognition, remorse, and resolve (also with interpersonal relational repair when necessary); see "Teshuvah, or Repentance," *My Jewish Learning.* Accessed September 14, 2021.

Part 5 | A Peace-Making, a Re-Making

but ever-trying struggle with said other/Other. Christianity, as it is known today, we found not to be the message of Yeshua; what was Yeshua's adopted task in life was a Judaism: a relating of human-divine, human-human, and one of many Judaisms that existed within his historical epoch. It remains thus, and we can espouse it or not, in parts or in whole. This is an utterly personal choice and we made no suggestions in regards to it or the related question of conversion; and nor would we dare to proffer any.

Here at the last we find that we are yet face to face with a picture(ing), an icon of our own construction, an image-idea/idea-image that turns, exits the frame, and re-creates (re-views) *us* as we have created (viewed) *it*. The approaches we take to Yeshua, to "the kingdom," to God/"God"—and to their combinations—these will ground whatever outcomes materialize, time and again, time without end. There is no need to be redeemed, there is nothing to fear, there is nothing waiting beyond what we ourselves give rise to, there is no eschatology, no telos, no soteriology; what *is* are only that: the ontology melts into the ontics, being is comprehended as a unified being-in-the-world, phenomenological transcendence is the immanence of the *this:* creature to creature, life to life, me to you: the human gift is that this is ours to effect. New interpretations of these image-ideas/idea-images which we hold can lead to new realities (the notion/event), they can establish new understandings, broader vistas, further horizons; current images may help point the way, or they may conceal. Everything, it seems, is up to us. Yeshua taught one way to be Jewish/"Jewish"; how might we respond? In our searching, what might be found? In our studying, what might be taken on? In our striving, what might be transformed? There are no finalities, and my prayer—I will call it that—is only this: That we follow Jacob and never stop struggling.

Bibliography

Alter, Robert. *The Wisdom Books: Job, Proverbs, and Ecclesiastes.* New York: W. W. Norton & Company, 2010.

Bataille, Georges. *Theory of Religion.* Translated by Robert Hurley. New York: Zone, 1989.

Barnstone, Willis, and Marvin Meyer, eds. *The Gnostic Bible: Gnostic Texts of Mystical Wisdom from the Ancient and Medieval Worlds.* Revised edition. Boston: Shambhala, 2009.

Barth, Karl. *God Here and Now.* Translated by Paul M. van Buren, new introduction by George Hunsinger. Abingdon-on-Thames, UK: Routledge, 1964/2003.

Belting, Hans. *The End of the History of Art.* Translated by Christopher S. Wood. Chicago: Chicago University Press, 1987.

———. *Likeness and Presence: A History of the Image Before the Era of Art.* Translated by Edmund Jephcott. Chicago: University of Chicago Press, 1994.

Benjamin, Walter. "On the Concept of History." In *Illuminations,* edited and introduction by Hannah Arendt, 196-208. Boston: Mariner, 1968/2019.

Benner, Jeff A. "Definition of Hebrew Words: Sin." Ancient Hebrew Research Center. Accessed September 10, 2021. https://www.ancient-hebrew.org/definition/sin.htm.

Berlin, Adele, and Marc Zvi Brettler, eds., *The Jewish Study Bible.* Consulting ed. by Michael Fishbane. Oxford: Oxford University Press, 2004.

The Bhagavad Gita. Translated and introduction by Juan Mascaró, new introduction by Simon Brodbeck. London: Penguin Classics, 1962/2003.

Bhagavad Gita: In the Light of Kashmir Shaivism. Revealed by Swami Lakshmanjoo, edited by John Hughes. Culver City, CA: Lakshmanjoo Academy, 2015.

Boyarin, Daniel. *Border Lines: The Partition of Judaeo-Christianity.* Philadelphia, PA: University of Pennsylvania Press, 2004.

———. *The Jewish Gospels: The Story of the Jewish Christ.* Foreword by Jack Miles. New York: The New, 2012.

———. *A Radical Jew: Paul and the Politics of Identity.* Berkeley and Los Angeles: University of California Press, 1994.

Bronner, Ethan. "Ancient Tablet Ignites Debate on Messiah and Resurrection." The New York Times. July 6, 2008. Accessed January 29, 2020. https://www.nytimes.com/2008/07/06/world/middleeast/06stone.html.

Brown, Raymond E. *The Death of the Messiah: From Gethsemane to the Grave: A Commentary on the Passion Narratives in the Four Gospels,* two volumes. New York: Doubleday, 1994.

BIBLIOGRAPHY

Buber, Martin. *I and Thou.* Translated, prologue, and notes by Walter Kaufmann. New York: Simon & Schuster, 1970.

Buddha (The). *The Dhammapada: Verses on the Way.* Translated and reading guide by Glenn Wallis. New York: The Modern Library, 2004.

Camus, Albert. *The Myth of Sisyphus.* Translated by Justin O'Brien. London: Hamish Hamilton-Penguin, 1955/2005.

Caputo, John D. *Cross and Cosmos: A Theology of Difficult Glory.* Bloomington, IN: Indiana University Press, 2019.

———. *The Folly of God: A Theology of the Unconditional.* Salem, OR: Polebridge, 2016.

———. *Hermeneutics: Facts and Interpretation in the Age of Information.* London: Pelican, 2018.

———. *The Weakness of God: A Theology of the Event.* Bloomington, IN: Indiana University Press, 2006.

Catholic Holy Bible, New Living Translation: Catholic Reader's Edition. Tyndale House Foundation. Carol Stream, IL: Tyndale House, 2017.

Cavarero, Adriana. *In Spite of Plato: A Feminist Rewriting of Ancient Philosophy.* Translated by Serena Anderlini-D'Onofrio and Áine O'Healy, foreword by Rosi Braidotti. Cambridge: Polity, 1995.

Chalmers, David J. *The Conscious Mind: In Search of a Fundamental Theory.* Oxford: Oxford University Press, 1996.

Cioran, E.M. *The Trouble With Being Born.* Translated by Richard Howard, new foreword by Eugene Thacker. New York: Arcade, 1976/2012.

Clark, T.J. *The Sight of Death: An Experiment in Art Writing.* New Haven, CT: Yale University Press, 2006.

Cohen, Richard A. "Levinas: Thinking Least about Death: Contra Heidegger." *International Journal for Philosophy of Religion* 60, no. 1/3 (2006) 21–39.

Cohen, Shaye J.D. "The Letter of Paul to the Galatians." In *The Jewish Annotated New Testament: New Revised Standard Version,* second edition. Edited by Amy-Jill Levine and Marc Zvi Brettler, 373. Oxford: Oxford University Press, 2017.

Critchley, Simon. *Very Little . . . Almost Nothing: Death, Philosophy, Literature,* second edition. New York: Routledge, 2004.

Crossan, John Dominic. *Jesus: A Revolutionary Biography.* New York: HarperOne, 1994.

Damásio, António. *The Feeling of What Happens: Body and Emotion in the Making of Consciousness.* New York: Harcourt Brace, 1999.

———. *Self Comes to Mind: Constructing the Conscious Brain.* New York: Vintage, 2012.

Danker, Frederick William, rev. and ed. *A Greek-English Lexicon of the New Testament and Other Early Christian Literature,* third edition, based on the sixth edition of Walter Bauer's *Griechisch-deutsches Wörterbuch zu den Schriften des Neuen Testaments und der frühchristlichen Literatur,* sixth edition. Edited by Kurt Aland and Barbara Aland, with Viktor Reichman, and on previous English editions by W.F. Arndt, F.W. Gingrich, and F.W. Danker. Chicago: University of Chicago Press, 2000.

Danto, Arthur C. *After the End of Art: Contemporary Art and the Pale of History.* Foreword by Lydia Goehr. Princeton, NJ: Princeton University Press, 1997/2014.

Bibliography

Davies, Brian. *The Thought of Thomas Aquinas.* Oxford: Clarendon, 1992.

Dennett, Daniel C. *Consciousness Explained.* New York: Little, Brown and Co., 1991.

DeTurris Poust, Mary. *The Essential Guide to Catholic Prayer and the Mass.* New York: Alpha, 2011.

Dijksterhuis, Ap. "Think Different: The Merits of Unconscious Thought in Preference Development and Decision Making." *Journal of Personality and Social Psychology* 87, no. 5 (2004) 586–98.

Durkheim, Émile. *The Elementary Forms of Religious Life.* Translated by Karen E. Fields. New York: Free, 1995.

Editors of Encyclopaedia Britannica. "The Acts of the Apostles." In Encyclopædia Britannica. Accessed January 23, 2020. https://www.britannica.com/topic/The-Acts-of-the-Apostles-New-Testament.

———. "Andromeda: Greek mythology." In Encyclopædia Britannica. Last revised and updated by Michael Ray, editor. Accessed June 15, 2020. https://www.britannica.com/topic/Andromeda-Greek-mythology.

———. "Babylonian Captivity: Jewish History." In Encyclopædia Britannica. Last revised and updated by Adam Augustyn, managing editor. Accessed April 22, 2020. https://www.britannica.com/event/Babylonian-Captivity.

———. "First Council of Nicaea." In Encyclopædia Britannica. Last updated November 29, 2019. Accessed January 20, 2020. https://www.britannica.com/event/First-Council-of-Nicaea-325.

———. "Pharisee." In Encyclopædia Britannica. Accessed March 18, 2020. https://www.britannica.com/topic/Pharisee.

———. "Revelation to John: New Testament." In Encyclopædia Britannica. Accessed December 24, 2020. https://www.britannica.com/topic/Revelation-to-John.

———. "Sadducee." In Encyclopædia Britannica. Accessed March 19, 2020. https://www.britannica.com/topic/Sadducee.

Edwards, Paul. "Heidegger and Death as 'Possibility.'" *Mind* 84, no. 336 (1975) 548-66.

Ehrman, Bart D. *How Jesus Became God: The Exaltation of a Jewish Preacher from Galilee.* New York: HarperOne, 2014.

———. "A Resurrection for Tortured Jews (2 Maccabees)." The Bart Ehrman Blog: The History & Literature of Early Christianity. August 17, 2017. Accessed December 16, 2020. https://ehrmanblog.org/a-resurrection-for-tortured-jews-2-maccabees/.

Ehrman, Bart D., and Plese, Zlatko, eds. and trans. *The Other Gospels: Accounts of Jesus from Outside the New Testament.* Oxford: Oxford University Press, 2014.

Endo, Shusaku. キリシタン時代：殉教と棄教の歴史[*Kirishitan Jidai: Junkyo to Kikyo no Rekishi*; The Christian Era: A History of Martyrdom and Apostasy (title translation by Stephen Turnbull)]. Tokyo: Shogakukan, 1992.

Falque, Emmanuel. *The Guide to Gethsemane: Anxiety, Suffering, Death.* Translated by George Hughes. New York: Fordham University Press, 2019.

Feyerabend, Paul. *Against Method,* new edition. Introduction by Ian Hacking. London: Verso, 2010.

Ford, Mike. "Bible Verses about Eye of a Needle." Bible Tools. Accessed November 11, 2019. https://www.bibletools.org/index.cfm/fuseaction/Topical.show/RTD/cgg/ID/3918/Eye-of-Needle-.htm.

Freud, Sigmund. "Our Attitude Towards Death." In *Reflections on War and Death,* translated by Abraham Arden Brill and Alfred B. Kuttner, 7-12. New York: Moffat, Yard and Co., 1918. Accessed January 13, 2021. Archived at: http://www.sophia-project.org/uploads/1/3/9/5/13955288/freud_waranddeath.pdf .

Fujimura, Makoto. *Silence and Beauty: Hidden Faith Born of Suffering.* Foreword by Philip Yancey. Downers Grove, IL: InterVarsity, 2016.

Funk, Robert W., ed., and the Jesus Seminar. *The Gospel of Jesus: According to the Jesus Seminar.* Salem, OR: Polebridge, 1999.

Funk, Robert W., ed., and the Jesus Seminar, trans. and comm. *The Acts of Jesus: The Search for the Authentic Deeds of Jesus.* San Francisco: Polebridge/Harper Collins, 1998.

Funk, Robert W. *Honest to Jesus: Jesus for a New Millennium.* San Francisco: Polebridge/HarperCollins, 1996.

Gadamer, Hans-Georg. *Truth and Method,* revised edition. London: Continuum International, 2004.

Gazzaniga, Michael S. *Who's In Charge?: Free Will and the Science of the Brain.* New York: Ecco, 2011.

Gilbert, Gary. "The Acts of the Apostles." In *The Jewish Annotated New Testament: New Revised Standard Version,* second edition. Edited by Amy-Jill Levine and Marc Zvi Brettler, 219-21. Oxford: Oxford University Press, 2017.

The Go-Anywhere Thinline Bible with the Apocrypha, New Revised Standard Version. National Council of the Churches of Christ in the United States of America. New York: HarperCollins, 2010.

Google Images. "マリア観音 [Maria Kannon]." Accessed November 12, 2019. https://www.google.com/search?rlz=1C1RUCY_enJP747JP747&q=%E3%83%9E%E3%83%AA%E3%82%A2%E8%A6%B3%E9%9F%B3&tbm=isch&source=univ&sa=X&ved=2ahUKEwjOrKCbtuPlAhUry4sBHah3DkoQsAR6BAgIEAE&biw=1920&bih=937.

Grant, Michael. *Constantine the Great: The Man and His Times.* New York: Charles Scribner's Sons, 1994.

Groys, Boris. *In the Flow.* London: Verso, 2018.

Gschwandtner, Christina M. *Welcoming Finitude: Toward a Phenomenology of Orthodox Liturgy.* New York: Fordham University Press, 2019.

Guenther, Lisa. "Being-From-Others: Reading Heidegger after Cavarero." *Hypatia* 23, no. 1 (2008) 99–118.

Hadot, Pierre. *Plotinus, or The Simplicity of Vision.* Translated by Michael Chase, introduction by Arnold I. Davidson. Chicago: University of Chicago Press, 1993.

Hagen, Steve. *Buddhism: Plain and Simple.* New York: Broadway, 1997.

Haidt, Jonathan. "The Emotional Dog and Its Rational Tail: A Social Intuitionist Approach to Moral Judgment." *Psychological Review* 108, no. 4 (2001) 814–34.

———. *The Righteous Mind: Why Good People Are Divided by Politics and Religion.* New York: Pantheon, 2012.

Bibliography

Harlow, Jules, ed. and trans. *Siddur Sim Shalom: A Prayerbook for Shabbat, Festivals, and Weekdays.* New York: The Rabbinical Assembly, United Synagogue of Conservative Judaism, 1989.

Harman, Graham. *Tool-Being: Heidegger and the Metaphysics of Objects.* Peru, IL: Open Court, 2002.

———. *Weird Realism: Lovecraft and Philosophy.* Winchester, UK: Zero, 2012.

Harrington, Daniel J. "Wisdom of Solomon." Oxford Bibliographies. Last modified on September 13, 2010, and last reviewed on September 21, 2016. Accessed June 09, 2022. DOI: 10.1093/OBO/9780195393361-0129.

healthline. "Is Mustard Good for You?" Last medically reviewed on January 10, 2020. Accessed July 17, 2020. https://www.healthline.com/nutrition/is-mustard-good-for-you.

Heidegger, Martin. *Basic Writings: Key Selections from Being and Time to The Task of Thinking.* Translated by HarperCollins Publishers, edited by David Farrell Krell, new foreword by Taylor Carman. New York: HarperCollins, 2008.

———. *Being and Time.* Translated by Joan Stambaugh, revised and foreword by Dennis J. Schmidt. Albany, NY: State University of New York Press, 2010.

———. *The Phenomenology of Religious Life.* Translated by Matthias Fritsch and Jennifer Anna Gosetti-Ferencei. Bloomington, IN: Indiana University Press, 2004.

Heschel, Abraham Joshua. *God in Search of Man: A Philosophy of Judaism.* New York: Farrar, Straus and Giroux, 1955.

Hofstadter, Douglas. *I Am a Strange Loop.* New York: Basic, 2007.

Hoover, Roy W., with Miller, Robert J. "The Historical Jesus Is Not History." *The Fourth R* 34, no. 4 (2021) 5–10, 20.

Hopkins, Gerard Manley. "Spring and Fall." Poetry Foundation: Poems. Accessed September 3, 2021. https://www.poetryfoundation.org/poems/44400/spring-and-fall.

Hunter, Regina L. "Why Do We Think Jesus' Ministry Lasted 3 Years?" Daily Bible Study Tips. May 23, 2009. Accessed January 21, 2020. http://www.daily-bible-study-tips.com/RQ_5_JesusMinistry.htm.

Husserl, Edmund. *The Essential Husserl: Basic Writings in Transcendental Phenomenology.* Introduction and edited by Donn Welton. Bloomington, IN: Indiana University Press, 1999.

IMDb. "The Good, the Bad and the Ugly." Accessed March 18, 2021. https://www.imdb.com/title/tt0060196/.

van Inwagen, Peter. *Material Beings.* Ithaca, NY: Cornell University Press, 1990.

Jackson, Frank. "Epiphenomenal Qualia." *The Philosophical Quarterly* 32, no. 127 (1982) 127-36.

Jeffries, Stuart. "The Storm Blowing from Paradise: Walter Benjamin and Klee's *Angelus Novus.*" Verso: Blog. August 2, 2016. Accessed February 7, 2020. https://www.versobooks.com/blogs/2791-the-storm-blowing-from-paradise-walter-benjamin-and-klee-s-angelus-novus.

The Jewish Annotated New Testament: New Revised Standard Version, second edition. Edited by Amy-Jill Levine and Marc Zvi Brettler. Oxford: Oxford University Press, 2017.

Bibliography

Jewish Virtual Library: A Project of AICE. "Quotes on Judaism & Israel: Rabbi Hillel." Accessed March 17, 2021. https://www.jewishvirtuallibrary.org/rabbi-hillel-quotes-on-judaism-and-israel.

Josephus, Flavius. *The Jewish War*, revised edition. Translated by G.A. Williamson, edited by Betty Radice, new editing, introduction, notes, and appendixes by E. Mary Smallwood. London: Penguin, 1959/1970; new material 1981.

Kahn-Harris, Keith. *Judaism.* London: Hodder Education, 2012.

Kahneman, Daniel. "A Perspective on Judgment and Choice: Mapping Bounded Rationality." *American Psychologist* 58, no. 9 (2003) 697–720.

———. *Thinking, Fast and Slow.* New York: Farrar, Straus and Giroux, 2011.

Kane, Robert, and Stephen H. Phillips, eds. *Hartshorne: Process Philosophy and Theology.* Albany, NY: State University of New York Press, 1989.

Kata Biblon: Greek Septuagint and Wiki English Translation. "2 Maccabees 7." Accessed December 22, 2020. https://en.katabiblon.com/us/index.php?text=LXX&book=2Mc&ch=7.

Kaufmann, Walter. "Existentialism and Death." *Chicago Review* 13, no. 2 (1959) 75–93.

Keller, Catherine. *Face of the Deep: A Theology of Becoming.* Abingdon-on-Thames, UK: Routledge, 2003.

Kimball, Roger. "The Perversions of M. Foucault." *The New Criterion* 11, no. 7 (1993) 10–18. Accessed March 26, 2020. Archived at: https://newcriterion.com/issues/1993/3/the-perversions-of-m-foucault.

Kirby, Peter. "4 Maccabees." Early Jewish Writings. Accessed March 23, 2020. http://www.earlyjewishwritings.com/4maccabees.html.

Knowing Jesus. "27 Bible Verses about All Have Sinned." Accessed March 18, 2021. https://bible.knowing-jesus.com/topics/All-Have-Sinned.

Koci, Martin. *Thinking Faith after Christianity: A Theological Reading of Jan Patočka's Phenomenological Philosophy.* Albany, NY: State University of New York Press, 2020.

Kohler, Kaufmann. "Pharisees." In Jewish Encyclopedia. Accessed March 18, 2020. http://www.jewishencyclopedia.com/articles/12087-pharisees.

Kohn, Daniel. "What Are Pilgrimage Festivals? Three Major Holidays Mentioned in the Torah: Passover, Shavuot and Sukkot." My Jewish Learning. Accessed November 11, 2019. https://www.myjewishlearning.com/article/pilgrimage-festivals/.

Kugel, James L. *The God of Old: Inside the Lost World of the Bible.* New York: Free, 2003.

Lander, Shira L. "The First Letter of Paul to the Corinthians." In *The Jewish Annotated New Testament: New Revised Standard Version*, second edition. Edited by Amy-Jill Levine and Marc Zvi Brettler, 321–2. Oxford: Oxford University Press, 2017.

Leloup, Jean-Yves, trans., intro., and comm. *The Gospel of Thomas: The Gnostic Wisdom of Jesus.* Translated from French and notes by Joseph Rowe, foreword by Jacob Needleman. Rochester, VT: Inner Traditions, 2005.

Lennon, John. "Working Class Hero." *John Lennon/Plastic Ono Band.* London: Apple Records, vinyl recording, 1970.

Lévi-Strauss, Claude. *Totemism.* Translated by Rodney Needham. Boston: Beacon, 1963.

Levinas, Emmanuel. *Time and the Other and Additional Essays.* Translated by Richard A. Cohen. Pittsburgh, PA: Duquesne University Press, 1987.

———. *Totality and Infinity: An Essay on Exteriority.* Translated by Alphonso Lingis. Pittsburgh, PA: Duquesne University Press, 1969.

Levine, Amy-Jill. *Short Stories by Jesus: The Enigmatic Parables of a Controversial Rabbi.* New York: HarperOne, 2014.

Lieber, David L., sr. ed. *Etz Hayim: Torah and Commentary, Travel-Size Edition.* The Rabbinical Assembly of the United Synagogue of Conservative Judaism. Philadelphia, PA: The Jewish Publication Society, 2004.

Llewelyn, John. "Review: *Heidegger on Death: A Critical Evaluation* by Paul Edwards." *The Philosophical Quarterly* 32, no. 129 (1982) 388.

Lords-prayer-words: Traditional and Contemporary Prayers. "The Lord's Prayer." Accessed September 18, 2019. https://www.lords-prayer-words.com/lord_traditional_king_james.html.

Luper, Steven. "Life's Meaning." In *The Cambridge Companion to Life and Death,* edited by Steven Luper, 198–212. New York: Cambridge University Press, 2014.

———. *The Philosophy of Death.* New York: Cambridge University Press, 2009.

Lycan, William G. *Consciousness and Experience.* Cambridge, MA: The MIT Press, 1996.

Marcus Aurelius. *Meditations.* Translated and introduction by Maxwell Staniforth. London: Penguin, 1964.

Marion, Jean-Luc. *God Without Being.* Translated by Thomas A. Carlson. Chicago: University of Chicago Press, 1991.

Marx, Dalia. "Hear, O Israel (Sh'ma Yisrael)." ReformJudaism.org. Accessed September 21, 2021. https://reformjudaism.org/prayer-hear-o-israel-shma-yisrael.

Melonic, Emina. "Done It Again." The New Criterion, May 6, 2020. Accessed May 8, 2020. newcriterion.com/blogs/dispatch/done-it-again.

Merleau-Ponty, Maurice. *Phenomenology of Perception.* Translated by Donald A. Landes, foreword by Taylor Carman. Abingdon-on-Thames, UK: Routledge, 2012.

Merriam-Webster. "History and Etymology" in entry for "Islam." In Merriam-Webster Dictionary. Accessed April 28, 2020. https://www.merriam-webster.com/dictionary/Islam.

Meyer, Marvin, trans. and intro. *The Gospel of Thomas: Hidden Sayings of Jesus,* revised edition. Notes by Marvin Meyer, interpretation by Harold Bloom. New York: HarperOne, 1992.

Miller, James. *The Passion of Michel Foucault.* Cambridge, MA: Harvard University Press, 1993.

Miller, Robert J. "Free Rain." *The Fourth R* 34, no. 1 (2021) 3–6, 20.

Mitchell, W.J.T. *What Do Pictures Want?: The Lives and Loves of Images.* Chicago: University of Chicago Press, 2005.

Mlodinow, Leonard. *The Drunkard's Walk: How Randomness Rules Our Lives.* New York: Vintage, 2009.

Molen, Steven. "The Identity of Jacob's Opponent: Wrestling with Ambiguity in Genesis 32:22–32." *Dialogue: A Journal of Mormon Thought* 26, no. 2 (1993) 187–200.

Müller, F. Max, trans. *The Thirteen Principal Upanishads.* Revised, introduction, and notes by Suren Navlakha. London: Wordsworth Editions/Bibliophile, 2000.

My Jewish Learning. "Jewish Resurrection of the Dead." Accessed September 15, 2021. https://www.myjewishlearning.com/article/jewish-resurrection-of-the-dead/.

———. "Teshuvah, or Repentance." September 14, 2021. https://www.myjewishlearning.com/article/repentance/.

———. "Tikkun Olam: Repairing the World." Accessed July 15, 2020. https://www.myjewishlearning.com/article/tikkun-olam-repairing-the-world/

Nagel, Thomas. "Panpsychism." In *Mortal Questions,* 181–95. New York: Cambridge University Press, 1979.

———. "What Is It Like to be a Bat?" In *Mortal Questions,* 165–80. New York: Cambridge University Press, 1979.

Nancy, Jean-Luc. *The Banality of Heidegger.* Translated by Jeff Fort. New York: Fordham University Press, 2017.

———. *The Ground of the Image.* Translated by Jeff Fort. New York: Fordham University Press, 2005.

———. *The Muses.* Translated by Peggy Kamuf. Stanford, CA: Stanford University Press, 1996.

Néret, Gilles. *Kazimir Malevich (1878-1935): and Suprematism.* Translated by Chris Miller. Cologne, Germany: Taschen, 2003.

The New Greek/English Interlinear New Testament: UBS fifth edition/Nestle-Aland twenty-eighth edition, with a literal English rendering and the New Revised Standard Version. Translated by Robert K. Brown and Philip W. Comfort, edited by J.D. Douglas and Jonathan W. Bryant. Carol Stream, IL: Tyndale House, 1990.

New World Encyclopedia. "Daniel, Book of." In New World Encyclopedia. Accessed December 21, 2020. https://www.newworldencyclopedia.org/entry/Daniel,_Book_of.

———. "Septuagint." In New World Encyclopedia. Accessed December 22, 2020. https://www.newworldencyclopedia.org/entry/Septuagint.

———. "2 Maccabees." In New World Encyclopedia. Accessed December 21, 2020. https://www.newworldencyclopedia.org/entry/2_Maccabees.

Niebuhr, Reinhold. *An Interpretation of Christian Ethics.* New York: Harper & Brothers, 1935.

Nietzsche, Friedrich. *Beyond Good and Evil: Prelude to a Philosophy of the Future.* Translated and commentary by Walter Kaufmann. New York: Random House, 1966.

———. *On the Genealogy of Morals.* Translated by Walter Kaufmann and R.J. Hollingdale; *Ecce Homo.* Translated, edited, and commentary by Walter Kaufmann. Double volume. New York: Random House, 1967.

———. *The Portable Nietzsche.* Translated, edited, and introduction by Walter Kaufmann. New York: Viking Penguin Inc., 1954.

———. *Thus Spake Zarathustra.* Translated by Thomas Common. Mineola, NY: Dover, 1999.

O'Meara, Dominic J. *Plotinus: An Introduction to the Enneads.* Oxford: Oxford University Press, 1993.

Oberg, Andrew. "Approaches to Finitude: Death, Self, Others." *Journal of Applied Ethics and Philosophy* 10 (2019) 8–17.

———. "Bloodying God: Crucifixion and the Image." In *Image, Phenomenon, and Imagination in the Phenomenology of Religious Experience,* Libri Nigri series. Edited by Martin

Nitsche and Olga Louchakova-Schwartz, series editor-in-chief Hans Rainer Sepp, 209-28. Nordhausen, Germany: Traugott Bautz GmbH, 2022.

———. *Blurred: Selves Made and Selves Making.* Leiden, The Netherlands: Brill, 2020.

———. "Prescience and an Early Death." *Think* 18, no. 53 (2019) 34–42.

———. "Reconsidering Euthanasia: For a Right to be Euthanized and for Recognizing Alternative End of Life Methods." *Journal of International Philosophy* 4 (2015) 297–305.

———. "Rereading the 'Vineyard' Parable: Squeezing the Grapes of a Fresh Hermeneutic for a Radical 'Kingdom' and a 'Weak' God." *Bulletin of the University of Kochi* 69 (2020) 17–35.

———. "Thinking Unempirically." Philosopher. July 3, 2017. http://philosopher.io/Thinking-Unempirically. Accessed October 10, 2019. Archived at: http://andrewoberg.blogspot.com/p/mind-and-language.html.

Osman, Magda, and Ruth Stavy. "Development of Intuitive Rules: Evaluating the Application of the Dual-System Framework to Understanding Children's Intuitive Reasoning." *Psychonomic Bulletin & Review* 13, no. 6 (2006) 935–53.

Oesterreicher, John M. *The Rediscovery of Judaism: A Re-Examination of The Conciliar Statement on the Jews.* South Orange, NJ: Seton Hall University Institute of Judaeo-Christian Studies, 1971.

Pelikan, Jaroslav Jan, and E.P. Sanders. "Jesus." In Encyclopædia Britannica. Accessed January 21, 2020. https://www.britannica.com/biography/Jesus.

Pels, Peter. "The Spirit of Matter: On Fetish, Rarity, Fact, and Fancy." In *Border Fetishisms: Material Objects in Unstable Spaces.* Edited by Patricia Spyer, 91–121. Abingdon-on-Thames, UK: Routledge, 1998.

Perowne, Stewart Henry. "Herod: King of Judea." In Encyclopædia Britannica. Accessed November 11, 2019. https://www.britannica.com/biography/Herod-king-of-Judaea.

Pinterest: Explore Ideas. Accessed August 14, 2020. https://pl.pinterest.com/pin/456904324682927968/.

Plaut, W. Gunther, gen. ed. *The Torah: A Modern Commentary, Travel Edition.* Central Conference of American Rabbis. New York: CCAR, 2005.

Pleasant, Barbara. "The Benefits of Growing Mustard." GrowVeg. August 16, 2013. Accessed July 17, 2020. https://www.growveg.com/guides/the-benefits-of-growing-mustard/.

Polanyi, Michael. *The Tacit Dimension.* New foreword by Amartya Sen. Chicago: University of Chicago Press, 1966/2009.

Powelson, Mark, and Ray Riegert, trans., footnotes, and eds. *The Lost Gospel Q: The Original Sayings of Jesus.* Preface and consulting editor Marcus Borg, introduction by Thomas Moore. Berkeley, CA: Seastone, 1996.

The Qur'an. New translation by M.A.S. Abdel Haleem. Oxford: Oxford University Press, 2004.

The Rabbinical Assembly. "Conversion to Judaism." Accessed June 17, 2021. https://www.rabbinicalassembly.org/jewish-law/conversion.

Ramachandran, V.S. *The Tell-Tale Brain: Unlocking the Mystery of Human Nature.* London: Windmill, 2011.

Raphael, Frederic. "Reflections on Anti-Semitism." *The New Criterion* 38, no. 7 (2020) 20–4.

Reps, Paul, compiler. *Zen Flesh, Zen Bones: A Collection of Zen and Pre-Zen Writings.* Parts I-III transcribed by Nyogen Senzaki and Paul Reps. New York: Anchor/Doubleday, 1961.

Reconstructing Judaism. "Reconstructionism." Accessed June 17, 2021. https://www.reconstructingjudaism.org/learn/reconstructionism.

ReformJudaism.org. "Choosing Judaism: Frequently Asked Questions." Accessed June 17, 2021. https://reformjudaism.org/choosing-judaism.

Rollyson, Carl. *The Last Days of Sylvia Plath.* Jackson, MS: University Press of Mississippi, 2020.

Rosenbaum, Stephen E. "How to Be Dead and Not Care: A Defense of Epicurus." *American Philosophical Quarterly* 23, no. 2 (1986) 217–25.

Russell, Daniel C., ed. *The Cambridge Companion to Virtue Ethics.* Cambridge: Cambridge University Press, 2013.

Ryle, Gilbert. *The Concept of Mind.* Introduction by Daniel C. Dennett. London: Penguin, 1949/2000.

Sacks, Jonathan. "Covenant & Conversation: Vayikra (5771) – The Dimensions of Sin." Jonathan Sacks: The Office of Rabbi Sacks. March 12, 2011. Accessed September 10, 2021. https://rabbisacks.org/covenant-conversation-5771-vayikra-the-dimensions-of-sin/.

de Saint-Exupéry, Antoine. *The Little Prince.* Translated by Katherine Woods. New York: Harcourt, 1943.

Sanders, E.P. "St. Paul the Apostle." In Encyclopædia Britannica. Last update March 10, 2020. Accessed March 17, 2020. https://www.britannica.com/biography/Saint-Paul-the-Apostle.

Sartre, Jean-Paul. *Being and Nothingness.* Translated and introduction by Hazel E. Barnes. New York: Philosophical Library, 1956.

Scheffler, Samuel. *Death and the Afterlife.* Edited and introduction by Niko Kolodny. Oxford: Oxford University Press, 2013.

SeetheHolyLand.net: . . . Your Guide to Seeing the Holy Places. "Gethsemane." Accessed October 27, 2020. https://www.seetheholyland.net/gethsemane/.

Sembera, Richard. *Rephrasing Heidegger: A Companion to Being and Time.* Ottawa: University of Ottawa Press, 2007.

Septuaginta: A Reader's Edition, volume 1. Edited by Gregory R. Lanier and William A. Ross. Peabody, MA: Hendrickson, 2018.

Seung Sahn (priestly name). *Ten Gates: The Kong-an Teaching of Zen Master Seung Sahn.* Edited and revised by Dae Kwang, foreword by Robert Aitken. Boston: Shambhala, 2007.

Shields, Charles J. *And So It Goes: Kurt Vonnegut: A Life.* New York: Henry Holt and Company, 2011.

Silk, Jonathan A. "Bodhisattva: Buddhist Ideal." In Encyclopædia Britannica. Accessed July 1, 2021. https://www.britannica.com/topic/bodhisattva.

Silverstein, Harry S. "The Evil of Death." *The Journal of Philosophy* 77, no. 7 (1980) 401–24.

Smith, David Woodruff. *Husserl,* second edition. Abingdon-on-Thames, UK: Routledge, 2013.

Solzhenitsyn, Aleksandr. *The Gulag Archipelago, 1918-1956: An Experiment in Literary Investigation,* three volumes. New York: Basic, 1997.

Spira-Savett, Jonathan. "Tzedakah in the Bible." My Jewish Learning. Accessed August 10, 2020. https://www.myjewishlearning.com/article/tzedakah-in-the-bible/.

Staples, Jason A. "The Length of Jesus' Ministry and Daniel 9." Jason Staples. October 14, 2019. Accessed January 21, 2020. https://www.jasonstaples.com/bible/new-testament/the-length-of-jesus-ministry-and-daniel-9/.

Stein, Edith. *On the Problem of Empathy*, third revised edition. Translated and introduction by Waltraut Stein. Washington, D.C.: ICS, 1989.

Steinbeck, John. *Of Mice and Men*. New York: Covici-Friede, 1937.

Takaki, Kyle. "Bullshit, Living, and the Future." *Journal of Philosophy of Life* 9, no. 2 (2019) 32–51.

Tanakh: The Holy Scriptures: The New JPS Translation According to the Traditional Hebrew Text. Philadelphia, PA: The Jewish Publication Society, 1985.

Taussig, Hal, ed. and comm. *A New New Testament: A Bible for the 21st Century Combining Traditional and Newly Discovered Texts*. Foreword by John Dominic Crossan. New York: Houghton Mifflin Harcourt, 2013.

Thich Nhat Hanh. *The Miracle of Mindfulness: An Introduction to the Practice of Meditation*. Translated by Mobi Ho. Boston, MA: Beacon, 1975.

Tilakaratne, Asanga. *Theravada Buddhism: The View of the Elders*. Honolulu: University of Hawai'i Press, 2012.

Tillich, Paul. *Dynamics of Faith*. Introduction by Marion Pauck. New York: Perennial, 1957/2001.

Tolkien, J.R.R. *The Silmarillion*. Edited by Christopher Tolkien with Guy Gavriel Kay. London: George Allen & Unwin, 1977.

Toy, Crawford Howell, George A. Barton, Joseph Jacobs, and Israel Abrahams, "Maccabees, Books of." In Jewish Encyclopedia: The unedited full text of the 1906 Jewish Encyclopedia. Accessed December 21, 2020. http://jewishencyclopedia.com/articles/10237-maccabees-books-of#anchor15.

Turnbull, Stephen. *The Kakure Kirishitan of Japan: A Study of Their Development, Beliefs and Rituals to the Present Day*. Abingdon-on-Thames, UK: Routledge, 1998.

Tversky, Amos, and Daniel Kahneman. "Judgment under Uncertainty: Heuristics and Biases." *Science* 185, no. 4157 (1974) 1124-31.

Walsh, Michael. *Roman Catholicism: The Basics*, second edition. Abingdon-on-Thames, UK: Routledge, 2016.

Watts, Alan. *The Way of Zen*. New York: Pantheon, 1957.

Wendel, JoAnna. "When Will the Sun Die?" Space.com. August 7, 2019. Accessed August 7, 2019. https://www.space.com/14732-sun-burns-star-death.html.

Westar Institute. Accessed July 6, 2021. https://www.westarinstitute.org/.

Westar Institute. "The Jesus Seminar." Accessed November 11, 2019. https://www.westarinstitute.org/projects/the-jesus-seminar/.

Whelan, Christal, trans., intro., and annotator. *The Beginning of Heaven and Earth: The Sacred Book of Japan's Hidden Christians*. Honolulu: University of Hawai'i Press, 1996.

BIBLIOGRAPHY

White, L. Michael. "Understanding the Book of Revelation." PBS: Frontline. Accessed December 24, 2020. https://www.pbs.org/wgbh/pages/frontline/shows/apocalypse/revelation/white.html#:~:text=The%20Book%20of%20Revelation%20was,1.10).

Whitehead, Amy. *Religious Statues and Personhood: Testing the Role of Materiality.* London: Bloomsbury Academic, 2013.

Wikimedia Commons. "File: Christ in Gethsemane.jpg." Heinrich Hofmann, Public Domain, via Wikimedia Commons. Accessed April 21, 2022. https://commons.wikimedia.org/wiki/File:Christ_in_Gethsemane.jpg.

———. "File: El Greco – Christ on the Cross, in a Landscape with Horsemen – 1610-14.jpg." El Greco, Public Domain, via Wikimedia Commons. Accessed April 21, 2022. https://commons.wikimedia.org/wiki/File:El_Greco_-_Christ_on_the_Cross,_in_a_Landscape_with_Horsemen_-_1610-14.jpg.

———. "File: Gethsemane Carl Bloch.jpg." Carl Bloch, Public Domain, via Wikimedia Commons. Accessed April 21, 2022. https://commons.wikimedia.org/wiki/File:Gethsemane_Carl_Bloch.jpg.

———. "File: Job Recounting His Experiences to His Daughters LACMA M.48.5.2.21.jpg." Los Angeles County Museum of Art, Public Domain, via Wikimedia Commons. Accessed April 21, 2022. https://commons.wikimedia.org/wiki/File:Job_Recounting_his_Experiences_to_his_Daughters_LACMA_M.48.5.2.21.jpg.

———. "File: Nikolay Ge 021.jpeg." Nikolai Ge, Public Domain, via Wikimedia Commons. Accessed April 21, 2022. https://commons.wikimedia.org/wiki/File:Nikolay_Ge_021.jpeg.

———. "File: Pietro Perugino cat20.jp." Pietro Perugino, Public Domain, via Wikimedia Commons. Accessed April 21, 2022. https://commons.wikimedia.org/wiki/File:Pietro_Perugino_cat20.jpg.

———. "File: 64 Agony in the Garden.jpg." Albrecht Dürer, Public Domain, via Wikimedia Commons. Accessed April 21, 2022. https://commons.wikimedia.org/wiki/File:64_Agony_in_the_Garden.jpg.

Wikipedia: The Free Encyclopedia. "Andromeda (Mythology)." In Wikipedia: The Free Encyclopedia. Accessed June 15, 2020. https://en.wikipedia.org/wiki/Andromeda_(mythology).

———. "Ardhanarishvara." In Wikipedia: The Free Encyclopedia. Accessed October 13, 2020. https://en.wikipedia.org/wiki/Ardhanarishvara.

———. "Jesus Seminar." In Wikipedia: The Free Encyclopedia. Accessed July 2, 2019. https://en.wikipedia.org/wiki/Jesus_Seminar.

———. "Ministry of Jesus." In Wikipedia: The Free Encyclopedia. Accessed January 21, 2020. https://en.wikipedia.org/wiki/Ministry_of_Jesus.

———. "Ousia." In Wikipedia: The Free Encyclopedia. Accessed March 26, 2020. https://en.wikipedia.org/wiki/Ousia.

———. "Simon bar Kokhba." In Wikipedia: The Free Encyclopedia. Accessed January 29, 2020. https://en.wikipedia.org/wiki/Simon_bar_Kokhba.

Bibliography

Wills, Lawrence M. "Daniel." In Berlin, Adele, and Marc Zvi Brettler, eds., *The Jewish Study Bible,* edited by Adele Berlin and Marc Zvi Brettler, consulting editor Michael Fishbane, 1640-2. Oxford: Oxford University Press, 2004.

Windeatt, Barry, trans. *Julian of Norwich: Revelations of Divine Love.* Oxford: Oxford University Press, 2015.

Wölfflin, Heinrich. *Principles of Art History,* sixth edition. New York: Dover, 1932.

Yamakage, Motohisa. *The Essence of Shinto: Japan's Spiritual Heart.* New York: Kodansha USA, 2006.

www.ingramcontent.com/pod-product-compliance
Lightning Source LLC
Chambersburg PA
CBHW080543230426
43663CB00015B/2696